Thinking *With*—Jean-Luc Nancy

Thinking *With*—Jean-Luc Nancy

Edited by
Susanna Lindberg, Artemy Magun, Marita Tatari

DIAPHANES

ISBN 978-3-0358-0552-9

Layout: 2edit, Zurich
Printed in Germany

The preparation of this book was in part supported by the
European University at Saint-Petersburg, which is a private institution
not affiliated with the Russian Government.

www.diaphanes.net

Table of Contents

Preface from the Editors

Soon after Jean-Luc Nancy's death, DIAPHANES invited us to prepare this trilingual and multidisciplinary collective volume. There are intellectual and biographical ties that bind us to the person of Nancy: we were and are a part of the Strasbourg school of philosophy. Strasbourg was a place where Nancy and Philippe Lacoue-Labarthe taught from the 1980s until Nancy became an Emeritus in 2002. Strasbourg was a place of intellectual intensity, around which thinkers from all over the world gathered at that time. The three of us met there, around the end of the twentieth century, and have since been engaged in a continuous dialogue with Nancy.

Nancy was not your isolated philosopher-genius, but a man of community and a community man. Together with Lacoue-Labarthe, he formed a school of thought, was a figure of personal, social, and intellectual attraction, and reflected himself in the work of his numerous disciples and friends. Jean-Luc's voice still announces tram stops in Strasbourg, (re-)orienting one in the physical and spiritual space of Europe, from within its geographical heart that was so often transposed back and forth between France and Germany. Strasbourg, for Nancy and Lacoue-Labarthe, echoed the romantic Tübingen and Jena at the threshold between the eighteenth and nineteenth centuries: the period that so attracted him theoretically and mimetically. The cloud of the sublime rose from his voice (the subject of Rodolphe Burger's contribution to this volume), enveloped this ancient city and plunged its dwellers into its atmosphere. This volume tries to reconstruct this dispersed existence of Nancy's thought through a constellation of voices, so diverse and so unanimous, from several generations and from several intellectual periods of Jean-Luc's thought that marked them most.

With this book, we would like to resume the discussion that Jean-Luc Nancy continuously engaged in during his life. This means not just reflecting *on* his work, but also *with* him, in keeping with the attitude characteristic of his thought. Indeed, as we know, Nancy took the old philosophical question of truth without any given measure, without comparison. This was a thinking responsible for the world from within the world, a speech that tried to correspond to the lasting mutation of our civilization.

The striving for autonomy, which inspired philosophy along with Western culture in its entirety, mutated into the autonomy of a colonializing techno-economical machinery: for this reason, Nancy insisted on finitude and heteronomy as our indispensable conditions. To hold on to the demand of sense amounts, according to him, to picking up, again and again, on this demand, and to opening sense to its unfitting outside: as the actuality of conversation, of address, of a relation, all of which we ourselves are.

Jean-Luc Nancy paid tribute to this infinite and uncanny relation through his own life and work. We would like to continue thinking together with him now, when his death holds open for us the relation to what is unrelated to anything: to what is open to its own infinite emergence.

We have divided the chapters in a thematic way. To start, there is an overview of the developments and pauses that Nancy's thinking went through over time. The introductory text poses the question of Nancy's unique standpoint. Then, under the title "*Lebentod*" ("Life-death"), follow some more intimate texts that enter into dialogue with the thinker or engage in an intellectual mourning. The subsequent themes are roughly chronological. They go from the "community" of the earlier period toward the deconstruction of Christianity, to the philosophy of history, and to contemporary approaches to ontology, nature, and environment. Two further important topics, mimesis/methexis and the question of art, close the volume.

The authors' approaches differ significantly, not just because they address different texts and periods but also because they continue Nancy's thought in various new directions. Jean-Luc Nancy valued estranging takes on his work and life. With this book, we would like to keep thinking with him, today, when his death opens up our relationship to what is itself without any relation and is thus open to us only in its infinite emergence.

Marita Tatari

"I am only asking that philosophy looks over its shoulder a little." Nancy's Standpoint

"Relation," "with," "commonality," "inoperative community," the "self-deconstruction of Christianity," and also, "body," "touch," "life," "sense," and its "mutations." Although Jean-Luc Nancy explicitly writes about these themes, a serious engagement [*Auseinandersetzung*] with his thought remains difficult so long as his standpoint, that is, the place [*Ort*] of his thought, remains unaccounted for. And while the primary demands of his work have remained constant—and with Borges he liked to say that he continuously wrote the same book—over time, distinct shifts from his earlier writings have become evident. To what can these be attributed? In whose name did they arise? Here, I present some of these shifts in order to demonstrate the necessity of a confrontation with the *standpoint* of Nancy's thought.

On the Political

Nancy has a leftist reception which reads him against the background of his 1980 co-founding of the *Centre de recherches philosophiques sur le politique* with Philippe Lacoue-Labarthe. In response to the power-politics [*Machtpolitik*] of China and the USSR, as well as the managerial coercion of Western techno-economic interests, Nancy and Lacoue-Labarthe sought to thematize "the withdrawal of the political." This attempted to extract "the political" from real existing forms of "politics" in order to "reactivate" it. They understood this to be a revolutionary gesture that was distinct from other Marxist-inspired movements, which for them were bound to empty and abstract visions of "people's power" [*Völkermacht*].[1]

Almost forty years later in 2021, Nancy writes, "In short, today with a certain distance, I would say that we were in this regard lost and confused."[2] The "political" had been a delusion [*"illusion"*]

---

1   Pedro Ebner, Marita Tatari, Facundo Vega, and Jean-Luc Nancy, "Heidegger Today," in *diacritics* (forthcoming 2023). In the following, I reproduce material offered by Nancy in this written interview from 2021.
2   Ibid. My translation.

that had contributed to a disdain for any actual politics, that is, all that was not an imaginary projection of ontological political truth, but instead, discussion and negotiation.

In 1984, the *Centre* dissolved. Nancy viewed the events of the *Solidarność* in Poland to have introduced a division between civil society and the state that betrayed the revolutionary perspective, an event that also initiated a major shift in his thought. Shortly thereafter, his work on the question of community would allow him to demystify his concept of the political. Community, he then says, is not to be primarily understood politically, but as belonging to a thinking of being-with that is itself irreducible to politics. This shift in Nancy's thought resonates with Derrida's observation that "politics" had become a confused concept. "Politics,", for 2021's Nancy, could no longer characterize our fundamental condition.

Potentiality vs. Actuality

There is a significant difference between Nancy's earlier and later positions. Whoever receives his thought from the horizon of the question of community as solely a political matter, fails to do justice to its philosophical stakes, which stem from a shift developed in (at least) two steps beginning in the 1990s:

First, Nancy shifts from 1983 to 1996, from *The Inoperative Community* to *Being Singular Plural*.[3] In the 1980s, Nancy had still understood the "common" or "sense," as "the political." There was still a necessity to deconstruct the (self)realization of community (the subject)—to expose it to its constitutive impossibility, an unworking [*désoeuvrement*] which simultaneously opens, maintains and reveals the possibility of relation along with the chance of an an-archistic politics.

However, the shift accomplished with *Being Singular Plural* exceeds this earlier deconstruction of the subject and with it the negative thinking that suspends (self)realization as such. This shift does not seek to provide an ontological foundation for togetherness or a philosophy of the social, but instead, a quasi-seismographically

---

3   Jean-Luc Nancy, *The Inoperative Community,* trans. Peter Connor, Lisa Garbus, Michael Holland and Simona Sawhney (Minneapolis and Oxford: Minnesota University Press, 1991), and Jean-Luc Nancy, *Being Singular Plural,* trans. Robert D. Richardson and Anne O'Byrne (Stanford: Stanford University Press, 2000).

recorded transformation of sense: sense,[4] the "ultimate goal" of the old theological-metaphysical language, that in modernity became the subject projected into the future as history's (self)realization, for example as the horizon of communism. Now, sense shifts. We enter another moment of its history, another sense of sense. Instead of being projected into the future, it takes its place, here and now.[5] Although Nancy's full confrontation with the historicity of sense would not be fully articulated in the 1990s, it was already pre-programmed. Only later in *The Creation of the World or Globalization*[6], and even more so in the first (2005) and second (2010) parts of *The Deconstruction of Christianity*, is it fleshed out in more detail.[7]

In *Being Singular Plural*, sense is thought as a transcendence of the given, not into some beyond, but as the self-difference of its taking-place, in and as the here and now (in the early 1990s, Nancy names this "transimmanence").[8] For Nancy, this opening of the "here," this "spacing"[9] of time, is the relation to an other. Relation, for Nancy, thus paradoxically almost precedes the beings that it relates—a relation that itself is unsubsumable to any consciousness. This is a non-phenomenological thinking of the "with" [*mit*][10] that Nancy develops through a critical engagement with Heidegger's "being-with" [*Mitsein*]. Crucial is that the "common," thought as "with," responds to the question of sense: to the questions of the last purpose and ultimate goal, and therewith to what is valuable in and of itself.

---

4   In French, as in German, "sense" [*sens, Sinn*], besides meaning "meaning," also has a strong directional, navigational, inflection.

5   *Being Singular Plural* begins and ends with the question of sense.

6   Jean-Luc Nancy, *The Creation of the World or Globalisation*, trans. François Raffoul and David Pettigrew (Albany: SUNY Press, 2007).

7   Jean-Luc Nancy, *Dis-Enclosure: The Deconstruction of Christianity*, trans. Bettina Bergo, Gabriel Malenfant and Michael B. Smith (New York: Fordham University Press, 2008), and *Adoration: The Deconstruction of Christianity II*, trans. John McKeane (New York: Fordham University Press, 2012).

8   Jean-Luc Nancy, *The Sense of the World*, trans. Jeffrey S. Librett (Minneapolis: Minnesota University Press, 1997).

9   "Spacing" translates the concept of "*espacement*," see Jacques Derrida, "Khôra," in *On the Name*, trans. David Wood, John P. Leavey, Jr. and Ian McLeod (Stanford: Stanford University Press, 1995), as well as Jean-Luc Nancy, The Technique of the Present: On On Kawara," *Multiple Arts. The Muses II*, trans. Alisa Hartz, (Stanford: Stanford University Press, 2006).

10   See Susanna E. Lindberg, "Pourquoi Jean-Luc Nancy n'est-il pas un phénoménologue?," *Lignes* 68 (2022), pp. 225–332.

Nancy thinks this primary "with" in *The Creation of the World or Globalization* as the opening or creation of world, "worlding." If sense had been projected into the future in modernity, and if the era of deconstruction had necessitated the thought of its constitutive (im)possibility, today, sense no longer gives itself as a (deconstructed) subject—the subject ends in globalization, in the techno-economic domination that converts all value (all that has value in and of itself) into the bad infinity of general equivalence, thereby liquidating it. For Nancy, the flipside of this nihilism is a transformation of sense: *nihil* as a singular opening of world. For this opening, which is sense within the conditions of globalization, it is necessary to fight ["*lutter*"].

The "with," as sense, is the good infinity of the finite here and now. This is presented in *The Truth of Democracy* as the "transformation of the order of ends": from the order of infinite (self)realization, to the here and now of a *punctual* infinity.[11] This is essentially the paradoxical thinking of singular plural sense, with which Derrida's "*destinerrance*" takes on almost "rhizomatic" features.

Nancy's thinking of finitude thus leads to a thinking of actual [*aktuellen*] infinity, an *actualitas* rather than a potentiality.[12] This is meant not as a pursuit of an infinitely receding goal, but as the actual effectivity of the present: "This doesn't mean that it is measurable or even generally determinable. It is the presence of the infinite in the finite, open in itself."[13] This is how Nancy interprets Derrida's *diff*érance: neither as "delay" nor "putting into reserve," but rather as "the absolute presence of the incomparable."[14] For infinite *diff*érance is finite.

The Nancy of this period, which perhaps was his most influential, is characterized by a distinct optimism. He was one of the few of his generation who saw in the nihilism of the omnipresent general equivalence of the market *qua* techno-economic hegemony, a simultaneous transformation of sense and therewith the taking-place of something valuable in and of itself. This value is no epiphany, but the unfolding that we *are* in our everyday existence.

---

11 See Marita Tatari, ed., *Orte des Unermesslichen. Theater nach der Geschichtsteleologie* (Zurich and Berlin: Diaphanes, 2014).

12 Michael Marder's work moves in a similar trajectory, see *Energy Dreams: Of Actuality* (New York: Columbia University Press, 2017).

13 Jean-Luc Nancy, *The Truth of Democracy*, trans. Pascale-Ann Brault and Michael Naas (New York: Fordham University Press, 2010).

14 Ibid.

"Adoration" describes this disposition towards finitude as actual infinity—the drive towards, and abandonment to, that which infinitely transcends us: the opening that *is* (as) the *here*.

This "post-deconstruction," as Derrida once described Nancy's thought (which Nancy appreciated), has been fruitful for many disciplines: for example in the philosophy of technology, which, as in Erich Hörl's "technological shift of sense," becomes a fundamental techno-ecology.[15] The arts also benefited from this thinking when, at least in the German-speaking world between 2005 and 2015, they departed from a deconstruction of representation (the "unrepresentable," "the ungrounding [*Verabgründung*] of the figure," etc.) and entered a "spatial turn," foregrounding a primary relationality beyond the so-called participatory art forms. Furthermore, Nancy's books on bodies, written in the early 1990s and received with some delay in the German-speaking world,[16] became highly influential in the fields of performance, dance, music, and beyond.[17] Therein Nancy presents the finite infinitude of sense as sensuousness, that is, as relation, that itself is always bound with the *unrelatable*, i.e. with finitude (to be thought with an immeasurable "distance" in the relating, or as the "emptying" of subjectivity, I would say—if this concept did not have such strong negative-theological connotations). This is an affirmation of finitude as a primary "with"—a celebration of an inappropriable alterity, as the "with."

Here, I would like to emphasize two aspects of this period of Nancy's thought:

1. Not everything is political

Unlike the thinking of self-realization and the projection of an unfoundable community onto history, the thinking of the singular plurality of sense firstly means that there is no all-encompassing sphere of sense. Nancy makes the consequences of this transformation of sense explicit for the understanding of politics in *Finite-Unfinite Democracy*, in which he still sought to find a positive conception of politics in the transformation of sense or the communal that would be distinct from its modern and post-modern versions:

15 See Erich Hörl and Marita Tatari, "Die technologische Sinnverschiebung. Orte des Unermesslichen," in Tatari, *Orte des Unermesslichen*, pp. 43–63.

16 See Jean-Luc Nancy, *Corpus*, trans. Richard Rand (New York: Fordham University Press, 2008).

17 See Marita Tatari, *Kunstwerk als Handlung. Transformationen von Ausstellung und Teilnahme* (Munich: Brill/Fink, 2017).

In recent years, various thinkers have offered us their take on the suspended revolution, on the insurrectional moment as opposed to the hardening into place of the revolutionary state, on politics as an ever-renewed act of revolt, critique, and subversion stripped bare of foundational pretense, on the option of continual harassment rather than overthrow of the state. (The word state means literally that which is established, guaranteed, and thus supposedly grounded in truth.) These ideas have merit [...]

It is necessary now to take a further step, to start thinking about how politics without foundation, politics in a state of permanent revolution (if that expression can stand) must permit spheres that are, strictly speaking, foreign to it, to expand on their own. The spheres I mean are those of truth and sense, the ones labeled more or less correctly art, thought, love, desire, and all the other possible ways of designating a relation to the infinite—or, to put it better, of infinite relation.[18]

Here, in Nancy's more optimistic period, politics is understood to provide everyone access to the spheres of sense or relation. These spheres, which are thus not political, are not pre-given, and this introduces admittedly significant difficulties for political thought.

2. Drive, Affect, Life, Environmentality

The sensuous relation, in which relation is thought as sense, is absolute—it is in and of itself valuable. An absolute is by definition not something that is given, but its own self-surplus, a transcendence that leads nowhere, an indeterminable alterity, like the "foaming infinity" at the end of the Hegelian *Phenomenology* which Nancy interprets as self-surplus and enjoyment. This indeterminable alterity, in the hands of Nancy, slips beyond consciousness. It is not considered, positively or negatively, from the perspective of the subject and its self-realization. Rather, such leads Nancy to a philosophy of life that is already pre-programmed in *The Sense of the World*, culminating in 2016 with *Sexistenz*,[19] which steps away from the "subject," "intentionality," "consciousness," and

---

18 Nancy, *The Truth of Democracy*, pp. 82–83. See Jean-Luc Nancy and Marita Tatari, "Kunst und Politik," in Tatari, *Orte des Unermesslichen*, pp. 23–41, also Philip Armstrong and Jason E. Smith, "Politics and Beyond: An Interview with Jean-Luc Nancy," *diacritics* 43, no. 4 (2015), pp. 90–108. The translation of the quoted passage is here slightly modified.
19 Jean-Luc Nancy, *Sexistence*, trans. Steven Miller (New York: Fordham University Press, 2021).

"self-realization," to a thinking of "desire," "drive," "affect," and "primary environmentality."[20] But this thinking of the affectivity of life comes with the following crucial difference from other popular affect theories: Nancy does not design an "epistemology of affects," which as a science would presuppose an unquestioned understanding of truth that legitimizes it. Nor does he design a theory of affective environmentality that grounds itself with a metaphysics. Far to the contrary, he confronts the question of sense, the question of the in and of itself valuable, from within the conditions of finitude.

Nancy describes finitude as actual infinity through a series of oppositions: Hegel's "good" or "concrete infinity" versus the "bad infinity of capital"; Derrida's *différance* as the presence of the immeasurable versus the general equivalence of money; the *nihil* of the opening of a world or worlding versus the *nihil* of globalization. Each of these oppositions indicates two sides of the same cultural moment. Actual infinity is not itself another moment, but (its) experience itself. However, experience here means: opening to an other as other—*relation*.

When Nancy describes the self-surpassing of humanity and repeatedly refers to Pascal's saying that "man infinitely surpasses man,"[21] he simultaneously turns against all transhumanisms and emphasizes the insurmountable finitude of human beings.[22] He insists on finitude as precisely that which opens and enables a thinking of the unconditioned.

This is a thinking of the absolute as paradoxically that of the autonomy of relation, for example as "sexistence." As such, it is fundamentally a matter of the communal, the enunciation of a "we" that is never given. It is noteworthy that Nancy will speak of this transformation of sense as a "mutation," because it itself transforms the understanding of nature and biology by foregrounding a primary technicity—the ever mutational, excessive drive of relationality. As he notes in *Sexistenz*: *technology is transcendence.*

---

20 On these questions, see Sandrine Israel-Jost's precise analyses in the present collection, "How Does Nancy Pursue the Thought of the Milieu by Other Means?," as well as Ian James' "Thinking Heteropoiesis with Nancy after History."

21 Blaise Pascal, *Pensées*, trans. A. J. Krailsheimer (Harmondsworth, Middlesex: Penguin, 1966), pp. 64–65, translation modified. Translator's note: Nancy also discusses this quotation from Pascal in Nancy, *The Truth of Democracy*, esp. p. 11.

22 See Jean-Luc Nancy, *An All-Too-Human Virus*, trans. Cory Stockwell, Sarah Clift and David Fernbach (Cambridge: Polity Press, 2021).

Historicity

The Deconstruction of Christianity presents the uncovering of the *with* (of sense as the with) from the heart of Christianity, interpreting the history of the becoming-global of the Occident as the unfolding of a self-deconstruction of Christianity. The tone of this period of Nancy's thought is affirmative and luminous, laudatory and celebratory.[23] In subsequent years, this will change.[24]

In 2021, Nancy writes that today, our thinking can no longer be led by the questions of "Being" or "the with."[25] Neither of these concepts is up to date. Rather, we should simply speak of "with" (without the "the")—as existence. We must turn away from "Being" in order to make the experience of existence (as being-outside, ex-posed). "We" are used, claimed—he takes the concept of "use [*Brauch*]" from Heidegger and similarly relates it to Augustine's *"frui"*: "enjoyment"— our heteronomy under techno-economic conditions is a form of such "use." The question is whether we are in the position to have the experience of what escapes us, or more precisely the experience of its escape from us, insofar as it gives us our truth only so long as it escapes us. Will we be in the position, not as subjects, but as a culture, to have the experience of and thus to have forms for this heteronomy?

As a culture, in fact, we are far from existing at all. According to Nancy, our forms and customs, languages and ideas, testify to

---

23 Of great interest is Lindberg's critique of Nancy's *lumonosity* in Susanna E. Lindberg, "Le christianisme et la pesanteur, ou Éclaircissements sur la 'déconstruction du christianisme' à partir de Schelling," in Gisèle Berkman and Danielle Cohen-Lévinas, eds., *Figures du dehors. Autour de Jean-Luc Nancy* (Nantes: Cecile Defaut, 2012), pp. 489–504. Also Lindberg's contribution to this present collection, "Splendid Splintered Being." See also Werner Hamacher, "Ou, séance, touche de Nancy, ici," in *On Jean-Luc Nancy: The Sense of Philosophy*, ed. Colin Thomas, Darren Sheppard and Simon Sparks (London and New York: Routledge, 1997), pp. 38–60.

24 See Jean-Luc Nancy, *Excluding the Jew in Us*, trans. Sarah Clift (Cambridge: Polity Press, 2018), and *The Fragile Skin of the World*, trans. Cory Stockwell (Cambridge: Polity Press, 2021); also "La fin de la philosophie et la tâche de la pensée," in *Philosophy World Democracy*, July 14, 2021, https://www.philosophy-world-democracy.org/other-beginning/la-fin-de-la-philosophie (accessed on September 19, 2022). See also in this book Jean-Luc Nancy, entretien avec Marita Tatari, "De l'esprit d'un changement d'époque," and Jean-Luc Nancy, *Cruor*, trans. Jeff Fort (New York: Fordham University Press, 2023). And finally, Ebner, Tatar, Vega, Nancy, "Heidegger Today."

25 "Heidegger Today." See also *The Fragile Skin of the World* on "*Brauch*" and "enjoyment."

an absence of innovation in favor of endlessly restarting, anxious and unstable "sensationalisms."[26] We are in a certain way outside of the world, in a techno-economic disruption that is no longer existence but which nevertheless determines it. Nancy suggests that all of these are dimensions of a general "diffraction," the experience of which has become impossible. Far from affirming a present mutation of sense, here he sees no contemporary experience of existence on the levels of society and culture. In "On the Spirit of the Turn of an Age" he writes: "Perhaps humanity is doomed to excess, it would not be surprising. Up to the excess of autonomy, which is the destruction of the self...."[27]

Such is not to be understood merely as cultural pessimism. Rather, and this is what interests me most here, such a statement should draw us closer to the place, the standpoint, of his thought.

On the Standpoint

According to Nancy, the preservation of life should not be seen as a self-evident value, not even in light of contemporary environmental catastrophes or public health crises. In an interview during the Covid-19 pandemic, Nancy persistently posed the question, "Why?": Why should life be preserved or prolonged? And in many of his writings, he doubted whether the (necessary) concern for equality was a sufficient response to the nihilism of general equivalence. For Nancy, previous forms of sense are in no way self-evident. They are today exhausted and the task is to co-respond to the current form, if there is one.

In this last period Nancy began to draw larger arcs of history understood as the history of the pursuit of autonomy (and no longer merely of Christianity); autonomy, which he writes in "Heidegger Today," is in all its forms, including automation, the proper name of our impasse.

Nancy's conception of history is determined by his confrontation with human conditionality [Bedingtheit]: the fact that humans are finite beings existing under always specific conditions. In this respect, he shows (despite their great differences) significant over-

---

26 Again from Nancy in "Heidegger Today."
27 "De l'esprit d'un changement d'époque."

laps with Hannah Arendt, which can help us uncover the place of his thinking.[28]

This history begins when people are first exposed to their conditionality as such. For Nancy, this takes place with the end of human sacrifice and the flight of the gods, which marked the end of the given, immobile world, and the exit from archaic hierarchies in which the "we" related to and distinguished itself from the gods through human sacrifice. Since then, the "we" has had to deal with otherness within itself, because it is exposed to its absolute limit: conditionality as such.[29] From this springs a concern for autonomy that animates not only philosophy but all aspects of Western civilization, as Nancy elaborates in his later texts.

The transformations of this history are strung together by Nancy (as by Arendt) as shifts between different dispositions and ways of dealing with this human conditionality. The desire for autonomy (for Arendt, the "one"), Nancy argues, took the form of expansion and enterprise in the Roman Empire, which strove to appropriate otherness as surplus and wealth. In Christianity, it took the form of a projection of otherness to heaven, and in modernity, a projection into the future as history and production. These successive forms of the pursuit of autonomy are forms of coping with an exposed human conditionality.

There is a certain continuity between these coping mechanisms, as these transformations, according to Nancy, arise from the fact that the concern for autonomy always unfolds aporetically. Since human beings are fundamentally finite and heteronomous, each attempt for autonomy fails and transforms into a new one. And

---

28 Especially interesting in this respect is the first chapter, "The Human Condition," in Hannah Arendt, *The Human Condition* (Chicago and London: University of Chicago Press, 2018). On the difference between Arendt and Nancy: Arendt opposes autonomy to a conception of the common understood as politics and the space of appearance, and to the subject she opposes the person. Nancy, however, does not affirm the common as being synonymous with the political. Nor does he stand for the person, as does Arendt, but rather a (non-individualistic) becoming, a drive as *with*.

29 See Jean-Luc Nancy, "Theater als Kunst des Bezugs, 2," in Tatari, *Orte des Unermesslichen*, pp. 101–108, here from p. 105: "The history of humanity is perhaps split into two parts. One part, where the heterogenous, that is, the sacred, presents itself as a being or beings, as a god or gods, etc. And another part of the history that no longer presents the sacred as a being or multiple beings, but instead as belonging to all beings, to all speaking living beings as a whole. The sacred takes on another name then, and is called, 'we'." [Translated by Donovan Stewart]

yet, Nancy (like Arendt) describes this history as a series of events without reason, without given necessity: unpredictable events that are not the results of an intention, project, or pre-given reason. This is precisely why Nancy's conception of history—like Arendt's and unlike Hegel's—is distinguished by the fact that it does not seek to sublate human conditionality with a form of autonomy. Nancy calls these incalculable events "spirit": that which is valuable in and of itself, and which in Arendt's version of history was first (in ancient Greece) the worldliness of the world, then in Christianity the sacredness of life, and next, in modernity, life as the highest good, and thus as self-preservation.

Nancy's guiding thread through this history of Western-global civilization is the question of transcendence: the successive transformations of the experience of that indeterminable alterity which becomes effective only when humans were exposed to the absolute limit of their finitude. From Empire to Christianity to production: each pursuit of autonomy inspired a new (necessarily impossible) form of appropriating alterity, up to the bad infinity of capital. At the end of this history, the question remains as to whether we can affirm our heteronomy in the form of an autonomy that is not "ours": "But this autonomy is what is realized precisely by going beyond oneself. Or, perhaps better, by never entering it."[30] *Cruor* describes the violent ambiguity of this pursuit of autonomy: the blood of human sacrifice that drew the border of the sacred is now the red thread of this story—the blood that is life and death. The glamor of *The Deconstruction of Christianity* disappears.

In his later years, Nancy saw no transformation of sense taking place, but only darkness and nihilism. "Politics" in the narrow and broad senses no longer occurred. In response, he insisted on keeping our eyes open in this darkness, to be able to respond if a transformation of sense arrived (a new "spirit").[31] For Nancy all contemporary proposals, for example a more ecologically-attuned state, remain projects and as such belong to the now-exhausted spirit of the subject that culminates in the techno-economic machine. Nancy's "transformations of sense" are thus not programmatic announcements, but on the contrary, indications of the place

---

30 Nancy and Tatari, "De l'esprit d'un changement d'époque," in this book in French. Here, Nancy describes this commonality as the "autonomy of a 'free run beyond itself' […] and even as the autonomy of singularity, which exists every time."
31 See Nancy, *The Fragile Skin of the World*.

of his thinking. A place that lies oblique to philosophy—a place where thought faces its presuppositions with a certain distance from the standpoint of the autonomy of the *logos*.

Looking Over the Shoulder

When Nancy historicizes sense and seeks to do justice to the present and co-respond to the "mutations" of sense taking place, he finds himself closest to Hegel, who also is concerned with the self-consciousness of cultural moments. At the same time, Nancy differentiates himself from Hegel, for his standpoint is not that of spirit's self-grasping, or, as for Heidegger, the question of Being (crossed-through or not). Instead, the place of his thinking is found, as is Arendt's,[32] simultaneously within and outside of philosophy. Thus, in his account of history, he describes the transformations of civilization as transformations of the pursuit for autonomy, doing so not, however, in the name of autonomy.

> I'm only asking that philosophy look over its shoulder a little. Because I think, we shouldn't cease to reflect—if not as an explication—on the fact that at a certain moment the given world (which, I forgot to mention, also included human sacrifice) came to an end—and from this moment on, from this event, which was in itself multiple, there emerged what we know today as civilization.[33]

The place of Nancy's thinking is where philosophy turns and looks over its shoulder. Rather than *philosophically* penetrating its cultural presuppositions, philosophy here asks, on the contrary, about

---

32 Arendt did not understand herself as a philosopher. Her standpoint was not the oneness of autonomy or the subject, but a fidelity towards human conditionality that does justice to the unconditionality of personal action and its primary, irrevocable plurality.

33 Alain Badiou and Jean-Luc Nancy, *German Philosophy: A Dialogue*, trans. Richard Lambert (Cambridge, Mass.: MIT Press, 2018), p. 44. In the original: "Je demande simplement que la philosophie tourne un peu la tête en arrière. Parce qu'il ne faut pas cesser de considérer, non pas une explication, mais le fait qu'à un certain moment le monde du donné – qui comportait d'ailleurs quelque chose que j'ai oublié de nommer, qui comportait en particulier le sacrifice humain –, ce monde est fini et, de ce moment-là, de cet événement, par lui-même événement multiple, sort quelque chose, qui, aujourd'hui, est la civilisation." Alain Badiou and Jean-Luc Nancy, *La tradition allemande dans la philosophie* (Paris: Nouvelles Ligne, 2017), p. 46.

the cultural events that have conditioned its pursuits. This results in a slight shift from the place of the autonomy of *logos*. I see this shift to not only be essential for understanding Nancy's thinking of history, but also as being indispensable today in light of the evident colonial implications of all philosophical universalisms.

In contrast to the poverty of opinions that today pose as philosophy, Nancy raises the question of wonder: the disposition towards that which is in and of itself valuable.[34] To grasp the cultural conditionality of philosophy rather than placing culture within a philosophical perspective means—with the radicality that characterized Nancy's thinking—to take no absolute value for granted, but to face the exhaustion of old values while refusing any cultural relativism that inevitably legitimizes itself with the same philosophical universalism of human dignity and equality. The desire to say "we" and to affirm a never-given commonality has to be led to that place which lies oblique to philosophy and its claims of autonomy.

Today, as the universal of the world has become technological, is that oblique place now the point where technology faces its worlding as itself culturally conditioned?

Translated by Donovan Stewart

---

34 In Nancy, "La fin de la philosophie et la tâche de la pensée."

Hélène Nancy

23 août 2022

À toi, Jean-Luc, ce poème d'Alejandra Pizarnik:

À ton anniversaire

Reçois ce visage mien, muet, mendiant.
Reçois cet amour que je te demande.
Reçois ce qu'il y a en moi qui est toi.[1]

Muito obrigada a Marcia Sá Cavalcante Schuback.

---

1   Alejandra Pizarnik, *Les Travaux et les nuits*, trad. Jacques Ancet, Paris, Ypsilon Éditeur, 2013.

Aukje van Rooden

Left in the Dark
Sharing Death with Jean-Luc Nancy

In one of his last video lectures before he died, a Q&A with Latin American scholars, Jean-Luc Nancy asks himself the question how to think the end, how to think in the light of the end, facing the imminent end of existence as such, of his own existence. It is, he explains, the ultimate uncertainty, the ultimate unpredictability. It is like thinking in the dark. Suddenly his eyes start to twinkle, as always when he realizes how things fall into place. He closes his twinkling eyes in front of the camera, moves his fragile body a little bit closer and stretches his speckled hands tentatively towards the camera. What do we do when we are left in the dark, he asks with his eyes closed. *Il faut apprendre à être dans le noir.* We have to learn to *be* in the dark. We have to learn it by touching our surroundings, stretching out our arms, by a form of thinking that is tentative, tactile, *tâtonnante.*[1]

This is how I feel, now that Jean-Luc is no longer here. Left in the dark. Trying to make sense of it, trying to make sense of the sudden deathliness, the sudden silence, the sudden immobility that started to permeate his texts from one moment to the other. Trying to make sense of the unbearable realization that we cannot continue our exchanges, the many many mails and meals and moments that we shared since we met fifteen years ago. I don't think this transformation is so visible, so tangible with other thinkers who passed away. There are thinkers and texts that already have a certain immobility about them even while their creator is still alive. But Jean-Luc is—was—a philosopher of *life*, in all its forms. Nancy's texts are living, breathing beings. How to touch upon the life, the liveliness, of this work, of this thinking, after August 23, 2021, the moment when Jean-Luc Nancy, at the age of eighty-one, died. How to be in the dark? How to *be,* to exist, in the dark with him? How to share his finitude?

Perhaps we need to take recourse to a thinker of death rather than life to guide us on this posthumous path. I am thinking of

---

1 The video can be found here: https://www.youtube.com/watch?v = WbBQW72knGI (last accessed on June 9, 2022).

Maurice Blanchot, one of Nancy's life-long interlocutors—though perhaps not the closest one, no doubt because Blanchot is indeed a thinker of death rather than life. So what does Blanchot teach us? Regaining or touching upon life after death, or *in* death, Blanchot says, is not a matter of hoping for resurrection, of praying that the deceased one will return on earth living and breathing in full glory. It is, rather, a matter of *descending into* death, as Orpheus descends into the underworld to reach for his beloved Eurydice.[2] Of course, it is Orpheus' job as a writer, a poet, to save Eurydice from obscurity, from oblivion, to "bring her back to the light of the day and to give [her] form, shape, and reality in the day."[3] And of course, we will do so in this volume, in our scholarly work. But bringing the deceased back into the light of the day is not Orpheus' primal concern, according to Blanchot. His primal concern is to see her *in her passing*, to touch upon her *absence*. He wants to see her "not as the intimacy of a familiar life, but as the foreignness [*l'étrangeté*] of what excludes all intimacy."[4] Indeed, descending like Orpheus into the underworld in order to touch upon Nancy's passing, we have to search for his absence. Not to scare away this uneasy, transformed presence with a flashlight, or by brusquely taking it by its arm and leading it back into our usual academic and personal lives, but by tentatively touching upon the dark, without being able to predict where this will lead.

We will have to look for Nancy with our eyes closed, stretching out our arms to touch rather than grasp. This is why Blanchot calls Orpheus' famous forbidden look at Eurydice a *gaze* and not a look.[5] According to Blanchot, both looking *and* not looking at Eurydice would betray her nocturnal condition. Instead, gazing at her in the darkness is the only way of seeing her, touching her as she is: absent, untouchable. The only way to ever come close is to throw

---

2   Maurice Blanchot, "Le regard d'Orphée," *L'Espace littéraire* (Paris: Gallimard, 1955). Translated as "Orpheus's Gaze," *The Space of Literature*, trans. Ann Smock (Lincoln, Nebr. and London: University of Nebraska Press, 1982).
3   Blanchot, "Orpheus's Gaze," p. 171.
4   Ibid., p. 172.
5   The difference between a *regard* (gaze) and *vision* (look or vision) is also emphasized by Émmanuel Levinas in his "Le regard du poète," *Sur Maurice Blanchot* (Montpellier: Fata Morgana, 1975). Translated as "The Poet's Vision," *Proper Names*, trans. Michael B. Smith (Stanford: Stanford University Press, 1996). For this reason, the translation of the *regard* from the title of his text by "vision" is a serious mistranslation.

what Blanchot calls a "weightless gaze,"[6] stealthily, furtively, indeed as if with the eyes closed. Touching upon the lost one, Orpheus is—that is, I am, we are—"no less dead"[7] than she is, Blanchot says.

But here Blanchot's posthumous path leads us *away* from Nancy, I think. Because, for Nancy, we are as much alive as he is, as he still is. This becomes clear from the lecture given by Nancy in memory of Blanchot's death in 2003.[8] In this lecture, called "Blanchot's Resurrection," like in his other readings of Blanchot, Nancy generously follows Blanchot's line of thought, but only to gently redirect it in the end. Both Blanchot and Nancy would say that what is touched upon or even resurrected in the Orphean gaze is not the one who died, but *death itself*.[9] But what does it mean to say that *death* is resurrected? Whereas Blanchot would stress that it is neither dead or alive, for Nancy, this means that death becomes a *living* thing, tangible, stroking or evading our hands, stealthily, unpredictably. Reading Blanchot against the grain, Nancy holds that the tentatively touching gaze "is not a crossing of death [*une traversée de la mort*], but death itself as crossing, as transport, and as transformation" revealing "the most precious point of life."[10] This most precious, most *living*, point of life revealed

---

6 Blanchot, "Orpheus's Gaze," p. 176.

7 Ibid., p. 172.

8 Jean-Luc Nancy, "Résurrection de Blanchot," *La Déclosion* (*Déconstruction du christianisme, I*) (Paris: Galilée, 2005). Republished in *Demande: Littérature et philosophie* (Paris: Galilée, 2015). Translated as "Blanchot's Resurrection," first by Michael B. Smith in *Dis-Enclosure: Deconstruction of Christianity* (New York: Fordham University Press, 2008); later by Robert Bononno in *Expectation: Philosophy, Literature* (New York: Fordham University Press, 2018).

9 Nancy, "Blanchot's Resurrection," *Expectation*, p. 177. The formulation of the "resurrection of death" is key to Nancy, but he admits that Blanchot, for his part, "may have mentioned it only once" (p. 178).

10 Ibid., p. 180. The phrase "the most precious point of life" is quoted by Nancy from Blanchot's novel *Thomas L'Obscur*. Also in the specific case of this phrase one could say that Nancy wilfully redirects its meaning. Making a comparison to Lazarus' resurrection from the tomb, Blanchot uses these words to describe his protagonist's resurrection: "He [Thomas, AvR] went forward [...] walking at an even pace which, for those men who are not wrapped in a winding sheet, marks the ascent towards the most precious point in life." Maurice Blanchot, *Thomas the Obscure*, trans. Robert Lamberton (New York: Station Hill Press, 1988), p. 38. This is not the place for an extensive elaboration of this point, but it is very well possible that, for Blanchot, "the most precious point in life" that marks the ascent of ordinary living men is *death*, i.e. the endpoint of life, the moment of completion where the liveliness of life, its changeability, can be put a stop to. Whether or not this is the case, Nancy, for his part, attributes almost the opposite meaning to this "most precious point of life."

in and by death is, according to Nancy, the "infinitely simple—and indefinitely renewed, indefinitely rewritable—experience in us of being without essence."[11] This indefinitely renewed and rewritable experience of being without essence, of the crossing of death in life, *qua* life, is, in Nancy's case, also always the personal experience of being a grafted organism, the receiver of a heart transplant. At the age of fifty one, Nancy's first heart stopped beating and he was to undergo a major and decisive experience of a heart transplant made in order for him to survive, an operation that did not fail to trouble him regularly for the rest of his life. Nancy, in other words, is not a Eurydice who suddenly lost life, but is a *grafted* life which *in* life, *qua* life, was already traversed by death, bearing its trace in the form of an interrupted but resumed beating of the heart, of more than one heart, of the most intimate sharing of finitude between mortal beings. It is a life that *as* life, *in order to* live, has already exceeded itself, opened itself in the most intimate way to what exceeds and surpasses. This most precious point of life as revealed by the crossing of death is the fundamental disposition of *being-with* that Nancy unremittingly brought to the fore in his life and work. It is also in this sense that Nancy's work, his thinking, has already grafted itself onto us, intruded *our* lives and thoughts, helping them to grow and transform—if not, I wouldn't have written this text, you wouldn't be reading it. Tentatively touching the crossing of Nancy's death, we also touch upon ourselves.

So what has Nancy's work grafted onto our collective thinking? In what way has he traversed it? Above all, he provided us with a new and challenging ontology. His philosophy of life, of the being-with, has no doubt most firmly altered our modes of thinking. As a reader of Heidegger, Nancy was interested in the most basic of questions, the question of what it means to be in the world. Avoiding all forms of essentialism, the answer to this question could only lie, for Nancy, in the each time singular, non-generalizable, manifestation of a being-with. Co-existence, co-implication, communication, and sharing always precede essence. Or rather, as he has it in *Le sens du monde*, co-existence "entrances essence," "traverses" each essence and "deprives it of its essentiality."[12] The relation is

---

11 Nancy, "Blanchot's Resurrection," *Expectation*, p. 184.
12 Jean-Luc Nancy, *The Sense of the World*, trans. Jeffrey S. Librett (Minneapolis: University of Minnesota Press, 1997), p. 31. Translation of *Le sens du monde* (Paris: Galilée, 1993).

primal here, in a more rigorous sense than we find in many other relational ontologies.

Especially in his earlier works like *La communauté désoeuvrée*, this relational ontology led Nancy to rethink the meaning of the word "community," and, in its wake, the meaning of politics. He has done so in such a way that thinking of "being in common"— within a group, a nation, or a world—no longer requires something like a "common being"—an essence, identity or ground—but needs nothing else than the mere fact of sharing existence, of being-together. There is no "'community' that precedes interrelated individuals," there are only "some ones *and* some other ones, or some ones *with* some other ones."[13] Community, in other words, is all about this "with" and this "and"; a "with" and "and" that manifests itself each time singularly, as a singular plurality, a *being singular plural*.[14]

Shifting our attention from the communal hope of sharing an essence to the way we share being, each time singularly, Nancy also shifts our attention to the *corporal* aspect of that being. Our being in the world, Nancy holds, is first of all a bodily affair, an exposition of bodies to other bodies, and of their mutual touching. As he explains in *Corpus*: everything that exists—animate and inanimate—exists in a bodily fashion.[15] To exist, for Nancy, is literally to stand forth as a body, to weigh with your body upon other bodies, skin upon skin.

Interestingly, this focus on the bodily side of being prepares a thorough rethinking of Christianity—one that does away with the dualistic image of a material, "worldly" world on the one hand and a divine, unworldly realm on the other. The Christian God becoming flesh, that is, emptying himself of his divinity to incarnate himself in the world, has, according to Nancy, *freed* the world of its divine outer realm, leaving us with *nothing* but *this* world *here*, this fleshy world of bodies that are exposed to each other, rather than to some divine beyond of the world.[16] This is what Nancy

---

13 Nancy, *The Sense of the World*, p. 71.
14 Jean-Luc Nancy, *Being Singular Plural*, trans. Robert Richardson and Anne O'Byrne (Stanford: Stanford University Press, 2000), p. 2. Translation of *Être singulier pluriel* (Paris: Galilée, 1996).
15 Jean-Luc Nancy, *Corpus*, trans. Richard A. Rand (New York: Fordham University Press, 2008). Translation of *Corpus* (Paris: Galilée, 1993).
16 See especially the two volumes of Nancy's deconstruction of Christianity, *La déclosion* (Paris: Galilée, 2005) and *L'Adoration* (Paris: Galilée, 2010). Nancy finds one of the expressions of this movement in Schelling's *Philosophy of Revelation*: "God himself presses so to speak in the direction of this world by

calls the "deconstruction of Christianity," or rather its "self-deconstruction," implying that Christianity, in principle, boils down to a form of atheism.

Beyond, or rather *through*, this rethinking of Christianity, of ontology, community and the body, Nancy has provided us with an important and far-reaching reconsidering of the concept of *meaning*. Asking himself what remains of the question of meaning when adopting a relational, bodily ontology of being-with, he cannot but conclude that our traditional views concerning meaning are in need of revision. For how to speak of meaning when there is no grand syntactic arrangement? Is there another meaning, one that would correspond to our everyday sharing of the world, without being a poor substitute for the grand and brilliant meanings that we have embraced up till now? Yes there is, Nancy assures us, and the notion he puts forward is the notion of *sense*. Being *the* central word in the philosophical lexicon of Nancy, "sense" encompasses sense in all its different senses: our five senses, sensuality, sensitivity, direction. The world, as Nancy famously puts it in *Être singulier pluriel*, does not *have* sense, it *is* sense and *makes* sense, in our exposition towards each other, in sensing each other. This ongoing circulation of sense between us "goes in all directions at once [and is] opened by presence to presence [of] all things, all beings, all entities."[17]

Shifting our attention from generalizable and decodable meaning, to the endlessly circulating, ungraspable, excessive sense of the world, it is no surprise that Nancy attached great value to the arts. Not to one particular artform, but—carried away, precisely, by their singularly exposed sense—to a whole spectrum of different artforms and artworks—from Christian painting, to modern dance, from poems by Hölderlin and Conrad Aiken, to the cinema of Abbas Kiarostami. If it were not for the life-long division of roles between himself and Philippe Lacoue-Labarthe—the latter identifying himself perhaps more, or also, as a man of theatre and literature, whereas Nancy would readily identify himself as a philosopher *pur sang*—if it weren't for that division of roles, I think that Nancy might have sooner developed creative ambitions

---

which he has finally cast all being outside of himself, in which he has a world free with respect to himself, a creation truly *beyond* him..., *this* world *here*, the world in which we actually find ourselves." Schelling, quoted in Jean-Luc Nancy, *The Sense of the World*, p. 25.

17 Nancy, *Being Singular Plural*, p. 2.

as well. The joy he had in acting, for instance, is so obvious from the way he performed, only a few months before he died, Goethe's friend Lenz, in a film shot by Rodolphe Burger.[18]

I have only touched upon some of the main themes in Nancy's work. The many-sidedness and immense vastness of his oeuvre—encompassing about 150 books—makes it certainly difficult to get a grip on. Nancy's work, so much is clear, does not have the logic of a philosophical system. Nevertheless, there is, I would say, one very clear impetus motivating all of his work, one *pulse* as Nancy would say, one pulsation or drive, and this is *love*.[19] The love for wisdom, certainly, *philo*-sophia, but not the moderate, deliberate, balanced love of the assiduous thinker. Not that kind of love, but rather *passion*, the crushing, quirky, physical love of amorous passion. If there is one intuition motivating his work, I would say that it is the intuition that to be, to exist, and therefore also to think, and to think being, should be an act of love—of an unpredictable, vulnerable movement of absolute exposition.

"In love we are two," Nancy writes in his *Petite conférence sur l'amour*, "[And] from the moment we are two, everything changes."[20] This also explains why his work is so personal, and tends to touch in a personal way. Reading Nancy is not a transfer of information, it is an experience of being addressed, being spoken to by this singular voice, oftentimes from a first-person perspective. And those of you who knew him personally, know that this extended well beyond the confines of his works—in his tireless willingness to *exchange*. A repositioning of his body when being addressed, an amused smile, the immense joy at a real exchange of words, of looks.

He was—he is—not the kind of person that wraps itself in a nocturnal veil, descending towards the underworld, patiently wait-

---

18 The short film created by Rodolphe Burger is called "Lenz au musée" and was part of the exposition *Goethe à Strasbourg, l'éveil d'un génie (1770–1771)*, presented by the municipality of Strasbourg in May 2021 at the Palais Rohan. It can be watched here: https://www.youtube.com/watch?v = F00s1MR9OZg (last accessed June 9, 2022).

19 I develop this hypothesis more profoundly in my article "Jean-Luc Nancy, A Romantic Philosopher? On Romance, Love and Literature," *Angelaki* 26, no 3–4 (2021), pp. 113–125.

20 Jean-Luc Nancy, "Love," *God, Justice, Love, Beauty: Four Little Dialogues*, trans. Sarah Clift (New York: Fordham University Press, 2011), p. 70. Translation of *Je t'aime un peu, beaucoup, passionnément...: Petite conférence sur l'amour* (Montrouge and Hauts-de-Seine: Bayard, 2008).

ing until someone—me, or you—asks him to follow the way back up. He is the kind of person who actively reaches out to you, who calls your name, from whatever region, who has already done so. "I have used your name," Nancy wrote me some time ago. He had to give a talk about Descartes, and wanted to compose a fictionalized letter to Descartes, supposedly written by Descartes' great-granddaughter, the one that issued from the love between Descartes and Descartes' life-long Dutch mistress, his beloved Helena Jans van der Stroom. History does not tell what their great-granddaughter was called, so Nancy wanted to give her my name, writing as it were from "my" perspective. This is typical for his mode of thinking and being: using your existence to move *beyond* himself—thinking through, *with* your existence, letting himself be taken by it, connecting his life, language, place with yours. No need to gaze over one's shoulder to catch a glimpse of Jean-Luc Nancy's passing. He is already under our skin, grafted onto us, his voice already resonating in our voices. So what did Jean-Luc make me, the fictionalized me, say in that letter to Descartes, to the great-grandfather of modern philosophy? "I think, therefore I am. [And] loving is still thinking, it is sensing and desiring and imagining, and first of all enjoying."[21] Let us, in our own work, enjoy Nancy's infinitely circulating thinking, and share all the different ways in which it has marked us.

---

21   Jean-Luc Nancy, "Lettre à Descartes," September 4, 2018, Stockholm (unpublished). My translation.

Marcia Sá Cavalcante Schuback

Le cœur [greffé] de la pensée[1]

> « Dès le moment où l'on me dit qu'il fallait me greffer, tous les signes pouvaient vaciller, tous les repères se retourner. »[2]
>
> Jean-Luc Nancy

La mort de Jean-Luc Nancy n'a pas été seulement la mort d'un grand penseur contemporain. Elle a été la mort d'un grand penseur qui était à la fois un grand ami, un ami aux nombreux amis, un grand ami du plusieurs. Que dire de cette expérience si rare où perdre un philosophe c'est perdre un ami – cet ami de chacun et du plusieurs qui a montré que la pensée est l'amitié du réel chaque fois plusieurs, ou pour le dire avec un mot de son dernier texte, l'amitié de l'« allotropie du réel »[3] ? Cette expérience rare demande plus que de rapprocher la pensée philosophique de son sens étymologique : un savoir de l'amitié, ou de l'autobiographie et ses confessions. Elle fait surtout signe vers un rapport entre la pensée et le cœur au cœur de la pensée, car la philosophie a manqué la pensée du cœur. Donc, la pensée, le cœur, le manque – de l'ami penseur.

Dans une entrevue donnée à Osamu Nishitani, Yotetsu Tonaki, philosophe japonais, ami et traducteur de Jean Luc Nancy, a décrit Nancy comme un philosophe, « capable de voir à travers une variété de thèmes car il voyait les situations selon la perspective d'un philosophe au-delà de la mort »[4]. Tonaki parle de la perspective d'« un philosophe au-delà de la mort » en plusieurs sens mais surtout de l'expérience de l'au-delà de la mort d'un philosophe qui a vécu avec une greffe du cœur pendant plus de trente ans,

---

1 Merci de tout cœur à Hélène Nancy pour l'aide apportée à la version finale de ce texte.
2 Jean-Luc Nancy, *L'Intrus*, Paris, Galilée, 2010.
3 Jean-Luc Nancy, « L'autre commencement de la philosophie », en ligne : https://www.philosophy-world-democracy.org/other-beginning/la-fin-de-la-philosophie [consulté le 07 mars 2023].
4 Osamu Nishitani, « Jean-Luc Nancy, A rare philosopher who lives beyond death », en ligne : https://www.philosophy-world-democracy.org/interviews-1/jean-luc-nancy-a-rare-philosopher [consulté le 07 mars 2023].

qui a pensé le monde et son allotropie selon la perspective d'un cœur transplanté. Une vie greffée est une vie au-delà de la mort et dans ce sens une vie ressuscitée. Si la pensée de Jean Luc Nancy est la pensée naissante d'un « au-delà de la mort » et ainsi une « *anastasis* », une certaine résurrection de la pensée[5], c'est au sens d'une pensée qui vit d'une « greffe du cœur ». Ainsi on pourrait dire qu'au cœur de sa pensée se trouve la question du cœur greffé de la pensée.

Le cœur greffé de la pensée – ce titre fait signe vers ce qui peut orienter une pensée qui pense avec Jean-Luc Nancy. Car ce penseur de l'être-avec a aussi rendu visible et nécessaire d'apprendre à penser-avec la pensée, de découvrir comme penser c'est penser-avec, plutôt que penser contre, pour, sur, à partir de, au-delà de – penser-avec, un nouveau verbe, qui dit comment les rapports conjuguent la pensée. Il s'agit d'un apprentissage du cœur. Ce que cette perspective d'un philosophe au-delà de la mort nous montre c'est une pensée qui a commencé le travail assez difficile de transplantation d'un autre cœur au sein du corps mourant du monde[6]. À la transplantation d'un autre cœur dans le corps d'un philosophe correspond en outre la transplantation d'un autre cœur dans le corps de la philosophie elle-même. Le rapport entre le corps et le cœur du philosophe et le corps et le cœur de la philosophie ainsi qu'entre le corps et le cœur de l'être du monde n'est pas un rapport métaphorique. Comme l'écrit Jean-Luc Nancy dans *L'Intrus* : « Une vie de *greffé.e* peut être considérée comme un microcosme de la mutation générale du monde et de l'humanité »[7], ce qui inclut sans doute la mutation de la pensée contemporaine. Ce rapport indique que l'acte de la pensée plus qu'autobiographique ou incorporé est un acte du cœur, au sens d'un acte qui « *takes to heart* », selon une expression chère à Shakespeare, c'est-à-dire qui prend au sérieux le cœur comme une question cruciale de la pensée. Au-delà de la mort, le cœur greffé fait attention à ses battements fragiles dans le creux du cœur comme le seul repère de

5   Cf. discussions sur l'*anastasis* de la pensée chez Jean-Luc Nancy proposées par Divya Dwivedi, Jérôme Lèbre, Shaj Mohan, Maël Montévil et François Warin, en ligne : https://twitter.com/PhilosophyWD/status/1480227639323287556 [consulté le 07 mars 2023].

6   Je garde toujours présente la question posée à Jean-Luc Nancy par Synne Myrebøe lors du colloque sur *L'amour cartésien* tenu à Stockholm en 2018 : « où trouver le cœur pour faire la greffe du monde ? »

7   Nancy, *L'Intrus, op. cit.*, p. 57.

l'être au monde. Ainsi, l'être même découvre son cœur comme ce qui bat entre être et néant[8].

Si la philosophie manque d'une pensée du cœur, on sait en revanche que les philosophes se sont bien intéressés au cœur. Au commencement de la philosophie, déjà dans les premiers vers de son poème philosophique, Parmenides parle du « thumos » : « Ἵπποι ταί με φέρουσιν, ὅσον τ' ἐπὶ θυμὸς ἱκάνοι,πέμπον [...], » (hippoi tai me férousin, hoson t'epi thumos hikanoi pémpon [...]), c'est-à-dire du cœur qui désire le lointain vers lequel les cavales emportent celui qui sait[9]. C'est vers le lointain du désir du cœur que les cavales emportent le philosophe. Parmenides parle aussi plus loin dans ce premier fragment du « cœur sans tremblement de la vérité, sphère accomplie « Ἀληθείης εὐκυκλέος ἀτρεμὲς ἦτορ » (aletheis eukúklos atremés hétor) lorsqu'il énonce qu'il faut s'instruire de tout, autant de ce que les mortels ont en vue, où l'on ne peut se fier à rien de vrai, qu'au « cœur sans tremblement de la vérité, sphère accomplie »[10]. Qu'est-ce que ce cœur qui désire le lointain vers lequel les cavales emportent le philosophe ? Et comment s'instruire du cœur sans tremblement de la vérité, sphère accomplie ? Le cœur de la vérité ne peut pas se dissocier de la vérité du cœur – s'instruire de cela, voilà ce que le premier poème philosophique énonce comme tâche philosophique. Beaucoup plus tard, Descartes, le philosophe inaugurateur de la philosophie moderne ayant opéré la rupture décisive et incisive avec toute la tradition précédente en imposant les lois d'une rationalité par principe détachée du cœur, était lui-même passionné du cœur. Pour Descartes le cœur est le principe de la vie, le lieu où flottent « les esprits animaux », l'intériorité pulsative de la vie, dont les mouvements involontaires sont à la base même des mouvements volontaires de l'esprit. On peut dire aux jambes : « marche » mais jamais on ne peut dire au cœur : « bat ». Ce sont les battements du cœur – la vie pulsative – qui nous permettent de marcher mais aussi de penser. La vision disséquante du cœur a révélé le cœur comme mouvements involontaires de la vie, excédant la volonté humaine, conduisant le sang du vivant, la source même de l'excès de la vie.

---

8 Jean-Luc Nancy, « L'amour en éclats » in Une pensée finie, Paris, Galilée, 1991.

9 « Les cavales qui m'emportent m'ont conduit aussi loin que mon cœur pouvait le désirer, puisqu'elles m'ont entraîné sur la route abondante en révélations de la divinité, qui, franchissant toutes cités, porte l'homme qui sait. » Jean Beaufret, Le poème de Parmenides, Paris, PUF, 1955, p. 77.

10 Ibid., p. 79.

La connexion du cœur désirant – du philosophe – avec le cœur sans tremblement de la sphère accomplie de la vérité [Parmenides] tout autant que la connexion des mouvements du cœur dans le corps du philosophe avec la nature pulsative de la vie [Descartes] situent dans le cœur la question philosophique du rapport entre pensée et vie. Non seulement comment la pensée pense la vie ou comment on peut rendre une pensée vivante et une vie pensive, mais surtout comment la vie se pense et indique ainsi comment la vie pensive se trouve immergée dans la vie de la vie. Dans sa longue histoire métaphysique, onto-théologique, arche-téléologique, la philosophie n'a pas entendu les battements de la vie se pensant lorsqu'elle vit chaque vie, à chaque instant exposant la vie en tant que vie de l'existence. C'est ce que la perspective du cœur greffé, de l'au-delà de mort de la pensée de Jean-Luc Nancy a rendu possible de penser. C'est selon cette perspective qu'il devient possible de penser comment le cœur est le battement de la condition *ad interiori* de la possibilité de la pensée. Ainsi, on peut dire que la pensée de Jean-Luc Nancy a mis à nu, de la manière la plus éclatante, le cœur greffé comme condition *ad interiori* de la possibilité de la pensée aujourd'hui.

Comment comprendre que le cœur est la condition intérieure – *ad interiori* – de la possibilité de la pensée aujourd'hui ? Aujourd'hui – comment l'aujourd'hui du monde nous frappe aujourd'hui ? Partout des expropriations appropriatives et des appropriations expropriantes, partout des exterminations de toutes sortes – génocides et homicides, multicides et urbicides et toutes leurs variations. Partout l'aujourd'hui du monde nous frappe par le fatal de la mort des mondes connus, et donc par un « plus jamais » ou un « *nevermore* », pour parler la langue corbeau de Edgar Allan Poe. Le « *nevermore* » d'un monde, cette terrifiante menace d'un avenir du monde sans monde, d'un « immonde » où l'avenir lui-même n'a plus aucun avenir, met en exergue une mort dépourvue de résurrection, d'*anastasis*, qui ne peut pas se lever de sa propre tombe, une mort sans aucun revenir à soi, où la représentation d'un retour, quel qu'il soit, disparaît de l'horizon du monde. Partout l'expérience de ne plus pouvoir rester en contact avec le monde en tant qu'ouverture – précisément dans un monde qui ne fait que se connecter à tout instant, dans une agrégation et agglomération qui ne font que ségréguer la vie de la vie, le monde du monde, le présent du présent, l'exister de l'exister. Si dans ce monde il semble impossible de rester en contact avec le monde de la vie dans la vie du monde, comment trouver un cœur pour ce cœur mourant du monde, comment trouver cette condition *ad interiori* d'une chance pour la pensée[11] – la pensée que depuis longtemps la philosophie a considéré comme le lieu atopique de la liberté ? Comment encore penser lorsque *la* pensée a du mal à se distinguer de la manière dont elle s'est établie, instituée, héritée, idéologisée, académisée, institutionnalisée, marchandisée, globalisée comme philosophie ? À la différence de Heidegger qui cherchait les voies d'un « autre commencement » du commencement lui-même, un « autre commencement » où la pensée aurait surpassé la philosophie, Jean-Luc Nancy ne cherche pas un « autre ». Pour lui l'autre est partout, est l'être lui-même, en effet, rien d'autre que l'en train d'exister de l'existence, irréductible, inidentifiable et non reconnaissable, se disant partout dans le langage d'un « ni-ni », « ni étant, ni néant », « ni silence, ni parole »[12]. L'autre c'est le réel et le réel est allotropique. Sa pensée reste en contact avec le rester sans contact du plus jamais, et c'est par là que sa pensée agite plutôt que cogite. Mue par une « sensualité spirituelle »[13], pour citer une de ses expressions, sa pensée reçoit plus qu'elle ne perçoit. Elle reçoit l'impossibilité d'un retour à soi qui se donne précisément dans l'excès autophagique d'un tournant qui ne fait que tourner autour de soi, où l'autre reste inidentifiable et non reconnaissable. Mais c'est en reconnaissant la non reconnaissabilité de l'autre, son irréductibilité et son inidentifiabilité, que l'autre émerge précisément en tant qu'inidentifiable et non reconnaissable à tout moyen d'identification et de connaissance qui opère pour réduire l'autre au même, toujours identifiable et reconnaissable. Le tournant qui ne fait que tourner autour de soi, dans l'automatisme de l'automatisation et de l'autonomie, dans le narcissisme automatique par des mouvements d'un en soi sans soi, réglés par des *selfies*, par l'obsession du à soi avec soi-même, ce tournant qui privatise non seulement des instances publiques mais aussi le privé de tout possible soi-même, ce tournant dans cet excès met à nu l'impossibilité d'un retour à soi et ainsi l'émergence de l'autre. On rencontre dans ce motif de la mise à nu du possible-autre –dans l'impossible-même – l'idée de mutation du monde dont Jean-Luc Nancy parle si souvent. En restant en contact avec le sans contact d'un soi-même qui ne fait

---

11 Juan Manuel Garrido, *Chances de la pensée. À partir de Jean-Luc Nancy*, Paris, Galilée, 2011.

12 Jean-Luc Nancy, « L'autre commencement de la philosophie », *op. cit.*

13 Jean-Luc Nancy & Jérôme Lèbre, *Signaux sensibles. Entretien à propos des arts*, Paris, Bayard, 2017.

que s'absolutiser, la pensée de Jean-Luc Nancy ne pleure ni ne se résigne, n'essaie de rappeler le passé ni de faire appel à un avenir perdu. Ce qu'elle fait c'est prêter attention, écouter le bruit de ce tour tournant autour du « à ». Elle prête attention à la partance en train de partir et non à son origine ou à sa destination. De cette manière, la pensée qui reste en contact avec le sans contact d'un soi-même infiniment absorbé par l'autoproduction et l'autoreproduction de soi et donc par l'extermination de tout autre, est une pensée qui reste en contact avec un reste qui n'est pas silence. C'est une pensée qui reste en contact avec le trouble des restes et de leurs silences et qui dit à ces restes : « Ne repose pas en paix », « *Do not rest in peace* », « levez-vous, restez sans contact », car ce qui reste, je cite Jean-Luc Nancy, « dans la déconstruction de soi à laquelle l'Occident est obstinément et rigoureusement employé [...] », « ce qui reste ou ce qui vient et ne cesse pas de venir en tant qu'un tel reste, nous le nommons l'existence »[14]. C'est donc au sein de cette autophagie de l'auto par l'auto que l'existence se met à nu, surgit à fleur de peau, et ainsi s'*expeause*, pour rappeler le verbe si précis signé par Jean-Luc Nancy. C'est du dedans, du sans sortie de ce tournant qui ne cesse de se tourner autour de soi qu'un autre sens du soi, un soi sans retour à soi qui n'est cependant que rapport à soi, nous touche. Ce qui est en question n'est ni un « soi-même » plus propre, ni aucun autre résidu d'une subjectivité généralisatrice mais une poussée vers l'autre, un « être-pour-l'autre »[15], un *soi-autre*. Qu'est-ce qu'un cœur greffé sinon un soi-autre ? Ainsi se trouve une possible formulation de la condition *ad interiori* de la possibilité de penser aujourd'hui, la condition d'une intériorité plus intérieure que toute intériorité, un « *interior intimo meo* », en rappelant la phrase augustinienne si chère à Jean-Luc Nancy, qui porte plus loin la pensée de ce que Hölderlin a compris comme *Innigkeit*, intimité. Une intériorité détachée de l'intériorité du soi-même, intimiste, séparée et ainsi absolutisée : l'intériorité du soi-autre du cœur greffé.

Que dire de ce cœur dont l'intériorité est un soi-autre expeausé dans le tournant autophagique du soi-même par soi-même ? La biologie nous rappelle que le cœur est un organe musculaire qui pompe le sang vers les vaisseaux sanguins pour le faire circuler par le corps entier à travers des contractions rythmiques. Parler du

---

14 Jean-Luc Nancy, *Le sens du monde*, Paris, Galilée, 1993, p. 202.
15 *Ibid.*, p. 55.

cœur greffé – « ce microcosme de la mutation générale du monde et de l'humanité » – c'est donc parler d'abord du sang circulant de l'existence au sein d'un monde où le sang s'écoule partout, tuant et menaçant toute forme d'existence. Comment sentir et faire sens du sang circulant dans le creux du cœur, du cœur sans cœur du monde qui fait s'écouler du sang partout ? Dans *Cruor*, Jean-Luc Nancy propose la pensée de ce qu'on pourrait appeler, à titre provisoire et à la suite de toute une tradition, une « différenciation sanguine » qui excède toute différence ontologique, phénoménologique ou cosmologique. Il s'agit de la différenciation entre le sang circulant dans le corps, *sanguis*, le sang qui configure la fécondité et sa périodicité, *menstruum* et le sang qui s'écoule au dehors et qui coagule, *cruor*. Autour de cette différentiation sanguine, une réflexion sur la cruauté du monde, sur la cruauté de notre monde se présente pour faire entendre le sang circulant lorsque le cœur mourant du monde a tant de mal à le pomper. Jean-Luc Nancy ne cherche pas les raisons et fondements de la cruauté du monde, de notre monde, de la souffrance et du mal du monde. Sa pensée du cœur greffé est en fait anarchique, car pour lui l'existence, comme la rose mystique, n'a pas de raison ni de fondement. L'existence existe ; « il y a l'il y a ». La cruauté du monde – le sang du monde qui s'écoule dehors et coagule formant une masse solide de sang cruel – est la cruauté de la plus grande des croyances, la croyance de la perte de toute croyance, la cruauté appelée nihilisme. Il s'agit de la cruauté générée par la croyance en la non croyance, croire que tout est permis, la grande confession de la révolte contre la gratuité de la vie et de l'existence. Si la vie est un œil qui voit et dit : « la vie n'a de sens que ce que vit la vie, plurielle », le nihilisme affirme que la vie n'a pas de sens et se rend sourd à l'affirmation que la vie se vit plurielle. Le nihilisme c'est la révolte contre la vie sans sens au dehors et au-delà de la vie, une révolte qui se volte et révolte sans cesse autour du « soi-même » d'un monde de la cruauté, un monde qui ne sait exister que comme sang écoulé et coagulé, comme *cruor*. Capitalisme c'est la loi vampirique d'un monde de l'équivalence générale qui ne peut se faire sans le sang écoulé, d'un vampire qui suce le travailleur et ne le lâche point tant qu'il lui reste un muscle, un nerf, une goutte de sang à exploiter, comme le disait Marx[16]. C'est le monde de la cruauté de

---

16   Karl Marx, *Le Capital*, I, en ligne : https://www.marxists.org/francais/marx/works/1867/Capital-I/kmcapI-10-7.htm#ftn166 [consulté le 07 mars 2023].

l'appropriation expropriatrice des pulsions, de la vie pulsive, du sang circulant et fécondateur. Il ne s'agit pas d'un dispositif externe imposé sur le corps du monde. Pour mettre à nu – car il s'agit de mettre à nu plutôt que de comprendre – la cruauté du monde, il faut penser le rapport entre *sanguis, menstruum* et *cruor*, un rapport qui laisse entrevoir dans cette cruauté elle-même le sang circulant de la vie. De même Jean-Luc Nancy insiste sur le besoin de comprendre comment la vie du cœur peut s'écouter à travers le creux du cœur, à travers des cœurs sans vie. La vie du cœur est selon lui vie désirante et reconnaissante, au sens d'une co-naissance qui se reprend sans cesse. Le désir, dit Jean-Luc Nancy, est la poussée vers l'autre de même que la reconnaissance du cœur pousse vers des lieux, des signes et des valeurs. Le nihilisme vampirique capitaliste fait de tout autre désiré un objet et fait de tout lieu, signe et valeur de reconnaissance, des non-lieux, des non-signes et des non-valeurs au point que la valeur perd sa valeur, le signe son signe de signe et le lieu son lieu de lieu. D'où l'urgence d'écouter dans l'équivalence générale anéantissante des mondes, les bruits et voix du tournant du monde se tournant autour de soi, car la voix des bruits du monde en tant qu'« auto-altération » coordonnée à l'auto-perception »[17] est déjà une voie.

Le soi-autre du cœur greffé est cependant surtout la pulsion rythmique de la vie qui assure la vie de la vie et pour la vie. Ainsi, écrit Jean-Luc Nancy aussi dans *Cruor* : « les battements du cœur donnent la cadence de la vie elle-même », une cadence selon laquelle « la vie vit à chaque instant, à chaque reprise de la pulsation »[18]. C'est le cœur qui montre sans métaphore que la vie n'est pas continuelle mais intermittente – car le cœur est lui-même intermittent, pour rappeler le titre proustien – que la vie donne et reçoit vie à soi-même de soi-même. Ce que le cœur nous apprend, selon Nancy, c'est que « le rythme du vivant expose le rythme en général comme un rapport à soi »[19]. Le soi-autre n'est pas un « lieu », « un point » ou un « refuge » « autre » mais un rapport à soi et ainsi un en soi hors de soi. Plutôt que d'auto-affection il s'agit d'auto-altération. Nancy le décrit comme « le rythme lui-même, la palpitation vive, vitale, vécue – ou bien l'inverse : la poussée palpitante de la vie [qui] s'élance et s'écoule, créant et irriguant à la fois le "soi" vivant, la vie en tant que "soi", poussée et retenue de soi. Avancée

17 *Ibid.*, p. 121.
18 Jean-Luc Nancy, *Cruor*, Paris, Galilée, 2021, p. 20.
19 *Ibid.*, p. 21.

et retrait – sans quoi il n'y aurait pas de soi : soi s'approche et s'éloigne de soi, c'est sa définition ou son essence. Cet aller-retour ou ce va-et-vient, cette alternance et cette altération ont lieu en lui comme l'aller-retour du sang ou de la sève »[20].

Du point du vue du cœur, de la greffe du cœur dans la pensée, le soi perd son autonomie et son auto-référence pour se découvrir comme « motif rythmique »[21], comme un soi-autre qui n'est qu'un rapport se rapportant aux rapports. L'autisme de la pensée du soi – auto-, du soi selon soi-même – *auto kat'auto* – qui a fondé un Occident philosophique, autocentré et auto-référent, est sourd à ce « motif rythmique », au soi en tant que scansion rythmique, qui fait retour, mais un retour qui en tant que rythme « n'est pas un retour à l'identique : au contraire, c'est un retour qui n'a pas encore eu lieu. Chaque contraction du cœur est une autre. La battue du cœur, la pulsion du sang identifie. Du même coup, l'identité se scande »[22].

Sans retour à soi lorsqu'il ne fait que retourner à un autre, le soi-autre entrouvre un autre sens du temps. Un temps qui n'est ni la forme du sens interne [Kant], ni la négativité de l'auto-division [Hegel], ni la durée [Bergson] ni la simultanéité du jeu entre les impressions primaires, les rétentions et les protensions [Husserl], ni même l'extase temporelle [Heidegger]. Ce qui s'entrouvre c'est le temps du sens, un temps qui est chaque temps, qui a lieu à chaque instant. Le cœur apprend le temps-espace du chacun, du chaque à-chaque-moment. Il apprend comment chaque existence est la forme d'un battement précis de vie. Chaque corps est le battement d'un rythme de vie. Loin des visions mécaniques, dynamiques et dialectiques de l'être de la vie et de la vie de l'être, Jean-Luc Nancy présente une vision pulsive, une compréhension qui part des leçons du cœur greffé. Dans cette compréhension pulsive de la vie de l'être, les corps ne peuvent plus être pris comme des configurations visuelles, des compositions de matière et d'esprit, des images ou des contours, ni même comme des organes, mais comme des rythmes et ainsi comme des « soi-autre », rapport se rapportant aux rapports. « *Taking to heart* », pensant avec le courage du cœur greffé, comment chaque corps, chaque existence est le battement du rythme de la vie et donc ce qui s'excède à soi, « en »-soi, comment chaque existence étant singulière-plurielle, il

---

20 *Ibid.*, p. 23.
21 *Ibid.*, p. 25.
22 *Ibid.*

faut que l'existence n'existe pas simplement mais que l'existence s'existe.

La s'existence de l'existence c'est le grand thème d'un autre livre de Jean-Luc Nancy, *Sexistence*, qui pense le rapport entre sexe et existence au sens que l'existence existe chaque existence, que la vie vit chaque vie. L'existence s'existant, existant chacun et chacune, rend compte du « chaque » de chaque corps, de chaque existence comme soi-autre, comme existence-avec, singulière-plurielle. « Or l'existence est avec ou bien rien n'existe »[23]. Mais pour comprendre que l'existence *est* avec, que l'acte d'exister est avec, il faut suivre la pensée de l'existence s'existant lorsqu'elle existe chaque existence. Il faut envisager le sens transitif de l'existence, le sens transitif de « être ».

La formule « sens transitif de l'être » vient de Heidegger, plus précisément de la conférence « *Qu'est-ce que la philosophie* ? [*Was ist das – die Philosophie* ?] », qu'il a faite en 1955 à Cerisy-la-Salle. Heidegger dit : « *Alles Seiende ist im Sein* » – je me permets une traduction littérale « tous étants sont dans l'être ». Il poursuit, pour le dire « de la manière la plus aiguë (*schärfer gesagt*) » : « *Das Sein ist das Seiende* ». L'être *est* l'étant, *ist/est* souligné. Et tout de suite après : « *Hierbei spricht "ist" transitiv und besagt soviel wie "versammelt"* » (Ici le "est" parle transitivement et dit autant que "rassembler" [traduction libre]).[24]

Il y a déjà eu de nombreux débats sur les différences entre le *Mitsein* heideggérien et « l'être avec », le commun, le *cum*, chez Nancy. Mais ce qu'il reste à penser, c'est-à-dire écouter, c'est le sens transitif d'être et d'exister, comment être est étant chacun. Comment « est » peut-il parler transitivement ? La langue mystique de Maître Eckhart nous enseigne la substantivation de *Ist – Istheit*. Cette substantivation de *Ist* en *Istheit* implique de considérer *ist* comme un verbe à part entière, le verbe *zu isten*. À ma connaissance, Heidegger ne le discute que deux fois[25]. Mais chez Heidegger le sens du verbe être, même sous la forme « *ist* », est presque toujours infinitif : *Sein ist zu sein*, être est à être. Ce n'est qu'à Cerisy qu'il parle du sens transitif. En plus, dire que l'être est l'étant

23 Nancy, *Le sens du monde, op. cit.*, p. 22.
24 Martin Heidegger, *Was ist das – die Philosophie*?, Pfullingen, Neske, 1976 [1956], p. 13.
25 Martin Heidegger, GA 82, p. 583 et GA 74. Cf. brève discussion de Ziarek K, *in Language after Heidegger*, Bloomington, Indiana University Press, 2013, p. 43.

au sens transitif de rassembler – donc que l'être rassemble l'étant, c'est encore ne pas entendre la transitivité de l'existence.

Nancy ne dit pas que *est*, qui parle transitivement, veut dire « rassembler ». Chez lui être-avec n'est pas rassembler – ce qu'il dit c'est : « l'être ne peut être qu'étant-les-uns-avec-les-autres, circulant dans l'avec et comme l'avec de cette co-existence singulièrement plurielle. »[26] D'abord être ne se distingue pas d'exister. Mais aussi il ne suffit pas de dire que l'être est étant. Il faut encore comprendre comment être est étant. Jean-Luc Nancy parle de : « la venue de tout à tout. De tout autre/même à tout même/autre »[27]. Cette venue est telle que l'existence non seulement se met à nu *en tant qu'étant*, mais surtout au sens que l'existence s'existe en existant chaque existence. Un des premiers aspects mis en exergue par la pensée de la transitivité de l'exister chez Jean-Luc Nancy c'est une compréhension de l'existence singulière-plurielle en tant que transit, circulation, passage : l'existence transite. Un autre aspect revient à l'appréhension que ce qui se transmet dans cette transitivité c'est l'acte d'exister, l'il y a en acte. L'existence s'existe en existant chaque existence : cela se met à nu lorsque la cruauté du monde, le sans sens du monde « en touchant du point absolu de l'existence »[28], laisse entrevoir que le seul reste c'est l'existence. De cette manière, la pensée de la transitivité de l'exister ne peut être qu'une pensée agrammaticale, car elle n'apparaît qu'en s'ex-crivant des données immédiates du monde. Elle ressort d'une écoute aux voix des bruits d'un monde qui désiste de plus en plus d'exister. L'excriture de la transitivité d'exister se rapporte à l'écoute du soi-autre au cœur creux du même. Sans rapport d'influence mais plutôt affinité de pensée, la manière dont Nancy laisse la transitivité de l'existence venir au langage de la pensée, très spécifiquement dans *Sexistence*, devient extraordinairement proche du langage littéraire de Clarice Lispector, la grande écrivaine de l'exister s'existant, nous existant, t'existant, m'existant, existant chacun[29]. Nous pourrions donc dire qu'il s'agit d'une transitivité saisie comme exister en étant existée par l'existence. En ce sens, l'existence ne précède l'essence ni ne succède à l'essence – l'existence se précède et se succède, car elle est à chaque fois existée par l'existence. C'est aussi en ce sens que l'on peut comprendre

---

26 Nancy, *Être Singulier Pluriel*, *op. cit.*, p. 21.
27 Jean-Luc Nancy, *Sexistence*, Paris, Galilée, 2017.
28 Nancy, *Le Sens du monde*, *op. cit.*, p. 127.
29 Cf. Clarice Lispector, *Agua* Viva, Paris, Des femmes, 2018.

ce que dit Jean-Luc Nancy lorsqu'il écrit que « l'existence est son propre tatouage »[30].

La pensée du cœur greffé est la pensée d'une écoute très attentive aux battements fragiles de l'existence s'existant en chaque existence dans un monde qui ne fait que désister d'exister. C'est une pensée qui écoute comment le cœur greffe l'autisme du soi-même, par ses battements arythmiques, et laisse entendre le soi-autre du même, lorsque tous les signes vacillent, et que tous les repères se retournent. Ainsi émerge selon Jean-Luc Nancy le besoin d'une transplantation, « d'un transport intégral de la force pulsionnelle vers un objet qui soit une forme à naître et non un objet à produire. Ce qui ne peut avoir lieu que dans les parages du *cosmos* et par une œuvre *poiétique* »[31]. Le soi-autre du cœur greffé oblige à une écoute des bruits et des voix du sang qui féconde même le sang de la cruauté. Une pensée comme une oreille collée au sol de la peau souffrante du monde, écoutant les battements arythmiques du cœur de l'existence qui [é- ins- ex]-crit :

Es ist Zeit, daß der Stein sich zu blühen bequemt,
daß der Unrast ein Herz schlägt.
Es ist Zeit, daß es Zeit wird.
Es ist Zeit.

Il est temps que la pierre veuille fleurir,
qu'un cœur palpite pour l'inquiétude.
Il est temps qu'il soit temps.
Il est temps.[32]

---

30 Nancy, *Le Sens du monde, op. cit.,* p. 98.
31 *Ibid.,* p. 96.
32 Paul Celan, « Corona », *in Pavot et mémoire,* trad. Valérie Briet, Paris, Christian Bourgois, 1987.

Marcus Coelen

Liebe Marita Tatari,

Ich danke Ihnen – sowie Susanna Lindberg und Artemy Magun – sehr für diese Einladung, an einem Band zu oder für, vor allem »mit« Jean-Luc Nancy teilzunehmen. Auch bitte ich zu entschuldigen, dass ich letztlich nur spät, und auch nur in wenigen Worten sowie in dieser Form eines Anschreibens Ihnen etwas zukommen lasse. Ich fühle mich derzeit nicht in der Lage oder mit denjenigen Bedingungen beschenkt, die erlauben würden, einen Artikel, eine Abhandlung oder einen Essay zu verfassen. Die Briefform – eine Einladung zu Direktheit, abgestützt auf eine formulierte oder angenommene Frage, aber auch, wie jede Form, eine Fiktion und somit ein Umweg oder Aufschub, oder die Ausstellung der Rede als Anrede – setzt mich zumindest teilweise frei von den Anforderungen der Abhandlung, und ich fühle mich besser, so vom Unfertigen zu zeugen. Sie ist aber auch, diese Form, glaube ich, ein Effekt seiner Lektüren und der Begegnungen mit ihm. Ich würde mich gerne noch einmal an ihn wenden, und tue es hier mittels einer Adressierung an Sie. Er hat etwas gegeben, das sich entzieht, das ich eher ansprechen als aussagen mag.

Man benutzt manchmal – obwohl ich es in den letzten Jahren weniger wahrgenommen habe – den Ausdruck, man »höre« einem Autor zu oder habe ihm »zugehört«. Sicher eine Wendung, die einem gefallen sollte, der sich der Bezeichnung »Psychoanalytiker« bedient, nicht um es zu sein – das wäre Hohn und Dummheit –, sondern um etwas von der Bedeutung der Benennung, dem Schein der symbolischen Bestimmung sowohl anklingen zu lassen als auch es sich und der analytischen »Sache« zunutze zu machen. Analytisches Hören gewinnt seine »Wirksamkeit«, die rätselhaft ist, aus einer Art von verkehrter Passivität; es ist nicht nur der Rhythmus, Puls und Schlag des Schweigens, für dessen poetischen Wert Nancy in Cruor eindringliche, verstörende Formulierungen gegeben hat – »das Wort ist das Blut, [...] Pulsieren« – es ist auch die geheimnisvolle »Sublimierung« in die Leichtigkeit, ins leonardische sfumato, von der er spricht, die in diesem so schlecht als »aktivem Hören« Bezeichneten seine ebenfalls schlecht benannte »Wirkung« entfaltet. Und auch – das ist diffiziles Terrain – hat Hören mit »Liebe« zu tun, mit der entgrenzten Mehrfalt von »Lieben«, für die Nancy ausgehend von Freud sehr hilfreiche, klärende und nun weiter zu bewegende Gedanken formuliert hat. Hören ist auch liebendes Umspielen dessen, was sich im Sprechen nicht gesagt hat, dort sitzt, hassvoll auf sich selbst harrt. Eine andere Art vom Zusammentreffen der Affektion – Liebe-und-Hass – mit dem Sprechen – Sprache-und-Puls – zu zeugen, und sodann dem Bezeugten etwas ablauschen zu können, findet sich auf den reichen Seiten des Cruor angerissen.

Es reizt mich also, vom Hören etwas vernehmen zu lassen. Und auch höre ich ihn immer wieder, habe seine Stimme im Ohr, eine große Verführung, ein großes Geschenk, die Gabe eines Stroms und seines Bettes, in das man sich einfließen lassen kann. Zum Gehör/A l'écoute hat so viele in den Bann ziehende Gedanken und Formulierungen gefunden, erfunden, die sich mit Cruor im Drängen des Triebes, im Rhythmus des Blutstroms, im Erspüren des Hörens in größerer Nähe zu Psychoanalyse wiederfinden. Im Verlauf dieses Flusses finde ich mich dann beizeiten etwas unentschieden: auf der einen Seite der Sog und der Drang, seine Rede, seine Texte, seine Stimme und seine Schrift, seine Bewegungen bis hin zu ihrem Abebben, Verschwinden, erneuten Aufleben weiterlaufen zu lassen, weiter hören, mehr davon, encore, mit großem Vertrauen auf etwas, das, zugleich einsam und mit anderen, so etwas wie eine »Inspiration« möglich macht; darauf, dass die Homofonie en corps klinge, sie vor allem aber auch selbst Körper annehme: er, uns voraus, wir selbst uns voraus, werden etwas – das mögen Ideen, Texte, Entwürfe, Bilder oder, und darum ist mir sehr zu tun, Einrichtungen sein – nicht produzieren (sehr dankbar bin ich für die Ausführungen zur Unterscheidung von Produzieren und dem Entstehen-Lassen von Formen), sondern sich so Gehör verschaffen, dass sie werden können. Das Verstehen, Vernehmen, Hören ist sinnliches Empfinden, Spüren – entendre est un sentir –, aber es spürt der Existenz des anderen entgegen, lockt sie hervor. Nancys Umwandlung der freudschen Annahme, dass die Dichter und die Künstler überhaupt den Analytikern voraus seien, lautet ja, dass die Dichter »anders oder besser« als die Analytiker hören würden; anders sicher, besser auch, aber die Aufgabe bleibt, vor allem für Analytiker, andere als anders-oder-besser zu hören, Hören anders zu hören, und damit etwas in die Existenz zu verführen: etwas, das eine andere Einrichtung, gar Institutionalisierung der Psychoanalyse erlauben könnte, über Psyche und Analyse hinaus.

Und es erhebt sich in diesem bewegten und rhythmisierten Mitbewegen mit dem Denken, das vom Sprechen handelt, eine andere Stimme, oder ein Impuls, appelliert an ein Innehalten, daran, mit ihm, angelehnt an ihn, gegen ihn, eine neue Form entstehen zu lassen, über die Form des Pulses, der Synkope hinaus, die keine Formen sind, aber bestimmte geben. Denn wie auf die zwei Exhortationen des Bandes Cruor hören – die eine richtet sich ans Begreifen oder Verstehen (des Oxymorons von Eros und Thanatos), die andere an die Dringlichkeit, dem Notfall der Welt ins Angesicht zu blicken. In diesem Blicken, sofern er möglich ist, erschreckt mich, dass was da kommen mag, ganz anderes Handeln und Denken erzwingen muss, als was Nancy uns vorgemacht hat – aber dann: wer hat mehr als er und Derrida, den Mut zum Denken des Erschreckenden, Grausamen auch in ihren noch unbekannten Erscheinungen gelehrt.

Aus Modestie, von seinem Platz her, den er denjenigen eines »Profanen« nennt, trennt Nancy die Praxis – oder Klinik – der Psychoanalyse deutlich von ihrem Denken. Als erstere müsse sie an sich glauben und müsse ein Wissen von sich vorgeben, letztere hingegen höre nicht auf, sich von sich zu verabschieden. Ich kann nur kurz, gedrängt, dringlich, gereizt, freudig erregt, traurig gestimmt von seiner Abwesenheit mit ihm, gegen ihn sagen, dass ich gegen diese Trennung aufbegehre, vom Denken her, von der Praxis her, vom geschichtlichen Geschehen her – mehr auf ihn hörend als ihm widersprechend. Über sein Denken Freuds, der Psychoanalyse, Lacans würde ich beizeiten gerne mehr sprechen, sich mehr entwickeln lassen. Ich hoffe es gibt da, vielleicht bald, ein Gespräch zu mehreren, zu dem ich gerne einladen würde; auch diese Sache drängt.

Was mich drängt, wäre das, was hier Denken heißt, das sich sozusagen als Denken Sagende, zurückzuwenden in eine Klinik – was einfacher scheint, das Hören hat dort schon den Raum bereitet – aber vor allem auch in die Praxis der Psychoanalyse, in ihre Einrichtungen, deren stetes Zuviel an Betrieb und Dominanz, in den Streit der Theorie und den Lärm ihres Geredes, ins Mitund-aus-einander der Analytikerinnen und Analytiker. Es gibt eine Chance, auch hier, und auch hier wissen wir nicht, »wohin, auf welche Seite es fällt«, dies »ungeheuerliche und maßlose Zusammentreten von Abspaltung und Beziehung« von dem seine kurze, letzte Leçon spricht, sich in eine Form individualisieren zu lassen.

Freud hat die Vereinigung der Psychoanalytiker von der Ambivalenz des Miteinander, dem Rätsel der Identifikation und der Instanz des Vaters her gedacht, sich so eine Gesellschaft vorgestellt, die etwas genuin Psychoanalytisches an sich hätte, auch darin, dass sie, wenn man Nancy folgt, den Mythos nicht verschmäht;

Lacan hat auf die antike Schule gesetzt und auf die Rede und Instanz des Maître in ihr, und versucht das Unbewusste, Verdrängte in Formen (cartels, passe etc.) sich artikulieren zu lassen, die Übertragung suspendieren oder neutralisieren sollten und seinerseits, vorgeblich außerhalb der École, seine Lehre als Dichtung – »je suis un poème« – ertönen lassen; es gab natürlich einige andere Unternehmungen, Kollektive oder Gruppen als Experimente in der Geschichte der Psychoanalyse; vor allem die größeren aber auch die kleineren Einrichtungen sind, so scheint's, vor den Anforderungen der kapitalistischen Unwelt aus Objektproduktion und Effizienzsicherung, ihrem eigenen Beharren in Dominanz oder durch naiv übernommene politische Repräsentanzformen mehr oder weniger stark eingeknickt und haben Psychoanalytisches zur Verwaltungssache gemacht; viele resignieren oder privatisieren angesichts dessen. Nancys Einladung, das Versprechen seines Denkens wäre hier, die Chance zu sehen, eine psychoanalytische Form des Miteinander entstehen zu lassen, die von seinem Trieb herkommt, und die den Trieb, so wie er ihn denkt, skandalös, vom Blutstrom her, vom Pulsieren, und nicht, wie Freud, vom Anspruch der Begriffe her auf sich nimmt.

Im so praktischen Denken wäre an der differenziellen Zusammenziehung von Trieb und Sprechen weiterzu- was soll man sagen? Wohlfeil ist -arbeiten, aber es verbietet sich aus Gründen, die vielfältig sind; -denken liegt nahe, zu nahe, man entzöge sich des Abstands vom Denken; -dichten wäre zugleich präzise und preziös, verriete die Differenz von Dichter und Analytiker, -sprechen wäre schlicht recht, ließe aber die hervorbringende Note aus; -setzen könnte man hier vieles noch: -träumen, -tanzen, -streiten, -basteln, -öffnen, -spüren, -machen, -lieben, -skeptizieren, -schreiben, -benennen, -… Ein offenes Weiterzu- wäre vielleicht ein Name für eine solche Einrichtung. Sie könnte als Praxis an sich selbst eine Hörkappe – oder Hörklappe, wie das freudsche Schema nach Celans Schief heißt, was Nancy in Cruor in Erinnerung ruft – tragen. Aber ich komme ins Schweifen.

Dies nun richtet sich nicht an Sie, nicht direkt, vielleicht über einen Umweg, dessen Erfahrung ich Ihnen unterstelle: auch Sie leben nicht nur in der Bedrängnis unserer Zeit, sondern auch in der Not, das Denken und seinen Trieb in der Institution zu wahren oder sogar seine Chance wahrnehmen, aufführen zu lassen, sie sich spürbar und sie wahrnehmbar machen zu lassen. Meine Worte richten sich an Analytikerinnen und Analytiker, gewisse, namentliche, anonyme, ihre Gruppe und Masse, an mich selbst. Aber

Psychoanalytiker – wer ist das? Wer sind sie oder Sie? Psycho-analytiker sind nicht nur die zu nennen, die sich so nennen: Psychoanalyse geschieht, Psyche heißt Ab- und Auflösen selbst, wem es geschieht in nennbarer, genannter oder ungenannter Form – das verschließt sich dem Wissen. Eine Diskrepanz von grammatischer Form, Benennung, Adressierung und Pronominalisierung überhaupt und Sein, großer oder kleiner Sprechform, eine Abdrift im Verb sein selbst, eine Ausrenkung im Sprechen, sogar im soi des soi-disant sozusagen selbst, die Sprache als ganz Fremde bleibt eine unerhörte Möglichkeit. Kurz gesagt, in Bezug auf die manchmal dramatischste Form: Die Psychoanalyse ist gehalten, von dem her zu denken und zu handeln, was man »Wahnsinn«, »Psychose«, »Irresein« oder anders nennt, und dieses Denkhandeln würde auch das affizieren, was von Nancy als Triebdenken und Triebsprechen gedacht und geschrieben wurde.

Hier liegt vielleicht eine Faltung von Trieb und Sprechen vor, die Missfaltung ist, die stets einreißt oder sich verpasst, fehlfaltet oder sich verheddert: einen kleinen Span oder eine Körnung von ganz fremdem Stoffgeschehen sich einlädt, einfängt, die sich in der Inkorporierung des Psychoanalytischen in das Trieb-Sprech-Sein-Selbstwahrnehmungs-Denken zu spüren geben, oder angenommen werden müssen. Psychoanalyse wäre der Name für eine Stätte, an der das Sprechen und die Triebe über ihre eigenen Fehlfaltungen wachen, in Grausamkeit sie betrachten, sie, die sich grausam einfinden, nicht um sie zu wahren, aber sie wahrzunehmen – was immer daraus folgen möge.

Wieder ganz mit ihm kann man hier schlicht sagen, dass auch hier kein Wissen gegeben ist, ob etwas, wie eine Form des Vernehmens, ein Stück Kosmos doch erspürt werden darf: Er gibt dieses Wort, sein Denken, und ich vernehme eine mal grausame, mal ermutigende Stimme, hier, den Blick nicht abzuwenden, sein Gemüt und seinen Leib nicht zurückzuziehen, und auch nicht zu unterlassen, Schritte zu gehen, nach anderen zu greifen, ihnen zuzurufen. Roh der Grausamkeit, grausam den Rohheiten begegnen – die psychoanalytische Stätte ist ein Aneurysma der Triebbahnen.

Weiter im Bilde, das an der Sache selbst partizipieren will, gesprochen: ein Strömungsort, ein Gefäß, für das Pulsieren, ein örtlicher Strudel, ist denkbar, er hat ihn schon gedacht, es denkt sich bereits; ein Umlaufgeflecht aus nach innen gefaltetem Außen im Fluss, wo Gerinnung ausgesetzt, darin aber der Grausamkeit eingedenk ist und Befreiung ermöglicht: Grausamkeit und Befreiung bieten sich mit ihm an, eine Metapsychologie und Poetik der institutionellen Psychoanalyse zu entwerfen, in der sich die vielleicht notwendigen, aber auch fade gewordenen Worte wie Transmission und Übertragung anders gesellen, sich anders zu Gehör geben. Eine Stätte also fürs Oxymoron von Eros und Thanatos, die neben dem Raum der Mutter und der Vatersehnsucht genug Raum und genug Sehnen für die Explosionen der Liebe und die Bannungen des Hasses verspricht, für eine Weile zumal, in aller Dringlichkeit.

Ich grüße Sie – von Herzen; die Wendung klingt nun, nach ihm etwas anders – und sage Ihnen noch einmal Dank dafür, ein Sprechen zumindest erlaubt zu haben, eines, das von der Sorge um die Psychoanalyse als Form des Triebs, des Sprechens, von anderem her sich bestimmt, sich erfinden und verlieren möchte.

Ihr
Marcus Coelen

Mysore, 25. August 2022

Helen Petrovsky

A Life with No Analogon
(Remembering Jean-Luc Nancy)

The world we are living in now is very different from the one that
Jean-Luc Nancy left less than a year ago. The rupture is harsh and
decisive. Indeed, February 24, 2022 marks a historical landmark
between "before" and "after," and if we know more or less what
"before" meant in terms of global politics and economics, the time
"after," which we are immersed in at the moment, has no such
clear or reassuring contours. Of course, many things have changed
already since the beginning of the global pandemic, and Jean-Luc
was there to evaluate the transformations taking place. He was
not at all put off by the fears of disruption or some kind of fateful
setback that were voiced at the beginning of this unexpected and
truly all-encompassing trial. Against the nervous, if not hysterical
outbursts of certain well-known scholars, deploring the growing
isolation of tech-savvy individuals (not to mention endless other
evils), he remained restrained and composed. His attitude was that
of a wise person, though not necessarily a sage. Jean-Luc's wisdom went hand in hand with his life experience, no doubt, but
also with the way in which he chose to treat the world around
him (to use his own philosophical term): I can think of no one
with the same degree of openness and interest in what is happening across the globe, with the same integral as well as integrating
vision. Knowing Jean-Luc's deep involvement in political affairs,
I am wondering what he would have said about the ongoing Rus-
sian-Ukrainian war, which from my side appears to be nothing less
than a total disaster.

I met Jean-Luc Nancy in Moscow in the winter of 1990, when
he came to the Institute of Philosophy to lecture along the lines
of what was planned as a preparatory visit. The event brought
together two distinguished scholars, namely, Jean-Luc himself and
the US political theorist Susan Buck-Morss, who was already a
close friend of members of the Laboratory for Post-Classical Studies in Philosophy headed by Valery Podoroga. This double visit
was supposed to pave the way for Jacques Derrida, another highly
welcome Western intellectual, who did arrive in Moscow one
month later accompanied by his wife Marguerite. Historically, it
was a very exciting moment known as *Perestroika*, and I daresay

that all our foreign guests were in one way or another captivated by it.[1] I even remember Jacques Derrida comparing *Perestroika* (literally *reconstruction*) to deconstruction, although later, regretfully, he went back on his words. The political movement for reform and freedom of speech found its immediate reflection at the academic level: visits of this kind would have been impossible during the Cold War, which divided not only countries and ideologies, but academic communities as well. The beginning of the 1990s was a turning point in all respects, and enthusiasts such as Susan Buck-Morss were instrumental in fomenting new ties. In the course of that memorable double visit Susan gave her insightful analysis of Derrida's reading of the Declaration of Independence, while Jean-Luc presented his own philosophy in a lecture entitled "Today."[2]

Working on the Moscow lecture was the beginning of our friendship, despite the fact that I felt a bit intimidated, considering the task assigned and my status as post-graduate student. No wonder, I was Jean-Luc's translator, and we had earlier agreed that he would speak in English, a language less exotic to the Soviet audience than French. On a frosty January evening we met at the Academy hotel to go over his notes together in preparation for the lecture. The place was rather rundown in those days. The only suitable working space was a small empty lunchroom, where we sat sipping tea from thick glass tumblers while Jean-Luc generously introduced me to his ideas and terminology, which (he would continue to insist) was not as untranslatable as Derrida's. The enterprise was challenging, to say the very least. And yet not everything could be foreseen. The next day, during the presentation, a sudden problem cropped up. Speaking of the subject capable of containing its contradictions within itself, a reference to late Hegel, Jean-Luc used a word that sounded like *law*. I translated it respectively. However, Alexei Garadzha, a brilliant professional translator who was present at the lecture, uttered the word *love*, quietly but very distinctly. An awkward pause ensued. The moment Jean-Luc realized what

---

1 See Jacques Derrida, *Moscou aller-retour. Suivi d'un entretien avec N. Avtonomova, V. Podoroga, M. Ryklin* (La Tour d'Aigues: Éditions de l'Aube, 1995).

2 Jean-Luc Nancy, "Segodnia. Lektsiia, prochitannaia v ianvare 1990 goda v Institute filosofii v Moskve [Today. Lecture Delivered in January 1990 at the Institute of Philosophy in Moscow]," trans. Helen Petrovsky, in *Ad Marginem '93. Ezhegodnik Laboratorii postklassicheskikh issledovanii Instituta filosofii Rossiiskoi akademii nauk* [Yearbook of the Laboratory for Post-Classical Studies of the Russian Academy of Sciences Institute of Philosophy] (Moscow: Ad Marginem Publ., 1994), pp. 148–164.

was being discussed, he turned to me and exclaimed: *"Ia liubliu tebia!* (I love you!)" This impromptu Russian explication nicely brought the issue to a close.

I was beginning to learn then, and I never stopped learning from Jean-Luc over the decades to follow. In "Today" one comes across many of his influential ideas formulated with incredible precision. They include the postulates that existence, being absolute and free, has no foundation whatsoever, that sense is essentially sharing, while communication is exactly this sense, which is offered to us as a gift, that philosophy, taken to its limits, has to think exteriority, which is just another designation for the "world." And, of course, the lecture touches on the concept of community that remains Nancy's distinct and indelible contribution to contemporary philosophical thinking. I am definitely referring to his classic book *La communauté désœuvrée* (1983),[3] but also to the ways in which he reduced both the rather unwieldy and technical *being-in-common* to the more elegant and laconic *avec*, trying to avoid a basic ambiguity attached to the very word itself (especially in its German translation as *Gemeinschaft*, reminiscent of the ominous *Volksgemeinschaft*) and perhaps also emphasizing the kind of relationality that takes us beyond the human condition as such. I remember that during Jean-Luc's last visit to Moscow in the fall of 2016 he confessed that he was more and more interested in the writings of Spinoza, something that philosophers are destined to confront at a later day in their lives. Still, he always emphasized that his concept derived from the Heideggerian *Mitsein*, where *Mit-* was already ascribed an existential and not categorical meaning.

What resonates most with the current state of affairs in this country is Nancy's vehement critique of a social totality engaged in producing its essence. He spoke of two such totalities, namely communism and fascism, and community for him is precisely that which avoids producing an essence. Its *désœuvrement*, i.e., inoperativeness and to a certain degree even idleness, consists in what is "subtracted" from it, in other words, in that which keeps retreating. What is implied here is nothing other than "work" (œuvre), which, if translated into political terms, is equivalent to some kind of fusion produced at the institutional level, be it the people, party, leader or the nation-state itself. Translated into

---

3   The book has seen many re-editions, one of them being Jean-Luc Nancy, *La communauté désœuvrée* (Paris: Christian Bourgois, 2004).

philosophical terms, "work" stands for substantial identity. And this is what community, being a communion of finite bodies and not infinite individuals (or simply subjects), strictly opposes. However, the historical moment we are living through now seems to be witnessing a dramatic reincarnation of an aggressively defined communal substance. Such is the inevitable consequence of war for a country that chooses to be the aggressor. Besides wondering about what Jean-Luc's comments might have been with regard to the conflict itself, I cannot help thinking of how he would have treated the changed attitude to everything Russian, including the classic writers that were widely read in his family. (This question is not an easy one, to be sure. Had we talked today, I would have probably suggested that the European—"rational"—layer of Russian imperial culture has to be appraised only in conjunction with a parallel reading of alternative or "minor" writings, in which the darker side of this culture is frankly revealed.)

Some time ago, after Jean-Luc's passing, I decided to return to my notes of his lectures, which I took way back in 1995–1996 during my stay in Strasbourg sponsored by the Bourse Diderot. It was an unforgettable academic and personal experience. Jean-Luc, then head of the philosophy department, was teaching two courses—one, for freshmen, on Hegel and the other, for postgraduate students, on Kant. His close friend and lifelong associate Philippe Lacoue-Labarthe was also teaching that semester, and his lecture courses on Rousseau and especially Hölderlin were a major attraction for listeners, who came from different parts of the world. So, no doubt, were Nancy's. While deciphering my notes on Kant, I was once again enthralled by the freshness and audacity of Jean-Luc's reading, who, besides offering an introduction to Kant's philosophy, was improvising during this regular course. The main question he addressed then may be formulated as follows: what does it mean to think of nature as technique? (In a later interview, he told me that at first he intended to take up Kant's idea of *als ob*, *as if*, that academic year, but switched over to the technique of nature instead.[4]) Of course, *technique* here is another designation for *ars* or *technē* (to remember the ancient Greeks) as well as for *savoir-faire*, which stands for *artfulness, skill*. However, the theoretical framework itself, calling for the use of this "art,"

---

4   "Tekhnika i priroda (interv'iu s Zhan-Liukom Nansi) [Technique and Nature (Interview with Jean-Luc Nancy)]," *Logos*, no. 7 (1997), pp. 130–145.

undergoes a most dramatic transformation in that epoch. Indeed, from now on one has to think of the world, i.e., creation, in the absence of any creator. The task, in other words, is to think of the world devoid of God, a guarantee of our actions and judgments, without losing one's way in its awe-inspiring manifoldness. This, in its turn, poses the following question: how is it possible to subsume the particular that is given, i.e., the manifold itself, under the universal that is no longer given?

I vividly remember, after all these years, how Jean-Luc once made an emotional and humorous digression. "Why," he asked rhetorically, "do they say that Kant was a boring person? He was not a bore at all! On the contrary, he was absolutely restless, his main concern being that of subsuming the manifold under some kind of unity. That was his real passion!" But to return to the lectures. First of all, Jean-Luc insisted on the fact that Kant was building a system. Within it, reason and understanding are complemented by a third faculty of the mind, namely judgment. It is judgment that performs the operation of connecting, while the ultimate goal of the system itself is to establish a connection between nature and freedom. And it is judgment that allows for the subsumption of the multiplicity of the given under the unity of a concept (or the concept of unity). Kant's third *Critique* is famously devoted to the faculty of judgment, which, it will be recalled, judges in the absence of concepts. In this sense, it is an "empty" faculty that adds nothing whatsoever to any kind of positive knowledge.[5] In the lectures that in one way or another embraced all three *Critiques*, Jean-Luc clearly prioritized the "First Introduction to the Critique of Judgment" (1789–1790), where Kant appears to be most explicit in setting out his aims. (The fulfillment of those aims, according to Jean-Luc, or the third *Critique* itself, is not quite as lucid and consistent as the conceptual outline of the "First Introduction...")

So, how is it possible to think of nature as technique? The answer might seem somewhat telegraphic: by turning to the idea of purpose. In order to think of nature, thinking has to have a support, and this is where purposiveness (besides the unity of experience) steps into the picture. Technique is presented as a relation to purpose. And this has to do with the modern image of a human being. Nancy interprets humans in terms of an infinite relation to a purpose, since they themselves are never given as a goal.

---

5   However, empty judgments are in no way nonsensical for Kant.

Now technique, according to Kant, is the very faculty of judgment, namely, the connecting of the manifold with the unity of representation. In Kant, one comes across two forms of technique, correlating with two distinct kinds of reflective judgments. First, this implies so-called "purposiveness without purpose," i.e., art in the narrow and conventional meaning of the term. In this case, nature should conform to a technique understood as human art, which presupposes a relation to form, while the latter, for its part, relates to nothing other than itself. We admire the beauty of a tulip, says Kant, because in our judgment of this beauty its purposiveness "is not referred to any end whatever."[6] Second, technique may assume the guise of inner purposiveness, which is manifested in a spontaneous organization of both animate and inanimate nature, be it flowers, animals or crystals. However, in each of these cases purposiveness is ascribed not to a creator, but to the human being as an actual bearer of judgment. In addition to other things, this allows Jean-Luc to characterize Kant's system in terms of *system-subject*.

It is not my task here to give a detailed overview of the lectures. Still, I do want to stress that Nancy's reading remains acutely fresh and inspiring. I will single out only two themes that I find especially relevant today. But before doing so, I would like to highlight Jean-Luc's idea that Kant's enterprise is formulated at a time when it is the modern subject, neither all-mighty nor immortal, that is assigned the task of cognizing the unity of nature (or the world), which is not given. Together with the exigency of the unconditional, such is the challenge that arises now from strictly human reason. And this is what ultimately accounts for Kant's decision to think of nature *as if* it conformed to our faculty of judgment, being somehow tailored to it. We are able to make sense of the multiplicity of things, bordering on chaos, only by accepting this necessary supposition. So what is it that strikes me today in Jean-Luc's interpretation? First of all, his reflections on receptivity and sensation in Kant's system as well as on the sensible aspect of thinking itself. Sensibility is precisely the "place" of the subject, that which allows for its return to itself, in other words, it is selfhood understood as a structure. At the same time, sensibility points to the presence of an outside, and this exteriority is not only a menace to reason, but also a constant challenge to it. However, the sensible is inseparable

---

6   Immanuel Kant, *Critique of Judgment*, trans. James Creed Meredith, rev. and ed. Nicholas Walker (New York: Oxford University Press, 1952, 2007), p. 67.

from reason itself. Nancy makes it clear that since cognition is connected with a primary feeling of pleasure, the sensible becomes a defining aspect of reason as such. Moreover, Kantian reason paradoxically tries to discover an a priori principle in the very feelings of pleasure and displeasure. And it succeeds, which brings us back to the concept of purposiveness. But the desired principle is also about universality in abeyance, i.e., *sensus communis*, when we demand or require agreement from other human beings.

The other theme is closely linked to the first and has to do with the definition of life. Despite his consistent transcendentalism and faith in metaphysics,[7] Kant acknowledges that life is self-organizing, following its own specific laws. The formula he comes up with is fairly well-known: life is that which has no analogon (*"La vie est sans analogon,"* to quote Jean-Luc from my notes). Nancy's interpretation may be treated in the following manner. Receptivity or sensibility—*se sentir*—and life are ultimate concepts in the sense that even for Kant, although being all-embracing, they are not definitive or exhaustive, seeming to have something like a reverse side: they communicate with other concepts in the philosopher's open-ended system. No wonder that, on the one hand, life ends up being identical with systematicity itself: it appears to be the very system that Kant is seeking to build. This is Nancy's conclusion. On the other hand, however, life points to the limit of the thinkable and of philosophy itself in its capacity as speculative system. Such a reading allows us to place Kant in the context of most recent explorations.[8] I will repeat that the expanded status of the sensible as well as the idea of the infinite manifold of life, resisting any subsumption whatsoever (it cannot be accounted for through

---

7   In his "Preface" to the first edition of the *Critique of Pure Reason* Kant boldly remarks: "Now metaphysics, according to the concepts we will give of it here, is the only one of all the sciences that may promise that little but unified effort, and that indeed in a short time, will complete it in such a way that nothing remains to posterity except to adapt it in a didactic manner to its intentions, yet without being able to add to its content in the least." Immanuel Kant, *Critique of Pure Reason*, trans. and ed. Paul Guyer and Allen W. Wood (Cambridge: Cambridge University Press, 1998), p. 104.

8   Among them, I would indicate a renewed interest in the writings of Peter Kropotkin, who formulated the concept of mutual aid as a law of evolution, which governs both society and nature. See, for example, Andrej Grubačić, "David Graeber Left Us a Parting Gift—His Thoughts on Kropotkin's 'Mutual Aid'," *Truthout*, September 4, 2020, https://truthout.org/articles/david-graeber-left-us-a-parting-gift-his-thoughts-on-kropotkins-mutual-aid/?fbclid = IwAR1aSmAFR9CS3BBM3N 0xDhPTvk89A3N6C-c-hoH21_4fgYF57dhn2WuHtJw (accessed May 22, 2022).

system-building efforts), fit well into the current picture. But this holds true for the notion of technique, which, while acquiring a human dimension in Kant, at the same time gravitates towards the unrepresentable, inasmuch as it is no longer attributed to any specific figure or form. According to Jean-Luc, it becomes increasingly a means'qua end in itself, which, one might conclude, stands for *change* pure and simple, and indicates the waning of representation as such.

There are many more things to be said and remembered. This will be done in due time. Ending this short memoir, I would like to note that Jean-Luc possessed an exceptional quality: he was someone you could rely on under any circumstances. And he was always wonderfully supportive of his family and friends. After my stay in Strasbourg we remained in touch on various occasions. In the years to follow we again met twice in Strasbourg, then three times in Moscow—in 2008, 2010 and 2016. Whatever the formal pretext (a defense, colloquium, public lecture or a conference taking place outside the city), there was always room for friendly and invigorating meetings or simply, I daresay, for fun. Indeed, no matter how earnestly Jean-Luc treated the people he met or the events that he attended, there was a strong affirmative feeling linked to his very existence. In this sense, his philosophy was a continuation of his life, and vice versa. I must also add that during all this time Jean-Luc was a regular and sympathetic contributor to my theoretical and philosophical journal *Sinii divan*. He would eagerly offer his published texts, but also respond with original pieces devoted to a special topic or theme. The most recent ones include "Lenin and Electricity" for an issue marking the 100th anniversary of the October Revolution and an earlier letter on the ascension of Islam, where Nancy prophetically speaks of the "delegitimization of violence" and the mutation that the "civilization of reason, technology and generality" has been undergoing already before World War II.[9] The very last text published in my journal is a translation of his beautiful essay "With, Being-with (*avec, l'être-avec*)," one of the thirty-eight entries comprising the *Glossary of a Time of Pandemic* that appeared in 2020.

Our last meeting took place in Paris in the rainy March of 2017. There was a formal occasion behind it, and a very exciting one, for

---

9   "Pis'mo Zhan-Liuka Nansi [A Letter from Jean-Luc Nancy]," trans. Alexei Garadzha, *Sinii divan*, no. 20 (2015), pp. 82–83.

that matter. A big show of Soviet unofficial art was on display at the Centre Pompidou, and the event we were invited to attend in the capacity of two interlocutors was dedicated to the memory of Dmitri A. Prigov, a renowned and versatile Russian conceptual artist. Having acquainted himself with Prigov's works well before the event, Jean-Luc suggested the following title for our conversation: "InARTiculation." We met early in the morning of that day and spent some time hanging out on the exhibition premises—drinking coffee, catching up and browsing through Prigov's works, this time as part of the show. At some point we sat on a bench facing the projection of one of Prigov's videos. In this short film, Dmitri Alexandrovich (Prigov liked to call himself exactly this way), displaying great satisfaction, was devouring a fried chicken to the poignant tune of Donizetti. Jean-Luc watched and laughed—he was visibly amused by the spectacle. He appreciated Prigov's irony and artistry, that was absolutely clear, an attitude he must have developed straight away. After our talk I saw him off to the railway station, although the commemorative event was still in full swing. What I can't help thinking, especially now, in this moment of an all-engulfing crisis, is that Jean-Luc's one-day trip to Paris was in fact a token of friendship, and my memory of that day, vividly acute, is interspersed with deep affection and a gust of sadness.

Dieter Mersch

Cum grano singularis
Jean-Luc Nancys ›negative‹ *koinōnia.*

»Das Bedeutendste und wohl auch Schmerzlichste, wovon die moderne Welt Zeugnis ablegt [...] ist das Zeugnis der Auflösung, des Zerfalls oder der Erschütterung der Gemeinschaft.«[1] Mit diesen Worten beginnt Jean-Luc Nancys – neben den späteren Arbeiten Être *singulier pluriel* (1996) und *Corpus* (2000) – wohl wichtigste Untersuchung *La communauté désœuvrée* (1986) – *Die undarstellbare Gemeinschaft.* Die Frage der *communauté,* der Gemeinschaft, deren Ausdruck in Deutschland durch den Nationalsozialismus diskreditiert, in Frankreich jedoch ohne Vorbehalt benutzt wird, hatte sich bereits 1983 anlässlich einer Einladung von Jean-Christophe Bailly für die Zeitschrift *Aléa* gestellt, deren Thema *La communauté, le nombre* lautete. Der Gegensatz ist erhellend: auf der einen Seite die ›Gemeinschaft‹, die einst Ferdinand Tönnies aus soziologischer Perspektive der ›Gesellschaft‹ als Inbegriff kollektiver, politischer und juridischer Organisation entgegengestellt hatte,[2] auf der anderen Seite die Zahl, die bloße ›Menge‹, bei der man sowohl an Gustave Le Bons *Psychologie des foules* von 1895 oder Hermann Brochs zwischen 1939 und 1948 entstandene *Massenwahntheorie* denken kann als auch an den mathematischen Mengenbegriff, dessen ubiquitäres Schema den damals erst im Entstehen begriffenen digitalen Technologien zugrunde liegen sollte. Es ist diese Vorahnung, dass sich im Rücken des kommunistischen Niedergangs in Gestalt ubiquitärer Vernetzung und ›sozialer Medien‹ neue *communities* zu formieren begannen, die gleichzeitig zu einer restlosen Disruption und Polarisierung des Gemeinschaftlichen führen sollten. Ausdrücklich hat Nancy später unter dem Titel *La communauté affrontée – Die herausgeforderte Gemeinschaft*[3] in Reaktion auf Maurice Blanchots *La communauté inavouable – Die*

---

1 Jean-Luc Nancy: *Die undarstellbare Gemeinschaft*, Stuttgart 1988, S. 11. Eine Neuübersetzung ist unter dem Titel: *Von einer Gemeinschaft, die sich nicht verwirklicht*, Wien 2018 erschienen.

2 Ferdinand Tönnies: *Gemeinschaft und Gesellschaft. Grundbegriffe der reinen Soziologie* (1887), München 2018.

3 Jean-Luc Nancy: *Die herausgeforderte Gesellschaft*, Zürich, Berlin 2007. Eine ausführliche Auseinandersetzung mit Blanchot geschieht darüber hinaus in ders.: *Die verleugnete Gemeinschaft*, Zürich, Berlin 2017.

uneingestehbare Gemeinschaft,[4] die sich ihrerseits als Antwort auf Nancys ursprüngliche Überlegungen verstand, diese Parallele gezogen.

Mit Anderen sein

Tatsächlich standen die Auseinandersetzungen von 1983 zunächst im Zeichen einer Erosion von ›Gemeinschaftlichkeit‹, wie sie sich in Bezug auf die gescheiterten Hoffnungen des kommunistischen Projekts abzeichnete. Dem stand das nicht weniger problematische Projekt einer Restitution des Kollektivs durch digitale Sozialtechnologien gegenüber, zwischen deren Extremen sich vor allem die Sartre-kritische Generation, der Nancy angehörte, zu entscheiden hatte. So war eine Opposition geboren, die Nancy allerdings von Anfang an kritisch zu unterlaufen suchte, denn *La communauté désœuvrée* stellte sich sowohl der sozialistischen Utopie einer ›Erarbeitung‹ oder ›Herstellbarkeit‹ (*œuvrée*) von Gemeinschaft entgegen, als auch sämtlichen Spielarten ihrer technischen Restitution. Entsprechend präzisierte Nancy seine Diagnose dahingehend, dass es nicht darum gehe, die *Idee* der Gemeinschaft zu erneuern, sondern darum, die Möglichkeit von Gemeinschaftlichkeit selbst zu befragen.[5] Die »Geschichte philosophischer Texte über die Gemeinschaft in den 1980er Jahren«, wie er später notierte, verdiene es, »mit großer Genauigkeit geschrieben zu werden, denn sie erhellt eine tiefgreifende Bewegung des Denkens in Europa zu jener Zeit«, durch die »das Motiv der ›Gemeinschaft‹«, anstatt es ans Licht zu bringen, es erst recht verdunkelte.[6] Dagegen setzte Nancy dort an, wo das Gemeinsame im Gemeinschaftlichen sich konstituiert, soweit es, wie der Bescheid in *La communauté affrontée* lautet, allenfalls als ein »Mit« unterschiedlicher oder auch gegenläufiger Kräfte denkbar sei, deren Gegenwarten in Wechselwirkung zueinander träten, miteinander konkurrierten oder sich aufeinander zubewegten und sich gegenseitig herausforderten.[7] Dieser Gedanke eines fundamentalen »Mit« bildet die paradigmatische Figur, unter der Nancy die Kategorie der Gemeinschaft diskutierte und deren Perspektive sich bis zu dem, kurz vor Nancys Tod erschienenen

---

4   Maurice Blanchot: *Die uneingestehbare Gemeinschaft*, Berlin, 2. Aufl., 2015.
5   Nancy: *Die undarstellbare Gemeinschaft*, a.a.O., S. 14.
6   Nancy.: *Die herausgeforderte Gesellschaft*, a.a.O., S. 17.
7   Ebd., S. 37.

Dialog *Begegnung* mit Carolin Meister hält, welcher die Flüchtigkeit und Unvorhersehbarkeit des *rencontre* als Modell für jede Art von Gemeinschaftlichkeit entwirft.[8] Dabei steht das »Mit« in der Bedeutung eines Zusammentreffens, eines Zusammen-Mit gerade für die Lücke des Gemeinschaftlichen ein, ihr Zwischenraum der Trennungen, die ebenso Verbindung ermöglicht wie vereitelt.

»Mit« gehört allerdings nach den klassischen Grammatiken zu den Synkategoremata, die selbst keine Bedeutung besitzen, sondern zwischen Partikeln und damit Bedeutungen vermitteln. In diesem Fall haben wir es mit einer Präposition zu tun, die räumliche und zeitliche Relationen ›modalisiert‹. Im Sinne einer performativen Modalität avanciert dann das »Mit« zum Schlüssel des Gemeinsamen, denn lateinisch *cum* bildet es in Form von Präfixbildungen wie ›Ko-‹, ›Kon-‹ oder ›Kom-‹, deren Bindestrich ihre Unruhe wie ihr Nichtaufgehendes bekundet, den zentralen Grundbaustein in nahezu sämtlichen Begriffsbildungen, die mit dem Gemeinschaftlichen des Gemeinsamen zu tun haben: *communitas* oder *communio* genauso wie *communicatio* und *coniunctio* wie auch die vielen anderen, durch die modernen Sprachen einverleibten Latinismen wie Korrelation, Ko-Existenz und Ko-Präsenz, aber auch Komparenz bzw. *Comparution* (Mit-Erscheinen) oder Koinzidenz, Konstitution (Zusammen-Setzung) und sogar Ko-Ipseität oder ›Con-science‹.[9] Viele ähnliche ›Kon‹nexionen, die Nancy nicht explizit nennt, könnten mitangeführt (*con-addere*) werden, man denke an Koordination, Kooperation, Kollaboration, Konfiguration oder Kollektiv – nicht zu vergessen der Kommerz als Gegenbild, der das Ko- oder *cum* durch den Warenfetischismus und dessen Imaginäres pervertiert.[10]

So bewahrt und verbirgt sich für Nancy gleichsam in einem exzessiv gedachten *cum* die grundlegende Frage nach der Gemeinschaft, die ebenso prekär bleibt, wie sie ›uns‹ immer schon vorausgegangen sein wird, denn das Gemeinsame, wie Nancy in *La communauté affrontée* schreibt, »ist uns gegeben, das heißt, uns ist ein ›wir‹ gegeben, ehe wir ein ›wir‹ artikulieren oder gar rechtfertigen können«.[11] Und doch bleibt die Weise dieses Gegebenseins chronisch unklar, offen, zuweilen dubios, denn das »Mit« kann so wenig selbst als gegeben gedacht werden wie ein ›Zusammen‹

---

8   Carolin Meister, Jean-Luc Nancy: *Begegnung*, Zürich 2021, S. 11, 14, 16 passim.

9   Jean-Luc Nancy: *singulär plural sein*, Zürich 2012, in der Reihenfolge S. 69, 57f., 73ff., 143ff., 70, 100, 96ff., S. 64f., 68ff., 76, 71 passim.

10 Vgl. ebd., S. 83ff., 117f.

11 Nancy: *Die herausgeforderte Gemeinschaft*, a.a.O., S. 38.

schon besteht, weil sie sich erst durch die ihm zugrunde liegenden Beziehungen performativ ergeben. Ähnlich hatte es auch Maurice Merleau-Ponty in seinem Vorwort zu *Humanismus und Terror* ausgedrückt, denn »eine Gesellschaft«, heißt es dort, sei »nicht der Tempel jener Wert-Idole, die auf dem Giebel ihrer Monumente oder in den Verfassungstexten stehen«, vielmehr seien sie »das wert, was in ihr die Beziehungen des Menschen zu Menschen wert sind«.[12]

Oikonomia und Koinonia

Nancy hat sich der Aufgabe der Erforschung dieses Wertes durch die Analyse der Logik des »Mit« und seiner Komposita gestellt, wobei es im Unterschied zum späteren Text Être *singulier pluriel – singulär plural sein* nicht um die Fundierung einer relationalen Ontologie, sondern um die Sozialphilosophie und deren eigentlichen Kern, die Voraussetzung des Sozialen überhaupt geht, die von einem ›Sein-mit-Anderen‹ ausgeht. Im Zentrum steht dabei von Anfang an die selbst bestimmungslose Mitte des ›Zwischen‹, die ohne Referenz auf ein Prinzip oder einen übergreifenden Sinn auskommt. Nancy packt also das Problem der Gemeinschaft an seiner Wurzel. Das macht die Radikalität seines Ansatzes aus. Denn die Wurzel ist die Fraglichkeit, aber auch die Fragilität des *cum*, das weder einer politischen Forderung genügen kann noch vom Politischen her zu erfassen ist, das auch nicht die Gemeinschaft als *Poietik* oder *technē* adressiert, sondern gleichsam jene Wendungen untersucht, die das Gemeinsame je um je hervorruft und offen lässt. Es geht also nicht darum, das Gemeinsame neu zu denken, es anders zu bestimmen, sondern in ihm ein immer erst Künftiges, noch Kommendes zu sehen,[13] denn die »Menschen-Gesellschaft« sei, wie es ebenfalls in Friedrich Nietzsches *Also sprach Zarathustra* heißt, ein »Versuch« – »kein Vertrag«.[14]

In der Tat bleibt jedoch die Frage nach der Gemeinschaftlichkeit der Gemeinschaft, nach dem was Menschen zusammenführt, was sie einbindet und füreinander engagieren lässt, was sie, mit anderen Worten, versammelt oder teilen lässt, eines der basalen Rätsel der Sozialphilosophie. Yuval Harari hatte es mit Blick auf kollektiv

---

12 Maurice Merleau-Ponty: *Humanismus und Terror*, Frankfurt/M 1966, S. 8.
13 Nancy: *Die herausgeforderte Gemeinschaft*, a.a.O., S. 26.
14 Friedrich Nietzsche: *Also sprach Zarathustra* (1883), Kritische Studienausgabe, München 1999, Bd. 4, S. 265.

erzählte Geschichten aufzulösen getrachtet,[15] Jürgen Habermas in Ansehung der intrinsischen Rationalität kommunikativer Prozesse,[16] Bruno Latour mit Bezug auf humane und non-humane Akteur-Netzwerke,[17] um nur einige zu nennen. Nancy sucht dagegen das Mysterium durch Rekurs auf die Präposition *cum* zu erhellen, das die Relationen zwischen uns, die Beziehungen modifiziert und damit eine mediale Funktion übernimmt, indem es in der Mitte (*medium*), als dem eigentlich Bindenden, eine Unbestimmtheit einträgt. Das Geheimnis der Gemeinsamkeit erscheint dann als ebenso nichtig wie unausräumbar.

Man täusche sich allerdings nicht: Nancy spielt auf diese Weise nicht Gemeinschaft gegen Gesellschaft aus, eher rekurriert er auf ein Begriffspaar, das in der Antike, der Spätantike zumal für die Erfahrung einer politischen Gemeinde (*polis*) einstand und quer zu den geläufigen Unterscheidungen zwischen Gemeinschaft und Gesellschaft verwendet wurde, nämlich *oikonomia* und *koinōnia*. Sie verweisen auf verschiedene Aspekte der Konstitution des Gemeinschaftlichen, wobei die *oikonomia*, die Aristoteles noch auf die Bewirtschaftung der Hausgemeinschaft bezog,[18] im Rahmen des Stoizismus als philosophisch-ethisches Pendant zur römischen Globalisierung als ein universales Konzept entstand, das vom frühen Christentum übernommen und theologisiert wurde. Sämtliche späteren Epochen einschließlich des Mittelalters und der frühen Neuzeit leiten aus ihm die Ordnungsseite der Gemeinschaften ab. Dagegen benennt die *koinōnia* das, was gleichsam das Versammelnde sammelt, das heißt dasjenige, was das Haus und seine Mitglieder zusammenführt und für Integration sorgt. Denn zielt die *oikonomia* wörtlich auf die ›Gesetze des Hauses‹, in der Spätantike als Ort der römischen *Civitas* und in der christlichen Welt als ›Haus Gottes‹, wie es symbolisch in der Kathedrale verkörpert war, steht die *koinōnia*, insbesondere bei Aristoteles, für den eigentlich politischen Sinn.[19]

Dabei schließt der *oikonomia*-Gedanke nicht nur im engeren Sinne die politische Ökonomie ein, sondern auch das Recht, die

---

15 Yuval Harari: *Kurze Geschichte der Menschheit*, München 2013.
16 Jürgen Habermas: *Theorie des kommunikativen Handelns*, 2 Bde., Frankfurt/M 1981.
17 Bruno Latour: *Eine neue Soziologie für eine neue Gesellschaft*, Frankfurt/M 2010.
18 Aristoteles: *Politika*, Philosophische Schriften Bd. 4, Hamburg1995, S. 14–22, 1256aff.
19 Ebd., S. 1, 1252a.

Geschichte und ihre Überlieferung wie ebenfalls die Institutionen der Regierung und die Organisation des Sozialen mitsamt der Person und ihrer Identität. Diese repräsentieren folglich die Kategorien, unter denen das Soziale bis heute diskutiert wird; gleichzeitig liegt in ihrer Kennzeichnung die Quelle der Interdependenz zwischen dem Sozialen und seiner politischen Gestaltung, die es den Direktiven der Machbarkeit unterwirft. Giorgio Agamben hat dies in seiner kleinen Untersuchung über den Begriff des Dispositivs herausgearbeitet, soweit die lateinische Übersetzung von *oikonomia* die *dispositio* bildet, die die Form und die Rahmenbedingung des Gemeinwesens allererst bereitstellt.[20] Dann spielen allein die Elemente und die Art ihrer ›Zusammen-Führung‹ eine Rolle, nicht die humanen Beziehungen sowie das, was ihr ›Ziehendes‹ ausmacht, was im eigentlichen Sinne wiederum der *koinōnia* zugeschrieben werden muss. Kenntlich wird so, dass sich mit der *oikonomia* eine verbindliche Struktur manifestiert, deren Domestikation die gesamte politische Philosophie von Thomas Hobbes über Adam Smith bis zu Hegel und Marx beschäftigen wird und deren Problem in der angemessenen Organisation und Gouvernementalität sozialer Verbindungen besteht.

Demgegenüber signifiziert der *koinōnia*-Begriff die nichtaufhebbare Ambiguität zwischen *oikonomischer Ordnung als sozialer Form* einerseits und dem, was auf der anderen Seite die *Sozialität des Sozialen*, die *Verbindlichkeit der Verbindung zwischen Menschen* konstituiert, noch bevor es Gemeinschaft oder Gesellschaft gibt. Wörtlich bedeutet der Ausdruck die Teilhabe (*koinos*) sowie das Gemeinsame (*koinōneō*), mithin also das, was uns dazu bringt, überhaupt von ›uns‹ zu sprechen, aneinander Anteil zu nehmen oder uns zuzuneigen (*clinamen*), ohne vorderhand schon auf ein Wir referieren zu können oder einen Grund für ein gemeinsames Leben zu besitzen. Der Ausdruck ist reflexiver Natur, ohne dass ihm bereits eine feste Bedeutung zukäme, sofern er lediglich für das steht, was im weitesten Sinne das Soziale erst zum Sozialen macht. Die Komplementarität zur *oikonomia* besteht insbesondere darin, dass dieser, als Bedingungsgefüge oder politisches Dispositiv, stets ein systemischer Zug zukommt, während die *koinōnia* dasjenige aufruft, was die Gemeinschaftlichkeit des gemeinsamen Hauses allererst ermöglicht und lebenswert macht. Entsprechend ist sie verschieden ausbuchstabiert worden – bei Aristoteles mit

---

20 Giorgio Agamben: *Was ist ein Dispositiv?*, Zürich, Berlin 2008, S. 19ff.

Bezug auf die *koinōnia politikē,* in christlicher Zeit mit Blick auf die *communion* und die Nächstenliebe und beim frühen Marx in Ansehung der »Allgemeinheit der Arbeit«. Arthur Schopenhauer spricht von »agapē«, George Batailles vom »Heiligen Eros«, Maurice Blanchot von der »Gemeinschaft der Liebenden«, Derrida von »Freundschaft«, Emmanuel Lévinas vom »Antlitz des Anderen« als erster Gabe und Gilles Deleuze und Félix Guattari schließlich von einer grundlegenden »Affizierung«. Edith Stein hat ihr ihren religiösen Anklang zurückerstattet, ebenso Vladimir Jankélévitch, wenn er vom »Verzeihen« als einer gemeinsamen Aufgabe spricht und dabei das Unverzeihliche anmahnt, während Michel Foucault ihr den Sinn einer »parrhesia« als Mut zum Wahrsprechen im Sinne des Bekenntnisses oder der Bezeugung des Zeugnisses zuspricht. »Die Gemeinschaft wird im Tod des anderen offenbart«, heißt es ergänzend bei Nancy, so werde sie »immer dem anderen offenbart. Die Gemeinschaft ist das, was stets durch und für den anderen geschieht.«[21] Die bindende Kraft der *koinōnia* ist dann an Endlichkeit und Sterblichkeit verknüpft, die uns in erster Linie an unsere Kreatürlichkeit erinnert.

Désœuvrement

Auch wenn diese verschiedenen Anrufungen nicht zur wirklichen Kennzeichnung der *koinōnia* taugen, sofern sich in ihnen vor allem die Zeit widerspiegelt, dokumentieren ihre Differenzen zur hegemonialen *oikonomia* das, was gegen diese und mit ihr auf dem Spiel steht. Dabei bildet die *koinōnia* keinen besonderen Modus von Sozialität, sie begründet keine Politik, keine Programmatik der Freiheit, vielmehr erfüllt sie sich einzig in ihrer Performativität. Dennoch verbirgt sich in ihr die stets unverwirklichte humanistische Seite der Gemeinschaft, der die oft trübe Realität der *oikonomia* entgegensteht. Die Schwierigkeit der Diskussion besteht deshalb darin, dass die *koinōnia* beständig von Neuem beginnen muss, indem sie aufbricht, und zwar im doppelten Sinne des Aufbruchs als eines Beginns sowie eines Risses, einer Spaltung, die das Gemeinsame der Gemeinschaft ebenso zusammenfügt wie teilt. In sie geht folglich etwas ein, was über die Sprache hinausgeht und zwischen den Teilhabenden erst manifest *werden* muss,

---

21 Nancy: *Die undarstellbare Gemeinschaft,* a.a.O., S. 38.

ohne dass ein Medium ausgewiesen werden kann, das deren Zusammen (*cum*) vermittelte.

Die Aufgabe einer jeden politischen Philosophie und Sozialphilosophie besteht entsprechend darin, *koinōnia* und *oikonomia* miteinander in ein angemessenes Verhältnis zu setzen und ihre möglichen Relationen zueinander in Bewegung zu bringen. Nancy nimmt darin insofern eine Sonderstellung ein, als er sich ihrer Konzeptualisierung verweigert und mit der problematisch gewordenen Gemeinschaft, ihrem epochalen Zerfall zugleich der Frage nach der Künftigkeit der *koinōnia* dadurch nachgeht, dass er ihre wesentliche Negativität herausstreicht. Hergeleitet einzig aus dem an sich leeren linguistischen Partikel ›Mit‹ und dessen anhängende Komposita beinhaltet es »[f]ür sich [...] nichts«,[22] weshalb die Gemeinschaft nur als ein schlechthin Unlesbares adressiert werden kann, das allein vermöge ihrer »Mit-Teilung« aufgeht.[23] Diese meint aber anderes als die Kommunikation und ihre Botschaften, noch geht sie in Partizipation auf, sondern sie unterstreicht die gemeinsame Teilung des »Mit«, sodass es nicht auf die Akt des ausdrücklichen Teilens, den Allmenden oder *commons* ankommt, sondern auf das immer erst vorläufige und prekäre Zusammen (*cum*). Es kann also auch nicht um die exklusive Idee einer neuen Gemeinschaft gehen, so wenig wie um ihre Wiederentdeckung, wie im Kommunitarismus, oder um ihre radikale Transformation wie im politischen Aktivismus, sondern ausschließlich um die Aufschließung eines stets noch Ausstehenden.

Daher die berühmte, sich an Blanchot anschließende Formulierung von der *communauté désœuvrée*, der nicht nur »undarstellbaren«, sondern auch »werklosen« oder »entwerkten«, sogar »unerwerkbaren« Gemeinschaft – einer Gemeinschaft, die sich »nicht verwirklicht«, die nicht einmal verwirklichbar wäre, ohne sich zu desavouieren.[24] *Désœuvrée* ist hier in seinen verschiedenen Bedeutungen zu verstehen: Vom Scheitern des Werkes über das, was überhaupt nicht Gegenstand einer Erwerkung oder *poiēsis* bzw. das Produkt einer *technē*, auch keiner politischen Technik sein kann. Keine Gemeinschaft ist im Wortsinn produzierbar, gestaltbar oder aneigbar, denn jede Produktion, Gestaltung oder Totalisierung durch das Gesetz oder die Macht zerschellen an deren

---

22 Nancy: *Die herausgeforderte Gemeinschaft*, a.a.O., S. 42.

23 Nancy: *Die Mit-Teilung der Stimmen*, Zürich 2014.

24 Vgl. auch die spätere Auseinandersetzung mit Maurice Blanchot in: ders.: *La communauté désaouvée (2014) – Die verleugnete Gemeinschaft*, a.a.O.,

Anmaßung und versagen am Widerstand der Einzelnen. »Entwerkung« (désœuvrement) meint deshalb immer das Un-Vollendete und Unvollendbare: Gegen jedes Phantasma einer Herstellung oder Konstruktion, sei es kommunistisch, kybernetisch oder performativ, sei es als Diktat und Diktatur oder durch Symbole, seine Geschichte oder durch politische Regulierungen insistiert Nancy auf einer entschiedenen Zurückweisung jeder Lenkung und Steuerung und damit auch eines einigenden politischen Willens. Der Grund liegt in der jeder »Mit-Teilung« inhärenten Singularisierung. Darum kann das Gemeinsame »weder ein Projekt« sein, wie Nancy betont, noch, »allgemeiner gesehen, ein auf ein Produkt oder Werk zielendes Projekt«, das das Alteritäre zugunsten des Gleichen vertilgte – »sie ist überhaupt kein *Projekt*«, wie er ausdrücklich hinzusetzt,[25] so wenig wie es *durch* eine kollektive Anstrengung, eine gemeinsame Erzählung oder »Mythation« erzeugt werden kann, denn die Gemeinschaft dient zu nichts, wie sie nichts verspricht oder in etwas fundiert werden kann und sei es die Familie, das Volk, Kirche, Nation, Partei oder Ähnliches.[26] Es gibt demnach auch »kein gemeinsames Erfassen der Gemeinschaft«, denn die »Mit-Teilung (begründet) kein Verständnis«, vielmehr verleiht sie »niemandem, auch nicht der Gemeinschaft selbst, die Verfügungsgewalt über das Gemeinsam-Sein«.[27]

Das Gemeinsame der Gemeinschaft im Sinne der *koinōnia* wird daher von Nancy als »das eigentlich Unmögliche« ausgewiesen. Beständig abwesend könne sie nirgends in sich selbst aufgehen, weil sie als »Mit-Teilung« der Singularitäten im doppelten Sinne des Genitivs im selben Maße von diesen je schon durchbohrt, aufgetrennt und beschnitten wie befremdet wird. Sie findet also nicht statt und hat, in gewisser Weise, noch nie stattgefunden, sondern bildet, im Gegenzug zur Ideologie der Einheit und der »ganze(n) Metaphysik der Einswerdung« ein stets Heterogenes, Unbeherrschbares und nicht zu Antizipierendes. Und trotzdem darf nicht unterschlagen werden, dass sie gleichzeitig für Nancy ein Unverlierbares bedeutet, denn »es ist uns nicht möglich, nicht zusammen-zu-erscheinen«, vielmehr haben wir es mit einer ununterbrochenen Werdung, einer »Gemeinschaft ohne Gemeinschaft« zu tun – mit einem »Zu Kommende(n) in dem Sinne, dass sie immer und unaufhörlich inmitten einer jeden Kollektivierung ankommt (und gerade

---

25 Nancy: *Die undarstellbare Gemeinschaft*, a.a.O., S. 38
26 Ebd., S. 153.
27 Ebd., S. 146.

weil sie dort unaufhörlich auftaucht, widersetzt sie sich ständig der Kollektivität selbst) [...]«.[28]

Mit-Teilung der Singularitäten und die Kraft der Konfidenz

Wird so die zweifache Schwierigkeit thematisiert, einerseits nicht schon von einem primordialen Wir ausgehen zu können, andererseits in der Teilung immer schon das Geteilte und Aufgeteilte, also die Unterscheidung wie die Notwendigkeit der Gemeinschaft mitzudenken, so ist die »Mit-Teilung« selbst chiastisch verfasst, weil sie je einzig geschieht und das Einzelne teilt. Partizipativität, wie sie in der politischen Theorie mitunter als Zauberwort einer umfassenden Demokratisierung heraufbeschworen wird, kann dann nichts anderes sein als ein permanenter Widerspruch, etwas, das sich nicht verwirklicht. Nancy hat dies zehn Jahre später, in seiner zweiten entscheidenden Studie über die Gemeinschaft nach *La communauté désœuvrée* unter den selbst schon zerrissenen Titel eines »être singulier pluriel« gebracht – eine fast nicht zu übersetzende Verkettung von Ausdrücken, deren eigene »Mit-Teilung« nach keiner Seite hin auflösbar erscheint. Die deutsche Übersetzung *singulär plural sein* versucht dem mit der doppelten Kennzeichnung eines Seins einerseits als Verbum, andererseits versehen mit den beiden kontradiktorischen Attributen des Singulären und Pluralen beizukommen. Maßgebend bleibt dabei aber die stets uneingelöste Praxis eines Teilens, die zur gleichen Zeit die Differenz mit sich führt, um die verschiedenen möglichen Verbindungen zu unterbrechen. Nirgends vollendet sich also das Gemeinsame in seiner Gemeinsamkeit, und zwar schon deshalb nicht, weil das Wir durch das Singuläre und Unvermittelbare des Anderen beständig wieder zerschnitten wird, denn jede »Mit-Teilung« bringt uns gleichzeitig als Nicht-Eines oder Uneiniges und Ungeeintes hervor.

Dann erfüllt die »Mit-Teilung« im Rahmen der Sozialphilosophie dieselbe Funktion wie die Derridasche *différance* in der Semiologie, soweit der Bindestrich gewissermaßen als Pendant zum Platztausch zwischen ›e‹ und ›a‹ fungiert. Dem orthografischen Fehler, der selbst schon eine Differenz anzeigt, entspricht so der Strich, der eint und spaltet. Die »Mit-Teilung« und ihre Singularität trägt also die *différance* phänomenologisch in das Geschehen der Gemein-

---

schaft ein und macht sie präsent. Deswegen spricht Nancy auch von der »herausgeforderten« (*affrontée*) Gemeinschaft als Affront, deren Provokationen in der unablässigen Konfrontation mit ihrer eigenen Heterogenität bestehen. Das lässt sich auch so ausdrücken: »Was die Gemeinschaft mit offenbart [...] ist meine Existenz außer mir«, das heißt das, was sich keiner Einheit fügt, was ein absolut Fremdes bleibt und sich der Vereinnahmung sperrt.[29] Die Gemeinschaft bildet folglich keine Instanz einer Verähnlichung, sondern ein Ort der Ungleichheit, der Disparität, der Inkommensurabilität. Die *koinōnia* setzt also die Fremdheit stets schon ›mit‹ voraus; umgekehrt können die verschiedenen koinonischen Gestalten nur rekonstruiert werden, wenn die Besonderheit unserer Beziehungen zum Fremden und Anderen ›mit‹bedacht wird.

Soziale Anerkennungstheorien wie auch Edmund Husserls Philosophie der Intersubjektivität[30] haben demgegenüber die Symmetrie und Spiegelung im Sinne einer Reziprozität von *alter* und *ego* betont. Stattdessen lässt Nancy das Alteritäre im Asymmetrischen wurzeln, sodass jede gleichberechtigte Verschränkung des Einen im Anderen in einer voreiligen Nivellierung münden muss. Das führt dazu, dass Nancy die »Mit-Teilung« als ein »Zusammen-Erscheinen« aus lauter »Singuläritäten« konzipiert, als eine *apparitio cum apparitio*, deren jeweiligen Erscheinungen eine unverwechselbare Färbung oder Maserung annehmen (*cum grano singularis*). Ihre Körnung determiniert das Gemeinschaftliche ebenso wie sie sie nuanciert. Die klassische Vorstellung eines sozialen Bandes, wie es sich vom Begriff der *religio* und seiner Geschichte herleitet, wird damit neu lesbar gemacht. Denn im *cum* bleibt das Problem des *Zusammen* sowie die Frage danach wach, *wie* und *auf welche Weise*, ohne forcierte Bindung, aus dem Nebeneinander ein *nexum* oder *conjungere* mit der Gleichzeitigkeit eines *disjungere* werden kann – sodass, um es anders auszudrücken, zum *cum* etwas hinzukommen muss, ohne es bereits als Religion, als politische Theologie, als Vereinnahmung durch einen organizistisch verstandenen Staat zu verklären.[31]

Lassen die früheren Texte Nancys zwischen *La communauté désœuvrée* und *Être singulier pluriel* oder zuvor *Le Partage des voix*

---

29 Ebd., S. 60.
30 Vgl. Edmund Husserl: *Cartesianische Meditationen und Pariser Vorträge*, Husserliana Bd. 1, Den Haag, 2. Aufl. 1973, S. 121ff.
31 Susanne Lüdemann: *Metaphern der Gesellschaft. Studien zum soziologischen und politischen Imaginären*, München 2004.

dasjenige, was den *Nexus* garantiert, offen, indem sie allein auf einen negativen Sinn der *koinōnia* und entsprechend der Negativität von Gemeinschaft rekurrieren, nehmen spätere Texte, wie das Vorwort *La communauté affrontée* oder *La communauté désavoue*, die beide die Auseinandersetzung mit Blanchot wiederaufnehmen, wie auch das erwähnte Gespräch mit Carolin Meister über »Begegnung« insofern eine interessante Wendung nimmt, als sie von der Teilung als Differenz zum »Geheimnis des Vertrauens« übergehen[32] und damit der *koinōnia* einen weiterführenden Sinn erteilen. Während das *cum* vormals das *dis*, den Riss unterstrich, nimmt es nunmehr die weitere Bedeutung von Konfidenz (*con-fidere*) an, der eigentümlich ist, dass sie sich auf sich selbst stützt und sich nur verdoppeln lässt, denn in Vertrauen kann man nur vertrauen. Implizit nähert sich damit Nancy der *communauté inavouable* Blanchots an, denn das Vertrauen ist das eigentlich »Unbekennbare«, soweit es dasjenige bezeichnet, was jede Kommunikation »gewährleistet und riskiert [...]«, wie es in *La communauté affrontée* heißt.[33] Die Kommunikation kann nämlich kein Ursprung sein, sondern erst das, was sie austrägt, ohne aber als solches durch einen kommunikativen Akt bezeugbar zu sein. Aus diesem Grunde betont die *confidentia* weniger das »Mit«, als dass sie sich, so Nancy weiter, »rückhaltlos gibt«, »sich hin(gibt)« an den Anderen, die Differenz preisgibt. Nicht wird die Fremdheit, der Unterschied oder die Disparität durch das Vertrauen aufgelöst, sondern das Vertrauen ermöglicht Gemeinschaft trotz der Differenz, denn ohne es ließe sich »nichts anfangen«, wie Nancy schreibt, soweit jedes konkrete Vertrauen bereits die Möglichkeit eines »unbegrenzten Vertrauens« voraussetzt: »So ist die äußerste Intensität der *fides* identisch mit der Nähe des *cum* im Sinne des ›Mit‹.«[34] Folglich sei die Gemeinschaft deshalb unbezeugbar, weil das Vertrauen unmittelbar noch in der Bedingung jedes »Mit« zu präsupponieren sei, denn Vertrauen ist weder eine Frage der Proklamation noch einer Produktion, sondern allein eines *Vorschusses*. Ähnliches gilt für das unter anderem von Donald Davidson ins Spiel gebrachte »principle of charity«,[35] dem wohlwollenden Verstehen, das einem ähnlichen Motiv nachgeht, wie gleichfalls Immanuel Kant in seinen *Vorlesungen über*

---

32 Nancy, *Die herausgeforderte Gemeinschaft*, a.a.O., S. 42.

33 Ebd.

34 Ebd., S. 43.

35 Donald Davidson: »Radical Interpretation«, in: ders.: *Inquiries into Truth and Interpretation*, Oxford, New York 2001, S. 125–140.

Logik auf die Kraft des »moralischen Glaubens« setzte. Demgegenüber zersetze die Ubiquität des Verdachts und der Täuschung bereits im Ansatz jede Grundlage einer gelungenen Kollektivierung, denn »derjenige«, so Kant, der umgekehrt einem »moralischen Unglauben« oder universellen Misstrauen fröne, »halt alle Menschen vor Lügner, er trauet keinem Menschen, er glaubet keinen Versprechungen, sonderen zweifelet immer an der Aufrichtigkeit anderer Leute. Ein moralischer Unglaube ist dem moralischen Fundament aller menschlichen Gesellschaft entgegen. Ohne Treu und Glauben kann [...] kein Staat bestehen.«[36]

---

36 Immanuel Kant: »Vorlesungen über Logik« § 213, Auszug in: Sybille Krämer, Sibylle Schmidt und Johannes-Georg Schülein (Hg.): *Philosophie der Zeugenschaft*, Münster 2017, S. 72.

Jacob Rogozinski

Die unmögliche Möglichkeit der Gemeinschaft

Lässt sich ein Gespräch, das vom Tod unterbrochen wurde, trotz Stille und Abwesenheit fortsetzen? Zweifellos kann es andere, spektralere Formen annehmen: Es kann im Schreiben erfolgen und vor allem im erneuten Lesen dessen, was der Tote uns hinterlassen hat. Aber was ist mit einem Gespräch, das unterbrochen wurde, bevor es überhaupt stattfinden konnte? Einem Gespräch, das sich viele Jahre lang vage abzeichnete, stets ersehnt und immer wieder verschoben wurde, bis es schließlich zu spät war? Was lässt dieses Gespräch, das seinen Ort nicht gefunden hat, von den Bedingungen einer Kommunikation oder gar einer Gemeinschaft zwischen Philosophen erahnen, die zwar der gleichen Institution angehören, dieselben Bücher lesen und dieselben Denkbewegungen bewundern, sich dabei in all ihrer Nähe aber dennoch fern sind? Und wird ein solches Gespräch nicht gerade in dem Moment, in dem es unmöglich geworden zu sein scheint, auf seine wesentlichste Möglichkeit zurückgeführt? Die Möglichkeit einer *denkenden* Gemeinschaft der Lebenden und der Toten, die einzig die Frage ihrer Möglichkeit teilt? Das heißt: die philosophische Frage par excellence, denn Jean-Luc Nancy zufolge sind »Philosophie und Gemeinschaft untrennbar« und »die Gemeinschaft ist das Thema aller Themen der Philosophie«.[1] Unter verschiedenen Namen – das gemeinsame Erscheinen, das *Mitsein* oder vielmehr das *Mitdasein*, das Singulär-plural-Sein, das Gemeinsam-Sein, die Koexistenz, das Wir, das Mit… – geht es ihm immer und immer wieder um die Gemeinschaft. Um ihre womöglich unmögliche Möglichkeit und um das Paradox, das diese Unmöglichkeit in Kraft setzt.

Dieses Paradox, oder diese Aporie, besteht in Folgendem: Die Ins-Werk-Setzung der Gemeinschaft ist historisch mit ihrer Selbstzerstörung zusammengefallen, mit dem Phantasma einer »einheitsstiftenden Verschmelzung« in der absoluten Immanenz, der Immanenz eines kollektiven Subjekts, das sich selbst erzeugt, indem es alles, was diese Verschmelzung zu behindern scheint, vernichtet. Gnadenlose, todbringende Logik »des Selbstmords der Gemeinschaft,

---

1 Jean-Luc Nancy: »Le sens en commun«, in: *Autrement,* 102/1988, S. 200–208, hier zit. n. Michel Gaillot: *Jean-Luc Nancy, la communité, le sens,* Paris 2021, S. 12. Übers. L.S.

die sich an [der Immanenz] ausrichtet«.[2] Nun öffnet jedoch gerade diese selbstzerstörerische Selbstverwirklichung der Gemeinschaft die Frage ihrer Möglichkeit:

> »Dass das Werk des Todes [...] im Namen der Gemeinschaft (hier der eines selbstkonstituierten Volkes oder einer selbstkonstituierten Rasse, dort einer selbstherausgearbeiteten Menschheit) vollbracht wurde, das bedeutete das endgültige Ende jeglicher Möglichkeit, sich auf irgendeinem wie auch immer beschaffenen *Gegebenen* des gemeinsamen Seins auszuruhen [...]. Die Aufgabe, die nun zutage trat, gilt dem *Gemeinsam-sein* [*l'être-en-commun*] jenseits des als Identität, Zustand und Subjekt gedachten Seins, dem Gemeinsam-sein, welches das Sein selbst tief in seiner ontologischen Textur affiziert.«[3]

Was Nancy hier »Werk des Todes«, manchmal auch »Gemeinschaft des Todes« nennt, ist zunächst die nationalsozialistische *Volksgemeinschaft*. Obwohl er Kommunismus und Faschismus nie gleichsetzen würde, gilt die Analyse auch für die andere Katastrophe des 20. Jahrhunderts: »Mit dem Kommunismus ist jedwede ontotheologische Auffassung von Gemeinschaft an ihre Grenzen gekommen, zu ihrer historischen Schließung gelangt.«[4] Wir wissen, welche Konsequenz Nancy aus dieser doppelten Katastrophe zog: Es ist an der Zeit, die Nostalgie einer verlorenen Gemeinschaft, die es neu zu gründen gälte, hinter sich zu lassen. Da sie nur als sich selbst verneinende und zerstörende geschehen konnte, müssen wir endlich anerkennen, dass »*die Gemeinschaft nicht stattgefunden [hat]*«[5]. Sie ist nicht das, was uns (durch die Moderne, den Individualismus, das Kapital, die Globalisierung usw.) entzogen worden wäre, sondern ganz im Gegenteil das, was »zu uns kommt«[6]: die Gemeinschaft als »ein à *venir*, die *Zukunft* eines *Kommens*, in dem Sinne, dass sie immer *kommt*, ohne Unterlass, innerhalb jeder Kollektivität«[7], was auch bedeutet, dass sie *immer (noch) möglich* ist. Wenn es bei Nancy eine Eschatologie gibt, das Äquivalent eines

---

2 Jean-Luc Nancy: *Von einer Gemeinschaft, die sich nicht verwirklicht*, übers. von Esther von der Osten, Wien, Berlin 2018, S. 24.

3 Aus dem Kapitel »Cum« in Jean-Luc Nancy: *Das nackte Denken*, übers. von Markus Sedlaczek, Zürich, Berlin 2014, S. 141f.

4 Jean-Luc Nancy und Jean-Christophe Bailly: *La comparution*, Paris 1991, S. 29. Übers. L.S.

5 Nancy: *Von einer Gemeinschaft, die sich nicht verwirklicht*, a.a.O., S. 22.

6 Ebd., S. 23.

7 Ebd., S. 121.

Messianismus ohne Messias, dann ist sie sicherlich an dieser Stelle auszumachen. Wobei sich das, was er Gemeinschaft nennt, immer schon der Ins-Werk-Setzung in einer einheitsstiftenden Verschmelzung widersetzt. Nancy schreibt, dass »[d]as schlichte, restlose Verschwinden der Gemeinschaft [...] ein Unglück« ist, »ein ontologisches Unglück«[8], und folgert daraus, dass diese Form der widerstehenden Gemeinschaft gar nicht verschwinden kann, da sie »der Widerstand selbst«[9] sei: das, was »einen Abstand offen[hält], eine Verräumlichung in der Immanenz«[10], eine Disjunktion, eine ekstatische Öffnung, die Möglichkeit der Koexistenz oder des Gemeinsam-seins. Daraus folgt: *Es braucht* die Gemeinschaft, als Imperativ und als Versprechen, und *es gibt* die Gemeinschaft, Spur oder Skizze dessen, was dem Unglück immer schon widersteht. So bezeichnet das Wort »Gemeinschaft« gleichzeitig ihre Selbstzerstörung im Werk des Todes *und* das, was sich dieser Zerstörung auf radikalste Weise entzieht. Nicht zuletzt benennt dieses Wort das, was niemals stattgefunden hat, was unaufhörlich ankommt und immer schon da ist ... Es wäre ein Fehler, darin eine Unentschiedenheit oder gar einen Widerspruch seines Denkens zu sehen. Diese Ambivalenzen entspringen der Sache selbst, dem paradoxalen, aporetischen Phänomen der Gemeinschaft, das Nancy zu denken versucht hat, um es zu dekonstruieren.

Dekonstruktion der Gemeinschaft: Wenn ich mich nicht irre, kommt diese Formulierung in seinen Schriften so nicht vor. Dabei arbeitet er genau daran, wenn er versucht, das einzugrenzen, »was die gesamte Tradition [...] eine Gemeinschaft nennt (einen identitären Körper, eine Intensität des Eigenen, eine natürliche Intimität)«[11], das heißt ein gemeinsames Sein, das sich auf eine vorgängige Gegebenheit gründet: »Blut, Substanz, Filiation, Wesen, Ursprung, Natur, Weihe, Erwählung, organische oder mystische Identität«[12]. Da dieser »abendländische« und »moderne« Gemeinschaftsbegriff aus der christlichen Tradition kommt, geht seine Dekonstruktion mit der des Christentums einher. Ob es einem gefällt oder nicht, die Dekonstruktion ist keine Destruktion, keine »nihilistische« Beseitigung der Tradition: Sie bemüht sich vielmehr, ihre Schließung zu markieren, um ihre Motive anders nachzuzeichnen

---

8   Ebd., S. 100.
9   Ebd., S. 101.
10   Ebd.
11   Nancy: *Das nackte Denken*, a.a.O., S. 143.
12   Ebd., S. 142.

und die Möglichkeiten und Versprechen, die diese Motive tragen, freizusetzen. »Dekonstruieren bedeutet abbauen, demontieren, auseinandernehmen, die Zusammenfügung lockern, ihr Spielraum geben, um zwischen den Teilen dieser Zusammenfügung eine Möglichkeit spielen zu lassen, von der sie herkommt«[13]. Worin besteht sie, die Möglichkeit, die sich aus dem Auseinandernehmen der Gemeinschaft, der *com-munauté*, ergibt, aus der Entkoppelung ihrer Bestandteile? Ist man nicht, wenn man den Gemeinschaftsbegriff dekonstruiert, gezwungen, auf das Wort selbst zu verzichten, da es doch einerseits so sehr von der abendländischen Tradition geprägt ist und andererseits durch die Schrecken der Moderne vollkommen kompromittiert wurde? Auch wenn er immer mehr dazu neigte, diesem Begriff andere, ihm durchaus »plumper« erscheinende Begriffe wie »Gemeinsam-sein« oder »Mitsein« vorzuziehen, hat sich Nancy nie dazu durchgerungen, ihn ganz aufzugeben. Dies war Gegenstand einer Meinungsverschiedenheit mit Derrida, der von sich sagte, dieses Wort »nicht sehr« zu mögen, ebenso wenig wie die Sache selbst.[14] Der freundschaftliche Streit zwischen den beiden fand unter anderem bei einer ihrer letzten Begegnungen im Juni 2004 in Straßburg statt, wohin wir Derrida einige Wochen vor seinem Tod für eine Würdigung seines Werks eingeladen hatten. »Bei dir«, merkt Nancy gegenüber Derrida an, »gibt es kein *Volk*, [...], du willst das Wort ›Volk‹ nicht verwenden. Ich benutze dieses Wort durchaus, aber du hast mir mehrere Mal bedeutet, dass du es beim besten Willen nicht anrühren willst. Genauso wie das Wort ›Gemeinschaft‹.«[15] Er scheint von Derridas Scheu, gewisse Worte zu gebrauchen, überrascht. Dabei hatte Derrida doch sehr früh die Notwendigkeit der *Paläonymie* formuliert, einer Wiederaufnahme traditionell überlieferter Begriffe, denen man durch Dekonstruktion ihren sedimentierten Sinngehalt entwinden und eine neue Chance geben könnte. Im Prinzip bieten sich sämtliche Wörter der Sprache für eine solche Wiederaufnahme an – und

---

13 Jean-Luc Nancy: *Dekonstruktion des Christentums,* übers. von Esther von der Osten, Berlin 2020, S. 251.

14 Jacques Derrida: *Auslassungspunkte. Gespräche,* übers. von Karin Schreiner und Dirk Weissmann, unter Mitarbeit von Kathrin Murr, Wien 1998, S. 359. Er habe »niemals auf eigene Rechnung [...] das Wort Gemeinschaft [...] schreiben können«, versichert er ferner in Jacques Derrida: *Politik der Freundschaft,* übers. von Stefan Lorenzer, Frankfurt/Main 2000, S. 407.

15 Jean-Luc Nancy, Jacques Derrida und Philippe Lacoue-Labarthe: »Dialogue entre Jacques Derrida, Philippe Lacoue-Labarthe et Jean-Luc Nancy«, in: *Rue Descartes,* 2/2006, S. 86–99. Übers. L.S.

doch scheint das, was für die Schrift, die Gerechtigkeit, die Freundschaft, das Ereignis, die Gabe, die Demokratie, den Messianismus und unzählige weitere Begriffe gilt, für die Gemeinschaft nicht zu gelten, ohne dass Derrida diesen Ausschluss jemals ausführlich erklärt hätte. Nancy verfolgt dieselbe paläonymische Strategie, dehnt sie aber noch weiter aus, da er ohne zu zögern Begriffe verwendet, die man bei Derrida vergeblich sucht: nicht nur die Gemeinschaft und das Volk, sondern auch das Sein, die Welt, den Sinn, den Körper. Worauf weist diese Differenz hin? Auf ein mehr oder weniger gefestigtes Vertrauen in die Ressourcen der Sprache? Auf einen mehr oder weniger starken Wunsch, »den Land- und Stammesworten [...] reinen Sinn zu geben«[16], sie gegen sich selbst zu wenden und sie ihren alten Verankerungen zu entreißen? Sicherlich nicht zuletzt auf ein anderes Verhältnis zu dem Philosophen, der von Sein, Welt, Sinn und manchmal auch von *Volk so großen Gebrauch machte: In ihrer »untreuen Treue« zum Denken Heideggers scheint es, als entschiede sich Nancy deutlicher als Derrida für die Treue.

Man könnte sich allerdings auch fragen, ob diese Uneinigkeit beim Thema der Gemeinschaft nicht eine radikalere Divergenz zwischen zwei verschiedenen Praktiken oder Stilen der Dekonstruktion belegt. Bekanntermaßen kann jede Aussage, die behauptet, die Dekonstruktion sei »dies« und »nicht das«, ihrerseits dekonstruiert werden. Trotzdem wagt es Derrida manchmal, die Dekonstruktion zu definieren, zum Beispiel, wenn er sie als »aporetische Erfahrung des Unmöglichen« bezeichnet. Die paläonymische Wiederaufnahme traditioneller Begriffe geht so mit einer Geste einher, die sie in Aporien umformt beziehungsweise die versteckten Aporien aufzeigt, die in ihnen verborgen liegen. Es geht also um die Affirmation ihrer *Unmöglichkeit*. So bezeichnet Derrida denn auch alles als Aporie, »was nur [...] als das Unmögliche [möglich ist]: Liebe, Freundschaft, Gabe, Anderer, Zeugenschaft, Gastfreundschaft, etc.«[17] Diese Aporien drücken sich in einer ganzen Reihe performativer Widersprüche aus, in denen Begriffe nur zum Ausdruck kommen, indem sie sich gleichzeitig annullieren: »Meine Freunde, es gibt keinen Freund«[18]; »Man kann nur das Nichtvergebbare

---

16 [Impliziter Verweis auf das Sonett *Le tombeau d'Edgar Poe* von Stéphane Mallarmé, hier zit. n. der Übersetzung von Franz Nobiling, *A.d.Ü.*]
17 Jacques Derrida: *Aporien. Sterben – auf die »Grenzen der Wahrheit« gefaßt sein,* übers. von Michael Wetzel, München 1998, S. 126.
18 Vgl. Derrida: *Politik der Freundschaft,* a.a.O.

vergeben«[19], »die Wahrheit der Gabe genügt, um die Gabe zu annullieren«[20]... Vor einem Missverständnis sollten wir uns jedoch hüten. Die *Möglichkeit des Unmöglichen*, die Heidegger dem Tod vorbehielt, während Derrida sie auf weitere Motive ausdehnt, ist nicht mit der *Unmöglichkeit des Möglichen* zu verwechseln. Denn während der erste Ausdruck eine Offenheit, ein Spiel, eine Chance bewahrt, schließt der zweite diese aus. Eine Aporie ist folglich nicht dasselbe wie eine Grenze oder eine Sackgasse: Sie ist für das Denken Bedrohung und Ressource zugleich. Dennoch zeugt sie von einer wesentlichen Unmöglichkeit, die es ohne den Versuch, sie zu überwinden, auszuhalten gilt. Etwas in eine Aporie zu übertragen erfordert eine hyperbolische Geste, durch die der jeweilige Begriff radikalisiert und unbedingt gemacht wird. Seine Unbedingtheit vermischt sich sodann mit seiner Unmöglichkeit. Dies ist beispielsweise bei der »reinen Gabe« der Fall, die so radikal ist, dass sie »nur unter der Bedingung stattfinden könnte, nicht stattzufinden«[21], beim »Ereignis des anderen«, der »nur dadurch kommt, dass er nicht kommt« [»n'arrive qu'à ne pas arriver«], oder bei einer »unendlichen Gastfreundschaft«, die nur als »Gastfeindschaft« vorkommt und sich zwangsläufig in Feindschaft verkehrt. Auch auf die Gemeinschaft trifft das zu: Auch sie ist nur als unmögliche möglich. In diesem Sinne teilt Derrida Nancys Diagnose der selbstzerstörerischen Selbstbestätigung der Gemeinschaft. Doch anstatt sie wie er auf die Extremfälle des Nationalsozialismus und des »Kommunismus« (oder vielmehr Stalinismus) zu beschränken, sieht Derrida darin eine Gefahr, der *jede* Gemeinschaft ausgesetzt ist: die Gefahr der tödlichen Autoimmunität, in der ein Schutzdispositiv zur Bedrohung für das wird, was es eigentlich beschützen soll. Der Name der Gemeinschaft selbst, *com-munitas*, bringt die Im-munität ins Spiel – sie wird sich der »allgemeinen Logik der Auto-Immunisierung«[22] also kaum entziehen können, jenem »Todestrieb, der stumm in jeder Gemeinschaft [communauté] und in jeder Auto-Ko-Immunität am Werk ist, der sie in Wahrheit als solche konstituiert, […] [als] ein Prinzip der opferhaften Selbstzerstörung«[23].

---

19 Vgl. Jacques Derrida: *Vergeben. Das Nichtvergebbare und das Unverjährbare*, übers. von Markus Sedlaczek, Wien 2018, S. 27.

20 Jacques Derrida: *Falschgeld. Zeit geben I*, übers. von Andreas Knop und Michael Wetzel, München 1993, S. 40.

21 Ebd., S. 51.

22 Jacques Derrida und Gianni Vattimo: *Die Religion*, Berlin 2001, S. 72.

23 Ebd., S. 85.

Derrida gebraucht das Wort »Gemeinschaft« fast nie (der soeben zitierte Texte ist sozusagen ein Hapax), weil er ihrer tatsächlichen Möglichkeit keine Chance lassen will. An diesem Punkt besteht zwischen ihm und Nancy nicht nur eine Meinungsverschiedenheit, sondern radikale Uneinigkeit, denn letzterer bemüht sich redlich, die Möglichkeit der Gemeinschaft gegen ihre Leugner zu verwahren. Davon zeugt sein Buch mit dem vielsagenden Titel *Die verleugnete Gemeinschaft*, in dem er auf diese auch einst mit Blanchot geführte Debatte zurückkommt. Am Ende einer sorgfältigen und geduldigen Lektüre kritisiert er hier das Verfahren, das »drauf hinaus[läuft], die Gemeinschaft zu verleugnen«[24], das sie zwar »jeder Herrschaft« entzieht, aber eben »auch jeder Beständigkeit«, sodass letztlich »[k]eine andere Gemeinschaft [anerkannt wird] als jene, die sich auflöst«.[25] Diese Kritik, die sich an Blanchot richtet, gilt sicherlich auch für Derrida; und derselbe Wunsch, das Versprechen einer Gemeinschaft offenzuhalten – jener Gemeinschaft nämlich, die Bataille die »Gemeinschaft der Liebenden« nannte – bringt ihn dazu, den lacanschen Aphorismus, es gebe keinen Geschlechtsverkehr[26], entschieden zurückzuweisen. Es kommt für Nancy also überhaupt nicht infrage, auf das Wort »Gemeinschaft« zu verzichten. Vielmehr geht es darum, ihm einen Sinn zu verleihen, der sich von seinem tradierten Gebrauch absetzt; es geht um eine neuerliche Affirmation der Gemeinschaft, die allerdings die Spur ihrer Dekonstruktion in sich trägt, sodass sich Gemeinschaft fortan als negativer Quasibegriff zeigt, den verschiedene Zusätze mit *ohne* jeder Bestimmung entziehen: »Gemeinschaft ohne Gemeinschaft«, Gemeinschaft ohne Kommunion oder Kommunismus, »entwerkte« Gemeinschaft, was bedeutet: ohne selbstzerstörerische Inswerksetzung, ohne Wesen, ohne eigene oder eigentliche Identität und ohne Namen.

Ist eine solche Gemeinschaft *ungestaltbar [infigurable]*? Nancy könnte es kaum häufiger sagen: »[D]ie Entwerkung ist dargeboten, wo die Schrift *eine Figur [...] nicht vollendet*«, dort, wo kein Heldenmythos mehr einer Gemeinschaft »gründende, ursprüngliche Figuren« aufbürdet, »Orte oder Mächte restloser Identifikation«.[27] Die Unterbrechung des Mythos, das heißt vor allem der

---

24 Jean-Luc Nancy: *Die verleugnete Gemeinschaft,* übers. von Thomas Laugstien, Zürich, Berlin 2017, S. 120.
25 Ebd., S. 122.
26 Vgl. Jean-Luc Nancy: *Es gibt – Geschlechtsverkehr,* aus dem Franz. von Judith Kasper, Zürich 2012.
27 Nancy: *Von einer Gemeinschaft, die sich nicht verwirklicht,* a.a.O., S. 132f.

»national-ästhetischen« *Mythenbildung* im Stile der Nazis, fällt auf
diese Weise mit einer Unterbrechung der Gestalt [figure] zusammen. An diesem Punkt zögert Nancy immer wieder, ebenso wie
er zögert, die Welt als Gestalt zu bezeichnen.[28] Er fragt sich, ob
es »ohne Figuration oder Konfiguration [...] noch Sinn [gibt]«, ob
»das Zusammen-sein ohne Gestalt auskommt, und folglich ohne
Identifikation«, obwohl die Gestalt doch das ist, »was in der Lage
ist, zum ›Mit‹ als zum Rand selbst und zur Grenze seiner Umrisse
hin zu eröffnen«[29]. Daraus folgt, dass eine Gemeinschaft ohne Ge-
stalt(en) mangels sie umschreibender Ränder unfähig wäre, die
Ko-existenz derer einzurichten, aus denen sie zusammengesetzt
ist: Sie wäre keine Gemeinschaft mehr, nicht einmal mehr eine
Gesellschaft, sondern eine amorphe, atomisierte Masse. Genau
diese Frage bildet die Grundspannung der Kontroverse mit Blanchot, denn Nancy besteht – wider den »aristokratischen Anarchis-
mus«[30] und die Verleugnung der Gemeinschaft, die er ihm ankrei-
det – darauf, dass es »sehr schwierig ist, das ›Gemeinsame‹ ohne
eine Form, um nicht zu sagen eine Gestalt zu denken«[31]. Dieselbe
Schwierigkeit taucht auf, als er versucht, die Demokratie zu denken: Selbst wenn sie in Wahrheit »nicht in eine Gestalt zu bringen«
ist, setzt sie doch voraus, »den gemeinschaftlichen Raum so zu
gestalten, dass sich darin die ganze mögliche Fülle der Formen
eröffnen kann, die das Unendliche annehmen kann«.[32] Wie aber
den Spielraum der Demokratie *gestalten*, ohne ihm *eine Gestalt* zu
verleihen? Wie einen *Rückzug des Politischen* verwirklichen, sodass es sich von den verfestigten historischen Gestalten ablöst und

---

28 Dies ist der Schauplatz einer weiteren freundschaftlichen Meinungsverschiedenheit, diesmal mit Lacoue-Labarthe. Ich verweise diesbezüglich auf Jacob
Rogozinski: »Face à l'im-monde«, in: *Lignes* 68/2022, S. 19–25.

29 Jean-Luc Nancy: *singulär plural sein*, übers. von Ulrich Müller-Schöll, Berlin
2012, S. 81f. Vgl. die erhellenden Bemerkungen in Joan Stavo-Debauge: »Dé-figu-
rer la communauté? – hantises et impoasses de la pensée (politique) de Jean-Luc
Nancy«, in: Laurence Kaufmann und Danny Trom (Hg.): *Qu'est-ce qu'un collectif?
Du commun à la politique*, Paris 2010, S. 137–171.

30 Nancy: *Die verleugnete Gemeinschaft*, a.a.O., S. 131.

31 Ebd., S. 119.

32 Jean-Luc Nancy: *Wahrheit der Demokratie*, übers. von Richard Steurer-Bou-
lard, Wien 2009, S. 57. Vgl. auch das Vorwort von Philippe Lacoue-Labarthe
und Jean-Luc Nancy: *Le mythe nazi*, La Tour-d'Aigues 1991, S. 12. [Ohne das
erwähnte Vorwort liegt der Aufsatz auf Deutsch vor als Jean-Luc Nancy und
Philippe Lacoue-Labarthe: »Der Nazi-Mythos«, übers. von Claus-Volker Klenke,
in: Elisabeth Weber und Georg Christoph Tholen (Hg.): *Das Vergessen(e). Ana-
mnesen des Undarstellbaren*, Wien 1997, S. 158–190, A.d.Ü.]

neu umrissen werden kann, eine Vielzahl neuer Formen hervor-
bringend? So lange diese Schwierigkeit – oder diese Aporie – nicht
überwunden ist, wird die Demokratie weiterhin der Bedrohung
eines »Rückzugs« des Politischen im landläufigen Sinn ausgesetzt
sein (der wachsenden Enthaltung und Passivität der Bürger nämlich, als Konsequenz einer »de-politisierten« technokratischen
Verwaltung), oder auch einer faschisierenden Um-Gestaltung um
die mythische Figur eines Helden beziehungsweise eines Führers
(oder einer Führerin). Um es mit Freud zu sagen: Hier geht es um
die Frage nach dem Übergang der »primären Masse«, die in ihrer
Liebe zum Oberhaupt und ihrem Hass für den Feind vereint ist, zur
»führerlosen Masse«, in der das Oberhaupt »durch eine Idee ersetzt
wurde«.[33] Mit Max Weber gesprochen gilt es, in Sachen Demokratie die Möglichkeit von Charisma zu denken, die Möglichkeit einer
gleichermaßen demokratischen wie charismatischen Legitimität,
die dem für die moderne politische Rationalität typischen Prozess
der Depersonalisierung etwas entgegenhalten kann.

Auf diese berüchtigten Fragen geht Nancy nicht wirklich ein.
Auch wenn er manchmal von einer Notwendigkeit spricht, der Gemeinschaft eine Gestalt zu verleihen oder sie zu gestalten, schlägt
er generell jedwede (Kon-)Figuration dem Mythos zu, was in den
Bedingungen unserer Moderne bedeutet: den »Identifikationsappa-
raten« eines totalitären Staates. Da er sich weigert, den Gemeinschaftsbegriff aufzugeben, bleibt ihm nichts anderes übrig, als ihn
zu entmythifizieren, zu entstalten und bis aufs Letzte zu reinigen,
alles entfernend, was einer Identifikation oder einer Gestaltung
Halt geben könnte. Am Ende dieser Askese »scheint der Begriff der
Gemeinschaft [communauté] nichts anderes mehr zum Inhalt zu
haben als seine eigene Vorsilbe, das *cum*, das der Substanz und
der Verbindungen entledigte *Mit*, dessen Innerlichkeit, Subjektivität
und Personalität abhandengekommen ist«[34]. Das *cum* – das *Mit* –
ist also das, was der Dekonstruktion der Gemeinschaft standhält,
die Entsprechung jenes Indekonstruktiblen, das für Derrida die Gerechtigkeit war. Wenn die Gemeinschaft ohne Gemeinschaft einen
Namen haben könnte, so hieße sie *cum*. Die elliptische Vorsilbe
wäre der Titel oder die Spur eines Ur-Ereignisses , einer Ur-Gemein-

---

33 Ist es Zufall, dass die freudsche Hypothese einer »Masse ohne Oberhaupt« in
Nancys und Lacoue-Labarthes Analyse der *Massenpsychologie* nicht vorkommt?
Vgl. Jean-Luc Nancy und Philippe Lacoue-Labarthe: *La panique politique. Suivi
de Le peuple juif ne rêve pas*, Paris 1979.
34 Nancy: *singulär plural sein*, a.a.O., S. 66.

schaft, die ursprünglicher wäre als jede Gemeinschaft: »was stets vorhergeht und was deshalb auch das unvordenklichste Ereignis schafft, ist wenn nicht das Kommune, so doch das *cum* [...], das bei weitem jeder Frage von Kommunität, ja sogar von Kopulation, Konjunktion oder Konversation vorhergeht.«[35]

Die Gemeinschaft [communauté] zu dekonstruieren, läuft demnach darauf hinaus, die Nominalwurzel vom Präfix zu trennen, das *cum* ohne das *munus* zu denken: ohne die Aufgabe oder die Schuld, ohne die Verpflichtung, die diesem Wort anhaftet. Im Lateinischen bezeichnet *munus* tatsächlich die Gabe, die man geben *muss*, um auf eine andere, bereits erhaltene Gabe zu antworten. Es wäre verlockend, darin eine »Ab-eignung« zu sehen, »welche das Eigentümersubjekt überfällt und dezentriert«, und davon ausgehend »ein[en] Strudel, eine Synkope, ein[en] Spasmus«[36], der jede Gemeinschaft destabilisiert – oder aber zu vertreten, dass es bei dieser Aufgabe »um unser *mit*, das heißt um *uns*«[37] geht, was darauf hinausläuft, das *munus* im *cum* aufzulösen. Aber tragen diese dekonstruktiven Interpretationen dem Wortsinn von *munus* ausreichend Rechnung? Hier haben wir es mit dem zu tun, was Anthropologen eine *Gegengabe* nennen, was das Gemeinsame und die Gemeinschaft in einer Ökonomie der Gabe und Gegengabe verortet, in einer Ökonomie des reziproken Austauschs, der sich insofern nicht zwingend, wie es Philosophen häufig glauben, auf einen interessegeleiteten oder kaufmännischen Handel beschränkt, als er auch Dankesgaben, Dankbarkeit und gegenseitige Anerkennung einschließen kann.[38] Die Gemeinschaft unter diesen Bedingungen auf das *cum* zu reduzieren und das *munus* auszustreichen, bedeutet, sie zu entlasten, sie von jeder Reziprozität, jeder Verpflichtung, jeder Schuld auszunehmen – kurz: sie zu im-munisieren, denn die *Immunitas* ist zunächst die Negation der (*Com-*)*munitas*. Man kann sich also fragen, ob diese entwerkte, gegen sich selbst immunisierte

---

35 Nancy: *Die verleugnete Gemeinschaft*, a.a.O., S. 150f.

36 Roberto Esposito: *Communitas. Ursprung und Wege der Gemeinschaft*, übers. von Sabine Schulz und Francesca Raimondi, Zürich 2004, S. 16 und 18.

37 Nancy: *Das nackte Denken*, a.a.O., S. 146. Der hier unter dem Titel »cum« veröffentlichte Aufsatz ist die überarbeitete Fassung des Textes »Conloquium«, das der französischen Fassung von Espositos *Communitas* (PUF 2000) als Vorwort vorangestellt ist.

38 Bezüglich dieser Frage verweise ich auf die Kritiken, die ein weiterer verstorbener Freund Lévinas, Derrida und Marion zuteilwerden lässt: Marcel Hénaff: *Die Gabe der Philosophen. Gegenseitigkeit neu denken*, übers. von Eva Moldenhauer, Bielefeld 2014.

und von allem, was eine Gemeinschaft bestehen lässt, befreite Gemeinschaft nicht Gefahr läuft, sich ebenso zwangsläufig wie die totalitären Versuche ihrer Ins-Werk-Setzung selbst zu zerstören. Mit anderen Worten: Genügt das *cum*, um Gemeinschaft zu werden? Stürzt man das Denken der Gemeinschaft nicht in eine ausweglose Aporie, wenn man sie auf ein Präfix reduziert?

Wenn wir auf diese Fragen antworten wollen, müssen wir uns mit dem Sinn des *cum* auseinandersetzen, mit dieser Ko-Ontologie des Mit, die Nancy uns nahelegt. Meistens bestimmt er das Mit als »Bindestrich, der ebenso ein Trennungsstrich ist«[39]: »Es gibt immer Konjunktion und Disjunktion, Diskonjunktion, Vereinigung *mit* Trennung, Nähe *mit* Ferne«[40]. Auf diese Weise hofft er, der doppelten Gefahr zu entrinnen, die der Gemeinschaft symmetrisch von zwei Seiten her auflauert: »weder Kommunion noch Atomisierung, lediglich das Teilen eines Ortes, allerhöchstens der Kontakt: ein Zusammen-Sein ohne Zusammenfügen«[41]. Ein gewisses Gleichgewicht zwischen Verbindung und Trennung wäre also zu wahren. Nancy allerdings legt den Akzent mitunter auf die Entkopplung, auf den »Abstan[d] im Herzen der Nähe«[42], den irreduziblen Abstand des *cum*, der jede Gemeinschaft mit einem Riss durchzieht. Zum Beispiel unterstreicht er, dass das *co-* wie ein *dis-* zu verstehen ist und das »Gemeinsam-sei[n] [*l'être-en-commun*] als *Dis-Position* (Dispersion und Disparität) der Gemeinschaft«[43]. An diesem Punkt grenzt er sich explizit von Heidegger ab, denn im gleichen Atemzug, wie er ihm vorhält, das **mit-* des **Mitseins* kleinzureden, wirft er ihm seine Privilegierung des **Zuseins* vor, des **Zuseins* als Zugang, Erreichbarkeit und Aneignung eines anderen Dings oder eines anderen Körpers:

»Warum müsste man *a priori* den ›Zugang‹ als die notwendige Weise eines Welt-Machens und eines In-der-Welt-Seins bestimmen? Warum wäre die Welt nicht auch *a priori* im Inmitten-Sein, Zwischen-Sein und

---

39 Nancy: *singulär plural sein*, a.a.O., S. 68.

40 Nancy: *Das nackte Denken*, a.a.O., S. 145 (Fußnote).

41 Jean-Luc Nancy: *Die herausgeforderte Gemeinschaft*, übers. von Esther von der Osten, Zürich, Berlin 2007, S. 31. Es gelte, die »singulären Daseine« nur »in dieser Kommunikation« zu denken, »*zugleich* ohne Band und ohne Kommunikation, in gleichem Abstand zu einem Motiv der Anbindung oder einer Verkoppelung durch das Äußere und zum Motiv einer gemeinsamen und fusionellen Innerlichkeit.« Nancy: *Von einer Gemeinschaft, die sich nicht verwirklicht*, a.a.O., S. 52.

42 Nancy: *Die herausgeforderte Gemeinschaft*, a.a.O., S. 31.

43 Nancy: *singulär plural sein*, a.a.O., S. 49.

Gegen-Sein? In der Entfernung und im Kontakt ohne ›Zugang‹? [...] Muss es nicht notwendig Nicht-Zugang, Undurchdringlichkeit geben, damit es auch Zugang, Eindringen geben kann?«[44]

Sicherlich, doch wer so sehr auf den Nicht-Zugang und das Ohne-Bezug besteht, läuft Gefahr, jedwede Öffnung zur Welt und zu den anderen zu verunmöglichen. Es sieht dann fast so aus, als würde das Denken der Gemeinschaft, um die schlimmste Gefahr zu bannen – die einheitsstiftende Verschmelzung unter dem Einfluss einer mythischen Figur –, in die entgegengesetzte Richtung umschlagen, in die der Zerstreuung, der Atomisierung einer Kollektivität ohne Gestalt und Kontur. Nicht selten wirkt Nancy gewillt, dieses Risiko einzugehen, zum Beispiel, wenn er die »Logik des Mitseins« mit der Logik »unorganisierter Gesamtheiten von Personen« gleichsetzt, die wie »Reisende in einem Zugabteil [...] einfach nebeneinander [sind], zufällig, willkürlich ganz äußerlich.«[45] Die Gemeinschaft löst sich sodann in dem auf, was Sartre »Serialität« nennt, in der passiven, ihrer »praktisch-inerten« Umwelt untergebenen Versammlung. Dem Autor der *Kritik der dialektischen Vernunft*[46] zufolge können die Menschen sich aus dieser seriellen Passivität befreien, indem sie sich in einer gemeinsamen Praxis engagieren. Diese »fusionierende Gruppe« kann, um nicht wieder in die Serialität zurückzufallen, in die »Terror-Brüderlichkeit« führen. Nancy untersteht sich, eine solche Selbstkonstituierung der Gemeinschaft anzustreben, nicht nur, weil er sich nicht mit den Bedingungen kollektiver Handlung, inklusive der Gefahr der Schreckensherrschaft, die sie mit sich bringt, auseinandersetzt, sondern auch, weil er allzu oft die äußerlichere Dimension des Mit privilegiert, die des Seite-an-Seite, des Einer-neben-dem-Anderen. Dies setzt er sowohl Sartre als auch Lévinas entgegen, wenn er »das wahrhaftige *Mit*« als »das Nebeneinander, das jedem Blick und jedem Von-Angesicht-zu-Angesicht vorgängige Seite-an-Seite« definiert.[47]

Woher kommt dieser Vorzug, den er der Entkoppelung, dem Auseinanderfallen erteilt? Da die »Ontologie des Mit-seins [...] eine

---

44 Jean-Luc Nancy: *Der Sinn der Welt*, übers. von Esther von der Osten, Berlin 2020, S. 89f.

45 Nancy: *Von einer Gemeinschaft, die sich nicht verwirklicht*, a.a.O., S. 151.

46 Jean-Paul Sartre: *Kritik der dialektischen Vernunft*, übers. von Traugott König, Reinbek bei Hamburg 1980.

47 Jean-Luc Nancy: »D'une mimèsis sans modèle. Entretien avec Philippe Choulet au sujet de Philippe Lacoue-Labarthe«, in: *L'animal*, 19–20/2008, S. 107–114, Übers. L.S.

Ontologie des Körpers [ist]«[48], ist der Hauptmodus des *cum* der körperliche Kontakt, wodurch die Möglichkeit oder Unmöglichkeit des Kontakts die Möglichkeit oder Unmöglichkeit der Gemeinschaft bedingt. »[D]och das Gesetz das Berührens ist Trennung«[49], sodass der Kontakt nie stattfinden wird. Das wird in einem seiner schönsten Bücher, *Corpus*, mehrfach bestätigt: »Kein Kontakt ohne Abstand«[50], kein Zusammen-sein der Körper ohne die Ausdehnung eines *partes extra partes*, wobei das Entscheidende der »Abstand des *extra*«[51] ist, sein beharrlicher Widerstand gegen jedwede Form der Annäherung. »Der Körper ist die Einheit eines Außerhalb-von-sich-Seins«[52]; er gibt sich vom Außen her und als Außen, aufgrund dieser *Ekstase*, die ihn seiner selbst entreißt. Was für den Körper gilt, gilt auch für das Sein, den Sinn, die Welt und für die Gemeinschaft: Ihre ekstatische Öffnung hält sie davon ab, in eine verschmelzende Immanenz abzudriften. Hätte man Nancy gefragt, inwiefern sich ein Außerhalb-von-sich-Sein auch als ein Mit-sein geben kann, hätte er wahrscheinlich im Anschluss an Heidegger und Bataille geantwortet, dass der Körper gerade durch seine Ekstase *mit* anderen Ekstasen sein kann, das sie *mit* ihm diese ek-statische Transzendenz teilen, die sie aus ihnen selbst hinausschleudert.

Dem wird man gerne zustimmen, doch kann man sich trotz allem auch fragen, ob es sich wirklich um *dieselbe* Transzendenz handelt, und ob die singulären Existierenden sich nicht jeweils in *ihre* ebenfalls singuläre Welt pro-jizieren, in einer Ekstase, die jedes Mal einsam bleibt. Ist dies der Fall, dann ist nicht sicher, ob ihr Außerhalb-von-sich-Sein eine hinreichende Bedingung dafür ist, dass es ihnen gelingt, Gemeinschaft zu werden. Dadurch, dass die Transzendenz einen Abstand zu sich selbst eröffnet, trägt sie zwischen sich und den anderen einen Abstand ein, der noch schwieriger zu überwinden ist. Muss man nicht, um mit jemand anderem in Kontakt zu treten oder sich einfach nur *außer* sich zu begeben, zunächst einmal man selbst sein? Und ist nicht diese Voraussetzung eines Selbst – das heißt letztlich eines *ego sum* – a priori die Bedingung jeder Gemeinschaft? Der Immanenzanteil, den jede Transzendenz erfordert? Wenn sich Körper, alle

---

48 Nancy: *singulär plural sein*, a.a.O., S. 131.
49 Ebd., S. 25.
50 Jean-Luc Nancy: *Corpus*, übers. von Nils Hodyas und Timo Obergöker, Zürich 2007, S. 58.
51 Ebd., S. 32.
52 Ebd., S. 123.

Arten von Körpern, menschliche und nicht-menschliche, lebende und nicht lebende, durch ihre irreduzible Äußerlichkeit auszeichnen, dann muss man, um die Möglichkeit einer Gemeinschaft zu bewahren, den Körperbegriff komplexer fassen und ihm eine *Reversibilität* einschreiben, eine doppelte Bewegung, in der »das Aussichherausgehen auch Rückkehr zu sich ist und umgekehrt«[53]. Wenn man aber nun befindet, dass eine solche Wendung nicht zum durch sein (Im-)Außen-Sein definierten Körper passt, muss man dann nicht auf eine Unterscheidung zwischen *Körper und *Leib zurückkommen, zwischen der weltlichen Transzendenz des Körpers und der Immanenz des Fleisches? Eines Fleisches, das als »*das Sinnliche im doppelten Sinne* des Empfundenen und des Empfindenden«[54] durch seine Reversibilität definiert wird, berührend und berührbar zugleich, sehend und sichtbar? Dehnte man diesen Chiasmus meines Fleisches auf das Fleisch der anderen und vielleicht der Dinge aus, würde es möglich, unser In-der-Welt-Sein und unser Zusammen-Sein auf eine andere Basis zu stellen, ohne dafür eine Gestaltwerdung oder Identifikation in Kauf nehmen zu müssen: auf den Modus einer »Zwischenkörperlichkeit« nämlich, einer fleischlichen Gemeinschaft der Monaden. Das würde bedeuten, auf Philosophen zurückzukommen, die Nancy nicht sonderlich schätzt, die er fast nie erwähnt, und wenn, dann nur, um sich von ihnen zu distanzieren: Husserl und Merleau-Ponty.[55] Was freilich nicht heißen soll, dass diese beiden Denker eine »Lösung« für die Aporien der Gemeinschaft gefunden hätten – ganz im Gegenteil: Die Schwierigkeiten, Sackgassen und Hemmungen, mit denen Merleau-Ponty beim Versuch zu kämpfen hat, die Möglichkeit der Verflechtung zu denken, in der sich die Ränder der »beiden Lippen« des Fleisches berühren, zeigen dies. Ihre Begegnung setzt eine »Dehiszenz« voraus, einen »Abstand« [écart], der sie von der Verschmelzung abhält – was wiederum an Nancys »Abstand« [écartement] erinnert –, sodass es sich im Grunde eher um eine »immerzu bevorstehende und niemals tatsächlich verwirklichte

---

53 Maurice Merleau-Ponty: *Das Sichtbare und das Unsichtbare. Gefolgt von Arbeitsnotizen*, übers. von Regula Giuliani und Bernhard Waldenfels, München 1986, S. 256.
54 Ebd., S. 327.
55 Für eine Vertiefung dieser Analyse sollte man Derrida zurate ziehen, der sich in Jacques Derrida: *Berühren, Jean-Luc Nancy*, übers. von Hans-Dieter Gondek, Berlin 2007 mit Nancys Begriff des Taktilen und des Unberührbaren auseinandersetzt, aber eben auch mit Husserl und Merleau-Ponty. Den Rahmen der vorliegenden Arbeit würde dies weit übersteigen.

Reversibilität«« [56] handelt. Statt von einem Chiasmus spricht Nancy allerdings lieber von *clinamen*. Das ist der lateinische Name einer begrifflichen Erfindung, mit der Epikur die Aporie des Demokrit auflöste, indem er in die parallele Laufbahn der Atome im leeren Raum eine geringfügige Abweichung einführte, einen minimalen Abstand, der den Kontakt erst ermöglicht und es dadurch den Atomen erlaubt, sich zusammenzufinden und eine Welt zu bilden. Zweifellos ist diese Entdeckung auch hilfreich, um die stets zufällige Eventualität einer Begegnung innerhalb einer atomisierten und von ihrem eigenen Vakuum gefährdeten Gesellschaft festzuhalten. Das Wort taucht in *Von einer Gemeinschaft, die sich nicht verwirklicht* gleich zu Beginn auf: »Gemeinschaft ist zumindest das *clinamen* des ›Individuums‹.« [57] In *Der Sinn der Welt* findet es sich wieder [58], ebenso wie in den letzten Zeilen von *Die verleugnete Gemeinschaft*: Hier spricht Nancy vom »schiefwinkligen Anstoß des Clinamen«, »ohne den die Atome allesamt und jedes vereinzelt in die grundlose Leere hineinstürzen würden« [59] – ganz so, als wäre dieses Motiv, das seinen Denkweg über dreißig Jahre lang ganz diskret begleitet, eine seiner heimlichen Signaturen. Ich für meinen Teil sehe darin ein Augenzwinkern, *un clin d'oeil*, ein Zeichen der Komplizenschaft, vom anderen Ufer herübergeschickt, als sollte es uns mitteilen, dass die aufgeschobene Begegnung letztendlich doch noch stattfinden wird.

Aus dem Französischen von Laura Strack

---

56 Merleau-Ponty: *Das Sichtbare und das Unsichtbare*, a.a.O., S. 193.
57 Nancy: *Von einer Gemeinschaft, die sich nicht verwirklicht*, a.a.O., S. 11.
58 Nancy: *Der Sinn der Welt*, a.a.O., S. 87.
59 Nancy: *Die verleugnete Gemeinschaft*, a.a.O., S. 150.

Gert-Jan van der Heiden

Thinking Hermeneutics with Nancy

1. The Dividing of Voices in Dialogue

It was his early study *Le partage des voix* that first drew me to Jean-Luc Nancy's oeuvre.[1] Since then I have often returned to it, not only because it has offered me the conceptual means to engage with Nancy's thought as a whole, but also because it has opened up a way for me to think with Nancy, especially concerning the question of what hermeneutics or interpretation might be in its most profound and original sense. Today, I tend to approach that question through the lens of the notion of testimony,[2] but the sharpening of this lens would have been impossible without the profound rethinking of hermeneutics and hermeneutical categories such as dialogue, interpretation, and translation initiated by Nancy.

If I would have to summarize, I would say that, for me, the importance of *Le partage des voix* is twofold. First, it is the text in which Nancy coins his conception of *partage*, which introduces and motivates much of his thought about both sense and being-in-common. To capture the ambiguity of the French term, it is often translated as "sharing in/sharing out." The French *partager* indeed means both "to share in"—including the sense of "to endorse" as in "to share the other's opinion"—and "to distribute"; yet, it also means "to divide." The first two senses are covered by the common translation of "sharing in/sharing out." The third sense, however, seems somewhat obscured by this translation. The title *le partage des voix* is an idiomatic expression in the French that signifies the tie that may occur when a particular subject matter has been *mis aux voix*, put to the vote, so that the voices may declare themselves in favor or against it. A tie indicates that the

---

1   Jean-Luc Nancy, *Le partage des voix* (Paris: Galilée, 1982). Translated by Gayle L. Ormiston as "Sharing Voices," in *Transforming the Hermeneutic Context: From Nietzsche to Nancy*, ed. Gayle L. Ormiston and Alan D. Schrift (Albany: SUNY Press, 1990), pp. 211–259.
2   See, for example, Gert-Jan van der Heiden, *The Voice of Misery: A Continental Philosophy of Testimony* (Albany: SUNY Press, 2020).

opinions that are voiced are not so much shared or distributed, but rather that the people casting their votes are completely *divided* over the subject matter. It seems to me that the French idiom has implications for what Nancy's notion of *partage* allows us to think concerning commonality, being-in-common and community but also—and chronologically in the first place—concerning hermeneutics.

Second, in *Le partage des voix*, Nancy provides a basic and new explication of "the original sense of *hermēneuein*" that Martin Heidegger announced in rather elliptic terms in reference to Plato's *Ion*.[3] Perhaps one should say that it has been Nancy who has kept and delivered Heidegger's promise and commitment—*Zusage*—to think the original sense of hermeneutics, but in that way, by keeping this promise and commitment, has opened a different path in the rethinking of hermeneutics than Heidegger's.

In this sense, Nancy's text enacts and presents a paradigmatic example of what *le partage des voix* means. Sharing in and responding to similar questions and concerns, to similar commitments, Heidegger's and Nancy's voices divide. If we understand Nancy's engagement with Heidegger as a dialogue, it is not a dialogue understood along the lines of "classical" hermeneutics. In this classical understanding, of which Hans-Georg Gadamer and Paul Ricoeur are the main representatives, a dialogue is understood as follows. It sets out with two, different voices, each voicing a different opinion about the subject matter under discussion, but it finds its fulfilment and completion in the unification of these voices, when both participants find the words to speak about this subject matter with one voice. For Gadamer, *Einverständnis, Einstimmung*, or *Einstimmigkeit* are terms expressing this "classical" goal of dialogue: they express the unification of understanding and of voices that bring a dialogue to its fulfilment.[4] Nancy's dialogue with Heidegger, however, does not find its fulfilment in this speaking with one voice. It is rather a conversation that allows each of the participants to find their own, singular voice in the first place.

---

3   Martin Heidegger, *Unterwegs zur Sprache* (Frankfurt am Main: Vittorio Klostermann, 1985), pp. 115–116; my translation.

4   Hans-Georg Gadamer, *Wahrheit und Methode* (Tübingen: Mohr Siebeck, 1990), p. 183, p. 296; Jean-Luc Nancy, *Être singulier pluriel* (Paris: Galilée, 1996), p. 110; Gert-Jan van der Heiden, *Ontology after Ontotheology: Plurality, Event, and Contingency in Contemporary Philosophy* (Pittsburgh: Duquesne University Press, 2014), pp. 90–92.

Hence, it is the sharing in the same subject matter that allows for a genuine division into singular voices. In this way, the *partage des voix* suggests a radical revision of the concept of dialogue at stake in this "original hermeneutics." The notion of *partage* contests the "obvious" presupposition that a philosophical dialogue begins with two different voices, as if everybody has always already found their own voice in advance, and that the only remaining task is to put these voices to the dialogical test of truth and correct the voiced opinions in accordance with the outcome of this test.[5] With Nancy, however, we may suggest that the goal of dialogue is rather to come into one's very own voice, to discover one's singularity in and by the plurality of *le partage des voix*. Only in dialogue with others, something like a genuine singular voice may appear in the first place—this singularity can neither be presupposed nor be found in the mere voicing of opinions.

2. Bringing into Circulation

The reinterpretation of dialogue discussed in the previous section is a first example of how Nancy's thought offers us conceptual means to rethink the nature and the essence of hermeneutics. Let us turn to a second one by considering his innovative reading of Plato's *Ion*. The reason to turn to this dialogue—for Heidegger, Nancy, and us—concerns the specific meaning of *hermēneuō* and *hermēneus* that is put to the fore in it. The interpreter is not so much the one who understands or has particular knowledge—in fact, the poet and the rhapsode are said to be out of their minds when they sing[6]—but is rather portrayed as the one who delivers or distributes. What type of movement and transfer do we encounter here in this original form and sense of interpretation?

The interpreter is not simply a vehicle or a vessel transporting a particular or fixed entity—a message, an idea, or a signification—from one place to another or from one mind to another. The movement at stake is definitely not the *kinēsis* studied in physics. Rather,

---

5   Plato, *Gorgias* 486d. Edition used: Plato, *Lysis. Symposium. Gorgias*, trans. W. R. M. Lamb, Loeb Classical Library 166 (Cambridge, Mass.: Harvard University Press, 1925).

6   Plato, *Ion* 534b. Edition used: Plato, *Statesman. Philebus. Ion*, trans. Harold North Fowler and W. R. M. Lamb, Loeb Classical Library 164 (Cambridge, Mass.: Harvard University Press, 1925).

it concerns the sense of movement that we refer to when we say that we are deeply moved or affected by something or when something has stirred our emotions. It is the movement and the being-moved of the soul. The intrinsic connection between hermeneutics and this form of movement is best laid bare in an analysis of poetry and rhapsody, as Socrates argues, because these concern a form of communication in which knowledge—and thus a particular sense of truth—as the goal of communication is suspended.

This change in focus raises important questions, especially when considered from a more classical perspective on interpretation. Should hermeneutics not be understood in one way or another as the art of understanding? That is, is the act of interpretation not always guided by the goal of understanding? So what does it mean to suspend this goal? To answer these questions, we first need to understand how knowledge, communication, and understanding function in a reflection on hermeneutics. At this point, Nancy's introduction of *partage* in his reading of the *Ion* paves the way for us.

Partage speaks of a poetic and rhapsodic participation. When we hear "participation" in relation to Plato, we tend to think of *methexis*, the participation in the idea as true being. Yet, *partage* is not introduced as a translation of *methexis*. Even though I have to admit that in the course of his text Nancy does relate *partage* to *methexis*,[7] this seems to me to be a somewhat problematic gesture slightly distorting the real discovery of *partage* as poetic participation.[8] *Partage* appears first as *partage divin*, translating *theia moira*, divine distribution.[9] More precisely, what is distributed poetically is not a truth or an idea, but rather a power, namely the *theia dunamis*, the divine power that makes poets and rhapsodes sing.[10] This power of movement is not the physical sense of *dunamis* in relation to *kinēsis* as spatial or qualitative movement, but is rather the power to stir, move, and affect the soul. In the *Ion*, Plato describes poets and rhapsodes as enthusiasts in the etymological sense of the word: the gods are in them; they are moved by a divine power and they are moved to speak. Their words are therefore not words of knowledge but rather of inspiration, and their words bring this particular power into circulation, sharing

---

7   See, for example, Nancy, *Le partage des voix*, p. 71.
8   Gert-Jan van der Heiden, *De stem van de doden. Hermeneutiek als spreken namens de ander* (Nijmegen: Vantilt, 2012), pp. 84–86.
9   Plato, *Ion* 534c.
10 Ibid., 533d.

it with their audience. Thanks to this circulation, poet, rhapsode, and receiver are moved by, engaged in, and committed to the same *dunamis*. This basic scene and sense of hermeneutics to which Nancy draws our attention, is important for (at least) two reasons in a reflection on hermeneutics, the second reason being addressed in the next section.

First, in some of its formulations and analyses, "classical" hermeneutics tends to portray the process of interpretation as a teleological or regulated process, attracted by an as yet hidden and absent, but nevertheless presupposed meaning—a "signifié transcendantal," as Jacques Derrida suggests[11]—which interpretation aims to approach and explicate. If the process of interpretation is an endless one, it is because of the finitude of the interpreters and the linguistic means at their disposal, which never allows the meaning to be present as such and in full. In this classical conception, therefore, interpretation is basically a representation or *mimēsis* of this ideal, transcendental meaning. Consequently, the truth claim of interpretation is based on a variation of Platonic *methexis*, of participation in a universal meaning or idea, or—in its modern guise—based on a variation of the Kantian regulative idea.

However, it remains to be seen whether such a metaphysical or transcendental presupposition is necessary. What happens if we understand the participation at stake in hermeneutics not based on the epistemological model of *methexis* but rather on the poetic model of *theia moira*? The problem of the presupposition of an ideal meaning—either universal for all who are rational or quasi-universal for those belonging to the same cultural and historical tradition—is that it solves the issue of communication before communication has taken place. The communicability—as well as the knowability—of an ideal meaning is grounded in this (quasi-)universality. Yet, by *presupposing* this communicability, hermeneutics runs the risk of obscuring its own provenance and *raison d'être*. Hermeneutics and interpretation have become a universal question and problem because of their particular modern predicament, by which all humans are recognized to have their own perspective on the world—and because this communication between these perspectives or horizons has become a *problem*. To ensure communicability by the presupposition of a "transcendental signified," a hermeneutic theory discards confronting the very problem that

---

11 Jacques Derrida, *L'écriture et la différence* (Paris: Seuil, 1967), p. 411.

defines it: How is communication possible, if and when humans are determined by their own life-nexus, *are* their own perspective on the world, unfolded by their singular experiences?

Exactly for these reasons, what an original hermeneutics needs to account for is not simply how this or that idea or message is communicated, but how, first and foremost, communicability itself is established in and by the act or enactment of communication. This, interestingly enough, is what defines sense in contrast to signification for Nancy: "Sense is consequently not the 'signified' or the 'message': it is *that something like transmission of a 'message' should be possible.*"[12] In the vocabulary of Plato's *Ion*, *theia moira* is exactly this, namely that the experiences which move and stir the speaker's soul now also move and stir the addressee's. This is the divine miracle of *partage*, namely that the experiences of the other do not remain mute or senseless to me, but rather speak to me, affect and move me—which is quite different from claiming that I understand them in the same way as the other does. In its original sense, *partage* concerns the constitution of this particular social bond: the interpreter enacts the communicability of what they transmit. Thus, Nancy's *partage* might in fact allow us to understand better what Gadamer means when he speaks of "hermeneutic experience" and when he notes that the true hermeneutic miracle of sense takes place when the world of the other is not only significant for the other, but can become significant for me.[13]

3. The Subject Matter of Communication

The second reason why the basic scene and sense of hermeneutics to which Nancy draws our attention is important concerns the following issue. When Nancy emphasizes that sense and *partage* concern transmissibility itself, one might wonder what has happened to the actual topic about which someone speaks. Perhaps, one might worryingly note, Nancy's reliance on the *Ion* implies that the emphasis on *dunamis* or power does not leave any room for the particular subject matter of a communication. Perhaps, his

---

12 Jean-Luc Nancy, *Le sens du monde* (Paris: Galilée, 1993), p. 184. Translation taken from *The Sense of the World*, trans. Jeffrey S. Librett (Minneapolis: University of Minnesota Press, 1997), p. 118.
13 Gadamer, *Wahrheit und Methode*, p. 445.

critical discussion of classical hermeneutics runs the risk of being overtaken by the opposition between sense and signification or between sense and transcendental signified. While the notion of *partage* insists that, in addition to this or that subject matter, communication also communicates the communicability of this subject matter, one might fear that the subject matter itself is lost sight of and erased because it is subsumed under the heading of signification and signified.

To address this worry, it seems to me, it is imperative to overcome the opposition between sense and signification and to understand the role and the place of the subject matter of communication differently. In order to do so, let us consider how both Heidegger and Gadamer prefer to use the German term *Sache* to refer to the subject matter of a communication. To capture this term's meaning, as Gadamer suggests, one needs to be aware that *Sache* translates *res* as well as *causa*.[14] It seems to me that each of these Latin terms captures an important aspect of what a subject matter or *Sache* actually is.

Res brings the dimension of reality and the real into play. The sense of the real does not concern an abstract or independent reality, but includes the human encounter with the subject matter as something real. The human who speaks, speaks about a *Sache* they encountered, were exposed to, touched on and were touched or affected by. The notion of *Sache* thus does not refer to a signified or a referent, independent from the one who experiences; rather, the *Sache* is experienced as that which can affect the individual human in a determinate way. The *dunamis* of which the notion of *theia dunamis* speaks can thus be made fruitful beyond the mere scenery of a poet inspired by a muse, as soon as we understand that the human encounter with and exposure to reality is not in the first place an encounter with something the human immediately grasps, understands or knows. Rather, the first significance of this encounter is that humans in this experience experience that they touch on the real, and are in this way committed to what they experience because *it is* (experienced as) real. The human is a place or locus where this reality is disclosed, announced, and made known *as real*. That the human encounters something real, albeit within the confines of their limited capacity to experience or

---

14 Hans-Georg Gadamer, "Die Natur der Sache und die Sprache der Dinge," in *Hermeneutik II* (Tübingen: Mohr Siebeck, 1990), pp. 66–76, p. 67.

perceive, makes it of human significance to the extent that humans are the beings interested in what is real.

With this sense of *Sache* as *res* we can also understand what it means to say, with Nancy, that communication is not simply the transfer of a particular signification or referent but rather concerns the communication of communicability itself. The original sense of hermeneutics as making known concerns the communication of the particular *dunamis* of the *Sache*—the potentiality to be affected and touched by the real as real and thus be committed to it—to the other; to share with the other that one has experienced something real that, *because it is real*, is significant to the other as well. Hermeneutics thus concerns the human miracle that the reality experienced by an individual can be shared and thus constitute a social bond sealed by the social significance of the individual's exposure to the real. Interpretation, in the more common sense of the word, departs from this exposure and is an attempt to understand the real by which one is touched and to which one is committed in and by this exposure.

In line with the idiomatic sense of *le partage des voix*, *Sache* as *causa* adds an important dimension to the previous account of the subject matter. *Causa* has a legal provenance and conveys that the *Sache* borne witness to is a subject matter *in dispute*: it can always be *contested*. A dispute presupposes plurality; there must be at least two contestants. To share in the significance of the subject matter means to be allowed to speak about it *with one's own voice*. With Nancy, we may indeed say that "sense is not what is communicated but *that* there is communication."[15] Original hermeneutics means that the interpreter communicates the human significance of the subject matter with others. Yet, at the very moment this significance is shared, it is divided. Once shared in a conversation, different voices articulate this significance differently. The movement of hermeneutics, exemplified by the model of dialogue, is not one-way communication—and it seems to me that exactly at this point the model of the *Ion*, from poet to rhapsode to audience, needs correction—but is rather a movement of to-and-fro. Each of the voices that speak out of their own exposure to the *res* at stake in the conversation, are now, in turn, exposed to the other's articulations and voicings. The goal of this exposure is not to reach an agreement with the other, but rather to allow the other's voice

---

15 Nancy, *Le sens du monde*, p. 178; *The Sense of the World*, p. 114.

to play a part in finding one's own voice. As I noted before, humans encounter something real within the confines of their limited capacity to experience and perceive. The model of dialogue shows how humans transgress these confines and limitations: not towards a more general or universal grasp, but rather towards their own singular voice.

4. The Ordeal of the Foreign

The emphasis on singularity in this conception of hermeneutics also brings out its mirror concept, namely alterity or strangeness. Nancy hesitates over whether classical hermeneutics is capable of allowing alterity to be brought into play in its proper sense. In discussion with Ricoeur, he notes: "[I]t would be necessary to analyze up to what point the alterity *of* meaning is put into play, and not only an originating meaning of an identified other (and because of that, endowed with an unchanged other [*non-altérité*])."[16] These comments are not dismissive, but rather express a genuine hesitation. Each and every encounter with an other person or with otherness, is a test. In the *Gorgias*, Socrates conceives of dialogue as a way of testing the quality of one's opinions; Platonic dialogue puts convictions to the test of truth. When rethinking hermeneutics with Nancy, the sense of this test changes. Within the realm of an original hermeneutics, the real test or trial at stake in a dialogue is the test of the foreignness that one encounters in the other's voice or language; it is *l'épreuve de l'étranger.*[17]

Antoine Berman introduces this beautiful expression as the title of his study on translation in German Romanticism.[18] Interestingly, it translates Heidegger's "die Erfahrung des Fremden," the experience or test of the foreign that one undergoes when engaged in the translation of a text.[19] One "passes" the test of the foreign not simply when one is capable of articulating the meaning of what is said in a foreign language adequately in one's own. Every translation

---

16 Nancy, *Le partage des voix*, p. 21; "Sharing Voices," p. 215; see also van der Heiden, *The Voice of Misery*, pp. 222–228.

17 Jean-Luc Nancy, "Echo by Jean-Luc Nancy," *Angelaki* 26, no. 3–4 (2021), p. 99.

18 Antoine Berman, *L'épreuve de l'étranger. Culture et traduction dans l'Allemagne romantique* (Paris: Gallimard, 1984).

19 Martin Heidegger, *Erläuterungen zur Hölderlins Dichtung* (Frankfurt am Main: Vittorio Klostermann, 1981), p. 115.

aims to integrate and appropriate a foreign text in one's own language. Yet, this implies that the particular struggle or ordeal of the foreign that the translator experiences in the act of translating is ultimately smoothed out in the translation the audience receives. If there are traces left of this ordeal, they are found in footnotes, a preface or an epilogue, excluded from the main text.

From the perspective of the audience, it seems that the hermeneutic act of translation is guided by the goal of discerning, discovering, and inventing similarities or comparables between what is expressed in the foreign language and what is expressed in one's own. Yet, the translator's experience of the foreign hesitates between similarity and difference, between that which can more or less adequately be phrased in the target language and that which resists translation. The ordeal of the foreign, expressed by *l'épreuve de l'étranger*, is thus itself marked by a hesitation between difference and similarity, by the fact that one may "comprendre" but not "entendre" what the foreign language says.[20] One hesitates and wonders whether "classical" hermeneutics does not tend to approach this test and the passing of this test mainly or even merely in terms of the similarity and accessibility of the foreign language by the linguistic power of expression offered by one's own language. If so, one needs to pose the question: Does such an approach not obscure the difference, the untranslatable remainder of which the translator is only too aware because it was this ordeal of the foreign to which they responded in the act of translating?

How to understand this hesitation? And can we only conceive of the untranslatable remainder as a *lack* of our language? The expression "die Erfahrung des Fremden" is only half of Heidegger's characterization of the dialogue between two languages in translation. The full expression shows more clearly in which sense the test of the foreign is a dialogical one: "die Erfahrung des Fremden und die Einübung des Eigenen." The experience of a difference and an untranslatable remainder is not abstracted or obscured in a one-sided embrace and appraisal of similarities between languages. Rather, the test of the foreign assigns a particular task to the translator: they have to translate the untranslatable. That is to say, they have to offer an interpretation of that which cannot be expressed in the same or in a similar way in their own language. Hence, they

---

20 Nancy, "Echo," p. 99; the verb *entendre* has a similar double sense as the German verb *verstehen*.

need to invent in their own language a new voice and a new articulation. In exactly this sense, the untranslatable remainder does not remain mute; in fact, the negative experience that the foreign cannot be rendered adequately in one's own language becomes productive in "die Einübung des Eigenen," in the practice of and the engagement with the power of expression that one's own language offers. This, I would say, is another paradigmatic example of Nancy's *partage des voix* on the level of translation: while the interpretation in one's own language does not say what the foreign text says, it is only thanks to *l'épreuve de l'étranger* that one discovers the singular power of expression of one's own language to share and express the significance encountered in the foreign text with different means and in its own singular way.

Juan Manuel Garrido and Alexander García Düttmann

Anyone, Someone, No One

In 2010, Jean-Luc Nancy published a short essay entitled *Identity. Fragments, Frankness*. It was a reaction to a populist and in the end unsuccessful debate launched by Éric Besson, head of a short-lived and infamous French Ministry for Immigration, Integration and National Identity during the presidency of Nicolas Sarkozy.[1] The fragmentary character of Nancy's essay in no way preempts a rigorous argumentative development that problematizes and re-news the political and philosophical conceptualization of "iden-tity." Besson's—and Sarkozy's—dysfunctional initiative cannot obscure the gravity of the question of national identity in a country and a continent that have experienced self-doubt of an increas-ingly brutal and destructive intensity in the last decades. As Nancy explains, "it is not merely 'national identity'—whether French or not—that seems to be threatened by other identities; in fact, all 'identities' are undergoing a general disidentification from what we used to call 'civilisation'."[2]

A question about identity—individual, collective or national—reveals itself to be pressing when what distinguishes us from oth-ers—friends or enemies—becomes blurred and our identification with a symbolic figure, a culture, a provenance or a destiny ceases to be available or self-evident to us. Our identity appears to be problematic at the moment we perceive our self to be threatened. And this threat must be a radical one. We risk more than dis-affection, transformation or alienation. We risk more than losing our home or homeland. We risk more than facing the intolerable prospect of migration. What we risk is destruction. The question of identity comes with a vital, existential, violently intimate anxiety: the anxiety that disidentification unleashes.

What happens with identity is the reverse of what happens with time, at least if we follow Augustine. That is to say, I know nothing about my identity unless someone asks me about it, compelling me to elucidate it. I am never simply something or someone. In order

---

1   Jean-Luc Nancy, *Identity. Fragments, Frankness*, trans. François Raffoul (New York: Fordham University Press, 2015). Originally published in French as *Identité. Fragments, franchises* (Paris: Galilée, 2010).
2   Ibid., p. 4—translation modified, J.M.G. and A.G.D.

to be something or someone I must be able to account for my identity. Therefore identity originates in its own mutation. And perhaps this implies, tragically, that identity emerges only when endangered, which means that it cannot be sought or produced without anxiety and violence. Simple, immutable identity, the identity of I = I asserts itself only in irrelevant and impotent modes, as the syntactic or semantic or administrative immutability of an x. Defending or acquiring an identity requires a process of reflection, in which an individual or a group of individuals distance themselves from identification as a mechanical operation of registration, verification, classification, and capture. Identity is either *thought*, that is, submitted to dis-identification and dissociation—or else it remains an external indifferent feature, even though much may depend on the possession of a national identity card in particular social, political and historical situations.

As identity seeks to emerge from an unquestioned state and constitute itself conceptually, in thought or reflection, it reveals a fissure and a tension, no matter how difficult it may be to discern them. It reveals a fundamental ambiguity that makes it all the more elusive and ties it all the more forcefully to an existential experience of anxiety and exaltation, lack and plenitude, downplaying and exaggeration, as if identity were always too much or not enough, or as if it were the most important thing in life and at the same time a negligible quantity, an ideological construct, a suspicious contrivance. No wonder that in the recent past, after a violent history of identitarian affirmation and cosmopolitan denial, a politics of diversity and pluralism has become dominant in the Western world that posits a settling, peaceful and comforting coexistence of different identities, so as to put an end to the turbulences that each of them may generate and that in the end may ruin them all. In his essay, Nancy thematizes the tension that arises within identity whenever questioned. He does not draw explicit attention to the ensuing ambiguity and yet it keeps transpiring in his argument.

The tension that splits identity can be described, when using Nancy's own terms, as a tension between, on the one hand, an indivisible, ineluctable, unintelligible point, the point of a "who," and, on the other hand, a labyrinthian course, itinerary or lineage, in which a "what" qualifies the presupposed "who," a "who" so entirely invested in its own ongoing qualification that it can barely subsist in the guise of a presupposition. The tension can also be described as a tension between something that remains in itself and something that exists for itself. Finally, it can be described as an unruly becoming that endlessly moves or unfolds between two extremes, between the intractable insistence of a point and the experience of an expansive journey. In truth, the tension that splits identity has a paradoxical aspect because its two extremes, absolute gathering and absolute dispersion, cannot be grasped. Identity in this sense amounts to a form of becoming deprived of both an identifiable beginning and an identifiable end. Such becoming must thwart any attempt to turn it into a mediating process between the extremes that seem to contain it. Where does identity stem from? Where is it heading? By definition, these questions cannot be answered. The point withdraws into an unfathomable impenetrability, the journey into an equally unfathomable openness. The "who" and the "what" are traces to be found in the becoming itself, in the becoming identical, and do not as such form stable and determinable poles. If this were indeed the case, they would collapse into each other, each one the pole of an absolute difference. They mark vanishing points and manifest their unattainable inconstancy as unexpected and unforeseeable discontinuities, gaps, interruptions, hiatuses, delays and blind spots.

The ambiguity that ensues from identity as a movement of becoming identical concerns the necessity and the impossibility of keeping the "who" and the "what" apart. "Who" and "what" must be kept apart, otherwise identity as logical requirement or administrative function could not be distinguished from identity as existential worry, as a disidentification of the self that calls for a becoming and entangles this becoming in a sort of bad infinity, relinquishing it to the proud or desperate reiteration of a tautology: "I am what I am." Consequently, Nancy separates the act of unambiguously declaring and unreservedly affirming one's irreducible, independent, free existence, the *whoness* of the one who speaks, as it were, from the act of affirming an identity with particular traits, characteristics or attributes, the *whatness* of the one speaking. Outspokenness in excess of any reason that would justify it, the contingency of my inalienable singularity: these lie at the core of any identitarian affirmation and provide it with its irresistible force. Yet simultaneously Nancy concedes that such identity admits of a plasticity that can create or recreate a lineage by shaping it according to different individual, collective, historical, social, biographical, psychological, or sexual features. If the "who" and the "what" could be kept apart, identity would fall prey to abstraction. Everything hinges on the sense of the specification to be encountered in the following passage of Nancy's essay: "Identity relies both on itself and on a lineage. More exactly: it is itself its own lineage."[3] Is identity provocative, disarming, intolerable, desirable because the structural straightforwardness of its constitutive speech act proves to be untouchable, outliving the life and death of the one who states it, or who looks his executioner in the eye, defiantly and unflinchingly? Or is it provocative, disarming, intolerable, desirable because the tension between a "who" and a "what" can never be located and ascertained, because any execution suppresses the very question of identity, as Nancy remarks?

The execution does not suppress the question of identity without first provoking the defiant and speechless gaze with which "I" stares at its executioner. What else could prompt such a self-affirming gaze if not the threat of suppressing the very question of identity? It is never a mere curiosity that raises the question "who am I?" or "who are we?" but a radical loss of identity. To what does the question of identity respond if not to a profound estrangement and ignorance? How then could this question be asked without the defiant and unflinching gaze of an "I" already lost in the indifferent opacity of the executioner's face?

In its self-affirmation, the "I" identifies with the frankness or veracity of its utterance ("I am, I exist"). But this identification entails a radical disidentification. The affirmation "I am, I exist" is true only if the "I" that utters it may cease to exist at the very moment of uttering it. "I am, I exist" means each time: "I have not ceased to be." "I" is each time a victory over the possibility of not being. Therefore, "being" and "existing" consist in more than truthful self-affirmation. They exceed and outlive the self-affirmation of the "I," leaving it exposed to what its veracity will not account for. They inscribe "I" in the possibility of not being and not existing. "I am, I exist" ultimately means that "I" is produced as the possibility of not being, that is, as the task of being, because its being is neither given nor guaranteed. No sooner is "I" enunciated than it is stripped of all identity, dis-identified or, put differently, identified with the task of being something that is neither given nor guaranteed; something that, in any event, is not what it is at the moment of the utterance. Being ("I am") dis-identifies the "I" from the act of self-affirmation and projects it beyond this act, throwing it into being, into what it is not. "'Become what you are!' This is very well said: You are not what you are; you have to become it;

---

3   Ibid., p. 17.

and nothing is given to you for this purpose since what you are is nowhere but at the end of your becoming. And at that point, you will not be there anymore."[4]

"'Here I am, forever unassailable'. This affirmation is at the basis of all affirmation of identity."[5] Therefore, the defiant veracity of the "I" is the crucial technology of identity. This defiant veracity is valid not because of what "I" knows but because of what it does not know. "I" comes into being by freeing itself from self-knowledge: "Affranchisement and independence are deeper than my dependency on myself (my taste, my desires, and my fears)."[6] The truthful affirmation of "I" does not affirm an indubitable "knowledge" about itself since the affirmation of "I" affirms much more or much less than "I" knows at the very moment of self-affirmation. "I" needs to identify itself defiantly with the unknown. "[...] [O]ne can have a great talent for introspection, but the first and last knowledge remains this: that there is nothing to know [...] What constitutes, with respect to identity, a great writer? It is that one can never claim to have discovered the ultimate identity of their characters. Think of James, Proust, and Faulkner. A bad writer, on the contrary, assembles a series of identified identities before he or she begins to write."[7]

"I" obeys the imperative of self-ignorance ("ignore thyself!") in the resolution to create itself ("become what you are!"). It stands for the apodictic abandonment of all self-knowledge and the obligation to produce knowledge that ultimately generates nothing other than questions. Perhaps "I" is always confronted with two different tasks and it is this confrontation that brings identity into play and turns it into a question, or, as shall become apparent, a quasi-question. Looking into the executioner's eyes, "I" is cut off from the historical intricacies of its lineage. Its lineage is reduced to the barest, most vulnerable and most unchallengeable expression, hovering undecidably between the abstraction of anyone and the concretion of someone. Anyone can be in the position of "I" and this position is always the position of someone, "I." Here, "I" affirms itself with a force, a force of being, that proves to be inextricably entangled with the force emanating from the vortex of non-being. The veracity of identity is the seal of this entanglement,

---

4   Ibid., p. 18.
5   Ibid., p. 14.
6   Ibid.
7   Ibid., p. 20—translation modified, J.M.G. and A.G.D.

a seal unavailable to whoever tries to appropriate it. For it is the mark of a twofold excess. Being and non-being come from beyond the act of resistance to the radical violence of a death sentence, in which identity becomes critical. Being and non-being are nothing but this coming that carries and undoes the "I" at the same time.

"I" can either engage in an endless process of identification and disidentification, a process called becoming, or else allow for the impossible, namely grasp the tip at which identification and dis-identification appear to touch each other. "I" can either take on the task of creating an identity for itself that it will never secure and that will keep giving birth to yet another executioner, or seek to maintain itself in the open and closed gap between identification and disidentification, in the gap where identification and disidenti-fication meet and also separate, instead of constantly being thrown from one side of the gap to the other. Can "I" somehow inhabit this gap or must it remain under the sway of the forces of identification and disidentification, being and not-being?

This second task is hardly a task, though—something that can be achieved or that leads to failure—and this is why the question of identity remains suspended in the choice between two distinct tasks, collapsing into a quasi-question. The second task resembles more a lucky coincidence or a stroke of good fortune that keeps occurring because of its very elusiveness: another "contingency," another "landing point"[8] or, better still, another relation opened up by "contingency." In the case of this lucky coincidence, "I" can neither be said to have an identity nor to lack one. It neither looks for an inexplicable identity nor incessantly produces one. It is neither ignorant nor knowing. Rather, "I" has become indis-sociable from its quotation marks and identity has ceased to be a tormenting question. The quotation marks do not so much point to a playful postmodern nominalism ("I" is no one and anyone, but never someone) or to the absolute hospitality of a shifter-function ("I" is anyone and someone, but never no one) than indicate that "I" is anyone, no one, and someone, all equally and simultane-ously. Is this a different manner of understanding becoming, one that no longer opposes becoming and standstill and that resembles the crystallization of a configuration pregnant with tensions? Such crystallization does not carry a revolutionary chance waiting to be seized, as in Walter Benjamin's "Theses on the Philosophy of

---

8   Ibid., p. 22.

History." For the emergence of an "I" that is equally and simulta-neously anyone, no one and someone must already be considered as the somewhat passive seizing of a revolutionary chance.

Yet are identification and disidentification not *acts I perform*? According to the dialectic of identity, disidentification is the flipside of the concrete and unplayful positioning of the self either as "I," "we" or something collectively shared and produced: a person, a couple, a species, a struggle for recognition, a friendship, a family, a society, a State, an action, a meaning, work, politics, freedom, war, hate, knowledge, action, justice, democracy. None of the elements or items listed are ever given once and for all but exist only qua the absolute and absolving becoming of the self's disidentification, that is to say, the resolute, defiant, reckless, unflinching separa-tion from everything that threatens to immobilize the self, to put "I" within quotation marks or to execute it. Saying veraciously "I" does not condemn me but frees me from death. It assigns me to the unpredictable lines of a veritable disappropriation. It inscribes me in a lineage that I trace or retrace by dint of remaining blind to my tracing. Every time my audacity surprises me and I ask myself who I am, I seek to make this lineage my own. And I seek to make it my own every time I resist the violence of grammar, objectification, or reification, ignorant of what, exactly, I am doing and who this "I" is. Even and especially when I subscribe to the statements I enunci-ate, I am not I.

The dialectic of identity claims that "I am" means: I disidentify myself, I separate myself from my identity with "I," I separate my-self from the empty identity $I = I$, and I become the being and non-being of becoming itself. "I am" is not, then, a pure abstrac-tion. Rather, it is an excription of my concrete (dis)identification. The identity $I = I$ is ultimately the identity of an object $(x = x)$, or it is identity as an object. So when I disidentify from $I = I$, I perform an act in which I cease to be an object and become a subject, the subject of a relation to the object or to another subject. I am released from being a being and take on the task of being. Or, more radically, I become the injunction of becoming who or what I am. This is why when we speak of "identity" we speak not of a proliferation of operations but of an act of self-identification and self-appropriation. We speak of a resolution to become and remain oneself. Yet I could not make such a resolution and bring about my identity without presupposing the possibility of a previous disiden-tification, or a sort of pure "I," an "I" purified of all particular identi-fication. For, on the one hand, the resolution to become and remain

111

oneself cannot be made by an I that has already acquired a specific identity, while on the other hand, the resolute I must be stable and constant enough to ensure that the subject's acts do not dissolve as they come into existence. Must then the disidentification that triggers the dialectic of identity involve the disidentification of a pure "I" that accompanies my acts, the acts a subject performs in the process of constituting itself? Can I engage in the dialectic of identity and become a subject if I do not accept that I am incapable of separating myself from objectivity, provided the identity of a pure "I" or of "I = I" is the identity of an object?

However, it seems no longer necessary, or even possible, to conceive of a unity of experience that keeps the world within the limits that render it recognizable and allow for its intelligible transformation. The concrete evolution of our knowledge and the life that this evolution enables do not presuppose the purity of a disidentified "I" that guarantees such experience. I am there where I *happen* to be. I am there more or less steadily.

Where I happen to be, I am anyone (an I equal to any other I equal to itself, "I = I") and no one (a pure I, "I = I") and someone (an I engaged in the dialectic of identity). As long as I try to shed the accidentality of my being there, I am like anyone who strives to be someone. In this strife, I shove off the pure I (the objectivity of identity) on which I also rely (only an I that is no one can ensure that the striving for identity takes place at all). I keep existing dialectically, under the spell of identification and disidentification. However, once I try *to be there* where I happen to be, I am anyone and someone and no one, all equally and simultaneously.

Apostolos Lampropoulos

From Debt-in-intimacy to Critical Intimacy[1]

The death of Jean-Luc Nancy was, for me as for many of those who had met and thought with him, an experience of intimate separation, of remaining one without a most inspiring and endearing thinker. Similarly, thinking further with Nancy is a debt to a philosopher that one can feel intimate with and who taught us much about intimacy. Even though he did not devote an entire book to this question, intimacy is anything but marginal to his work. Whether one reads him as a philosopher of the community, of the body, of touch, of the "there is" of sexual relation, of painting, of the singular plural being, or of Christianity, intimacy remains at the core of proximity, sharing, being-together, taking pleasure and accepting risk in enjoying the warmth of another body or shivering with it.

Thinking further with Nancy is debt-in-intimacy also in that he expanded on this issue repeatedly over the course of the last few years. In *Sexistence*[2] he explored sex-related issues varying from devouring to singular plural sex, and from love-to-death to love-to-life. This essay was followed by the dialogical book *The Deconstruction of Sex* (co-signed with Irving Goh and published posthumously in English),[3] which attenuated possible misinterpretations of *Sexistence* in the North American academic context. Nancy adopted a similar approach in one of his last talks, "Touche-touche,"[4] that he gave in the context of the public program of the *Intimacy: New Queer Art from Berlin and Beyond* exhibition[5], which I co-curated

1   This publication was partly funded by the Deutsche Forschungsgemeinschaft (DFG, German Research Foundation) under Germany's Excellence Strategy in the context of the Cluster of Excellence *Temporal Communities: Doing Literature in a Global Perspective* – EXC 2020 – Project ID 390608380.
2   Jean-Luc Nancy, *Sexistence*, trans. S. Miller (New York: Fordham University Press, 2021[2017]). E-book.
3   Jean-Luc Nancy and Irving Goh, *The Deconstruction of Sex* (Durham, N.C.: Duke University Press, 2021).
4   Jean-Luc Nancy, "Touche-touche," trans. B. Wocke, online lecture, March 24, 2021, https://www.ici-berlin.org/events/jean-luc-nancy-intimacy/ (accessed August 17, 2022).
5   See Peter Rehberg and Apostolos Lampropoulos, *Intimacy: New Queer Art from Berlin and Beyond*, exhib. cat. (Berlin: Schwules Museum, 2021).

with Peter Rehberg for the Schwules Museum of Berlin in 2021; written in French and read in English by way of Brendon Wocke's beautiful translation, it relaunched a discussion on touching "closer than what the decorum would allow"[6] and readdressed, counter-intuitively, touching as a mode of divergence between bodies. All these texts resonated with a playful online discussion with Peter Banki, "Sex and Philosophy with Jean-Luc Nancy,"[7] offering hints regarding the potential of a discourse on sex.

The connections between this body of work and some of Nancy's most well-known texts such as *The Inoperative Community*, *The Intruder*, and *Corpus* are numerous. This same work is all the more pertinent in the context of the Covid-19 pandemic and an experience of distancing that cannot leave one's perception and practices of intimacy unharmed. With the publication of *An All-Too-Human Virus*[8] and his participation in Annebeth Jacobsen's documentary À fleur de *peau*[9] in which he addressed the question "Who were we when we could still touch each other?," Nancy gave us reasons to think about how we became unsynchronized with each other—unshared time, so to speak—during the pandemic. I read this as a reminder that, during this period, several intimacies have been in suspense and pending, triggering a kind of intimacy hunger.

Drawing on such a debt to Nancy, as well as on the insights that he offers us in his aforementioned contributions, I will suggest a programmatic approach to the notion that I term "critical intimacy." This notion stems from an open dialogue with the work of Nancy, rather than from its interpretation in a stricter sense. With this notion I do not seek to introduce a special type or new categorization of intimacies, but rather I pursue a series of positions that will allow me to formulate a clear stance vis-à-vis intimacy and its representations, mainly literary and artistic. My assumption is that intimacy has only occupied a minor position in the theoretical vocabulary of the last decades, and consequently it carries the weight of an underworked term often perceived as relatively

---

6 Nancy, "Touche-touche."

7 Jean-Luc Nancy and Peter Banki, "Sex and Philosophy with Jean-Luc Nancy," online discussion, February 18, 2016, https://www.youtube.com/watch?v=UPccnKA-X88 (accessed August 17, 2022).

8 Jean-Luc Nancy, *An All-Too-Human Virus*, trans. C. Stockwell, S. Clift, and D. Fernbach (Cambridge: Polity, 2022 [2020]).

9 Annebeth Jacobsen, À fleur de peau. *Une histoire des caresses, câlins et autres étreintes*, documentary (Arte, 2021).

unpolitical. The notion of critical intimacy sees representations of intimacy as deserving special attention and being, themselves, a precious tool for the analysis of issues varying from community to citizenship, public health, subcultures, and many more. I also think that intimacy is critical in that the representations and practices of intimacy matter, politically and otherwise, in our everyday lives as the mode par excellence of connecting, harmoniously or acrimoniously, with other bodies.[10] Finally, I forge the notion of critical intimacy with the intention of enhancing the visibility of the most diverse intimacies, allowing them to become both the topic and the site of a vivid debate.

The term "critical intimacy" has already been theorized some twenty years ago by Mieke Bal[11] in a very different sense than mine. Working on Spivak and tackling it in the context of teaching theoretical texts, Bal opposes critical intimacy to "unacknowledged complicity."[12] She writes: "Complicity—historically inevitable, presently fatal—can only be neutralized by working through it. Critical intimacy with an 'other,' someone who is not a clone of oneself, offers an arena where you can do that working through with a measure of safety."[13] In what follows, I am keeping this mode of alertness and awareness in relating with otherness,[14] while at the same time I am moving the focus to representations of queer corporeal, and often sexual, intimacies. All kinds of intimacy are potentially concerned, my take on it echoing Nancy's position that "sexual liberation brings out into the open as much misery as jubilation."[15] In this text, though, I will focus on three main aspects of critical intimacy, illustrating them with brief references to theoretically informed art and literature.

By adding the adjective "critical" to an understanding of "intimacy" inspired by Nancy, I am deliberately opting for a somewhat

---

10 See also Apostolos Lampropoulos, "Intimacy is Critical," in Rehberg and Lampropoulos, *Intimacy*, pp. 6–7.

11 Mieke Bal, *Travelling Concepts in the Humanities: A Rough Guide* (Toronto, Buffalo and London: University of Toronto Press, 2002), pp. 286–323.

12 Ibid., p. 295.

13 Ibid., p. 319.

14 See also Apostolos Lampropoulos, "Entre hospitalité et intimité, droit de regards pour plus-d'un," in "Derrida 2021: Déconstruction et biopolitique," ed. Stéphane Lojkine and Francesca Manzari, *Malice. Le magazine des littératures & des cultures à l'ère du numérique* 13 (2022), https://cielam.univ-amu.fr/malice/articles/entre-hospitalite-intimite-droit-regards-plus-dun (accessed August 17, 2022).

15 Nancy, *Sexistence*, p. 103.

ambiguous gesture. Thinking further with Nancy will be to some extent thinking with him, but also thinking beyond and away from him. More precisely, when I qualify the thinking of/through intimacy as "critical," I refer to the critical thinking that aims to destabilize any monolithic mode of thought presenting itself as devoid of the possibility of a contestation. Nancy remains skeptical of this type of critical thinking that I insert here, because the thought it contests is itself "deployed out of the dissipation of a long series of critical thoughts (or 'alternatives' [...])."[16] On the other hand, in critical intimacy I only see a grain of the "crisis" that, according to Nancy, "strays away from critique," even when we "critique crisis to master it."[17] The distinction between critique and crisis is important for Nancy, because the former "presupposes its own criteria, and consequently the principle of its own resolution as well," while the latter "is without criteria and without ground."[18] I join what I see as the spirit of Nancy's distinction in that I do not introduce the notion of critical intimacy as the starting point of a ready-made critique of intimacy, but as a way to work on intimacy's quicksand. I would not go as far as Nancy goes with "crisis," but, as I explain in my first section, I would rather consider the term "trouble" as more appropriate with regards to handling the question of intimacy. Hence, by elaborating on the notion of critical intimacy, I am only half-following Nancy—in fact, I am only critically, yet contentedly, intimate with his thought. In any case, the notion of critical intimacy is conceived in such a way so as to add words to the *cri*[19] of intimacy (that is to say a trouble in, rather than a crisis of, language, a certain interruption of language[20] during intimacy), while maintaining something of what can only be inarticulate in a joyous scream, a striving cry, or a muffled voice during an intimate encounter.

---

16   Jean-Luc Nancy, "Critique, Crisis, Cri" [2016], trans. P. J. Lyons, *Qui Parle* 26, no. 1 (2017), p. 6.
17   Ibid., p. 11.
18   Ibid., p. 14.
19   Ibid., pp. 14–16.
20   Ibid., p. 14.

Embracing the Trouble in/of Intimacy

The Intruder, Nancy's account of his heart transplant, offers two important insights regarding intimacy. Intimacy with someone or something (here with an old and a new heart) is inseparable from the appearance of a crack within one's interiority—in Nancy's words, from a "trouble in the midst of intimacy."[21] This happens when the old sick heart no longer belongs there and appears as a foreign body with which intimacy will have to be scrupulously thought. Moreover, intimacy with someone or something cannot exist without exposure to an external gaze. Nancy explicates this point referring to Saint Augustine's *interior intimo meo*:[22] modelled on the exposure of one's interiority to the divine gaze during confession, Nancy's troubled intimacy with his hearts is inextricably linked to its exposure to the quasi-omniscient medical gaze before, during, and after the surgery.[23] Intimacy (etymologically the superlative of interior) is thus not privacy, looking after secrecy or invisibility, neither is it placed somewhere between the private and the public. Intimacy is the trouble of relating to what dissolves the continuum of one's interiority or privacy, and letting one's relating be seen.

The notion of critical intimacy, as I understand it, embraces this double trouble as a questioning of subjectivity and identity, and as an exposure of all of this to a contemplative exteriority. It addresses the process by which one is readjusted in terms of pleasure in agreeable intimacy, of tension within dysfunctional intimacy, and of all the range of experiences and feelings which lie between the two. It is also a way of formulating an approach regarding unnoticed, underestimated, clandestine, guilt-ridden, or censored attachments and proximities, or even hitherto unheard-of modes of relating. Nonetheless, the notion of critical intimacy is to be understood neither as an impediment to relating or sharing, nor as a way of moderating the temperature of an encounter. It sees the troubling experience of intimacy as a site wherein subjectivities

---

21 Jean-Luc Nancy, "The Intruder" [2000], in *Corpus*, trans. R. A. Rand (New York: Fordham University Press, 2008), p. 161.

22 Ibid., p. 170.

23 See also Apostolos Lampropoulos, "Des yeux au cœur, l'intime comme exercice en théorie," in "Renewing Theory," ed. Stéphane Lojkine and Francesca Manzari, *Malice. Le magazine des littératures & des cultures à l'ère du numérique* 16 (2022), https://cielam.univ-amu.fr/malice/articles/yeux-coeur-lintime-exercice-en-theorie (accessed August 17, 2022).

and identities are tested, whether it be in the context of a well-prepared meeting, of a hazardous crossing of paths, or of a love affair. By that, it is meant to place intimacies, spectacular or discrete, under scrutiny in order to sharpen our approach to the very trouble caused by and happening in intimacy without seeking or pretending to fully grasp what the intimate subjects are or become. In that sense, working with the notion of critical intimacy is a difficult exercise: reflecting on the context and the terms in which intimacy happens; then proposing insights into how the intimate subjects evolve within it, while at the same time renouncing the attribution, inevitably reductive, of fully intelligible identities to them. If there is no intimacy without trouble, critical intimacy works its undecidedness and approximation.

But where exactly within the trouble in/of intimacy is criticality to be inserted? Nancy sees separation, distance, and exteriority in even the closest proximity: "Only a separated body can touch."[24] In this logic, skin-to-skin contact is not fusion or a first phase of becoming-one,[25] but rather a passing contact between two or more. This is the zone within which closeness occurs, succeeds or fails, is prolonged or interrupted, practiced, and thought of, reevaluated, compromised or reconfirmed, yet always with an important degree of uncertainty because "I represent the touched substance to myself [...] but representation is less immediate when we touch."[26] Togetherness is not inseparability, adjacency is not confusion, and even the closest contact announces an impending re-splitting, the reappearance of a caesura at the heart of a coming-together. Within this zone of divergence-in-closeness (Nancy says: "*Touche-touche*: it touches and moves away in touching itself"[27]), I situate both the certainty that the outcome can only be a separation of sorts, and the undecidability of what this separation will look or feel like. This same zone is where trouble happens and where the external gaze intrudes. But, with the notion of critical intimacy, I take one step further than, or even away from Nancy. Where he sees divergence-in-closeness, I additionally see a space within intimacy calling for the critical intervention of queer and, more broadly, literary and cultural theory: neither an idealization nor a condemnation or even an a priori cancelation of the various repre-

---

24 Nancy, "Touche-touche."
25 Nancy and Goh, *The Deconstruction of Sex*, pp. 54–55.
26 Nancy, "Touche-touche."
27 Ibid.

sentations of intimacies, but a way of addressing the lack, the excess, or the supposed normality of intimacy. In that sense, I do not see the trouble in/of intimacy as leading to an aporia, but rather to always more nuanced representations and discourses of intimacy.

This critical intimacy was the main thread of my co-curation of the abovementioned exhibition *Intimacy: New Queer Art from Berlin and Beyond*, exploring forms and nuances of predominantly sexual queer intimacies. Reading and rereading Nancy throughout the preparation for the exhibition allowed me to think about what troubling intimacies were to be shown, and what trouble they were meant to cause once they were seen. The thirty-odd positions were organized in four chapters—namely "Look at us," "Our bodies in time," "(Y)our sex power," "More parties for us"—which recapitulated some of the most critical aspects of intimacy: the construction of a we/us/our; the provocative invitation to external gazes; the historicity, temporality, and temporariness of intimacy; the power of and within sexual intimacies; the intertwining of intimacy with conviviality, assemblies, or even sexual excess in public. In all these cases, the exhibition addressed the trouble that establishing intimacy can result in and the trouble that depicting intimacy can incite, both from an esthetical and from a political point of view. The exhibition addressed issues that resonated with sensitive debates, such as intimacies within queer families (Eva Giannakopoulos), sexual intimacy and aging (Roey Victoria Heifetz), the memory of intimacies during the HIV/AIDS pandemic in the era of PrEP/Pre-Exposure Prophylaxis (Marlon Riggs, AA Bronson, Simon Fujiwara), digitally-mediated intimacies (Sholem Krishtalka), the interweaving of queer intimacies and the gentrification of public space (Rafael Medina)—to mention but a few. In all these variants of trouble, critical intimacy was for me a lens of crucial importance allowing an understanding of post-blood links, mourning, experiencing time, new medialities or the evolution of urban spaces.

Nancy underlines that the "broad, encompassing control of sexual activity bears witness to the possibilities of disorder that it entails."[28] Likewise, the exhibition considered the ambiguities of queer intimacies becoming visible and shared publicly, the variety of topics to which they are explicitly linked, and the consequences that the rethinking of the latter through intimacy will probably

---

28 Nancy, *Sexistence*, p. 80.

have. It showcased various depictions of intimacy, not only questioning heteronormative positions but also diversifying queer ways of relating. Embracing the various (and often much needed) trouble that intimacy is, brings, and alludes to, it showed part of the ongoing "theater of disorders, illnesses, crimes, deviations, betrayals, infamies, as well as comedies"[29] that sex has always been to be critically tackled as trouble and as disorder, rather than as an occasion to multiply the categories and names which order sexuality. More generally, if critical intimacy goes further along the direction which leads from sexual undifferentiation to sexual pluralization,[30] then it is indissociable from the positions that "sex promises an end while hiding that it might become infinite"[31] and that it relates to the inappropriable.[32] I would tend to see these positions not as an aporia, but as an incitement to explore the as yet uncharted, and as such potentially troubling, intimacies.

Caring for the Sex of Others

The broad and evolving terrain of queer intimacies offers a most compelling set of cases in which critical involvement could be tested. Articulating Nancy's sexual thought with queer theory will no doubt sound paradoxical to some of those who identify as researchers in the field. The late work of a white male straight ablebodied (his heart transplant is already described as stemming from a chronological privilege[33]) French philosopher with a prominent presence on the Western philosophical stage for many decades might not be an obvious choice for some of those working on the intersection of theory and activism. Nancy's abstract and often hard to grasp manner of addressing sex, along with his recurrent references to reproduction, might also lack the necessary appeal to many. His reticence to prioritize race—more understandable in the context of mainstream color-blindness in France—or identity for the understanding of sex might also seem to be only an average fit

---

29 Ibid., p. 103.
30 Ibid., p. 99. The original French reads: "[Le sexe] se précède *dans une indifférenciation sexuelle du sexe lui-même* et se succède dans une pluralisation sexuelle"; the part of this phrase that I have here put in italics does not appear in the English translation.
31 Ibid., p. 17.
32 Ibid., p. 43.
33 Nancy, "The Intruder," p. 162.

for the intersectional approach that is currently dominant in queer theory.

Such elements might indeed hinder the reception of Nancy's late work by queer theory. I believe, however, that the notion of critical intimacy can unleash the dynamics of this conjuncture. Unlike hard identity and representation politics, Nancy's approach is only to a lesser extent compatible with a line of thought that sees sexuality primarily or uniquely as the epicenter of inequalities, as an activity mostly dissociated from pleasure, or as a site of occasional pleasure that does not deserve an adequate amount of critical attention.[34] Nancy remains suspicious of the possibility to pre-calculate the effects of sex and of the variable geometry of intimacies that emerge from it. Instead, and without letting this sound like an outdated plea from a post-1968 era, his main concern is to maintain the undecidability of sex, also as an entrance point to other, equally complex, issues. Quite characteristically, he says that "there is no love without some touching, there is no love without a little bit of sex, and there is no sex without a little bit of love."[35]

All these little bits are a place where the notion of critical intimacy can intervene in order to re-articulate the disorder of sex and the queer, and to offer a nuanced thinking of what happens in and with sex, spelling out and reclaiming its significance as a means of becoming-other. Already in *The Inoperative Community*, Nancy stated that "lovers know joy in drowning in the instant of intimacy [...]. In the instant, the lovers are shared, their singular beings—which constitute neither an identity nor an individual, which effect nothing—share each other, and the singularity of their love is exposed to community."[36] Critical intimacy is meant to inspect the each and every time newly born non-identity of the lovers, to elucidate the gains and losses of this unbecoming-one, and to add more fluidity in queerness. Instead of approaching sex in the name of one or the other subjectivity, sex is to be studied in its capacity to revisit, partly undo, and further complexify them.

---

34 Oliver Davis and Tim Dean, *Hatred of Sex* (Lincoln: University of Nebraska Press, 2022), p. xiv.
35 Nancy and Banki, "Sex and Philosophy with Jean-Luc Nancy."
36 Jean-Luc Nancy, *The Inoperative Community*, trans. P. Connor, L. Garbus, M. Holland, and S. Sawhney (Minneapolis: University of Minnesota Press, 1991[1986]), p. 39.

Even more importantly, critical intimacy is a way of responding to the challenge that represents the always unique sex of others, as disorienting as this may seem. Half-joking half-serious,[37] Nancy says that he would seriously consider visiting a gay sauna, but his overall health condition would not allow him to do that. Later, he comments on the practice of glory holes insisting on the "gentlemen's agreement" to omit any attention that could be paid to the face contact which is usually essential to launching an encounter. I would tend to see the very playfulness of Nancy's somewhat unexpected examples as a lesson in critical intimacy: the philosopher with health issues who has written on the face and the portrait is the one who opens his thought to the sexual practices of others and to how otherness may be experienced in sex.

What counts here is not so much an elaborate philosophical position, but Nancy's gesture and the moderate tone of his theoretical curiosity. What I retain from this is the way in which critical intimacy should tackle sex: as a question rather than as a site for identification, but also as a challenge to togetherness and as an occasion for understanding the togetherness of others. Even more, I see critical intimacy as caring about the sex of others, the one that seems weird or eccentric, and calls for work on the challenge that sex represents for the idea of community. In that sense, it can be a potentially significant intervention in the currently undersexed field of queer theory, and a way of reinforcing the presently underestimated contribution of sexual thinking to emancipatory everyday queer politics.[38]

This is the case of the installation *Queer Time: Kinships & Architectures* proposed by the Indian collective Party Office and the artist-curator Vidisha-Fadescha in the context of the fifteenth edition of the exhibition documenta held in Kassel in 2022. Curated by the Indonesian collective Ruangrupa, documenta 15 invited mainly art collectives from the Global South and most artworks addressed issues of social and global justice. Very few collectives and artworks identified as queer and even fewer involved a sexual component. *Queer Time* was described as a "multifunctional party space, dungeon, dark room, reading room, public programming space," offering the basement of the venue WH22 to "crip and kink

---

37 Nancy and Banki, "Sex and Philosophy with Jean-Luc Nancy."
38 Davis and Dean, *Hatred of Sex*, pp. 45–86.

subjectivities, encouraging visitors to party and play,"[39] where also parties, considered as sites of liberation, could take place. A series of HyperVigilant parties, open to BIPOC and FLINTA people, were scheduled as part of the work.

I read *Queer Time* as experimenting with critical intimacy, introducing a highly sexualized type of space in a very political, yet fairly sexless, exhibition. It invited us to rethink a politics of touch, including emancipation through touching each other "respecting absolute singularity"[40] and through some welcome confusion in a room seeking to welcome crip and kink people, offering them a space for working, clubbing, and playing. It summarized essential aspects of critical intimacy: engaging with and exposing unfamiliar intimacies through reflecting on how to touch bodies that are often discriminated against by being perceived as less touchable, on how they touch back, and on sexual intimacy as a major component of critical community building. The cancelation of the HyperVigilant parties, following incidents of racist and transphobic harassment in the city of Kassel,[41] aptly reminded us that community building on a sexless ground is bound not to last long, because it insufficiently thinks, tests, and encourages intimacies of those different from and perhaps more vulnerable than us. As Nancy says, "community does not lie beyond the lovers, it does not form a larger circle within which they are contained: it traverses them [...]. Without such a trait traversing the kiss, sharing it, the kiss is itself as despairing as community is abolished."[42] In a similar vein, critical intimacy does not seek to reinject sex into the queer only for the sake of re-introducing an element missing in intersectional thought. It is meant to address the limits of envisaged and politicized intimacies, and to trigger reflection on why some intimacies are possible, while others (and especially those of others) are not, and under what conditions.

---

39 Ruangrupa and Artistic Team, *documenta fifteen Handbook* (Berlin: Hatje Cantz, 2022), p. 165.

40 Jacques Derrida, *On Touching: Jean-Luc Nancy*, trans. C. Irizarry (Stanford: Stanford University Press, 2005 [2000]), p. 114.

41 Renée Reizman, "Queer Arts Space Cancels Documenta Programming After Harassment Incidents," *Hyperallergic*, July 8, 2022, https://hyperallergic.com/746222/queer-arts-space-cancels-documenta-programming-after-harassment-incidents/ (accessed August 17, 2022).

42 Nancy, *The Inoperative Community*, p. 40.

Thinking an Ethics of Withdrawal

The installation *Queer Time* encouraged intimacy and at the same time prevented contact with random threatening bodies. Organizing a withdrawal into well-thought hypervigilance, it allowed a retreat into the intimacies of and with vulnerable and, in any case, greatly diversified bodies. Placed in the basement of a venue, both connected to and detached from other exhibits and with a differently planned publicity, this artwork can only remind me of the way in which Nancy understands *expeausition* (skin-show) in *Corpus*[43]:

> Bodies [are] always about to leave, on the verge of a movement, a fall, a gap, a dislocation. [...] A departing body carries its spacing away, itself gets carried away as spacing, and somehow it sets itself aside, withdraws into itself—while leaving its very spacing "behind" [...] *in its place* [...]. This spacing, this departure, is its very intimacy, the extremity of its separation (or, if we prefer, of its distinction, its singularity, even its subjectivity). The body is *self* in departure, insofar as it parts—displaces itself right here from the *here*.

In this passage, a body is to be understood in its ripping itself away from a *here* which is most probably a *here-with*, somehow parallel to being as being-with. In my reading, the body might also be withdrawing from the experience or the perspective of intimacy with other bodies—an intimacy which is no longer wanted, or no longer safe, or not sufficiently pleasurable, or not agreeably exciting, or too narrowly associated with the possibility of a fusion. Whatever the contact preceding the withdrawal of a body from a body-with, this is also the moment when critical intimacy becomes possible and necessary: firstly, as a review of the intimacy, blissful or ungratifying, that has just expired; secondly, as part of the process of becoming available for intimacies to come, whether this takes the form of vivid eagerness or of extreme caution; thirdly, as the crucial link between the memory that there was already some withdrawal within intimacy and the unique self that the withdrawal leaves behind.

Critical intimacy is thus an exercise in thoughtfulness, watchfulness and anticipation linked to the skin that is being untouched and shows anew. This is also a refreshed or timeworn skin with

---

43 Jean-Luc Nancy, "Corpus" [2000], in *Corpus*, p. 33.

an extended memory nourishing the criticality of the intimacies to come. Therefore, critical intimacy does more than sampling the innumerable past intimacies between bodies. It reflects on ramifications of the intended or fortuitous touchings, the occasions on which skin folds back upon itself in order to regain its troubled exteriority or the occasions on which it stretches in order to offer even more space to a welcome caress. It scrutinizes the surface of the bodies, itself *expeausé* following their withdrawal from a body-with. But it is neither a prefabricated judgment or a straightforward celebration of past intimacies, nor the path away from intimacy altogether. Through its very criticality, it is meant to extend and multiply the points of contact between bodies, the variety of their interactions, as well as the subtlest aspects of the intimacies experienced and observed. In that sense, critical intimacy renders the mutual touching of the bodies denser, as it pixelates skin-to-skin and magnifies one-off or repetitive pleasures and acute tensions.

Critical intimacy as work on withdrawal is, I would even say, a way to reflect on who comes after sex.[44] Nancy says that "even though sex or 'sexistence' teaches us, or gives us, the experience of being 'more than one' or 'being singular plural,' this experience can only last during sex."[45] This is precisely what happens in a text such as Arthur Dreyfus' *Journal sexuel d'un garçon d'aujourd'hui*.[46] This book of about 2,300 pages takes the form of a diary (a *journal intime* in French), organized around the narration of sexual encounters arranged through dating applications. Dreyfus presents the book in the following terms:[47]

> One day, it seemed impossible to have what is called a sexual relationship without mentioning it in a computer document. It had to be told. For this diary, I multiplied my experiences, diversified my practices, gave up certain encounters, when I imposed others on myself. Several times, I interrupted the act to take notes. [...]. This is the meticulous diary of a crazy addiction, punctuated by Grindr use. [...] Above all, it is the story of a contemporary odyssey, and of redemption.

Written, in some cases, during a visit at someone's home or in the stairwell of a building after leaving someone's apartment, it

---

44 Nancy and Goh, *The Deconstruction of Sex*, pp. 53–69.
45 Ibid., p. 62.
46 Arthur Dreyfus, *Journal sexuel d'un garçon d'aujourd'hui* (Paris : POL, 2021).
47 Ibid., back cover (my translation).

consists in the numerous episodes of the story of a body experiencing serial intimacies and being in an equally serial critical retreat, offering itself, by way of the systematic, if not obsessive, self-observation, unto the gaze of the reader. The biggest part of the book was literally written in the moments which lie between culminating intimacies and the *expeausition* of the gay body. This writing thus coincided with the moment when intimacy was fading away and being transformed into a site of critical contemplation. Intense and poignant, Dreyfus' text epitomizes the work of critical intimacy as a systematic rethinking of withdrawal—the mutual withdrawal of bodies which enjoyed or irritated one another, and now leave place for the inspection of what this coming-together meant. Following this logic, critical intimacy is looking back at the moment when one finds oneself alone or leaves someone alone, exposing oneself to the possibility of a new rapprochement, acceptable in terms of decorum or not. It is therefore a key to an ethics of withdrawal, because it focuses on what comes after intimacy and on how to live-apart after having been-with.

The notion of critical intimacy addresses the drama of exteriority after intimacy, therefore after what, for a few seconds or much longer, allowed the lovers to hope for a seamless fusion, or which was the non-lovers' nightmare. This is the time of criticality and of reflection on what intimacy was, could have been, and persistently is or is not. Just as community is perceived in the process of its unworking, as an entity that "encounters interruption, fragmentation, suspension,"[48] intimacy is thought retrospectively, presupposing the distancing that comes after it. This is also when the effect that intimacy had upon the body becomes clearer: the scars, the bruises, the persevering sensations, and all of these as sexual trophies, unbearable traumas, or ambiguous corporeal trajectories. Writing critically on this crepuscular moment of intimacy, as Dreyfus does, can only be illuminating for what Nancy describes as "what [lovers] show in their communal aspects and intimacy. [...] For the community, lovers are on its limit, they are outside and inside, and at this limit they have no meaning without the community and without the communication of writing: this is where they assume their senseless meaning."[49] The withdrawal from intimacy might then be the moment when intimacy becomes more intel-

---

48 Nancy, *The Inoperative Community*, p. 31.
49 Ibid., p. 40.

ligible and its conditions more transparent, when it can be lucidly celebrated or mourned. If critical intimacy is also an ethics of withdrawal, this happens because it shows us how to live-apart well, reconsidering past and upcoming intimacies as most demanding exercises in being-with.

* * *

In my programmatic theorization of critical intimacy, I engaged with the sexual thinking of the late Jean-Luc Nancy, organized around ideas such as the trouble intimacy represents and provokes, the care for the sex of others, and the development of an ethics of withdrawal. The core of my analysis could be summed up in two positions by Nancy who says, first, that "the whole question of dignity is played out in sex,"[50] and, second, that "as soon as my body approaches that of another—whether the other is inert, of wood, of stone or of metal—I move the other—even if it is to an infinitesimal degree—and I move away from it, in a sense I withdraw."[51] Rather than a strict calculation of what is happening in intimacy, an apology or a regret for having been too close to the other, the notion of critical intimacy is an investigation of how what happened between the bodies was made possible, what was excessive in the excess and what was excessive reticence in the withdrawal, what should be avoided and what deserves to be repeated, how intimacy is to be reconsidered and, perhaps most of all, how to re-desire or recover from intimacy. Critical intimacy is thus a renewal of relating and an investment in a temporary withdrawal feeding into a future rapprochement. As intensive work on the grey zones of being-together, and as has to happen after the death of Jean-Luc Nancy, it is a way of maintaining a *with* within a living-apart.

---

50 Nancy and Banki, "Sex and Philosophy with Jean-Luc Nancy."
51 Nancy, "Touche-touche."

Philipp Stoellger

Deconstruction of Christianity as a Self-Transgression of Theology

1.
Setting the Framework

Philosophy has (re)discovered the theological heritage given urgent questions of the present: universalism, ethics, human rights, the political, community theory, anthropology as well as questions of violence. Lévinas serves here as an example, and also Ricoeur, Derrida and Vattimo or Marion: theological texts and themes from all places, but all this often without seeking dialogue with contemporary theologies. As attentively as theology listens to philosophers, this is usually not reciprocal. Philosophers do *theology from outside*—a theology without theology?

In this respect, Nancy differs from the others, *differently* different. First of all, anyone who does not know Jean-Luc Nancy is to be envied. For one still has an educational event ahead of oneself, spiced with singular pleasure and plural impetus – if there wasn't something irritating that recurs throughout his work: that he refers to central themes of Christianity in an original and incisive way. His treatise entitled *Corpus* is *about the soul*, and has as its motto *Hoc est enim corpus meum*. The text is—in theological perspective—as much a doctrine of the soul as it is a tract on the Lord's Supper.[1] His two books on *community* are an examination of too narrow, if not totalitarian models of community—including those of Christianity. Thus, the book is a text about and against many ecclesiologies and about the political in theological perspective.[2]

---

1 On this subject, see Philipp Stoellger, *Passivität aus Passion. Zur Problemgeschichte einer 'categoria non grata', Hermeneutische Untersuchungen zur Theologie*, vol. 56 (Tübingen, 2010), pp. 59–62, 256–261; Philipp Stoellger, "*Dekonstruktion des Christentums?*—Eine Antwort auf Jean-Luc Nancy," in *Evangelische Predigtkultur. Zur Erneuerung der Kanzelrede*, ed. Alexander Deeg and Dietrich Sagert (Leipzig: Kirche im Aufbruch [KiA)] Reihe eins, 2011), p. 131.

2 Philipp Stoellger: "Mit-Teilung und Mit-Sein: Gemeinschaft aus 'Neigung' zum Anderen: Zu Nancy's Dekonstruktion der Gemeinschaft," in *"Mit-Sein". Gemeinschaft – ontologische und politische Perspektivierungen*, ed. Elke Bippus,

And Nancy's works on *image theory* are one of the greatest challenges for theology. *The Skin of Images* or *At the Bottom of Images* show how and what moves *an image*, how demanding and significant images are for human beings. In this way, one might think he is speaking with Aaron's voice, while the Jewish tradition adheres to Moses—and in Christianity the image, especially its religious significance, is still not disputed today.

Nancy is characterized by a cultural context that is clearly different from the German one. In Paris, there is an old tradition of occasional confessional secularism, not least against the prevailing Catholicism. Thus, *Corpus* begins: "*Hoc est enim corpus meum*: nous provenons d'une culture dans laquelle cette parole rituelle aura été prononcée, inlassablement, par des millions d'officiants de millions de cultes [...]."[3]

Nancy thinks of the human being and the community in a decidedly *different* way than the Catholic tradition. A *critique* of Christianity, a critique of theology and the church thus is to be expected. Nancy also meets this expectation insofar as he repeatedly presents (above all) the Aristotelian and Thomistic theology of Catholicism as an opponent against which he raises his voice. And suddenly and unexpectedly one finds oneself in the neighborhood of Protestantism—which, in the form of Luther, tirelessly criticized precisely the same tradition, albeit with a delay.

Nancy is not *only* a secular critic of Christianity. The gesture, the style of his thinking is not simply that of destruction. And that makes the whole matter exciting from a theological perspective. If it is neither destruction nor simply reconstruction to affirm and celebrate the *return of religion*, what is it then?

Deconstruction *exists* for Nancy in three dimensions: as a dynamic of phenomena, as a method (in a particular form) and as a specific feature of Christianity, thus stipulating a *primal leap*, an (anarchic) *arché* of deconstruction.

Jörg Huber and Dorothee Richter (Zurich, Vienna and New York: Springer, 2010), pp. 45–64; Philipp Stoellger, "*Kirche am Ende oder am Ende Kirche? Auf welche Gemeinschaft dürfen wir hoffen?*," in *Grenzgänge der Gemeinschaft*, ed. Elisabeth Gräb-Schmidt and Ferdinand Menga (Tubingen: Mohr Siebeck, 2016), pp. 149–186.

3   Jean-Luc Nancy, *Corpus* (Paris: Métailié, 1992), p. 7.

2.
Autodeconstruction of Christianity: Opening Answers

The latter is grounded in Nancy's guiding thesis of the "autodeconstruction" of Christianity,[4] which has five aspects:

1. "[L]e monothéisme est en verité l'athéisme."[5] For the uniqueness of God means "le retrait de ce dieu hors de la presence [dans le monde] et donc aussi hors de la puissance ainsi entendue."[6] This intensifies in the "figure du Christ," in which the "renoncement même à la puissance divine et à sa presence qui deviant l'acte propre de Dieu, et qui fait de cet acte son devenir-homme."[7] Thus, God is hidden, *absconditus*, absent. Monotheism therefore dissolved theism (understood as the presence of power and metaphysical *meaning*). Faith then becomes "fidélité à une [i.e. son] absence."[8]

From a theological perspective, one is probably both attracted and irritated, while others may be outraged or repelled. On the one hand, the *critical* potential of monotheism and Christology is correctly articulated: Monotheism sharply distinguishes between God and the world—and therefore the world is neither divine nor is God a piece of the world. He is *beyond being*, as Plato, or thoroughly differently Lévinas, would have formulated.

Only—is monotheism therefore the same as atheism? This sounds strange, but it is easy to understand if one understands *a*-theism as the destruction of theism. For this has been theologically acceptable and common in the metaphysical critique of theology since Luther at the latest, and intensified by Jüngel, for example. For Tillich, too, God (in a Christian sense) does not exist because he is not part of the world (as existence). Therefore, Tillich enthused about the *God behind God*—even if this could be a hypertheism.

Only Nancy gives his thesis a *negative* twist: not understanding God as power and not as presence (as christologically only too fitting), he leads further into hiddenness and absence. To put it further: into the *real absence* of God—as if he were not (*etsi non*

---

4   Jean-Luc Nancy, *La Déclosion (Déconstruction du christianisme, 1)* (Paris: Galilée, 2005), p. 55.
5   Ibid.
6   Ibid.
7   Ibid., p. 56.
8   Ibid.

daretur). "Le christianisme, en d'autres termes," Nancy says, "indique de manière la plus active—et aussi la plus ruineuse pour lui-même, la plus nihiliste à certains égards—comment le monothé-isme abrite en lui [...] le principe d'un monde sans Dieu."[9]

On the one hand, this is theologically acceptable, even plausible, if not trivial: nothing in or about the world is God (and *vice versa*), otherwise the theological difference between God and the world would be misunderstood. Therefore, *there is* also no *immortal soul* as something divine in man. On the other hand, it is also theologically unacceptable: Because the reason for why this is *ruinous* or *nihilistic* is misunderstood. What could be meant that God as the epitome of meaning is not the world or something in the world—and therefore the world is meaningless? The transgression would be wrong. For the relationship to God and his broken presence in Christ are neither ruinous for monotheism nor nihilistic for the world. At this point it thus is necessary to differentiate and to set a definite *no*. Nancy is too undifferentiated.

2. The second aspect of autodeconstruction is *demythologization*.[10] The self-understanding of Christianity becomes "de moins en moins religieuse au sens où la religion implique une mythologie (un récit, une representation des actions et des personnes divines)."[11] And this characteristic of religion is erasing Christianity.

This is again half true, half doubtful. The theologies of Israel (exemplified by the priestly scriptural school, the Deuteronomistic historical work and the prophets) are already deeply critical of myth. Therefore, as is well known, Genesis 1 is already a form of demythologization, in which the ancient oriental heaven of the gods or the king's deified court are brought *from heaven to earth*—for the sake of a worldly world and the transcendence of God. But demythologization does not mean *demythification* as the destruction of myths. Bultmann has clarified this sufficiently: it is a matter of interpreting myths, of their hermeneutics (even if Bultmann remains committed to Heidegger), not of destroying or disregarding them. Moreover, myths are not the *conditio sine qua non* of religion. These are short-circuits Nancy succumbs to.

Nevertheless, there is definitely a *deconstructive* trait at work in criticism of myths and hermeneutics of myth. For a deconstructive

---

9   Ibid., p. 55.
10 Ibid., p. 57.
11 Ibid.

shift in form and meaning sets in when creation is narrated as in Genesis 1, in distinction to other religions of the ancient Near East. And this shift intensifies in the story of Paradise and the Fall, in its continuation in Paul and its variation in Augustine, etc. Shifting and variation of meaning as work on myth dissolves the stable, supposedly timeless validity of such stories. This culminates in the incarnation and passion—when God on the cross refutes all common prejudices about religion.

3. Christianity is *a limine* a "composition" of Judaism and Greco-Roman philosophy.[12] Its identity is therefore not seamless. It never was nor is it identical with itself without distinction, but has sources, origins that live on in it. This is evident in the different theological traditions as well as in the conflictively plural Christian denominations. Philosophically quite traditionally, Nancy concentrates this in the (alleged) *split of faith and knowledge*: "Cette unite de soi divisée du monothéisme fait le plus proprement et donc aussi le plus paradoxalement l'unité du dieu unique. On pourrait dire, avec toutes les résonances possible, que ce dieu se divise— voire s'athéise—*à la croisée du/des monothéismes.*"[13]

This thesis again provokes a decisive *yes* and *no*. For here, despite all the deconstruction and its differentiation, a little *more* differentiation is necessary and sensible in order to open up the thesis instead of closing it (as Nancy insinuates). On the one hand, it is clear that Christianity carries heterogeneous traditions within itself, which are expressed in theological differences and religious diversities. This is not so different in Judaism. The hybridity of sources and origins, and therefore also the hybrid transculturality of both Judaism and Christianity, has been studied many times in history and cultural studies and has actually been clarified.

But to conclude the thesis that God is splitting, or even *atheizing himself* is as appealing to read as it is to contradict. This is to be affirmed at least once: for when God's Word became *flesh*, it led to an ultimate conflict—on the threshold of God and God. Luther dared to say of Golgotha: "*da streydet Got mit Gott*"[14]—the Word made flesh against his Father. This is a conflict in which the Word turns against its originator—and the powerlessness gets frustrated with the power of the origin. *Nemo contra deum nisi deus ipse* has

---

12 Ibid.

13 Ibid., p. 58.

14 *Weimarer Ausgabe (WA)* 45, p. 370.

its original seat in life at this point, or more precisely in death, and be it the *death of death* (more simply: the creative annihilation of a God-relationshiplessness) or, according to Jüngel, the *death of God*. This certainly is a critique of theism, as well as a *whole death thesis* on the Son of God, but as a split it is still a relationship—in or as a rift.

Nancy's thesis therefore also provokes objection, since it not only includes a schism or atheism, but also a thorough or abysmal redefinition of the meaning of God and therefore also of monotheism, as the doctrine of the Trinity (albeit mostly metaphysically pre-stabilizing). The power and presence of God are condemned in their meaning. But this is not a celebration of atheism—unless what is meant here is merely *a*-theism, the negation of the metaphysical theism against which theology since Luther, Schleiermacher, Tillich and Jüngel has been thinking.

After an affirmative and a negation now another *affirmative*. For in essence, Nancy seems to represent an ambivalent position: to go beyond Christianity in such a way that it would possibly remain on the track of history—or be deconstructively brought to the track? The division and atheization is not only described, but also pursued, and apparently pursued *in such a way* that the person doing the driving shows himself to be driven: driven to describe Christianity in such a way that it disintegrates in origin and essence because of this *division*. Does it really have to be this way?

With Nancy, it is helpful and also theologically leading to understand God and Christianity *no longer* in the Platonic or metaphysical tradition of the philosophy of identity: from the One the Many back into the One. For only the One is the true and truth is always unity. Nancy thus offers and pursues a *difference-theoretical* view of Christianity and God. In this, Nancy also encounters the more recent attempts at a de-platonized *hermeneutics of difference*, which does not start from consensus and moves towards consensus, but rather starts from strong differences and deals with them in a way that preserves difference.[15]

4. The fourth aspect of the autodeconstruction indicates that Christianity is "lui-même un *sujet*" that is "dans une recherche

15 See, among others, Philipp Stoellger, "Hermeneutik am Ende oder am Ende Hermeneutik? Möglichkeitsbedingungen einer Hermeneutik angesichts ihrer Kritik," in *Hermeneutik unter Verdacht*, ed. Andreas Kablitz, Christoph Markschies and Peter Strohschneider (Berlin and Boston: De Gruyter, 2021), pp. 115–164.

de soi, dans une inquiétude, une attente ou un désir de sa propre identité."[16] This can be seen as a reference to the futuristic of eschatology and the messianic of Christology, which can be well followed theologically. Only: in the logic of desire, the self-reference of this self "ne peut être qu'infini," in which lies an "échappée à soi."[17] This can easily tip over into the incomprehensible: as if it were a tragic or unhappy self-relation in bad infinity.

To see this as an insight into the logic of *faith as desire* is certainly appropriate—which does not live from fulfilment, but towards it, in the sustained awaiting of fulfilment. *This* opens up an understanding of Christianity that does not see the *beati possidentes* administering their *thesaurus gratiae*, but rather precarious self-relations that live and believe in what is yet to come. Wouldn't that be faith under the sign of love and hope as intensified desire?

5. Christianity is *a limine* in a process "d'autorectification ou d'autodépassement."[18] This is perhaps the crucial point. The call *ecclesia semper reformanda* articulated what has been determinant since Reformation times. Tillich would have called this the *prophetic principle* and thus characterized Protestantism.

Nancy sees Christianity as determined by an antagonism: on the one hand, "une affirmation de puissance, de domination et d'exploitation théologico-économico-politique"; on the other, "une affirmation inverse de dépouillement et d'abandon de soi dont le point de fuite serait l'auto-évanouissement."[19] That is quite accurate. On that basis, Nancy could have a weighty critique of the history of Roman Catholicism in mind, which brings him into a noticeable proximity to Protestantism (without this being named anywhere by him). However, it only becomes decisive when the relationship between this antagonism is dealt with descriptively and normatively. Similar to Marie-José Mondzain's[20] distinction between incarnation and incorporation, a critique of the corporate economy of salvation is possible and necessary on the one hand; on the other hand, a normative (and affirmative) argument in favor of divestment is also necessary for this critique: Is there

---

16 Nancy, *La Déclosion (Déconstruction du christianisme, 1)*, p. 59.
17 Ibid.
18 Ibid.
19 Ibid., p. 60.
20 Marie-José Mondzain, *Können Bilder Töten?* (Zurich and Berlin: Diaphanes, 2006).

always a preceding and more weighty labilization, no matter how great the stabilization? Is it this dynamic that Nancy latently argues for in the sign of deconstruction?

In any case, it is remarkable that Nancy sees further and takes a more differentiated approach than Giorgio Agamben. His *Il Regno e la Gloria* argues that Christian theology from the very beginning has stood under the sign of economy (of housekeeping and business management)—in a rather single-minded orientation towards power and its administration.

Nancy sees this differently, with good reason. *Theological-economic-political exploitation* is certainly a feature of the history of Christianity. But it is not the whole of Christianity. In all denominations, the opposite trait is at work at the same time: towards divestment and self-sacrifice. No denomination can consider itself so fortunate as to have completely renounced the former. One should not misjudge that this antagonism also recurs in Protestantism—the older the Reformation became.

At this point, Nancy goes a little further—and perhaps too far. The divestment to the point of self-sacrifice, the prophetic of Christianity, leads in his perspective to a strange limit: "dépassement dialectique, decomposition nihiliste, ouverture de l'ancien à l'absolument nouveau."[21] Now these are three very different determinations. The *opening to the absolutely new* (?) could be understood as the original foundation of Christianity—the beginning of theology in the passion and total death of Christ. The *dialectical transcending*, on the other hand, would be as a dialectic a movement of thought that always remains abolishing and seeks to *heal* or close the liminal rift. The *nihilistic disintegration*, on the other hand, breaks in here unexpectedly. Should this be a sign that Nancy is marking his own path here: into a beyond of Christianity, into a *post-Christian* world? This can be understood as an invocation of Nietzsche, whereby the question would be whether this reflects his respect for Jesus against Paul, or Nietzsche's opening for a *theology beyond theology*.[22] But it can also be understood more simply: insofar as Christianity per se is *post-Christian*, not only *post Christum natum*, but *post festum*—in times of Christ's withdrawal.

---

21 Nancy, *La Déclosion (Déconstruction du christianisme, 1)*, p. 60.
22 See Christian Jung, *Die Sprache im Werk Friedrich Nietzsches. Eine Studie zu ihrer Bedeutung für eine Theologie jenseits von Theologie* (Tubingen: Mohr Siebeck, 2013).

Therefore, all presence can only be presence in withdrawal (or conceived *as* withdrawal of presence).

3. Nancy's Deconstruction

In all five points of the autodeconstruction, it became noticeable how not only something is *described*, but it is deconstructively re-written and perpetuated: *operated*, that is. On the one hand, Nancy perceives and takes up a prophetic, myth-critical, progressive, self-critical trait of Christianity. On the other hand, he *exaggerates* in the direction of a self-abolition of Christianity.[23] Why and to what end?

On the one hand, Nancy dares to operate as a thinker of God. His work on the concept of God, while not always clear, is clear enough to recognize. It is reminiscent of what Eberhard Jüngel called the *de-platonization of Christianity*: a thinking of God and the world that does not follow the logic of Parmenides and Neoplatonism, the primacy of the One, against which all difference is considered onto-logically inferior. Thus Nancy writes: "l' 'un' du 'dieu' n'y est pas du tout l'Unicité en tant que substantielle, présente et réunie à elle-même: au contraire, l'unicité et l'unité de ce 'dieu' [...] consistent précisément en ce que l'Un ne peut y être posé, présenté ni figuré réuni en soi." [24] This is a trinity-theologically partly familiar, partly explosive thesis: jointless unity; differenceless monotheism, that would not be God, but at best a philosophical concept of the One (*Hen*). Even Hegel criticized misunderstanding God in this way.

But Nancy also deconstructs a trinitarian-dialectical mediation that understands the difference of the three as a teleological-har-monic unity (against Hegel). Rather, his concept of God is deter-mined by a strong difference that does not understand God as iden-tical with himself. "Qu'il soit dans l'exil et la diaspora, qu'il soit dans le devenir-homme et dans un être-triple-en-soi [...], ce 'dieu' [...] exclut absolument sa propre présentation [...]."[25] This could vehemently oppose the Bishop of Rome's claim to representation; but it goes further. No church, no word and no sacrament *present* God. That would be serious: no presence of God at all in Word and

---

23 Whereby exaggeration (as in hyperbole) would by no means be an illegiti-mate procedure. See Alexander García Düttmann, *Philosophie der Übertreibung* (Berlin: Suhrkamp Verlag, 2014).

24 Nancy, *La Déclosion (Déconstruction du christianisme, 1)*, p. 62.

25 Ibid., p. 62f.

Sacrament? A God without being would be one without ever being present? No Christus *praesens*? Wouldn't God then be thought completely hidden—and the point of Christology missed? For one must conclude: Christ was not a *presentation* of God either.

This is due to the radically negativist concept of God that Nancy represents here: a God who does not appear, who does not present himself—and this because he is not identical with himself in himself. He is not an identity, but is essentially difference—a torn One? Not a One, but a rift? Would there then be a difference between the One thus torn apart and the torn world? Why should one then speak of God as God at all? And why should one speak of presence? And think against it?

Nancy notes or professes to find his view of God already in the *great mystics* of all three monotheisms,[26] without elaborating. Somehow—and here it remains unclear—he joins the mystical tradition. Not destruction, but deconstruction; not mere critique of Christianity, but deconstruction as a dynamic in and out of Christianity, so far so good. But not only in and out of Christianity, but also beyond it? That doesn't sound like a theology *for the church*, but against it and out of it? One does not have to follow that. But the critical thing about it remains the disturbing thing in it. Not to think of Christianity as unity, God as original difference, without him being present and presentable somewhere in *real presence*, always in withdrawal—and yet hoped for, longed for, desired, without this coming to an end or a goal. A disturbing view, but a view of Christianity.

What remains is above all a figure of hope: as an intentionality of the future, as a being-out-of the *coming*. Christianity to come, like community to come, unworked?

In any case, Nancy indirectly indicates his point of view and his perspective: to think Christianity without negating it, but also without returning to it,[27] and thus to open up thinking (including that of theology) "sur un avenir du monde qui ne serait plus ni chrétien, ni anti-chrétien, ni monothéiste ni athéiste ou polythéiste, mais qui s'avancerait précisément au-delà de toutes ces categories […]."[28]

---

26 Ibid.
27 Ibid., p. 54.
28 Ibid.

4. Deconstruction of Christianity—explicit

Nancy mentions two rules of his thinking about Christianity. Firstly, only a Christianity that looks at the present possibility of its negation can be current (here Nancy cites Luigi Pareyson, Eco's teacher). And secondly: "Seul peut être actuel un athéisme qui contemple la réalité de sa provenance chrétienne."[29] He does *not* consider the possibility of thinking *etsi Deus daretur*, which would mean: only an atheism that considers the possibility of its negation could be current. He is not concerned with attacking Christianity, nor with defending it. It is not the time, "parce que le christianisme lui-même, le christianisme comme *tel* est dépassé."[30] Here, the deconstruction thesis (on monotheism) returns: it is obsolete "parce qu'il est lui-même et par lui-même en état de dépassement," in an "état d'autodépassement."[31] The autodeconstruction condenses in Christianity: it can never simply be and remain what it was or meant to be. *Semper reformanda* and the *Protestant principle* resonate. But it is about more and different things: Christianity has ceased "de faire vivre dans l'ordre du *sens*."[32]

The *division of God*, his non-identity and essential self-difference, returns here as a basic figure of Christianity: being in difference—and not a difference to be abolished or overcome. Only this is not understood as tragedy or self-failure, but rather: the "distension de soi" is "le cœur de ce movement d'ouverture," so that he determines "l'essence du christianisme comme ouverture: ouverture de soi et soi comme ouverture."[33] "[O]uverture comme ipséité chrétienne," as "distension de soi."[34]

One might be inclined to agree with this happily, especially as a Protestant. But does this also mean: Christianity as the epitome of deconstruction, and deconstruction as essentially Christian? At any rate, this is how Nancy constructs it—and thus, of course, comes into conflict, with deconstruction and its adherents, who see themselves as far removed from Christianity, and with *these* Christians and theologies, who want to have as little to do with deconstruction as possible.

---

29 Ibid., p. 205.
30 Ibid., p. 206.
31 Ibid.
32 Ibid.
33 Ibid., p. 210.
34 Ibid., p. 211.

Valentin Husson

Se relever – avec Jean-Luc Nancy

« *Fall if you but will, rise you must* »
James Joyce, *Finnegans Wake*, 4.35–17.

Comment écrire sur celui qui fut son maître ? A tous les sens de ce mot : le maître à penser, bien sûr, celui qui nous a appris à prendre à bras le corps les questions les plus urgentes, afin de penser la chose même sans s'autoriser des autorités diverses qui souvent musèlent celui qui écrit, mais encore au sens du *magister*, c'est-à-dire au sens de celui qui émancipe, libère, nous apprend à n'avoir d'autre maître que nous-même. Comment écrire à propos de Jean-Luc Nancy, maintenant, du vivant de sa mort, si j'ose dire, car Nancy reste vivant pour moi, chaque jour, à chaque instant, à chaque fois que je pense et écris, non pas comme une autorité surplombante et intimidante (je crois qu'il n'aimait pas cela), mais comme une inspiration, un souffle, un allant. Comment *se relever* de sa disparition, alors que sa présence était pour nous si réconfortante ou consolatrice dans le désert ambiant ? Comment se relever pour penser à nouveau, et à nouveaux frais ? Comment avoir la force de se lever contre le nihilisme qui croît ? Comment avoir la force, sinon la folie, de se relever pour assurer la relève de cette pensée, ou de cette séquence philosophique française à laquelle Jean-Luc Nancy participait ?

L'*anastasis* : se relever de la *relève* hégélienne

Si le verbe « relever » vient si souvent sous mon clavier, c'est qu'il est peut-être le mot et la chose de Nancy. Le *relever* de Nancy n'ayant que peu à voir avec la relève de Hegel : l'un se dit en grec *anastasis*, quand l'autre se dit en allemand *Aufhebung* (Lacoue-Labarthe proposait même de traduire ce terme par le grec : *catharsis*). On a souvent traduit *anastasis*, via la tradition chrétienne, par « résurrection » ; Nancy, lui, l'a toujours compris comme le fait de re-susciter, de susciter à nouveau, de se relever de tout, même de la mort, de se relever vivant de celle-ci, d'être la levée vivante de la mort que nous sommes. La résurrection est ainsi « la surrection qui dresse la mort dans la mort comme une mort vivante »[1]. Comme une échappée belle, comme le beau risque couru par un corps qui vit à tombeau ouvert. En ce sens, l'*anastasis* a bien quelque chose à voir avec cette relève hégélienne, par laquelle la vie la plus vivante est celle qui « supporte » la mort « et se maintient en elle »[2] ; reste que ce mouvement par laquelle la vie se relève ne dit pas le tout de l'*Aufhebung* hégélienne, en ceci que cette dernière détermine encore un procès dialectique et une téléologie où toute chose se déploie de manière déterminée dans la clôture de son propre sens et de son existence, que l'on peut justifier rétrospectivement dans sa nécessité. *Muss es sein ? Es muss sein !* Chez Nancy, la relève n'est pas une thé(lé)ologie : si pour se penser, elle s'inspire de la levée du corps christique, elle n'ouvre à aucune promesse eschatologique quant à une quelconque résurrection effective des corps : la revivance commence ici et maintenant. *Ressusciter est possible ici-bas, non pas comme une vie nouvelle mais comme une vie renouvelée.* La relance de son allant ou de son allure tient à une vie qui est tout entièrement en-vie, entrain de vivre, pulsion d'être, jaillissement, explosivité, ex-stase. Comme il y a des morts subites, il y a « la vie subite » – selon le beau titre d'un livre de Michel Deguy, lui aussi désormais disparu.

Au reste, la relève n'est pas simplement un motif ontologique, il emporte avec lui l'ensemble de l'œuvre de Jean-Luc Nancy, tant ce mot articule les choses de sa pensée : la relève du sens d'après la signification, la relève du monde d'après l'immonde de la mondialisation, la relève du christianisme d'après la clôture de son sens, la relève du corps d'après sa dévaluation occidental au profit de l'esprit, la relève de la communauté d'après l'échec du communisme étatisé et de l'individualisme forcené (à quoi on pourrait ajouter, la relève de la liberté d'après son aliénation dans les totalitarismes du 20e siècle).

---

1   Jean-Luc Nancy, *La Déclosion, Déconstruction du christianisme*, I, Paris, Galilée, 2005, p.146.
2   G.W.F. Hegel, *Phénoménologie de l'esprit*, « Préface », trad. B. Bourgeois, Paris, Vrin, 2018, p.106.

Le signifiance du sens commun sans signification

Le sens, d'abord, ce motif qui fut si mal compris, alors qu'il occupa grandement Nancy, comme une sorte d'évidence et d'arrière-fond à toute entrée dans l'existence, à toutes les façons de se rapporter à soi comme existant ou autres existants. Le sens, pour lui, est la chose du monde la mieux partagée. Car le sens est avant ce qui partage les existences, et ce que les existences partagent. Cessons de philosopher, et regardons la chose même : le sens est ce qui à chaque fois circule de manière incandescente quand les existences se touchent, par exemple, à la terrasse d'un café, que les voix se mêlent et se démêlent, que les rires éclatent, que la discussion s'échauffe lorsqu'on refait le monde attablé.e.s entre ami.e.s, lorsque l'on s'escrime pour du beurre sur des sujets sensibles, lorsque l'on prend la main de quelqu'un, lorsqu'on l'embrasse, lorsqu'on le regarde pour briser la glace, lorsqu'on glisse un mot doux dans son oreille, lorsque des mains s'effleurent dans le tram, lorsque l'on demande son chemin à quelqu'un, lorsqu'on fait l'amour à son aimé.e ou à un.e inconnu.e, lorsque donc, toujours déjà, l'existence s'expose, s'exhibe, et se laisse toucher par l'autre, lorsque le sens (la signifiance) circule en tous les sens (physiologiques), lorsque donc l'existence est électrisée, changée, affectée, par ce que son corps voit, sent, entend, goûte ou touche du bout des doigts. Les existences baillent signifiance – comme le disait Levinas –, et cela se fait par le langage, et à sa limite – quand les corps parlent pour nous, et quand le silence est parlant.

Et c'est ce sens-là, immanent, si l'on peut dire, qui se relève fièrement de la signification finissante. Puisque de signification, nous n'en avons plus : les grands récits se sont essoufflés, et avec eux les idéologies politiques. Qu'on imagine la vie au début du 20e siècle : la signification de celle-ci était allouée par le Parti (on était communiste, et être communiste signifiait un certain rapport à l'Histoire, à l'avenir, à la pratique politique, au militantisme), par l'Église (on allait à la messe tous les dimanches, la vie était rythmée par le calendrier liturgique, quand ce n'était pas la vie privée elle-même, jusque dans sa chambre à coucher, qui était commandée par les commandements divins : mariage, enfants, mort), par le travail (qu'il soit libre, aliéné, ou domestique, le travail tanne les peaux, et forge le caractère à défaut d'épanouir, il est l'honneur des hommes et des femmes – l'horizon indépassable de leur vie), par la Nation ou la Patrie (l'on part encore volontairement au front afin de mourir pour la Patrie, et pour que le sang impur de l'ennemi abreuve nos sillons – comme dit l'hymne français). Mais une fois que l'essentiel de ces régimes de signification sont tombés en désuétude, que reste-t-il ? Le sens, pardi ! Ce qui expose les existences dans la convivialité (que les arts de la table occupent le devant de la scène médiatique désormais n'y est pas pour rien : c'est le sens qui y circule à tous les sens, et en tous les sens).

Cette question du sens charrie, chez Nancy, celle du monde, en ceci que le monde est sens et que le sens est monde. La structure mondaine de nos existences est tissée comme un réseau de signi-fiance, où choses comme existants font réciproquement sens. Le monde est ceci que nous touchons, en tous les sens, à tous les sens ; par nos sens physiologiques, toujours en éveil, mais encore par le partage du sens que le langage, dans ses formes intersubjec-tives, organise. Reste que cette circulation est court-circuitée par l'im-monde, c'est-à-dire la globalisation marchande qui détricote la pelote signifiante de l'existence collective. La langue a été rempla-cée par la communication, et la sensualité de nos vies par le « sans-contact » et le distanciel. Dans quel monde vivons-nous, dès lors ?

Le monde contre l'immonde de la mondialisation

À l'instar de la signification, formant la cohérence signifiante d'une représentation commune (la Patrie, l'Église, le Parti, etc.), le monde fut depuis les Grecs considéré comme une structure unifiée, harmonieuse, ordonnée. Le *kosmos* des Grecs disait le bon et bel ordre des choses. Depuis, le monde a perdu la signification qui en formait l'unité : il n'est plus *kosmos*, *harmonia mundi*, mais un monde disséminé, disloqué, anarchique. Dieu formait le principe et la fin de ce monde : il en était le Créateur et le Destinateur. La mort de Dieu a émondé le monde de sa signification en le laissant à l'immonde. Le Dieu-argent a remplacé ce Dieu du monothéisme qui s'est retiré. De là que le monde indique dès lors une simple mondialisation économique, une globalisation des échanges, transformant celui-ci en village planétaire. Si planète dit bien en grec : l'astre errant, l'errance d'un caillou sans destination précise.

Règne, dès lors, la globalisation de l'im-monde, l'extension in-définie du marché, et du nihilisme l'accompagnant, où les valeurs sont dévaluées, et où le principe même d'extension du capitalisme est la dévaluation des choses et des individus. C'est pourquoi la crise économique et les soldes (le *Black Friday*, dit-on maintenant) sont la manière même dont le capital se déploie : premièrement en réajustant son empire dès qu'il rencontre une contradiction le menaçant, et deuxièmement par la liquidation des stocks favorisant le remplacement des anciennes marchandises par de nouvelles.

En partant de Nancy, l'on pourrait parler d'une création d'un monde à partir d'une *praxis* commune venant de rien, ne s'autorisant d'aucun principe ; création anarchique d'un sens nouveau, en deçà des idéologies ; création, partant, démocratique, en cela que la démocratie est la dimension anarchique de la politique : c'est la communauté qui s'autorise d'elle-même dans les pratiques qu'elle engage, dans les lois qu'elle choisit, et dans lesquelles elle se reconnaît. Le gouvernement du peuple, par le peuple et pour peuple, ainsi que le dit la devise française, en tant que cette gouvernance ne prédestine pas une programmatique figée (je dirais, pour ma part, que l'on constate d'ailleurs que les programmes politiques sont avant tout des effets d'annonce, et qu'ils ne sont jamais suivis par les faits), mais une inventivité inouïe et sans modèle prédéfini. Des expérimentations démocratiques ne cessent pas d'avoir lieu, ici ou là, des expérimentations associatives, aussi, et à chaque fois, c'est une manière de faire monde qui s'invente, une manière de faire sens, de faire du sens commun, et communément du sens (Nuit debout ou les Gilets jaunes participèrent d'une telle expérimentation – et ces exemples montrent bien l'actualité de la pensée de Jean-Luc).

Si la signification est en assomption, et d'une certaine façon toujours transcendante, le sens circule à même le monde, de manière immanente, entre les « gens », comme l'on dit. Si bien que je soutiendrais, depuis Nancy, que l'action politique, désormais, ne se passera plus dans les partis, ni même dans l'État, mais dans ce qu'on appelle de manière courante « les mouvements sociaux », qui ne sont rien de plus que le mouvement du sens comme socialité, c'est-à-dire être-avec. De tels mouvements n'ont en définitive qu'une seule demande : instiller de l'inéquivalence dans l'équivalence généralisée, créer des conditions nouvelles de vie, lutter pour la reconnaissance des singularités et l'égale liberté des individus, reconnaître, par conséquent, à chacun qu'il est sans équivalent, c'est-à-dire inégalé. Ce que Nancy dit ainsi :

> *Créer le monde* veut dire: immédiatement, sans délai, rouvrir chaque lutte possible pour un monde, c'est-à-dire pour ce qui doit former le contraire d'une globalité d'injustice sur fond d'équivalence générale. Mais mener cette lutte précisément au nom de ceci que ce *monde* sort de rien, qu'il est sans préalable et sans modèle, sans principe et sans

fin donnés, et que c'est exactement *cela* qui forme la justice et le sens d'un monde.[3]

Cette « création *ex nihilo* » ne reconduit pas ainsi, selon une provenance théologique, une mythologie de la création divine : elle dépose radicalement cette position religieuse. C'est donc le monde à l'envers ! : c'est le vivant (humain et non-humain !), et non pas Dieu, qui crée à tout instant, d'une sorte de création continuée, ce monde-ci. Ce n'est qu'à ce prix que le monde peut se relever l'immonde ; et que la mondialisation – au sens du faire-monde – peut se relever la globalisation.

La représentation du monde, en ce sens, a pendant longtemps été rapportée à une orbe crucigère. Le Christ régnait sur le monde comme son sauveur. La peinture occidentale y trouva l'inspiration pour inventer le Christ sauveur du monde – le fameux *Salvator mundi*. Par suite, le nihilisme aura fait une croix sur la croix christique et la mort de Dieu aura libéré l'orbe terrestre de son roi, et par là de son régime de signification, où le sens de l'existence résidait dans notre foi, et dans une doctrine du salut définie par notre incorporation au corps salvateur du Christ. Comment le christianisme peut-il donc résister à la fin de cette hégémonie ? Quel avenir pourrait-il encore ouvrir, lui qui a largement structuré la signification de notre monde depuis l'Antiquité ? C'est justement à cela que J.-L. Nancy répond en engageant une déconstruction du christianisme.

Déclosion du christianisme : se relever d'entre les morts

La déconstruction du christianisme – appelée par Nancy : déclosion – indique une manière de se relever de la théologie, et je dirais même de l'Église, qui, en tous les cas, dans le Nord de l'Europe, ne pèse plus de tout son poids sur l'existence des individus. Cette déclosion avait pour but de déclore la clôture de sens, dans lequel le christianisme était pris, « dans la mesure où le christianisme peut et doit être considéré comme une puissante confirmation de la métaphysique [...], le christianisme et avec lui tout le monothéisme ne font que conforter la clôture et la rendre plus étouffante. »[4] Clô-

---

3   Jean-Luc Nancy, *La création du monde ou la mondialisation*, Paris, Galilée, 2002, p. 63.
4   Nancy, *La déclosion. Déconstruction du christianisme*, I, *op. cit.*, p. 16.

ture largement déterminée ou surdéterminée par Hegel, et sa volonté de faire concorder le destin du monde dans l'esprit chrétien
auto-réalisant l'Histoire dans son déploiement. Quel sens, dès lors,
le christianisme peut-il encore délivrer ? Qu'est-ce que le christianisme peut-il encore pour nous, si celui-ci recouvre le procès de
la vérité historique, comme Histoire de l'Esprit libérant l'esprit ?
Quel avenir pour le christianisme si celui-ci a atteint, selon Hegel
(et si l'on en croit Hegel – ce qui est une autre paire de manches,
car rien n'est moins certain), au XIXᵉ siècle la pointe extrême de
sa parousie en mettant un point final à l'Histoire humaine, et en
réalisant pleinement son sens ? Quel sens, en somme, peut avoir la
religion qui a clôturé le sens ?

Tout l'effort de Nancy fut de montrer que le mouvement même
du christianisme est de sans cesse se déclore, d'être animé par
une transgression inhérente le portant au-delà de toutes limites.
Ce mouvement de déclosion, Kant le nommait *inconditionné*. La
raison est elle-même mue par une pulsion qui l'emmène vers plus
qu'elle-même, vers un sens par-delà le sens, ou vers une transcendance contenue dans l'immanence. Au fond, pour Nancy, le
christianisme est le nom de cette pulsion, de cet excès, de cet infini
dans le fini, ne se laissant jamais capter et claquemurer dans une
finitude toujours déjà éclatée sur ses bords par le débord d'un désir
qui est plus forte qu'elle, et se dérobe à elle. Par là, il y a toujours
plus d'un christianisme, et le verrouillage de la métaphysique ne
peut plus tenir. Le verrou lâche et cède, et le christianisme revient
nous hanter, et nous ouvrir à autre chose, un autre sens. Hors de
son Église et de sa théologie, c'est-à-dire hors de son régime de
signification connu et peut-être daté. De fond en comble, la déclosion du christianisme par lui-même laisse apparaître un fond insu
et inestimable, qui ouvre la pensée à l'impensé, c'est-à-dire à ce
qu'il nous reste impérieusement à penser dans le temps de détresse
qui est déjà le nôtre. Cet impensé n'est peut-être plus quelque
chose de chrétien, ou qui appartient au christianisme, même s'il
en provient et s'en inspire ; cet impensé se libérant de la déclosion
du christianisme se tient peut-être au-delà de lui, en cela qu'il ne
requiert aucun acte de foi.

Ce « chantier à ciel ouvert »[5], que Nancy ouvre, emporte avec
lui « l'infini en acte », ou « l'infini actuel »[6] que le christianisme

---

5   *Ibid.*, p. 17.
6   *Ibid.*, p. 20.

ouvre en son cœur, et qui fait signe pour lui vers l'infinitude finie de l'existence, le fait qu'ex-ister, c'est être ouvert, dédié infiniment à plus que soi par un inconditionné qui nous pousse au-dehors de nous. Le christianisme est ainsi le prête-nom de cette existence se passant infiniment (selon le mot de Pascal que Nancy lui reprend souvent : « l'homme passe infiniment l'homme »), et que le christianisme nomme *anastasis* : résurrection – laquelle est pour le penseur français : levée, ou relevée d'entre les morts ou de la mort. Ce que la déclosion nous laisse entrevoir est dès lors la déclosion même de l'existence qui, bien que finie, est l'infini étendu actuel. Corps glorieux : corps se relevant de la mort pour affirmer infiniment son élan, son allure, sa foi dans son mouvement excédentaire.

Le corps glorieux

« Je suis la résurrection et la vie » (11:25), cette phrase de Jean, pourrait très bien s'entendre chez Nancy comme suit : « je suis la relevée et la vie », je suis celui qui se relève de tout, en vie, et même de la mort. Et si cela est vrai, elle ne peut se départir totalement de la place qui est faite au corps dans l'évangile johannique : car si la vie s'est faite chair, elle ne se relève que comme incarnée, corps glorieux, haut-le-corps, sursaut de l'existence vers plus qu'elle-même, vers sa transcendance horizontale, sa transimmanence.

Le corps glorieux est la vérité du corps pour Nancy. La vérité, oserais-je dire même, de son corps. Lui qui aura subi une transplantation cardiaque, dont son livre *L'intrus* témoigne, vivant dès lors dans un corps qui aurait dû mourir, si la technique ne l'avait pas aidé à survivre ; vivant, en somme, avec le corps d'un mort-vivant, c'est-à-dire avec le cœur d'un mort vivant en lui, ou lui ayant re-donné vie. Ainsi, « l'existence n'est pas «pour» la mort », mais « «la mort» est son corps ». « Toute sa vie, le corps est aussi un corps mort, le corps d'un mort, de ce mort que je suis vivant. »[7] Et c'est cela que l'on peut nommer avec Nancy, *corps glorieux*, la surrection d'un corps mort, par-delà la mort ; la re-suscitation de la vie dans la mort ; le haut-le-corps d'un existant en qui la vie est suscitée subitement.

Le corps a l'existence sur les os, il est l'étendue d'une pulsion de vie, de mort, l'extension d'une pulsion de sur-vie, à tous les sens de

---

7   Jean-Luc Nancy, *Corpus*, Paris, Métaillé, 2006, p. 17.

ce mot, au sens courant de qui se maintient en vie vaille que vaille, mais encore au sens de qui affirme la vie à tout prix, c'est-à-dire à corps perdu. Le corps vit à tombeau ouvert : il est l'ouverture d'un beau risque – sur le fil du rasoir. La ligne de crête sur laquelle le corps se meut n'est pas celle partageant la vie et la mort, mais celle partageant la (re)naissance de la mort. Il n'y pas a pas de ré-surrection au sens strict du terme, pas d'autre vie dans « une autre vie » : il y a en revanche « le «redressement» du mort […] comme renaissance, recommencement de la vie, régénération. »[8] La re-sus-citation de la vie encore et en corps. Tout philosophème est un biographème : Nancy était un roc, un mort-vivant plus vivant que les vivants, l'incarnation de cette levée ou de cette relève d'entre les morts. De ce lever de la vie au crépuscule de chaque instant recommencé de celle-ci.

Comparution immédiate : la justice de la communauté

Si le corps s'exhibe, s'expose, comme ce corps glorieux, c'est qu'il participe d'un corps social ou politique, que Nancy nomme : communauté. S'il refuse le nom de « corps social » ou « politique », lui le penseur du corps, c'est avant toute chose car ce corps collectif forme une unité factice, totalisante, où le singulier est arasé, subsumé le plus souvent sous une signification qui étouffe le sens commun, et la communion véritable qui est comme-union, c'est-à-dire une effusion sans fusion. Le thème de la communauté arrive sous la plume de Nancy, au moment même où les expériences d'étatisation du communisme sont à bout de souffle : deuil de l'échec du communisme, où le commun était unité fusionnelle, ordonnée à même destin morbide. Loin de cette morbidité, la communauté, chez Nancy, est con-vivialité. Certes, ce qui forme la communauté, pour lui, est notre commune finitude, car « rien n'est plus commun que la commune poussière où nous sommes promis »[9] , mais il n'en reste pas moins que de cette finitude procède le rapport infini de la vie à elle-même. La singularité plurielle se partage sur cette limite, tant et si bien qu'elle partage avant tout une vie commune, où la mort de chacun commande de veiller sur chaque autre. Cet être-en-commun n'est toutefois pas morose, mais « *communia gaudia*, […]

8   Jean-Luc Nancy, *L'Adoration. Déconstruction du christianisme*, 2, Paris, Galilée, 2008, p. 129.
9   Jean-Luc Nancy, *Vérité de la démocratie*, Paris, Galilée, 2008, p. 55.

joies partagées »[10], dit Nancy en se référant à Lucrèce. Les vivants humains « paraissent vouloir l'union, mais ils veulent son simulacre – sinon sa simulation – par quoi se relance l'ardeur qui donne le plaisir si vif du désir dans son élan. »[11] Il y a donc : comme une envie de s'exhiber. C'est-à-dire : une *commune envie de sexhiber.* De partager, de jouer, de provoquer, de taquiner, de piquer, d'ironiser, de rire, de discuter, car le temps est compté, et que la vie fait sens, aussi et avant tout, dans cet allant vivace qui nous pousse à aller vers l'autre, à entrer en contact avec lui (ce que le confinement a mis au jour : le *zoon politikon* est, par essence, un être sociable fait pour vivre en communauté).

« La finitude comparaît, c'est-à-dire est exposée : telle est l'essence de la communauté »[12] : cette comparution, cette manière d'apparaître ensemble, doit aussi être entendu au sens de la justice – la communauté est toujours déjà une comparution devant la justice du monde, sa manière de paraître ensemble lui intime une responsabilité, une manière de répondre de l'existence de chacun, autant que de l'existence commune : sa finalité – sans fin – est de créer, ici et maintenant, un monde plus juste. La communauté est ce qui comparaît devant du différent, et des différents, et ces différences, ces singularités d'existence appellent justice, réajustement, justesse de la réponse, ou choix judicieux, précisément parce que dès qu'il y a du différent, il y a du différend, et ce différend est ce qui commande toute justice.

Ainsi, le sens commun, fondant par là même, le sens du commun, provient de ce que nous sommes mortels. Chose que nous comprenons très bien, ne serait qu'en scrutant l'actualité récente : ce qui a organisé nos vies depuis 2019 a résidé précisément dans ce commun souci de nos vies fragiles et exposées à un virus mortel. La pandémie de la Covid-19 nous a fait sentir qu'un commun sort nous liait, à savoir notre commune finitude. Plût au ciel que celle-ci nous aide également à sortir de la catastrophe écologique dans laquelle nous nous trouvons, en comprenant que notre vie commune est menacée, non pas simplement pour nous autres humains, mais également pour les vivants non-humains. Seule la création d'un nouveau sens commun, loin du nihilisme marchand des États survivalistes hantés par leurs intérêts privés, pourra nous

---

10 Jean-Luc Nancy, *Sexistence*, Paris, Galilée, 2017, p. 16.

11 *Ibid.*

12 Jean-Luc Nancy, *La communauté désœuvrée*, Paris, Christian Bourgois, 1999, p. 73.

prémunir d'une disparition prématurée de la Terre. Un tel sauve-tage n'aura lieu que pour autant que nous comprenons, qu'au-delà de nos identités particulières (culturelles, nationales, etc.), le sens du monde est le sens de notre vie commune. Nous partageons en cela un même sort : celui de notre commune fin que nous pouvons communément éviter.

Ce que Nancy disait peut-être ainsi, en nous renvoyant une tâche infinie qui était également une lutte : « La communauté nous est donnée – ou nous sommes donnés et abandonnés selon la com-munauté : c'est un don à renouveler, à communiquer, ce n'est pas une œuvre à faire. Mais c'est une tâche, ce qui est différent – une tâche infinie au cœur de la finitude. « Une tâche et une lutte, cette lutte dont Marx eut le sens [...]. »[13] Elle n'est pas une œuvre, car il ne peut y avoir d'œuvre communautaire que de mort : tout com-munautarisme est morbide, voire mortifère, en tant que cet être-en-commun se referme sur soi, selon une logique auto-immune, que Derrida avait analysé, dans *Foi et savoir*[14], où se gardant du différent, le corps politique œuvre à la mort et à sa propre mort, en excluant, rejetant, persécutant ce qui n'est pas lui. Discrimination de l'ami et de l'ennemi, de ce qui appartient organiquement à la communauté, et à son identité, et de ce qui en diffère. Ce puri-tanisme communautariste s'expose toujours à une épuration. Or désœuvrée, la communauté a pour tâche, au contraire, non pas de nous précipiter vers cette œuvre sacrificielle, mais de sacrifier à l'infinité de la vie, qui est « dur désir de durer » (Char).

Loin d'être un commun désaffecté, ou décharné, la communauté telle que pensée par Nancy était peut-être la communauté du «

---

13 Nancy, *La communauté désœuvrée, op. cit.*, p. 89.
14 Qu'entend Jacques Derrida par cela ? Pour le comprendre, il faut en revenir à la dimension biologique de cette expression. Qu'est-ce que l'immunité ? C'est la capacité de l'organisme à se défendre contre une agression infectieuse, ou contre une maladie donnée. Néanmoins, cette logique peut se retourner contre elle-même. L'immunité peut devenir auto-immunité. En d'autres termes, ce qui conserve la vie peut se retourner contre la vie, et la rendre malade, ou la faire dépérir. Les maladies auto-immunes sont une inflammation de l'organisme liée à une hyperactivité du système immunitaire. Ce qui devait permettre la vie, la rend impossible. Ce qui devait faire vivre, fait mourir. Les auto-anticorps peuvent empêcher le travail des anticorps luttant contre la maladie, par exemple. Au fond, les auto-anticorps sont des anticorps qui se retournent contre l'organisme qui les a produits. Tout organisme, en voulant préserver la vie absolument, peut produire une réponse auto-immunitaire qui lui nuit également. Pour le dire encore autrement : à trop surprotéger la vie d'un péril, on l'expose à un péril tout aussi grand, sinon pire.

dérèglement des sens » (Rimbaud), celle du tact et du contact. Il n'est pas de trop de le rappeler à une époque où le « sans contact » a contaminé toutes nos existences : puritanisme des sites de rencontres où la séduction se fait à distance et par écrans interposés (qu'on songe à Tinder) ; société hygiénique où le gel hydroalcoolique, le check poing contre poing, les gestes barrières, remplaceront bientôt les embrassades de la franche camaraderie ; et où l'économie, elle-même, nous fait désormais cracher notre argent par des paiements « sans contact ». Bien loin de tout cela, donc, Nancy était certainement, selon les mots de Derrida dans un livre qu'il lui consacra, intitulé *Le toucher, Jean-Luc Nancy*, « le plus grand penseur du toucher de tous les temps »[15], c'est-à-dire aussi le plus grand penseur du contact, du tact, de la franchise et de la droiture des relations humaines, là où l'existence prend toute la couleur de son sens lorsqu'elle est « touchée », comme on dit, émue, électrisée par les rencontres qu'elle fait. Par-là, l'existence est toujours déjà « expeausée » (Nancy, *Corpus*) à de l'autre ; jamais recroquevillée sur elle-même, jamais claquemurée dans une identité par trop destructrice lorsqu'elle se fait revendication « identitaire ». Par-là, encore, autre mot sublime de Jean-Luc Nancy, l'existence est tout entièrement « sexistence »[16] : vie sexuée, c'est-à-dire destinée à être touchée (passion amoureuse, joie amicale, plaisir esthétique, enthousiasme politique, etc.), de quelle que manière que ce soit, par (de) l'autre (l'aimé.e, l'ami.e, le ou la camarade, une œuvre ou un.e artiste, voire une découverte scientifique).

La déclosion : déconstruction et restitution

La séquence philosophique du XX° siècle fut largement déterminée par la déconstruction, dont les noms propres furent : Heidegger et Derrida. La *Destruktion* ou l'*Abbau* heideggeriens cherchaient à extraire des ruines du temps, ce qui s'était fait jour au commencement de l'Occident, en étant, tout aussitôt, recouvert et enseveli dans l'oubli. Déconstruire, ce fut ainsi, pour Heidegger, sortir de l'oubli ce qui s'était au commencement oublié, afin d'en recycler les restes de pensée, et à penser (l'être, l'*alethéia*, la *moïra*, le *kreon*, etc., etc.) La déconstruction derridienne cherchait, quant à elle, à

---

15 Jacques Derrida, *Le toucher, Jean-Luc Nancy*, Paris, Galilée, 2003, p. 14.
16 Nancy, *Sexistence, op. cit.*, 2017.

rouvrir les brèches entre nos concepts traditionnels, afin de laisser luire un nouvel éclairage sur eux, ou sur leur prétendue opposition conceptuelle désormais ruinée. La déconstruction allait à la trace, aux traces restantes, à la restance – autre motif de Derrida – de la trace. A la fin de sa vie, Derrida lui-même en venait à dégager des indéconstructibles – la démocratie, la justice –, comme si la déconstruction était nécessitée, depuis toujours déjà, non par ce qui était, en droit, déconstructible, mais ce qui, de fait, ne l'était pas. Au fond, tous ces gestes de pensée avaient affaire avec des ruines, avec des restes. Avec une certaine architecture ou architectonique.

Le premier postdéconstructeur, de l'aveu même de Derrida, fut J.-L. Nancy. Son geste fut celui d'une *déclosion*. Il s'agissait, pour lui, de déclore la clôture métaphysique, afin de restituer la trace d'une énergie inaliénable qui s'y était réservée sans s'y essouffler. C'est à ce déverrouillage que s'employa Nancy, en vue de montrer ce que le christianisme pouvait receler comme reste glorieux. Une fois « démonté de fond en comble », le christianisme pouvait délivrer une nouvelle clarté, un impensé : une levée se relevant de la mort du religieux, et qui n'est autre que la levée – l'*anastasis* – de l'existence comme sens, pouvant nous libérer du nihilisme nous condamnant à l'im-monde et au non-sens.

On pourrait en ce sens dire, au-delà des motifs que l'on a ici exhumés (le sens, le monde, le corps, la communauté) afin de monter que l'*anastasis* était au cœur de la pensée de Nancy, que la pensée nancyéenne appartient pleinement de droit à la période déconstructive, mais s'en excepte absolument et sans aucune contradiction. *Déconstruction – restitution, c'est au creux de ce dispositif que se tient son geste novateur. La déclosion est le nom de cette opération : déconstruire un édifice pour en libérer, en restituer une part inaliénable, une énergie emmagasinée, un reliquat enfoui qui peut encore irradier la pensée de tout son impensé. La restitution est la relevée de ce qui s'est essoufflé sans s'être totalement épuisé. Elle est la relève de toute relève hégélienne, en ce que son geste ne concorde pas avec un achèvement recollectant un sens clos sur luimême, mais avec l'ouverture infinie d'une irradiation du sens en excès sur la signification verrouillée et achevée.*

Reste cela à penser. Reste les restes à méditer. Avec Jean-Luc Nancy pour boussole et excavateur. La restitution se voudrait donc, avant tout, une extraction des restes, une libération et une rénovation. Réhabiliter, libérer, rénover sont donc les maîtres-mots de celle-ci. « Restituer » se devrait d'avoir trois sens :

1) il signifierait le fait de rendre les reliquats qu'il nous reste à penser ; d'extraire, donc, les indéconstructibles. Car les restes sont, de fait, des indéconstructibles, des restes inconditionnels, des absolus non-relatifs. Il s'agit, ainsi, de réhabiliter certains objets de pensée dans ce qu'ils ont d'opératoire pour notre temps ; de les dépoussiérer, et de les rendre à leur intempestivité et à leur capacité de penser l'à-venir. *La restitution est, partant, une réhabilitation.*

2) il indiquerait le fait de libérer, pour l'à-venir, une énergie inouïe et insoupçonnée encore contenue dans ces restes ; car le système de la philosophie peut encore restituer de l'énergie nouvelle, un élan nouveau, qu'il aurait emmagasiné à son insu ; il peut nous apprendre à nous libérer de la ruine pour penser à nouveaux frais, voire à libérer cette ruine comme une pensée nouvelle. Restituer, c'est ainsi restaurer, comme un organisme se restaure afin de pouvoir ré-emmagasiner de l'énergie, et la dépenser. *La restitution est, en cela, une libération* (et non pas une restauration – à moins de l'entendre au sens physiologique et gastronomique du terme).

3) il ferait signe, enfin, vers une rénovation, étant entendu que « rénover » ne signifie pas créer du nouveau à partir de rien, mais réhabiliter, restaurer, refaire à neuf, ou plus précisément encore, *ravoir*, c'est-à-dire se réapproprier une tradition afin d'y puiser du nouveau. Et c'est ici la philosophie qu'il nous faudrait réhabiliter (en rendant compte de son impériosité en temps de détresse), en recyclant certains concepts tombés dans l'oubli ou en désuétude. Si la philosophie a toujours eu à restituer ce qui restait à penser, à et de l'avenir, et pour modifier l'à-venir, sa tâche s'aggrave désormais et se déploie dans sa pleine essence. *Par quoi, la restitution est, dernièrement, une rénovation.*

C'est peut-être cette relève, cette restitution sans relève hégélienne, que Nancy nous aura appris à méditer, et qu'il aura ouvert comme une chance pour l'avenir. Cela même qu'il résumait ainsi : « la portée véritable de la déclosion ne peut être mesurée qu'à ceci : oui ou non, sommes-nous capables de nous ressaisir – par-delà toute maîtrise – de l'exigence qui porte la pensée hors d'elle-même, sans pour autant confondre cette exigence d'une irréductibilité absolue avec une construction d'idéaux ni avec un barbouillage de fantasmes ? »[17] Ouvrir, ainsi qu'il le disait encore, « un *chantier* à ciel ouvert »[18], où ce qu'il reste à penser comme l'im-

---

17 Nancy, *La déclosion, op. cit.*, p. 23.
18 *Ibid.*

pensé même de notre Histoire devrait être réhabilité, libéré, afin de penser à nouveaux frais ce qui arrive d'inouï. Nancy a embrassé ce geste toute sa vie durant : faire entrer les vieux concepts de la métaphysique dans un lever unique, qui était une manière de les faire se relever de leur oubli ou de leur mort programmés. Ainsi en est-il de ces mots vieux comme la philosophie, le sens, le monde, le christianisme, le corps, la communauté, mais encore, s'il fallait en ajouter d'autres, dans un relevé lexical qui ne clôt aucun compte, et qui dépasse bien largement le choix arbitraire et non-exhaustif qui fut le nôtre : âme, vie, mort, être, soi, propre, appropriation, art, liberté, démocratie, justice, Dieu, amour, adoration, création, etc. A chaque fois, ces motifs se sont relevés d'on ne sait où pour libérer une radiation de sens nouvelle. A chaque fois, nous avons appris à nous relever de l'oubli de la pensée et de la mort avec Jean-Luc Nancy. Qu'il soit rassuré, sa relève est là, et se prépare – en toute fidélité à lui, à sa pensée vivante, à sa vie.

Artemy Magun

A Conspiracy of Hymn

Introduction

If we look at the sentimental side of European and American culture from the 1980s to our present time, we first of all find a tendency toward melancholia, eschatology, and trauma. Several books are dedicated explicitly to this disposition, such as Wolf Lepenies' *Melancholia and Society*,[1] Wendy Brown's *States of Injury*,[2] or Mark Fisher's *Capitalist Realism*.[3] Film's turn to Gothic, anxiety-driven genres and to images of devastation (Lars von Trier, Michael Haneke) is accompanied by the hypochondriac, "therapeutic" turn of mass culture.[4] In continental philosophy, Slavoj Žižek developed a philosophy of a transcendental negativity that is only to be overcome through a heroic, *self-sacrificial*, ethical act.[5] Even the objectivist "speculative realism" often ends up in a horror-like estrangement of nature as monstrous (Donna Haraway,[6] Reza Negarestani,[7] Timothy Morton[8]) and in the apocalyptic atmospheres of "Anthropocene." In 1991, Jean-Christophe Bailly published a collection of essays under the title *The End of the Hymn*.[9]

---

1 Wolf Lepenies, *Melancholy and Society* (Cambridge, Mass.: Harvard University Press, 1992).

2 Wendy Brown, *States of Injury* (Princeton, N.J.: Princeton University Press, 1995).

3 Mark Fisher, *Capitalist Realism: Is There No Alternative?* (Winchester: Zer0 Books, 2009).

4 See for instance Roger Foster, "The Therapeutic Spirit of Neoliberalism," *Political Theory* 44, no. 1 (2015), pp. 1–24.

5 For instance, Slavoj Žižek, in Judith Butler, Slavoj Žižek, Ernesto Laclau, *Contingency, Hegemony, Universality* (London: Verso, 2000), p. 237; Slavoj Žižek, *Event: A Philosophical Journey through a Concept* (New York: Penguin, 2014), p. 46.

6 Donna Haraway, *The Promises of Monsters* (New York and London: Routledge, 1992).

7 Reza Negarestani, *Cyclonopedia: Complicity with Autonomous Materials* (London: re:press, 2008).

8 Timothy Morton, *Hyperobjects: Philosophy and Ecology after the End of the World* (Minneapolis: University of Minnesota Press, 2013).

9 Jean-Christophe Bailly, *La Fin de l'Hymne* (Paris: Christian Bourgois, 1991).

Bailly argues that the hymnic mentality in poetry is analogous to façade-centered architecture and to stage-centered performance: it concentrates the gaze on the *subject,* unlike contemporary aesthetics, which *fragments* both the subject and the gaze.

This new unhappy consciousness was a response to a pre-existing forced official optimism characteristic of both capitalist and socialist countries in the 1950–1960s ("the spaces of celebration," to paraphrase Mikhail Ryklin on Stalinist culture[10]): a heterodox push to existential sobriety and mistrust. But while sometimes playing a positive critical role, this emotional regime provides a subject with a negativist ideology of alienation that justifies her social passivity and cynical egoism. In my *Negative Revolution,*[11] I explain public melancholia in a Freudian way through the withdrawal of affect from Soviet authorities and the communist project back to civil society. The tendencies of the 2010s seemed to transform this melancholia "back" into hysteria where it became bound provisionally to this or that aggressor.[12]

If we look for affirmative countertendencies, we find them in two areas: the aforementioned cultivation of the heroic revolutionary act (Slavoj Žižek, Alain Badiou, Judith Butler), and the theories of true love (Alain Badiou again,[13] but also Jean-Luc Marion[14] and Jean-Luc Nancy[15]). The problem of both these tendencies, in my view, is their idealistic character, which can only dismiss the subject's or the pair's actual societal existence: the moralistic activism culture that ends up reinforcing the status quo, and love as the sentimental *ideology* that sustains the bourgeois ultra-narcissism.

In this article, I will focus on a wave of thought in the 2000s that took a surprising interest in the genre of *hymn* and, more generally, in a mood of celebration. In 2000, the leading Russian philosopher Vladimir Bibikhin taught a course on the grammar of

---

10 Mikhail Ryklin, *Prostranstva Likovania* (Moscow: Logos, 2001).

11 Artemy Magun, *Negative Revolution* (New York and London: Bloomsbury, 2013).

12 Artemy Magun, "Hysterical Machiavellianism," *Theory and Event* 19, no. 3 (July 2016).

13 Alain Badiou, *In Praise of Love* (New York: The New Press, 2012).

14 Jean-Luc Marion, *The Erotic Phenomenon* (Chicago: Chicago University Press, 2006).

15 Love, and the related topic of sexuality, are discussed throughout the work of Nancy. See the chapters by Helen Petrovsky and Apostolos Lambropoulos in this volume, as well as Aukje van Rooden "Jean-Luc Nancy, a Romantic Philosopher?," *Angelaki,* 26, no. 3–4 (2021), pp. 113–125.

poetry, dedicated to the ethical thrust of hymn as embodied in the Sanskrit *Rig Veda*.[16] In Italy in 2007, Giorgio Agamben published his *The Kingdom and the Glory*,[17] a significant part of which is devoted to Christian, Indian, and modern postromantic hymns as the verbal mode of glorification: glory being, according to Agamben, constituting sovereignty in the sense of the first figure of the Trinitarian relationship.

Jean-Luc Nancy, the hero of this commemorative volume, would seem to be marginal in this context, since he never refers to hymn explicitly. But, on reading his *Adoration*[18] and some other adjacent works as a theory of hymn, I will demonstrate his proximity to the Italian and Russian philosophers. In all the three cases (Bibikhin, Agamben, Nancy), a turn to hymn is motivated by an intellectual interest in Christianity, Catholic or Orthodox, taking into account the relative opposition of these two confessions to the darker mood of contemporary Protestantism. In the three cases, we are also dealing with the (indirect) disciples of Martin Heidegger who, in the 2000s, elaborated on the hymnic mood that is so characteristic of Heidegger's works after the *Kehre*, unlike his earlier writings on anguish and Nothingness.

Bibikhin

Vladimir Bibikhin (1938–2004) is today recognized by many as the most important Soviet/Russian philosopher of the second half of the twentieth century. His public lecture courses in the 1990s, in the tradition of Jacques Derrida and Jacques Lacan, enjoyed a boom in popularity, and almost every course later became a thick philosophical treatise. One of the recurrent themes in Bibikhin is a mood of enthusiasm and powerful thrust: a *Stimmung* of "captivation" that he found in the historical moments of the Italian Renaissance, Peter the Great's Russia and, cautiously, in his own time of the emancipated post-Soviet society. In a Bergsonian mood,

---

16 Subsequently published as *Grammatika Poezii* (Saint Petersburg: Ivan Limbakh, 2009).

17 Giorgio Agamben, *The Kingdom and the Glory: For a Theological Genealogy of Economy and Government*
(Stanford: Stanford University Press, 2011).

18 Jean-Luc Nancy, *Adoration* (New York: Fordham University Press, 2012 [2010]).

Bibikhin also describes the thrust of life, as exemplified in birds' migration and their pecking with a quasi-phallic beak.[19]

Unsurprisingly, when turning to what he calls the "philosophical grammar" of hymn and to the close reading of the *Rig Veda* in his *Grammar of Poetry*, Bibikhin (who had studied Sanskrit as a linguistics student) associates the affirmative and festive literary genre with a historico-political movement: the early "Aryan" nomads that were the *Rig Veda*'s authors. But as in other cases, the poetical and philosophical *event* is more significant than the empirical conquests of the Indo-European tribes.

> The picture of the Aryans, quick and powerful, few in number, but hence even more stupendous, invading India from somewhere in the North (from the Arctic, according to one of the theories…), who would spread through the enormous Indus Valley in demolishing the preexisting clay cities: is not this a rather naïve projection, a geographic extrapolation of what one has read in the Rig Veda itself. The main theme of this book is the spreading of space.[20]

This, however, is not just a trivial juxtaposition of the ideal register with the empirical. Bibikhin presents things in a more speculative way:

> But archaeology, is it not intense all along the Indus, have not lots of cities been excavated? Strangely, archaeology says nothing about the Aryans themselves, these cities had most probably been destroyed by Aryans… . the Aryans of the Rig Veda period did not have cities or stable villages. Houses were light huts, without basements, easy to disassemble… . Such light constructions were bound to disappear without trace. There were no traces also from the burials. The corpses were burned in cremation fires… . A strange impression! It appears as though this light people would have made it on purpose that the lightning-like poetic texts would be the only thing remaining after it. There is a general question about the very possibility of the Veda archaeology: nothing *is* left (objectively), or nothing *was* left, on purpose?[21]

It looks like the historical event has the character of self-destruction, akin to sacrifice, which leaves poems as its remains. Time is

---

19 Vladimir Bibikhin, *The Woods* (London: The Polity Press, 2021).
20 *Grammatika Poezii*, p. 21. Translations from this book are mine—A.M.
21 Ibid.

being destroyed (through speed), so that space stretches out: such is the logic of event embodied in hymn. The shining effect of hymn is a goal in itself.

Hymn is a sacrifice, an offered word-thing.[22]

Addressing gods, whose names are confused, dream-like, with each other, is one aspect of a hymn. Another is the descriptions' thick materialism. Bibikhin, here as elsewhere, underlines the drug-like immersion of humans into events, and ties up hymns, cautiously and metaphorically, with the ritual feasts of inebriation:

> Poetry is a title of a mystery outside of which we are positioned just by virtue of naming it. Separated from us by seven locks, a sacrifice is taking place. We do not know how a poet sings, how s/he hears or selects words: we tried to learn this, but in vain. To feel the distance, let us imagine that we started to sing and, instead of talking, keep singing throughout the day. Let us imagine that the verse and the music of this song is our own. We probably need to be in a special condition to do that. For instance, having drunk a lot. Searching for a condition in which the poets were, and are, we inevitably paint ourselves a *different* condition, for instance, in the Veda case, a drugged one: a "narcotic culture." Such hypotheses are untestable, we should not play around with them, but their very existence reminds us of a distance.[23]

Bibikhin further reminds us, in a Hölderlinian or Bakhtinian fashion, of the festive and ritualistic context of hymn:

> Life is created by a harsh law that suddenly turns, by instantly changing its face, into the violent force of Indra, a rash energy, a drunk inspiration, a wild triumph.... . In the *Rich*, the mad riot of being does not require a justification, it justifies everything by itself, and this is the very essence of the "battle for the sun" that Indra conducts. Everything is from the very start plunged into a feast of victory, war becomes a parade, and after the breakthrough even the riot becomes too ceremonial. Knowing no obstacles, the Aryans crush, with an unimaginable lightness, the countless multitudes of enemies. In the Indian epic, this

---

22 Ibid., p. 30.
23 Ibid., p. 73. "Seven locks" is a Russian idiom meaning something inaccessible and hidden.

superpower of heroes is already ornamental, and its festive origin fades into a ritual.[24]

The sacrificial character of poetry in hymn implies a reflexive turn. Hymnic words often tend toward an auto-description of poetry (instead of a description of deity). A modern would say that hymn is a discourse of the subject, and one of reflection. Hymn is "a glimpse into what it is impossible to glimpse: the glimpse itself."[25]

For example, one of the most famous hymns from the *Rig Veda* compares poetic speech to frogs' croaking:

As soon as the season of rains has come, and it rains upon them who are longing, thirsting for it, one approaches another who calls to him, 'Akhkhala', as a son approaches his father.

One of the two greets the other as they revel in the waters that burst forth, and the frog leaps about under the falling rain, the speckled mingling his voice with the green.

When one of them repeats the speech of the other, as a pupil that of the teacher, every piece of them is in unison, as with fine voices you chant over the waters.

6. One lows like a cow, one bleats like a goat; one is speckled, one is green. They have the same name but they differ in form, and as they speak they ornament their voices in many ways.

7. Like Brahmins at the overnight sacrifice who speak around the full bowl of Soma, so you frogs around a pool celebrate the day of the year when the rains come.[26]

Notable is the auto-referential nature of the hymn, the use of glossemic abracadabra in reference to language, and, as Bibikhin remarks, a "deconstruction of syntax": not "the first day in the rainy season" but, literally, "the day that became for the rains a beginning."[27]

Bibikhin further points at the availability of the poetic sentence's cosmic scale. Along with treating the *Rig Veda*, Bibikhin evokes relatively recent poets, mostly Velimir Khlebnikov and Rainer Maria Rilke. But in spite of their cosmic addressing, this poetry is

24 Ibid., p. 77.
25 Ibid., p. 100.
26 *The Rig Veda. An Anthology*, translated and edited by Wendy Doniger (New York: Penguin Books, 1981), p. 737. Verse VII.103.
27 *Grammatika Poezii*, p. 236.

different from classic hymn because, unlike the hymn, it "looks back" and expresses a split between the sacred and the profane. Unlike this recent poetry, then, "the hymn wants to rattle in the very midst of things."[28]

Thus, Bibikhin overall reads hymn's "grammar" as an argument for his own materialist phenomenology that celebrates enthusiasm and event, by combining Heidegger with the aestheticism of Russian thought, from Pavel Florensky to Alexey Losev.

Agamben

Bibikhin died in 2004, around the same time that Giorgio Agamben, of course independently, began his project on glory. In 2005, Agamben began presenting about it in public lectures (I first heard one in Saint Petersburg, Russia), and in 2009, his seminal *Kingdom and Glory* appeared in Italian.[29] Like Bibikhin, Agamben focuses on hymn: about one hundred pages of the book are devoted to this poetico-religious genre, with a reading of, among other works, the *Rig Veda* and Rilke's *Duino Elegies*. Unsurprisingly, Agamben makes many of the same observations as Bibikhin. Relying on Marcel Mauss, he says that hymn is a material thing, food for gods, analogous to Christian liturgy:

> "The divine essence," concludes Mauss, "was, from this point of view, a food, nutrition itself. God was food" (ibid.). Among the papers that refer to the incomplete study of nourishment in the Brahmana, there is a brief article, "Anna-Viraj," in which the theory of anna is taken in an unexpected direction. The viraj is a metrical Vedic form composed of three feet of ten syllables each (the title could be translated as "nourishment-hymn"). The Brahmana regards this metrical form as itself possessing a fundamental and specific nutritional virtue... . the eating god, creator of the world (Mauss 1974). What is decisive here is that the hymn, the viraj, does not simply produce the food, but is food in itself.[30]

---

28 Ibid., p. 114.
29 Agamben, *The Kingdom and the Glory*. Agamben, *Il Regno e La Gloria*. Torino: Universale Bollati Boringhieri, 2009.
30 Ibid., p. 237.

Hymn is not a substantive message but a speech that loses its meaning. The word "Amen," as spoken in Judeo-Christian prayers, is a characteristic example of such meaningless words.

> The hymn is the radical deactivation of signifying language, the word rendered completely inoperative and, nevertheless, retained as such in the form of liturgy... . The discourse that resonates has no content: it is a pure will to discourse.[31]

Another instance of such meaningless names is a proper name. Names in hymn are structured paratactically, without a common logic.

> In hymn, all names tend to be isolated and become desemanticized in the proper names of the divine.[32]

Both Bibikhin and Agamben point at the *relational* character of being as revealed in hymn. Bibikhin points at the indistinction between the subject and god. There is, he says, a "fusion in war of god's riches, and ours."[33] To Agamben, glory is the relationship within the trinity, a relation that precedes the relata. Moreover, it relates the two "trinities," the sacred and the political one, as says Agamben, quoting Louis Bréhier:

> "when the pope goes to Constantinople, in the course of the sixth and seventh centuries, the emperor adores him, but at the same time he adores the emperor."[34]

Agamben's general argument is, of course, different from Bibikhin's. Glory, he claims, presents god as "inoperative." It attempts to take him out of action. The very language of hymn is also empty and inoperative. Agamben needs this argument for his intricate theory of "economy" that ties together the theological trinity with the modern state's political structure. In both cases, the higher sovereign entity (god-father) receives glory but is de-activated. If, in theology, this operation gives due respect to the transcendence and to the "sabbatical" understanding of human good, in politics,

---

31 Ibid.
32 Ibid., p. 238.
33 Bibikhin, *Grammatika Poezii*, p. 73.
34 Agamben, *The Kingdom and the Glory*, p. 193.

it produces a hypocritical structure of mutual reference where the first person of the "trinity," the sovereign, remains nominal, and the actual authority belongs to the "government," the analogon of Christ. Agamben thus points at the practical ambivalence of glory: appropriate in ritual and ethics, it becomes "captured" by a politico-theological machine in Western "democratic" politics. God receives glory; the king, and today, the sovereign People receive acclamation and as a result can reign without ruling.

Like in Bibikhin, there is here a secular prosaic element to the hymnic attitude: for the former, inebriation and aesthetic delight, for the latter, public opinion and the media (the democratic version of acclamation). The festive element remains in an authentic, higher inoperative version, but it is presented differently than in Bibikhin: not through Dionysian delight but, rather, through rest and emptiness. Both underline hymn's materiality, but if the former demonstrates the sacredness of life, the latter testifies to its inoperativeness: *modo privativo.*

Nancy

Now, let me finally move on to Jean-Luc Nancy's thought.

From his early work, Nancy developed a philosophy of affect that still awaits a systematic summary. Being critical of sentimentalism, Nancy at the same time cherishes passions, whose passivity is, to him, the result of sense's lack of reflexivity.[35] An affect, like the drive, its active side, is an effect of the impenetrability of sense, which does not redouble and therefore remains somewhat mysterious for the subject. Nancy's major theme is the homonymy of sense and sensibility, thus also of sentiment.[36] But passion is not identical to sense; it is precisely sense taken as senseless. This special affect has two further characteristics:

1) An affect fleetingly *touches* upon sense, being unable to fix it or to objectify it.[37] It is therefore an eventful, surprising affair.

---

35 "There is no sense of sense": this recalls the analogous formulae of Heidegger that there is no being of being, no form of form, etc.

36 Jean-Luc Nancy, *The Sense of the World* (Minneapolis: University of Minnesota Press, 2008).

37 "The sense of the world as its very *concreteness,* that on which our existence *touches* and by which it
is *touched,* in all possible senses. Sense is concrete: that is, it is tangible *and* impenetrable (these two attributes mutually imply each other)." Ibid., p. 10.

Affect's shocking character, which under the current emotional re-gime leads to the order of "trigger warnings" and the "noli me tan-gere" of the "glass skin," about which Aïcha Messina writes in the present volume,[38] is due to anxiety about affect as such. The very fact of affect is shocking. This is a reduplication of sentiment, a sen-timent about sentiment, which, in Nancy's thought, is a forbidden operation, the same as the search for a sense of sense. Thus, the "glass skin" or "snowflake" generation of the 2010s arguably gets the sense of sensibility *right*; the problem, as Messina again rightly notes, is that it (the generation) is not prepared to tolerate it.

2) Affect emerges where a subject senses/touches *herself* as an irreducible aspect of feeling something about an outside thing or situation. Implicitly relying on Kant and on Heidegger's reading of Kant, Nancy unites affect with a broader topic of *self-affectation*. While sense is not reflexive, the subjective praxis aimed at it (for instance, sentiment), for this very reason, can be reflexive, turn-ing inward. It is one thing to redouble an affect (a bad reflection), another thing to sense oneself (a good reflection). Hence Nancy's consistent strategy to conceive the being ethically, through the self, all the while deconstructing the inertial understanding of the sub-ject as a unitary instance. Nancy's theological project, for instance, differs from Jean-Luc Marion's in that it emphasizes the subjective (faith, prayer, virtue), not the objective side of religion.[39]

In a 2011 interview with Philip Armstrong and Jason Smith,[40] Nancy notes that there is an affective unbinding in the contemporary capi-talist world:

---

38 Messina connects the two features of modern culture, the plastic narcissism of virtuosity, and the vulnerability to offence, in one metaphor of "glass skin." Is not what she calls a "skin without skin" a materialization of Nancy's "sense without sense"?

39 Jean-Luc Nancy, *Dis-enclosure* (New York: Fordham University Press, 2008), p. 153: "I understand perfectly well that Marion, in speaking of 'saturated phe-nomena,' is not talking about a phenomenon like faith, but rather of phenomena that would offer themselves as faith, or that would entail faith; nevertheless, I leave open the question of whether faith might not be such a 'saturated phenom-enon,' or even, perhaps, saturation itself." See also Ashok Collins, "Towards a Saturated Faith: Jean-Luc Marion and Jean-Luc Nancy on the Possibility of Belief after Deconstruction," *Sophia* 54 (2015), pp. 321–341.

40 Jean-Luc Nancy, Philip Armstrong and Jason E. Smith, "Politics and Beyond: An Interview with Jean-Luc Nancy," The Prepositional Senses of Jean-Luc Nancy (2), *Diacritics* 43, no. 4 (2015), pp. 90–108.

Money dominates today, both in politics and over politics. More precisely, we have granted power to money that we no longer could or wanted to distinguish in terms of sense. At the same time, the affective powers (*puissances*) that are attached to sense, to power (*pouvoir*), to recognition, and to domination were unbound and gained autonomy from the entanglements—admittedly relative, incomplete—that they formed in a prior mode. In this independence, the hunger for domination appears, as well as the desire for sense and the ambivalence of recognition between "subjects." The result is a sort of general wandering of the passions that diminishes the image of power to an exercise or even a cynical game of greed and exploitation.[41]

The question now is whether this loose energy is bound to produce a constant public unhappiness, mixed with hedonistic narcissism, or whether there is an alternative, which Nancy seems to find in the affective politics of (Catholic?) Christianity. Because this religion does not really put the person in direct contact with its god, it combines an introspective whirl of passions with their messianic readdressing.

Nancy's project of deconstructive theology, as developed in the 2000s, is different from that of Bibikhin and Agamben. Bibikhin, a Christian thinker, endeavors to give a secular, phenomenological philosophy that would depict the world as it appears against the background of Christianity in its horizon. Agamben, whose personal attitude to faith appears to be complicated, uses theology as a critical tool to reveal politico-theological structures. Nancy, somewhat like Ludwig Feuerbach, provides a primary transcendental structure of a world that makes religion possible but not necessary: the mythological deities hide the infinite and open nature of being, and of the human relationship to it. There is a negativity of "disenclosure" concealed under the hypostasizing of sovereign gods.

> It is necessary, if possible, to extract from a ground deeper than the ground of the religious thing [*la chose religieuse*] that of which religion will have been a form and a misrecognition [*méconnaissance*].[42]

Nevertheless, like the two other philosophers, Nancy cherishes and even advocates religion's *celebratory* mood, which he notices

---

41 Ibid., pp. 100–101.
42 Nancy, *Adoration*, p. 26.

in the phenomena of prayer, address, and salutation. He calls this attitude "adoration," understood literally as an "ad-oration," an addressed speech. Any ontic address is made possible by the transcendental condition of an infinite attitude to an absent or distant interlocutor.

Adoration is the praise of the infinite [mutual] referral.[43]

Adoration is a relational structure: its possibility consists not only in the divine's exuberance but also in the position of the subject who feels diminished, humbled, by the abyss of being.

The openness of this attitude is expressed in art, most importantly in music.

[Adoration] is nothing other, at least in the form in which it is born, than the movement of singing that comes to the throat and the lips for no reason, from nowhere, in an uncertain cadence, in a tune still lacking precise melody, and in an issuing that is withdrawn from the formed, speaking voice. This song would be held and stretched between the full, worked-out form of the *oratorio* and the formlessness of *humming* [*fredonnement*]—whose name takes us back to babbling or spluttering and even to the chirping of birds and the thrumming of cicadas. The murmur and stammering of a celebration and an invocation, of an exclamation that comes from before language and outlasts it... . Or again: the world saluting itself, via all of "nature" up to "mankind" and its "technology," engendered by nature in order to get to the end of its creation [*art*]: a know-how of the impossible, the incommensurable, and the infinite—the revelation that the world is not there in order to remain there, laid down on itself, but on the contrary in order to open this "there" onto unheard-of, exalting or catastrophic, sublime or monstrous distancings, and perhaps all of this comes down to a single coming. A sole, unique, trembling coming, perilous and yet resolved, which is also the coming of song itself, its beating.[44]

The overarching theme of Nancy's *Adoration* is that sense has no further sense, which "is not a negative proposition."[45] It is a way to conceptualize the role of nonsensical or self-referential elements in hymn and acclamation. Paradoxically, even though these forms are

---

43   Ibid., p. 13.
44   Ibid., p. 64.
45   Ibid., p. 12.

made for addressing to gods, they are also speaking of themselves: the *Rig Veda* hymns, for instance, speak much of the priests, the *brahmans*, and of poetic speech (which it compares to the sounds of frogs). Nancy, accordingly, believes that adoration is practiced by a subject: the "subject" being here not a caricatural unitary center, but a "subject of relation," the "I am" addressed to the indefinite others. Gods need humans so that they sing their glory, as Agamben also notes.[46]

A hymn, paradoxically, speaks of itself: this is an auto-affection of the adoring person, which, as we have seen, is the condition of sending sense (*sense-sending*) to an infinitely distant interlocutor. Nancy in the *Adoration* speaks not of hymn but rather of an "oratorio" (a religious opera). The theme of hymn is, however, present in the "Dis-enclosure," where the author, speaking of prayer, explicitly questions Bailly's and Philippe Lacoue-Labarthe's "dismissal of hymn."[47]

There are important motifs that unite Nancy with one or both of the aforementioned theorists of hymn. Like Bibikhin, he points at the position of the adoring subject "in the midst of the world," at the point of intensity within it. Like both Bibikhin and Agamben, he notes the self-referential and content-less nature of the adoring address. Where Bibikhin appeals to the stretching of space and the amplitude of the world as manifested in hymn, Nancy speaks of a characteristic "spacing":

> The Christian "god," insofar as we can name him as such, is not posed, not even self-posed. There is neither a ground nor a space for this: there is neither world nor afterworld, but an opening of sense that produces the spacing of the world and its relation to itself.[48]

A long-time follower of Georges Bataille, Nancy, like Bibikhin, sees adoration realized in ecstatic relations such as sexuality and festivity. Bataille plays for Nancy the same role as Pavel Florensky does for Bibikhin.

Following on from his older work, *Corpus*,[49] Nancy depicts the body's proto-theological nature as a site of sensuous reception and

---

46 Agamben, *The Kingdom and the Glory*, p. 234.

47 Nancy, *Dis-enclosure*, pp. 133–134.

48 Nancy, *Adoration*, p. 31.

49 Jean-Luc Nancy, *Corpus* (New York: Fordham University Press, 2008).

expository incarnation, an "exposure of a soul."[50] He even adds to this, mixing religion and sexuality in a characteristically naughty way:

Bodies are adoration in all their openings.[51]

Developing the "Inoperative Community,"[52] Nancy points at the infinite relationship's ecstatic and festive nature that links not just human to human, but, maybe more importantly, human to the higher entities. Community is not a contractual nor fusional collection, not a union for collective action, but an unlikely mutual attitude that negates; one that dis-encloses and inebriates its participants.

Sense in adoration is suspended, and, moreover, breaks down. Nancy lingers on this particularly in his earlier work, *The Sense of the World*, arguing for a materialization and *fragmentation* of language that is simultaneously responsible for its openness to new meanings.[53] The tendency of hymnic language to turn on itself, sometimes even bordering on nonsense (as in the word "Amen" that Agamben uses as an example of hymnic desemantization), is another instance of the sense without sense, a sense that actively resists itself to preclude this second reflexive "sense" from emerging. Sense sacrifices itself (perhaps to prevent human subjects from doing so).

Inoperativeness, says Nancy, is characteristic of faith as a dis-activating act,[54] and is inherent in adoration as long as it is a kind of phenomenological reduction: a suspension of sedimented senses, and even of the object-like *intention*, in order to achieve its "extension,"[55] that is, its cosmic ambition.

In *Adoration,* Nancy goes even further and associates Christian *virtue* (faith, hope, justice) with what in Freud's metapsychology is called "drive" (*Trieb*): an infinitized version of desire. The proto-religious world is a world of insatiable *forces*, which pull and push (instead of delimiting and stopping, as we would normally think of

---

50 Nancy, *Adoration*, p. 28.

51 Ibid., p. 20.

52 Jean-Luc Nancy, *The Inoperative Community* (Minneapolis: The University of Minnesota Press, 1991).

53 Nancy, *The Sense of the World*, pp. 2; 58ff.

54 Nancy, *Dis-enclosure*, p. 52.

55 Nancy, *Adoration*, p. 87.

ethical virtue). This is a materialist/ontological ethic which, again, is very close to Bibikhin's reading of the *Rig Veda* as a celebration of power (but not magic).

Conclusion

To synthesize all three authors, a spatial and temporal *concentration* of forces intensifies and extends being but, at the same time, reduces humans to an evanescent point. Their own force comes to them, as though from outside, their ecstatic affectivity takes on a communicative and expositive role, that of a *gesture* (Nancy and Agamben) or *posture* (Bibikhin). Bound by the form of space and time to repeat, humans use ritual repetition to expose themselves in their senselessness (*alogon*) and corporeal impenetrability, sensing themselves as addressed (through attention, or admiration), and addressing in response, thus miming the meaningless message of the facticity, with its positive, affirmative mode of donation. But the blinding light of this donation blocks the potential donor, so that glory is sung to the glory itself, thus playing the role of a certain screen: an invitation, for god, to withdraw.

I suspect that the tendency I have described here has to do with the non-Protestant (post-Catholic and Orthodox) reaction to the negativistic, critical/melancholic tonality predominant today.[56] Nancy confirmed as much, prompted by Pierre Jandin, by defending joy against the dangers of nihilism:

> Sure, with law, with good theology, or good Christian spirituality, salvation must tendentially be identical to joy, which means that the saved person is in permanent jubilation to be in the presence of God, etc. But in everyday practice, in ordinary Christianity, Protestantism pushed joy into the background. Then the possibility opens for what you have placed in your expression "nihilism or joy": I like this

---

56 In saying this, I recall the historicity of these three denominations, as there is an internal tension between the negative and affirmative in each of them, in their own right. Moreover, it is probably impossible to build an objective picture of any of them without taking a viewpoint of another. However, one can speak with more certainty of a historical-cultural nexus that today, in the last hundred years, allows us to distinguish among the denominations as specific traditions of sensibility and thought. On Protestantism as a nihilistic philosophy, see an excellent book by Michael Gillespie, *The Theological Origins of Modernity* (Chicago: University of Chicago Press, 2008).

question's position, which I've never thought about: Nihilism is perhaps the absence of joy before anything else.[57]

That said, in *Adoration*, Nancy's attitude to Christian confessions is more qualified. There, he actually praises the Protestant for bringing forth secularization, that is, trying to accomplish and self-dissolve Christianity into "an irrigation system for the culture of the modern world (its morals, its law, its humanism, and its nihilism)."[58]

We are dealing with two different Protestantisms, or with the internal split of the Reformation. But, since "nihilism" is mentioned, it can be conjectured, with Nietzsche, that the moment in which Christianity decided to focus on the inner-worldly, it built on the death of god event and thus, along with sentimentality, has secularized despair.

The post-Heideggerian authors reverse nihilism with an invitation to "salute" and hold on to the void, but without pretending that it is occupied. The problem, however, is the critical work of cleansing this space. No-one argues against the need to remove fetishes, but the post-Protestant critical stance should itself be put into question: whether it is not only meant for intellectuals, or whether it does not involve the enormous negative effort of "dis-enclosure," which may, in and by itself, bring back anxiety and guilt. A certain speed and ambition of proceeding seems to be key here. Nevertheless, a question remains, most explicitly approximated by Agamben, where we are dealing not just with the adoration/glorification, but also with the ritual *expulsion* of deity. Adoration is sacrificial also because a certain substance is dismissed there in favor of form. No wonder that the ecstatic sentiment emerges: the God himself is now dead, and the trinity remains. (The theme of relationality, so popular in the last decade, is often subject to criticism for the very reason that it potentially removes the relata[59]).

This role of negativity is a suspicion to be pursued in the future, to restore confidence in a world increasingly driven by self-hatred. Bibikhin, Nancy, and Agamben show that there is in fact a strong background of enthusiasm and adoration that gets wasted or dis-

---

57 Jean-Luc Nancy, *The Possibility of the World: Conversations with Jean-Pierre Jandin* (New York: Fordham University Press, 2017), p. 131.
58 Nancy, *Adoration*, p. 13.
59 As in Graham Harman, *The Quadruple Object* (Winchester: Zer0 Books, 2011).

regarded by the fetishisms of the benign or malign gods. The task of philosophy, according to them, is to clean up and restore the originary picture, to hear an *addressed* message behind each pathological condition. The situation, however, is symmetrical: there is a profound negative impulse of self-humbling and self-sacrificing behind any adoration. A hymnic song of adoration requires a rhythm that would allow for alternating between the two sides of the tragic, not-quite-sacrificial, disposition.

Marita Tatari – Jean-Luc Nancy

De l'esprit d'un changement d'époque

Marita Tatari : Cher Jean-Luc, tu parles depuis des années non pas seulement d'une *Epochenwende*, mais d'une transformation très profonde de notre civilisation occidentale-mondiale, voire même d'une mutation, comparable à la fin du monde ancien. Tu dis que ce qui est en jeu dans cette mutation est un esprit, un esprit nouveau.

L'esprit de l'Europe chrétienne trouvait la valeur de la vie en la rapportant à une transcendance. Il a été suivi par l'esprit de production, qui projetait la vie dans l'avenir et trouvait sa valeur dans ce que Marx appelait l'équivalence. Cet esprit du monde de production est aujourd'hui épuisé et avec lui la confiance au progrès et à l'histoire maîtrisée. Nous nous trouvons dans cet épuisement et nous ne pouvons pas nous représenter ce qui va venir, car notre représentation ressort de l'esprit de la production, et ce dont il s'agit, dis-tu, est d'un autre esprit.

Ta considération de l'Occident résonne à certains égards avec celle d'Hannah Arendt dans *Vita activa*. Dans cet ouvrage, Arendt ne parle pas d'esprit, mais plutôt de l'histoire comme d'une suite d'événements ; et, comme toi, elle parle d'une conduite, d'une manière de se tenir par rapport à la condition humaine de la finitude. Mais pour Arendt, cette conduite est celle de l'action et du lieu d'apparition, qu'elle comprend comme politique, alors que pour toi l'Occident même s'est épuisé. S'il s'agit, non pas de se représenter ce qui va venir, mais – comme tu le dis dans ton dernier ouvrage *La peau fragile du monde* – d'une *praxis*, d'un *ethos*, d'une disposition vécue et vivante que nous connaissons déjà sans le savoir et qui s'écarte de la logique usagère et usante de la production. Alors au nom de quoi peux-tu faire cet écart ? Veux-tu expliquer pourquoi tu insistes sur le mot esprit ?

Jean-Luc Nancy : Chère Marita, tu me poses une question très embarrassante car je n'ai pas de réponse simple ni claire. C'est d'ailleurs une très bonne raison pour te remercier de la poser. J'utilise le mot « esprit » par pur défaut : je ne peux pas me servir du mot « politique » qui est devenu extrêmement confus – surtout avec la distinction entre « le » et « la » politique, distinction que j'ai utilisée moi-même mais dont j'ai fini par comprendre qu'elle brouille la perception. On croit qu'il y a « une » politique faite d'intérêts, de rapports de forces, de stratégies et de négociations et « un » politique (en allemand « *das Politische* », en anglais « *the political* ») qui serait une sorte d'élément éthéré de l'ensemble de tous les rapports et aussi pour finir de toutes les destinations. C'est un peu de ce « politique » qu'il y avait chez Arendt. Pourtant elle savait aussi que l'art, l'amour, les œuvres de l'esprit (comme on dit en français pour les arts, la littérature et la pensée) ne se laissent pas comprendre dans la politique – bien qu'ils aient avec elle des rapports nécessaires. Mais Arendt me semble être restée prisonnière d'une vision idyllique de la *politeia* où elle voit la réalisation de la réalité humaine dans la délibération publique (malgré, je le répète, ce qu'elle sait de l'amour et de l'art). Or d'une part cette vision est fausse du point de vue historique, d'autre part Arendt elle-même sait qu'il y a autre chose que la place publique.

Aujourd'hui il se produit que la sphère politique est presque entièrement prise à l'intérieur du complexe techno-économique qui gouverne le monde. Comme il y a des peuples – réalité très réelle que l'internationalisme, malgré toutes ses vertus, nous laissait oublier – il faut que subsistent des organes de gestion et de décision propres à ces peuples (et je néglige ici la question très complexe de la transformation ou du brouillage relatif, aujourd'hui de ces peuples eux-mêmes). Mais une grande partie du possible de ces gestions et décisions dépend du complexe dont j'ai parlé. Lequel en outre produit en même temps un horizon général de destination – pour tous les peuples – qui est justement la satisfaction de la grande machine productiviste-consommatrice.

En 1919 – déjà ! – Valéry écrivait *La Crise de l'esprit* – et dans le mot « esprit » il ne mettait évidemment rien de ce que le « spirituel » évoque trop souvent. Il nommait ainsi ce qu'on pourrait aussi nommer la conscience ou bien l'âme voire la culture ou la civilisation si chacun de ces mots n'était pas trop étroit et trop peu dynamique pour désigner ce dont il s'agit. Dans le cas de « civilisation » il faut rappeler que c'est ce livre qui commence par la phrase fameuse : « Nous autres, civilisations, nous savons maintenant que nous sommes mortelles. » Valéry parle d'un « Hamlet européen ». Il écrit : « Il médite sur la vie et la mort des vérités. Il a pour fantômes tous les objets de nos controverses ; il a pour remords tous les titres de notre gloire ; il est accablé sous le poids des découvertes, des connaissances, incapable de se reprendre à cette activité illimitée. » Plus loin : « Mais moi, ne suis-je pas fatigué de produire ? N'ai-je pas épuisé le désir des tentatives extrêmes et n'ai-je pas abusé des savants mélanges ? Faut-il laisser de côté mes devoirs difficiles et mes ambitions transcendantes ? Dois-je suivre le mouvement et faire comme Polonius, qui dirige maintenant un grand journal ? Comme Laertes, qui est quelque part dans l'aviation ? Comme Rosenkrantz, qui fait je ne sais quoi sous un nom russe ? »

Avec les retouches nécessaires, on ne peut que constater l'actualité de ce texte qui date d'un siècle entier. Ce que Valéry nomme l'esprit n'a rien de spiritualiste : c'est au fond simplement ce qui ne se réduit pas à la servilité de la production, du calcul – fût-il celui des « tentatives extrêmes » ou des « savants mélanges ». L'esprit est ainsi à peu près ce que Bataille nomme « l'hétérogène ». Ou bien ce qui n'obéit pas au « projet » mais qui a le sens de l'inutile et de l'impossible. Ce qui avant tout se comprend soi-même comme infiniment dépassé par un réel qu'il n'est pas question de maîtriser.

Bien sûr l'« esprit » a servi à beaucoup d'usages asservis à des finalités comme le divin ou la patrie, comme le peuple ou même la vérité (scientifique). Il faut relire le *De l'esprit* de Derrida – mais il faut ne pas méconnaître qu'il cherche pour finir à défier toutes les spiritualités pour s'ouvrir à un esprit tout autre – tellement autre que Derrida le sent plus s'échapper que se laisser saisir.

Tout cela dit, très vite, en raccourci, je cite à nouveau la phrase de Marx que j'ai citée vingt fois. Comme tu sais Marx dit que la religion – l'« opium du peuple » – est « l'esprit d'un monde sans esprit ». Ce qui veut dire qu'il y a un faux esprit et un vrai. Marx ne dit pas quel est ce vrai. Il est clair que pour lui c'est l'appropriation par l'homme de sa valeur propre – et que dans tous ces termes il y a une quantité de pièges et de difficultés, aujourd'hui pour nous, repérés et déconstruits mais pas pour autant remplacés. Je dirais donc qu'aujourd'hui l'« esprit » est le seul mot disponible pour parler d'un « homme » qu'aucun humanisme ne connaît et d'une « valeur » inévaluable. Ou plus exactement, pour désigner l'attitude en face de ces réalités ou de ces significations inconnues. Attitude autant de sentiment que de pensée, autant d'énergie que de sensibilité. Je pourrais lui donner le nom de « souffle » qui est le sens premier de « esprit ». Mais c'est pour nous trop sportif. Je pourrais aussi parler de « caractère » au sens où on dit « le caractère d'un peuple », ce qui distingue et « caractérise » – justement – une façon d'être au monde. Mais on perd alors la transcendance qui caractérise l'esprit : le rapport à un réel avec lequel aucun rapport ne peut être noué. Exactement sans doute ce que « Dieu » a étouffé sous le poids de son cadavre. ...

Je vais en rester là pour le moment. Mon embarras reste le même et j'ai déjà l'expérience du fait que si je prononce ce mot en public immédiatement quelques bonnes âmes spiritualistes me font savoir qu'elles se réjouissent... Aussi j'évite de le prononcer mais parfois, tout de même, je me risque... J'ignore ce qui viendra plus tard... Mais je partage avec Marx la déploration d'un « monde sans esprit »... Et d'autant plus que l'« opium » aujourd'hui est encore plus répandu qu'au temps de Marx... Sous forme de drogues et sous forme de spiritualités diverses, évangéliques ou chamaniques, scientifiques aussi ou politiques (je parle des imaginaires politiques, non des pratiques), technologiques, etc.

MT : L'esprit, comme à chaque fois l'esprit d'un moment du monde et à la fois comme ce à partir de quoi ce moment est possible, fait en effet penser à Heidegger et à *De L'Esprit* de Derrida. Car comme rapport à un excès ou un surplus absolu, il est en effet le corrélat de la logique d'investissement que – encore dans *La Peau fragile du monde* – tu vois à l'œuvre dans les divers moments de l'Occident, la logique visant à l'appropriation de cet excès : l'empire romain se donnerait un projet qui serait sa propre production et son exportation ou son extension. Le judéo-christianisme viendrait comme réponse à la richesse que Rome employait à des opérations de rapport (comme le commerce – l'entreprise). Et il répondrait par la richesse des cieux, tout en transmettant le terrain de sa réalisation dans l'homme même, l'invitant à se renouveler. Le capitalisme représenterait ensuite le développement de ce principe d'investissement et d'expansion de telle sorte que la richesse – tendanciellement tout usage – investisse dans l'accroissement de sa propre capacité à s'investir.

Si aujourd'hui l'Occident même s'épuise, cette affirmation n'a rien, dis-tu, d'une vision téléologique ou destinale : la limite de l'investissement ne peut consister que dans une déperdition des possibilités d'investir. Derrida, à la fin de *De l'Esprit*, dit : il suffit de continuer à parler. L'esprit, dit-il, fera le reste, « à travers la flamme ou les cendres, mais comme le tout autre, inévitablement ». Ce qui ne nous empêche pas de poser encore la même question : s'il n'y a aucune logique destinale à l'œuvre, au nom de quoi – à l'inverse des « transhumanismes » – se tenir aujourd'hui dans l'attitude, la *praxis*, l'*ethos* du rapport à cette transcendance finie, cet excès absolu ? N'est-ce pas parce que depuis la fin du monde archaïque du donné et encore aujourd'hui, « nous », le commun, est exposé à soi-même ? Se tenir à cette exposition ?

« L'anthropocène », désignant la substitution de l'homme aux forces naturelles et annonçant la maîtrise et l'autonomie de l'homme, refoule, dis-tu, l'énorme incertitude, voire l'égarement dans lesquels cette maîtrise s'engage. Aujourd'hui, au lieu de chercher la maîtrise et le bon usage, et au lieu de se représenter un avenir par exemple écologique, s'agit-il, peut-être, dis-tu avec Heidegger et Augustin, d'affirmer la valeur autonome du *Brauch* de l'existence humaine : les humains comme *gebraucht*, employés, utilisés par leur simple mise en jeu, et comme sa propre fructification infinie – à la place de l'homme autonome. Comment est le commun mis en jeu dans cette hétéronomie de l'homme utilisé, s'il ne l'est pas sur le mode politique ?

JLN : Au préambule de ta question je voudrais ajouter une précision. A la façon dont tu présentes les deux aspects du commencement occidental – Rome d'un côté, le judéo-christianisme de l'autre – on pourrait croire à une opposition tranchée. Je reconnais que j'ai sans doute moi-même dans certains textes donné prise à cette lecture de l'histoire. On pourrait souligner ce qu'il y a de Heidegger en arrière-plan – sauf que lui a escamoté le judéo-christianisme, peut-être pour le métamorphoser en sa propre pensée, ce qui en fait accentue l'opposition entre un côté d'« oubli de l'être » et un côté de fidélité au sens de l'être.

Or Heidegger lui-même inscrit l'« oubli » en question dans l'« envoi » même de l'« être ». C'est ainsi d'ailleurs qu'il en vient à dire que la technique est le dernier envoi de l'être – et c'est ainsi aussi qu'il a pu vouloir imputer au « type d'homme » juif la charge (ou la mission ?) de « déraciner tout l'étant de l'être » (je cite de mémoire). Mais justement avec cette figuration du « juif » il introduit un manichéisme qui en toute rigueur contredit l'unité de l'« envoi » et de l'« oubli ». Il faut donc se débarrasser de cette contradiction. Ce qui veut dire entrer dans une complexité, voire dans une obscurité très incommode mais qui est inévitable.

En effet cela revient à dire qu'on ne peut pas simplement opposer un côté à un autre et qu'au-delà de l'Antiquité et jusqu'à nous, il faut considérer ce qu'est *aussi* en dépit de tout l'œuvre de l'Occident. C'est-à-dire une civilisation imposante. D'une part en effet, elle a atteint un degré d'élaboration technique qui fait aujourd'hui problème mais qui n'en représente pas moins une ingéniosité, un investissement intellectuel autant que matériel – investissement qui n'est pas seulement calcul du « retour sur investissement » mais aussi engagement, aventure et risque de toute la science moderne et *même* du capitalisme qui a impliqué au cours de son histoire beaucoup de témérité dans l'ambition et de risque dans le calcul. D'autre part, en dehors de la technique (mais à certains égards en rapport avec elle, comme dans la conception des instruments de musique ou du traitement des couleurs et des vernis en peinture) un déploiement artistique et spirituel qu'on peut dire somptueux et qui n'a pas à rougir devant les richesses des cultures asiatiques, africaines, amérindiennes ou autres. Giotto ou Beethoven, Dante ou Ibn Arabi, Faulkner ou Nietzsche sont devenus des trésors de l'humanité au même titre que Lao-Tseu, le *Dit du Genji* ou la sculpture Yoruba.

Il faut donc méditer sur ce qu'on pourrait emblématiser par cette remarque : l'art de la Renaissance européenne a été fortement lié au premier essor du capitalisme. Ou pour reprendre tes termes : la richesse des cieux et celle de la bourgeoisie se sont autant accouplées qu'opposées. Et lorsque la seconde en vient à s'enfermer dans un mécanisme d'auto-développement privé de finalité, c'est aussi toutes les pensées et tous les arts de l'esprit humain qui tombent en panne…

Cela signifie peut-être au moins – et ainsi je vais vers ta question – que s'il y a un avenir, il n'est pas détachable de la technique ni par conséquent d'une économie de l'investissement. En un sens c'est ce que désirent tous ceux qui, n'ayant pas le bien-être des sociétés développées, veulent l'acquérir tout en gardant ou en renouvelant les richesses de toutes les cultures. Et en effet cela ne peut pas se faire par un simple projet écologique. L'écologie, sous quelque forme qu'elle se présente et aussi inventive qu'elle soit, ne fait pas naître un « esprit » pour reprendre ce mot. Ou bien ne montre pas, jusqu'ici, en quoi il consiste. Lorsqu'on parle de « la terre » ou de « la planète » par exemple, de quoi parle-t-on ? Du sens cosmo-géo-graphique de ces termes ou bien de valeurs symboliques ou métaphysiques (comme lorsque Heidegger parle de « la terre » , lorsque la Bible dit : « toute la terre chante la gloire de Dieu » ou Rimbaud : « je suis rendu au sol, avec un devoir à chercher, et la réalité rugueuse à étreindre ! Paysan ! ») ?

Tu te réfères au *Brauch* de Heidegger qui est en effet une façon de renverser la domination du monde par l'homme en le faisant « employé » par l'« être » ou bien offert à la jouissance de l'être (dans *La Parole d'Anaximandre* Heidegger traduit *brauchen* par le latin *frui*). En tout cas une hétéronomie. L'hétéronomie est la grande affaire : comment l'homme relève d'autre chose que de lui-même…

Ne faut-il pas dire que c'est justement de son rapport à l'autre que l'homme tient sa spécificité ? Les autres vivants n'ont pas ce rapport – dont le langage est à la fois l'expression et la mise en œuvre. Quel autre ? Si ce n'est ni Dieu, ni l'Autre lacanien – pour chacun des deux je dirais qu'ils sont, chacun à sa façon, des témoins de la clôture de l'Occident (le premier par sa « mort », le second par son caractère structurel plus que dynamique).

Le « commun » alors, pour finir de te répondre, serait un langage – forcément commun – capable d'ouvrir à une altérité qui prendrait en charge notre *Gebrauchtsein* – c'est-à-dire peut-être notre « faire sens » ou « être dans le sens » – par cela même qui fait que nous ex-istons, que nous sommes hors de nous, y compris dans la technique mais de telle façon que celle-ci ouvre sur l'altérité. Cela n'a ni nom ni figure et ne peut pas être anticipé. Ça ne peut que *venir*. Mais ce pourrait être aussi bien notre disparition… L'« homme » disparaissant dans la venue de l'autre…

MT : Oui, Heidegger lui-même nous fait entrer dans cette complexité, n'opposant pas simplement à l'oubli de l'être une fidélité au sens de l'être (dont l'expérience est la langue), mais en inscrivant cet oubli dans l'envoi de l'être. Et pourtant c'est comme s'il trahissait les prémisses de sa propre pensée, ou, pour reprendre le terme de Lacoue-Labarthe, comme s'il était dans un *double-bind* que Lacoue-Labarthe décrivait comme symptomatique pour l'Occident même et repérait – bien avant la publication des *Cahiers Noirs* – dans le rôle qu'Heidegger accorde à la poésie de Hölderlin.

Parler de l'hétéronomie du *Gebrauchtsein* de l'homme, au lieu de chercher des alternatives devant les catastrophes dont nous sommes actuellement témoins (au lieu de plaider pour une écologie, une bonne politique, des stratégies pour le renversement du capitalisme en vue d'un commun à venir…), me semble d'une probité intellectuelle sans compromis. Il s'agit alors de cor-respondre aux transformations qui ont lieu mais d'y cor-respondre à partir de la condition humaine de la finitude. L'écologie, les stratégies alternatives, etc… Même si elles correspondent aux transformations actuelles, s'inscrivent malgré tout dans le projet impossible de l'autonomie (débouchant aujourd'hui à la domination techno-économique). Mais les transformations à venir – mutation ou *Epochenwende* – ne sont pas notre projet : ta distinction entre « l'esprit à venir » et « l'écologie sans esprit », semble souligner qu'il ne s'agit pas de faire de cet esprit un projet.

Intéressante est ta remarque sur ce que veulent ceux qui n'ont pas le bien-être matériel des sociétés développées, à savoir entrer dans la technique et l'investissement et, pourtant, non pas affirmer leurs identités, mais garder ou renouveler, si je te comprends bien, un autre rapport à l'altérité : les « richesses » de toutes les cultures. Je trouve intéressant aussi que, à propos de l'art de la Renaissance, tu parles de l'accouplement de la richesse des cieux et de la bourgeoisie. Dans un interview, tu as lié l'événement de la polyphonie dans la Renaissance à l'entrée de l'excès (du « plus ») dans le domaine de la production.

En distinguant du caractère « structurel » de l'Autre lacanien (qui témoignerait de la clôture métaphysique) un caractère « dynamique » de l'altérité, est-ce à la motilité comme technicité de l'existence que tu penses ? Et donc à une mutation de l'être-humain en cours (qui reste tout de même humaine car émanant de la condition humaine de la finitude) ? Le langage qui prendrait en charge l'hétéronomie de l'homme en tant qu'il est *gebraucht* tout en s'ouvrant à une altérité, ne présenterait-il pas tout de même et malgré tout une sorte d'autonomie paradoxale – une forme ? Non pas une autonomie de l'homme, mais du fait de son ex-ister « comme tel », ne revenant pas à un soi ; le libre cours de son aller par-delà soi-même : « sexistence » (pour reprendre un de tes termes) ?

JLN : Se détacher du projet c'est aussi se détacher du sujet. Il est remarquable que depuis le 18e et même avant chez Pascal, le « moi » est l'objet des plus fortes suspicions. Cela s'accentue avec par exemple Schelling puis Nietzsche, cela rebondit avec Kierkegaard, Heidegger et notre modernité la plus récente. Pourtant en même temps le moi ou le soi, le « par soi-même », le « *self-made man* » ou le peuple autogéré sont de puissants modèles, ou plutôt des schèmes pour des modèles rarement présentables. Il en va de même avec « l'autre » : on ne cesse de prôner l'ouverture à l'autre, le partage, etc., les valeurs démocratiques oscillent entre solidarité et fraternité mais cela reste de « bonnes intentions » (on pourrait dire une forme imaginaire du projet). On n'accède pas à une pensée « radicale » (j'emploie ce mot avec distance car il me déplaît) de l'altérité de l'autre comme inatteignable, inidentifiable même. Tu évoques mon titre « sexistence » : au fond j'ai écrit ce livre pour essayer de dire que le sexe nous confronte à l'autre – aussi en nous-même – et que cela est loin d'être simple. Mais on fait aujourd'hui du sexe : projet de consommation ou de choix de genre (je ne critique pas la pensée des genres, mais je regrette que

sa vulgate se ramène à une autonomie de choix qui tendanciellement voudrait qu'on ne doive son genre qu'à soi-même et qui
aussi ne considère pas assez l'infinie complexité interne de chaque
« genre »).

Mais le plus frappant est la disparition effective de tout projet social véritable sans que cela débouche sur un autre type de contestation et de révolution – car le projet révolutionnaire était, au moins
très souvent, un projet allant au-delà du projet, cherchant un accès
à un tout autre monde. Au contraire, l'effacement du projet so-
cio-politique se fait parce que le grand projet techno-économique
absorbe tout.

De même, tout ce qu'il y a eu de vigoureux et aussi d'utopique
(même chez Marx, même dans l'anarchisme) c'est-à-dire de rapport à une vraie altérité, sur tous les registres, tout est emporté
dans le même grand projet auquel pour finir se rallient sans le savoir ceux qui veulent réformer, améliorer, combattre l'injustice. Il
n'y a pas d'idée de la justice (sinon qu'elle est « indéconstructible »
comme dit Derrida).

Quant à l'autonomie d'un « libre cours au-delà de soi », oui,
certes et même aussi l'autonomie de la singularité existant chaque
fois. Mais cette autonomie est celle qui se réalise justement en
sortant de soi. Ou bien, peut-être mieux, en n'y entrant jamais.
Où est soi, quel est-il ? Rien avant qu'il existe, et dès qu'il existe
il s'échappe. L'enfant à peine conçu a déjà échappé à un « soi »
qui se perd en arrière dans sa généalogie et va se perdre en avant
en se séparant de sa mère, puis du sein de sa mère, puis de tout
ce qui peut l'identifier. Ainsi il devient « quelqu'un.e » – qui ne se
confond avec aucun autre malgré tous les conformismes sociaux,
culturels, affectifs, linguistiques. Ce devenir dure toute la vie et ne
cesse de devenir. Il coule comme un fleuve et « on ne se baigne
jamais deux fois dans le même fleuve ». Et ce devenir est ce qu'il
y a de plus riche dans la vie. (Bien sûr il y a des traits d'identité
physiques, affectifs, etc. Ils sont nécessaires pour que le soi-même
et les autres se repèrent. Mais le noyau ou le cœur de cet ensemble
de traits n'est pas identifiable).

Avoir 80 ans m'a porté à jeter un œil sur toute ma vie et j'éprouve
un sentiment très paradoxal : je sais que c'est moi – ici ou là, en
telle année, faisant ceci ou cela – et pourtant je n'éprouve pas
vraiment ce « moi ». Au contraire, ça me paraît bizarre que ces
situations et actions puissent être attribuées à « moi ». A Jean-Luc
Nancy, oui, mais ce nom est de pur hasard et arbitraire.

Je pense qu'avant l'époque de l'« individu » chacun.e se sentait plus pris dans un ensemble qui le dépassait – que ce soit dans l'ordre du groupe social ou bien des pulsions qui l'entraînaient. Et en ce sens chaque existence finie appartenait à une forme d'infini ou du moins d'indéfini. Notre culture a profondément changé lorsque nous avons pensé maîtriser l'infini et que nous l'avons transformé en la croissance exponentielle des biens produits et consommés, des droits des subjectivités et de l'appropriation des richesses par un nombre plus restreint repoussant ainsi un nombre toujours plus large de pauvres.

Comment l'infini de l'existence s'est-il converti en développement exponentiel de la technique, de la richesse et de la pauvreté, de la vie bourgeoise et de la famine ou de l'épidémie ? Il n'y a pas de réponse, mais c'est bien ce qui nous est arrivé. Peut-être l'humanité est-elle vouée à l'excès, ce ne serait pas surprenant. Et jusqu'à l'excès d'autonomie qu'est la destruction de soi...

Erich Hörl

The Break In and With History: Nancy's Thinking of History in Light of the Disruptive Condition

> We must therefore think this: it is the "end of the world," but we do not know in what sense. It is not merely the end of an epoch of the world or the end of an epoch of sense because it is the end of an epoch—an epoch as long as the "Occident" and as long as "history" itself—that has entirely determined both "world" and "sense," and that has extended this determination over the entire *world*. Indeed, we cannot even think of what is happening to us as a modulation of the same world or sense.[1]

1. Getting Out of History

There is a far-reaching theory of history running through and, indeed, grounding Jean-Luc Nancy's thinking. It exposes—this is the claim—the key moment of our epochality. Time and again, he highlights "getting out of History" [*sortie de l'Histoire*] as the fundamental movement happening to us, "the event of a rupture of and in History"—a movement that inaugurates "a thinking of time itself as disjunction rather than continuity [*enchaînement*], as secession rather than succession," a movement that also touches on thinking as such and, in so doing, is to trigger a "profound mutation of thought" and a shift of "the entire regime of thought."[2] This may be the core mutation toward a suspension such as has never existed, one that unfolds and manifests in the intertwined

---

1   Jean-Luc Nancy, *The Sense of the World*, trans. Jeffrey S. Librett (Minneapolis: University of Minnesota Press, 1997), p. 6, Nancy's emphasis.
2   Jean-Luc Nancy, *The Truth of Democracy*, trans. Pascale-Anne Brault and Michael Naas (New York: Fordham University Press, 2010), pp. 13 and 9. Even if the sentences just quoted concretely refer to May 1968, they also point us to the much wider reflection on the theory of history I sketch in this chapter, which forms the backdrop against which Nancy develops his reading of '68 in the first place and '68 acquires its special (sense-)historical position.

mutations of sense, of community, and of the world as Nancy's work posits them as the defining presents of our thinking.[3] Inversely, the mutations of sense, of community, and of the world—which, according to Nancy, together, in their intertwining, form the signature of our present, and which he devoted all his philosophical attention to working through—acquire their full virulence and impact only in light of this core mutation of a suspension of history that, in them, reveals all its radicalness. This, precisely, is where the immense presentness of this thinking of suspension finds its firm foundation.[4]

The "getting out of History" Nancy conceptualizes thus undoubtedly represents more than just a critical reaction to the "end of history" so frequently invoked since 1989, particularly in the wake of Francis Fukuyama.[5] From the eschatological philosophical-historical depth flow since Hegel, it takes up the manifold and ramified problem of the end: the end of philosophy, the end of sense, the end of the subject, the end of representation, the end of

---

3   Nancy's use of the concept of mutation deserves special attention. It undoubtedly becomes a central concept of the theory of history: "Mutation signifies profound, even complete change. It is more than 'transformation' and even more than 'metamorphosis.'" This is his answer to the question about what questions he seeks to capture with the idea of mutations. He uses the concept in the continuation of the concept of mutation in the theory of evolution, he explains, to emphasize the central moments of "rupture" and "inauguration," which are such central moments for the history of Mediterranean-Western civilization. The mutation at issue here takes three forms: capitalism, technics, and democracy. They are three aspects of one and the same process, which Nancy calls "production," his name for "investment in the service ... of an exponential development of given purposes." Juan-Manuel Garrido and Jean-Luc Nancy, "Phraser la mutation: entretien avec Jean-Luc Nancy," in Les Cahiers philosophiques de Strasbourg, no. 42 (2017), pp. 15–25, here pp. 15 and 16. Other civilizations may be familiar with accumulation or with profit, he stresses, but they are not familiar with "production." Nancy subsequently elaborated the mutation via the trinity of "technics, domination, and wealth" that has "determine[d] the slow gestation of the West" since Roman antiquity. "A Time to Come Without Past or Future," in The Fragile Skin of the World, trans. Cory Stockwell (Cambridge: Polity, 2021), sect. 4.
4   In gathering and condensing these mutations in the mutation of history, Nancy proves to be a great reader of Hegel. And indeed, the entire trajectory of his thinking, along which his particular thinking of history takes shape, is the expression and the consequence of a Hegel driven through Nietzsche, Marx, Heidegger, and Bataille, and, moreover, syncopated by a structuralist break with history that took place in the 1960s.
5   See Francis Fukuyama, The End of History and the Last Man (New York: Free Press, 1992).

metaphysics, the end of the human, the end of art, the end of the West, and so on. After 1950, all these ends, according to Jacques Derrida, represent the daily "bread of apocalypse"; they strike the "apocalyptic tone in philosophy."[6] Nancy brings them together precisely in and as the movement of getting out of History, be they followed by getting into a different history, into the outside of history, or into something other than history. It is, in other words, a history busy with its own deconstruction, indeed, it is the autodeconstructive movement of history that shatters itself as history: as history of sense and as sense of history, and as history of the sense of the world and as the history of the world of sense, which Nancy has absorbed in all its facets since the mid-1980s at the latest and which, in his works, seeks to be expressed.[7]

The notion that we might be "outside history" or "perhaps exposed to another kind of 'history,' to another meaning of it or perhaps to another history of history," is first developed in the 1988 lecture "Finite History"—explicitly as "sketch[ing] only the outline of a possible approach to thinking history today."[8] There, it is still charged with hope, optimistically invigorated by a possible communal reappropriation of history as *our* history that would be mindful of all these ends and take them into account. Some thirty years later—not just any years, but long winter years of an increasing crisis of deworlding globalization and the emergence of anthropocene devastations, during which the full breadth of the question of history becomes ever more significant for Nancy and urges him to give further explications—the notion is further developed in a number of texts collected in *The Fragile Skin of the World*. It now appears—not least on the basis of the increasing inclusion in Nancy's work of capital and technics as the two great drivers of the comprehensive movement of destitution, of what Heinz Dieter Kittsteiner calls an undeniable and undoubtedly destructive emergence of the "non-availability of history"[9] that now interrupts any

---

6   Jacques Derrida, *Specters of Marx: The State of Debt, the Work of Mourning and the New International*, trans. Peggy Kamuf (London: Routledge, 2006), p. 16, and "Of an Apocalyptic Tone Recently Adopted in Philosophy," trans. John P. Leavey, *Oxford Literary Review* 6, no. 2 (1984), pp. 3–37.

7   Nancy, *The Sense of the World*, p. 5.

8   Jean-Luc Nancy, "Finite History," in *The Birth to Presence*, pp. 143–166, here pp. 149–150 and 143.

9   Heinz Dieter Kittsteiner, *Out of Control: Über die Unverfügbarkeit des historischen Prozesses*, ed. Jannis Wagner (Hamburg: Europäische Verlagsanstalt, 2021), p. 12.

thought of a reappropriating making—as rather a sober statement of the profound exhaustion of the western world.[10] An exhaustion, yes, but one that, with a peculiar *Gelassenheit*,[11] might allow for, if not a communal reappropriation, then at least a "reopening and … revival" of history after history, or beyond it, namely as "*the technical creation of the singular-plural world*," and "this is what we are called upon to think now, at the beginning of the twenty-first century."[12] This is the spectrum of Nancy's reflections on the theory of history that I will lay out in what follows.

The question of history becomes a pressing one for Nancy at the latest in 1986, in *The Gravity of Thought*. He is already wrestling with the question of a different history, namely as the line of flight of his contemporary reflections, which are still largely concerned with the history of sense but already set out to unearth our epochal determination along the lines of a notion of exhaustion. The path here leads from the meanings that are exhausted and suspended to the exhaustion and suspension of history as such. The intrusion [*Einbruch*] of an unheard of, inappropriable exteriority that signals the beginning [*Anbruch*] of a different, non-signifying sense, here sweeps up history as such, shows itself to be the effect of a movement of exteriorization that suspends history itself, a movement that, as Nancy will gradually bring to light, is none other than technics.[13] From the conception of "Nietzsche's age [as] the age when all the projects of Humanity come to recognize themselves under the heading of 'nihilism,' that is, as doomed from the outset and by essence to the exhaustion of their signification," Nancy distils the central insight

---

10 Nancy, "A Time to Come without Past or Future," in *The Fragile Skin of the World*, sect. 4.

11 I use the term *Gelassenheit* on purpose, for in a way, Nancy adopts the attitude that Heidegger calls for as an openness to the as yet concealed sense of the far-reaching "change" of the technical world, to the fundamental change in and through the exit from history that his thinking not only seeks to work through but to which it also seeks to live up.

12 Nancy, "Taking on Board (Of the World and of Singularity)," in *The Fragile Skin of the World*, Nancy's emphasis. For Nancy, the end of history increasing proves to be the question of the end of the world, both questions can increasingly be mapped onto one another: "*the end of the world*, which is, in short, the ground plan of the set of *ends* that we are in the process of *traversing*." *The Sense of the World*, p. 5, Nancy's emphases.

13 See Erich Hörl, "The Artificial Intelligence of Sense: The History of Sense and Technology after Jean-Luc Nancy (By Way of Gilbert Simondon)," *Parrhesia*, no. 17 (2013), pp. 11–24.

that this event has happened, and that it is still under way (which does not mean that it is alone on this path ...), the fact that *history*, whose "meaning" has itself been suppressed, has at least this deep scansion, this caesura or syncope of signification—and that this inevitably delivers us over to *another history* which opens up before us beyond signification, a history whose meaning could never consist in a return of "meaning."[14]

It is this first reflection on an *other* history—other than a history full of sense, infatuated with it, laden with it, driven by it—that a short time later, in "Finite History," becomes the foundational notion of a theory of history in which a caesura in the history of sense and in the history of the world characterizes our present as a whole. This caesura completely absorbs history as such: "Our time is no longer the time of history, and therefore, history itself appears to have become part of history. Our time is the time, or a time (this difference between articles by itself implies a radical difference in the thinking of history) of the *suspense* or *suspension* [*suspens*] of history."[15] This moment of "suspense" is absolutely central to the entire conceptualization of "getting out of History": "Between both possibilities, to be outside history or to enter another history (for which the name 'history' no longer perhaps applies), is the 'suspense' specific to our time."[16]

At the end of the 1980s, the end of sense, of purpose, and of project, the end of history as subject, the end of History, appears as the basic moment and main marker (one Nancy returns to time and again) of this vast movement of suspension that suspends modern history as a whole:

First of all, history is suspended, or even finished, as *sense*, as the directional and teleological path that it has been considered to be since the beginning of modern historical thinking. History no longer *has* a goal or a purpose, and therefore, history no longer *is* determined by the individual (the general or the generic individual) or the autonomous person that Marx frequently criticized in the speculative, post-Hegelian way of thinking. This consequently means that history can no longer be presented as—to use Lyotard's term—a "grand narrative,"

---

14 Jean-Luc Nancy, *The Gravity of Thought*, trans. François Raffoul and Gregory Recco (Amherst: Humanities Books, 1997), p. 44, Nancy's emphases.
15 Nancy, "Finite History," p. 144.
16 Ibid., p. 150 [translation modified].

the narrative of some grand, collective destiny of mankind (of Humanity, of Liberty, etc.), a narrative that was grand because it was great,
and that was great because its ultimate destination was considered
good. Our time is the time, or a time, when this history at least has
been suspended: total war, genocide, the challenge of nuclear powers,
implacable technology, hunger, and absolute misery, all these are, at
the least, evident signs of self-destroying mankind, of self-annihilating
history, without any possibility of the dialectic work of the negative.[17]

The time of the suspense of history—a suspense or suspension in
very close proximity to Kojève's and Bataille's inactive negativity,
mere happening and acceptance of the negative without history
being sublated in a sense or a project—marks the point where a
further historical-theoretical reflection sets in that articulates the
radical consequence of this engagement for the thinking of history
itself and conceptualizes another history. In so doing, Nancy explicitly situates his work on the thinking of history in the wake of
Marx. He insists that, "in a quite different historico-philosophical
context"—and to what extent this context might be completely different, wholly other, is something we will see in a moment in reflecting on the disruptive condition—his goal is "nothing other than
a reelaboration" of the thesis Marx opposed to "the representation
of history as a subject," the thesis "that history is 'the activity of
man.'"[18] That is decisive and shows the special, perhaps even constitutive importance the reflection on the theory of history has for
Nancy's entire agenda. He undertakes this new elaboration within
the framework of his coexistential ontology via, precisely, "the determination of history as something common, or its determination
as the time of community," the determination of "the 'communi-
tarian'" or "'communist' aspect of history."[19] And perhaps we can
also say, inversely, that the project of coexistential ontology simply
draws the conclusions from the getting out of History Nancy ob-
serves, which as such seeks to correspond to this very movement.

---

17 Ibid., pp. 144–145, Nancy's emphases. Obviously, this central antiteleologi-
cal determination of history, which characterizes Nancy's end of history, strikes
at the heart of the notion of the end of history being conjured up around 1990
and shows it to belong to and depend on an obsolete teleological concept of history: Fukuyama's end of history clings to the telos of progress, an ideal finality,
an absolute orientation toward the alliance of liberal democracy and free market;
see Derrida, *Specters of Marx*, p. 72.
18 Nancy, "Finite History," p. 409, n1.
19 Ibid., p. 151–152.

This is, if you like, Nancy's first thesis on history, which dislodges and uses the suspension of history for a radical inauguration and reconceptualization: "history is community ... the proper and singular mode of common existence, which is itself the proper mode of existence."[20] It is followed immediately by a second thesis on history: history is essentially "finite history," understood as "the happening of the time of existence, or of existence as time ... *infinitely exposed to its own finite happening as such.*"[21] That is to say, "finite history is the presentation or the becoming present of existence insofar as existence itself is finite, and therefore common."[22] And in that—this might be called, finally, Nancy's third thesis on history—it is no longer a question of time; more precisely, it is not a question of "temporal succession"[23] or sequence, which the modern thinking of history granted pride of place in the form of causality, thereby turning history, strictly speaking, into a matter of nature. Instead, it now is a question of "the spacing of time itself, by the spacing that opens the possibility of history and of community."[24] From this perspective, history is now a "coming" [*venue*]—coming into presentness, a coming that does not represent the present but presents [*gegenwärtigen*] it, that lets it come—and "happening" [*arrive*]—the happening of an alterity.[25] "Coming" and "happening" are undoubtedly the main terms of this first great text on the question of history. In close proximity to Walter Benjamin's "now-time," Nancy articulates them coexistential-ontologically as "we, now":[26]

Time opened up as a world (and this means that "historic" time is always the time of the changing of the world, which is to say, in a certain sense, of a *revolution*), time opened up and spaced as the "we" of a world, for a world or to a world, is the time of history. The time or the timing of nothing—or, at the same time, the time of a filling, of a fulfilling. "Historic" time is always a *full* time, a time filled by its own *espacement.*[27]

This full time—"a time full of 'now' [as] a time full of openness and heterogeneity"—is "our time" in the most emphatic sense,

---

20 Ibid., p. 156.
21 Ibid., p. 157, Nancy's emphasis.
22 Ibid., p. 158
23 Ibid., p. 161.
24 Ibid., p. 160.
25 Ibid., p. 161.
26 Ibid., p. 166.
27 Ibid., p. 165, Nancy's emphases.

"our epoch" insofar as that means "we, filling the space of time with existence."[28] The "we, now" thus marks a radicalized participation at the heart of this theory of history, and it bears a historical index as to its appearance: "to be exposed together to ourselves as to heterogeneity, to the happening of ourselves"—for Nancy, this is ultimately a matter of decision.[29] That, in any case, is how he sees it at the end of the 1980s (and, in a reading after the fact, has seen it since '68), at a time that is very far from us today, as an originary possibility opening up in getting out of History: "We have to decide to ... be in common.... . We have to decide to make—to write—history, which is to expose ourselves to the nonpresence of our present, and to its *coming*."[30] A remarkable formulation—both as concerns the "we have to" and as concerns the "making" of history—whose problem must also be read in a proximity to Heidegger's essay "The Time of the World View," which, too, is a version of the end of the world and of history: for this "history making" by a "we" can no longer be understood in the modern sense of making, where the producing and imagining of the modern subject are intrinsically entwined, no longer in the sense of an enterprise and project,[31] let's say: no longer in the sense of production, which for Nancy—in the form of growth and thereby exceeding mere reproduction—"forms the heart of the modern time such as it began with the Roman, Christian, and bourgeois West."[32] Instead, it represents a making without making, which Nancy subsequently spells out repeatedly as creating—his counterconcept to production—and which will become a central moment of the problem he outlines.[33]

Already at this point, we must pause for a moment to ask where Nancy takes this thinking beyond production from, this beyond of production, as the innermost possibility of the historical moment

---

28 Ibid.
29 Ibid., p. 166.
30 Ibid., Nancy's emphasis.
31 Nancy, "A Time to Come."
32 Nancy, "Right Here in the Present," sect. 3, in *The Fragile Skin of the World*.
33 This takes place primarily in Jean-Luc Nancy, *The Creation of the World or Globalization*, trans. François Raffoul and David Pettigrew (Albany: SUNY Press, 2007). It is evident just how much the problem of creation, and especially the problem of creation, becomes virulent for Nancy thanks to the problem of history. I discuss his rearticulation of creation in the spirit of technology, which claims to be leading technics beyond the time of production, in greater detail in Hörl, "The Artificial Intelligence of Sense."

of suspension he is bearing witness to, for example when we think of the reflections by his friend Gérard Granel on the becoming-total of production, which sweeps up all domains of being, ideas he presented a few years later but which had been maturing for many years.[34] Today, in any case, after some thirty years of a techno-capitalist mobilization of hyperproduction, even the last illusion of a communal reappropriation shining through this "we have to make history" seems to have dissipated. That, in any event, is the ground Nancy's late development of his intervention in the theory of history in *The Fragile Skin of the World* stands on. It starts from what he succinctly calls the "collapse" [*effondrement*]. Yet for Nancy, "this 'collapse' is not an accident: it is, in a sense that has no precedent, the rational principle of our history, its reopening and its revival."[35] Confronted with "the growing dissipation of all possible ends"[36]—which, as I intimated, has been the problem that supports Nancy's history of sense, which opens up the entire problem of history but has, in the meantime, been elaborated as the truth of the nihilism of technics, as a becoming-technological of technics that leaves all finality behind—he sees us dominated, for half a century already, by a "mourning of history"[37] from which we must finally liberate ourselves. "The history of progress is complete, another history has begun in this very completion."[38] Nancy also calls this time the "ripening of the present," to which "corresponded ... the withering of the future. Hymns to tomorrow have grown muffled, blurred, and have now almost faded away. The difference between a future [*futur*]—projection and promise—and a to-come [*à-venir*]—unforeseeable, indeed unidentifiable—has imposed itself on the thinking of history."[39] As difference, the difference between *futur* and *à-venir* (so prominently staked out by Derrida) for Nancy ultimately conveys the historical mutation

---

34 Gérard Granel, "La production totale," (1992), in *Granel, l'éclat, le combat, l'ouvert*, ed. Jean-Luc Nancy and Élisabeth Rigal (Paris: Belin, 2001), pp. 37–43. I collected Granel's scattered and in part unpublished work on production in a commented edition: Gérard Granel, *Die totale Produktion. Technik, Kapital und die Logik der Unendlichkeit*, ed. Erich Hörl, trans. Laura Strack (Vienna: Turia + Kant, 2020).

35 Nancy, "Taking on Board." (Translation amended].

36 Jean-Luc Nancy, "The Accident and the Season," sect. 4, in *The Fragile Skin of the World*.

37 Nancy, "A Time to Come," sect. 1.

38 Ibid., sect. 2.

39 Nancy, "Right Here in the Present," sect. 4.

193

in question, this "getting out of History" his entire oeuvre testifies to. For the emergence of this difference as such is to mark no more and no less than this very getting out of and the possible beginning of another history from out of the collapse of the history of progress, the very History Nancy capitalizes as L'Histoire. The "coming," a coming "without past or future," here appears as the central category of the other history—characterized by a mere "emergence" [surgissement]. "The world is an emergence," we now read;[40] at least after the end of the world and all the ends tied to it, that, together, are "the end of an epoch—an epoch as long as the 'Occident' and as long as 'history' itself—that has entirely determined both 'world' and 'sense,' and that has extended this determination over the entire world,"[41] to take up once more the quotation I prefaced these reflections with. The "future," by contrast, is still and primarily a category of the history of progress, its remnant, which within the framework of the techno-economical mobilization of the present still encloses what is to come, and this remnant, according to Nancy, is precisely what the reopening of another history as reopening of world is attacking.[42]

2. The Disruptive Condition

We can and must question Nancy's far-reaching reflections in the theory of history, which define our epochality as the time of the suspension of History taking place along the unfolding of a logic of collapse [Zusammenbruch] and new beginning [Neuanbruch], as to what remains unthought in them. Nancy undoubtedly understands this logic to be at a remove from and a deconstruction of Heidegger's thinking of "an 'other beginning'"—a deconstruction that is necessary because in the latter, "the ontological logic of the starting point, of the principle—and thus of the end"[43] is still at work, a logic whose suspension, in light of the exit from History, is the matter at hand. Moreover, Heidegger's logic of the other beginning resides in close, indeed too close proximity to the "decline of the West." Inscribed in the first beginning is the "ne-

---

40 Nancy, "A Time to Come," sect. 2.
41 Nancy, Sense of the World, p. 6.
42 Nancy, "Overture," sect. 4, in The Fragile Skin of the World.
43 Ibid.

cessity of a decline"[44]—in Heidegger, the "collapse" [Einsturz] of the world and the "devastation" [Verwüstung] of the earth—he considers indispensable for the occurrence of the other beginning. Here, in this ontohistorical overbidding of Spengler's decline, all of Heidegger's antimodernism comes together. But is the logic of collapse and new beginning, which organizes the reflections on getting out of History, at far enough a remove from this problematic constellation of the Western to avoid being contaminated by it? It is, after all, the last insistence of a figure of sense that still, and precisely, endows the collapse with sense, namely the sense of the new beginning. The question of the historical signature of Nancy's peculiar mutationism arises because this mutationism itself, precisely in the logic of suspension at work in it, may not all that easily escape the eminent destructiveness of this extremely phantasmatic figure of the theory of history.

And what if the historical framework changed, if the collapse that according to Nancy allows the other history after History to begin turned out to be no beginning at all or at least to be less opening than supposed and possibly even to be closing, to be one big breakoff [Abbruch]? What if the entire figuration of collapse and beginning, which here comes to break through [Durchbruch] as the leitmotif of a thinking of history as mutation, referred us first of all to the emergence and the insistence of the break [Bruch] as such, to a pure immanence of the disruptive, a vertigo of interruption of the kind we have already been swept up in (a key trait of our epochality)? What if it thus referred us to an epochality that could be described as the epoch of the epokhē itself, since its basic moment represents the suspension as such and nothing but the suspension, a suspension become total, as it were? Have not technics and capital, which precisely in acting together under the auspices of total production triggered a destructive movement of infinitization,[45] brought us to this absolutely vertiginous abyss of a bad infinity of interruption, which

---

44 See Jean-Luc Nancy, *Banality of Heidegger*, trans. Jeff Fort (New York: Fordham University Press, 2017), p. 19. At this point, Nancy also stresses "that the anti-Semitic motif is inscribed very clearly at the heart of this configuration: the Jewish people belongs in an essential way to the process of the devastation of the world," p. 20.

45 See Erich Hörl, "Die Problematik Granels," in Granel, *Die totale Produktion*, pp. 7–37.

threatens to indeed devour history, devour it in something other than history, to be sure, but something we must conceive of as *the disruptive condition*?

In the end—this is my basic thesis—the getting out of History Nancy is laboring to describe marks the transition to the time of disruption.[46] "The disruption" here is understood as *our historical experience*, namely *after* History—historical experience in the time of the suspension and suspense of History, in which break, interruption, discontinuity take on a very different hue than in modernity, become structurally hegemonic in a peculiar way, and begin to dominate the entire ontoepistemological constitution as well as sociohistorical reality all the way down. While break, interruption already constitutively belong to incipient modernity, it is in the "saddle time" examined by Reinhart Koselleck—that is to say, the period of the transition to modernity from about 1750 to 1850— that they are always already sublated in the collective singular of the one history (no longer "history of" but "history itself") said to be borne by progress, embedded in a history of improvement and emancipation, and placed in the open horizon of (a) future. Koselleck effectively captures the significant moment of incipient modernity in his model of the separation [*Auseinandertreten*] of "space of experience" and "horizon of expectation," and it is in and as this separation that the break (of continuity), the gap, appear as characteristic of the epoch, precisely because they institute sense though the essential moments of world renewal they are coupled with—futurality, progress, emancipation, improvement.[47]

---

46 This would be the point to cross Nancy's thinking of suspension with another thinking of suspension that even, in the end, explicitly unfolded as, precisely, a critique of disruption: the thinking of Bernard Stiegler. An attempt at developing the problem of our epochality as an epoch of suspense and suspension would have to run patiently alongside their encounter, out of their encounter, indeed as their encounter. Only this encounter allows for radically developing the problem as our problem in the form I'm calling the disruptive condition. For reasons of space, I will make that attempt elsewhere. See Bernard Stiegler, *States of Shock: Stupidity and Knowledge in the 21st Century*, trans. Daniel Ross (Cambridge: Polity, 2015), and *The Age of Disruption: Technology and Madness in Computational Capitalism*, trans. Daniel Ross (Cambridge: Polity, 2019), as well as Erich Hörl, "A Thinking of Suspension: Melancholy and Politics Where There Is No Epoch," in *On Bernard Stiegler: Philosopher of Friendship*, ed. Jean-Luc Nancy (London: Bloomsbury, 2023).
47 See Reinhart Koselleck, "'Space of Experience' and 'Horizon of Expectation': Two Historical Categories," *Futures Past: On the Semantics of Historical Time*, trans. Keith Tribe (New York: Columbia University Press, 2004), pp. 255–275.

Yet since the 1970s at the latest, we have been witnessing the decay of just this structure of sense in the most varied domains. Nancy locates this moment already in the 1960s, of which he says that in them, "a form of civilization, and thus a figure of existence began to show the marks, the fissures, the tendencies of its fading away and thus also those of its metamorphosis into another configuration."[48] This has since amplified dramatically. Today, the aspect of catastrophe and crisis no longer represents the exception but the new normal. We are confronted with anthropocene devastations from climate change to the collapse of biodiversity, with pandemics and (civil) wars, market crashes, interruptions of supply chains and infrastructure, and radical contestations of democracy. In the course of the continuing dialectic of enlightenment, which thereby stages, in an unsurpassably dramatic way, how radically unfulfilled they are, the collective singulars "progress" and "history" have completely lost their conjuring power as transcendental categories. In the process, a broad closing down of future has been, and is, happening, precisely to the extent that knowledge of the future has increased, that future has been formatted, not least of all by mediatechnical procedures and the dispositifs of information, to become a programmed future. The planning of scenarios and simulations going all the way to "algorithmic governmentality," which no longer aims to predict but to preempt,[49] but also the cultivation of the future thanks to financialization, testify to the establishment of an automatic future that has been inexorably on the march since the 1970s.[50] The release, in getting out of History, of what is to come—which Nancy in his attempt to see disruption as sense considers in the sense of a radicalization of the open as the characteristic of the time that is beginning—this release has precisely not taken place; indeed, it has turned into the opposite

---

48 Jean-Luc Nancy, *La pensée dérobée* (Paris: Galilée, 2001), p. 239.
49 See Antoinette Rouvroy, "The End(s) of Critique: Data Behaviourism Versus Due Process," in *Privacy, Due Process and the Computational Turn*, ed. Mireille Hildebrandt and Katja de Vries (Abingdon and New York: Routledge, 2013), pp. 143–167, as well as Erich Hörl, "Critique of Environmentality: On the World-Wide Axiomatics of Environmentalitarian Time," trans. Nils F. Schott, in *Critique of the Digital*, ed. Erich Hörl, Nelly Y. Pinkrah and Lotte Warnsholdt (Zurich: Diaphanes, 2021), pp. 109–146.
50 See Joseph Vogl, *Capital and Ressentiment: A Brief History of the Present*, trans. Neil Solomon (Cambridge: Polity, 2022).

of the complete occupation of the open. The revolution has lost its efficacy as the historical hope for a renewal of the world.[51]

What thus emerged as structural characteristics and now develops a true power to shape experience are shock, break, and interruption—without any sublation. This is central: the only thing that remains in the suspension of History that Nancy's thinking of suspension has drawn our attention to is the experience of history as the pure repetition of its crisis aspect that radically breaks with any form of continuity except that of discontinuity itself. Disruption appears as the experience of history in the decay of a collective singular of History—an experience of history in which all of today's experiencing of, talking about, or also strategic deployment of disruption have their starting point.[52] "The disruption" thus describes a double suspension: what is suspended is not only the experience of history in the sense of the collective singulars discussed above— progress, revolution, emancipation—so is, congruently, the very possibility of such concepts as transcendental concepts that lay out and capture historical experience.[53] "The disruption" has not simply taken the place of history and inherited its transcenden-

---

51 See Enzo Traverso, *Left-wing Melancholia: Marxism, History, and Memory* (New York: Columbia University Press, 2016).

52 On the question of the historicity of the collective singular "history," see Reinhart Koselleck, "History, Histories, and Formal Time Structures", in *Futures Past*, pp. 93–104.

53 Nancy thematizes this two-fold suspension in terms of a decay of legitimacy. Thus we read in *Cruor*, for instance: "Our [civilization] draws its legitimacy entirely from the technoscientific rationality on which all legitimacy is said to be modeled. This immediately gives rise to the question: can there be a legitimacy that would stand on its own? For the moment, we observe a self-destruction rather than a self-foundation… . The question of the 'legitimacy of the modern age' is not new. But it has been visibly transformed or altered from that point onward when that which constituted, under the name of 'progress,' a potential legitimacy in the strong sense of the word vanished. For what has become doubtful are not the effects of technical progress alone but also those of the possibility of adding, opposing, or substituting another (a moral, a religious, an ideological) perspective for it. Along with progress, the project in general has passed a threshold." Jean-Luc Nancy, *Cruor* (Paris: Galilée, 2021), pp. 13 and 14. See also Jean-Luc Nancy and Marita Tatari, "Vom Geist der Epochenwende," https://www.zflprojekte.de/zfl-blog/2020/12/14/vom-geist-der-epochenwende-marita-tatari-im-gespraech-mit-jean-luc-nancy/ (accessed February 13, 2023). "What is most striking, however, is the effective disappearance of any social project worth the name without this [disappearance] leading to another kind of contestation and revolution—for the revolutionary project was, at least very often, a project that went beyond the project, seeking an access to an entirely different world. On the contrary, the erasure takes place because the great techno-economical

tality. It means that we do not even live under the shelter of the disruption; the "transcendental homelessness" Georg Lukács already spoke of becomes total only under the disruptive condition. Hermann Schweppenhäuser made this point already in the 1960s: "The next blow is already threatening. Life takes on the intermittent, interruptive aspect that the technical way of seeing things associates with the concept of the discontinuous... . Under the existential concretism of shelterlessness [*Unbehaustheit*], existence makes shelter [*sich einhausen*] in discontinuity." What reigns in the disruption, to use Schweppenhäuser's term, is "a chaos full of blind order."[54]

We live at the bidding of the disruption.[55] The description of our epochality as disruptive condition is the task before us. We must wonder what makes "the disruption" so convincing and acceptable that not only was it able to become the epitome of what change means in general (change today is disruptive or it isn't change), it also requires us to think Being today not so much as Being-with than as Being-in-the-disruption.[56] In this endeavor, we can draw on the heritage of a thinking of suspension that problematized and charted this getting out of History as such (which marks the beginning of the time of disruption) but in so doing was not sufficiently aware of the unparalleled violence asserting itself in this profound mutation, the violence of the disruption—a heritage, in any case, that must be deciphered, at least in part, namely insofar as it bets on a break and on interruption, as itself a manifestation of the disruptive condition.

---

project absorbs everything." (My thanks to Marita Tatari for making the French transcript of the conversation available.)

54 Herrmann Schweppenhäuser, "Diskontinuität als scheinkritische und als kritische geschichtstheoretische Kategorie," in *Tractanda: Beiträge zur kritischen Theorie der Kultur und Gesellschaft* (Frankfurt am Main: Suhrkamp, 1972), pp. 68–91, here pp. 76 and 70.

55 I would like to thank Christoph Görlich and Christian Voller, as well as Christina Wessely, Orit Halpern and Lars Koch for intense conversations about the socio-historical experience of disruption.

56 When I speak of *being-in-the-disruption* here, I do so in the sense of defining disruption as a historical-ontological condition. Nancy, for his part, increasingly turned his back on the concept of Being as such, first in favor of *Being-with*, then of *with*. See his conversation with Pedro Ebner, Marita Tatari, and Facundo Vega in the forthcoming special issue of *diacritics* on "Heidegger Today." (My thanks to Marita Tatari.)

Aïcha Liviana Messina[1]

Crystal Skin

A paradox seems to cut across Jean Luc Nancy's thought. On one hand, Nancy is a thinker of the mutation, which is to say, of a radical change that sticks to the processes that make possible the formation of life and thought. For Nancy, we might be at the end of an era called the West, an era that is the result of a mutation. On the other hand, and paradoxically, Nancy is a thinker of history. "The history of progress has come to an end. Another history has begun in this completion," he writes in *The Fragile Skin of the World*.[2] Thus, for Nancy, the end of history is only the end of *a* history, one that has thought events in relation to a teleological scheme. Now, how can we think the mutation and history *at the same time*? If we face a process of radical change, is it not the very ground of history, which is to say, not so much the reason that would act in it as the human being that is made through it, that is forced to be interrupted? Isn't to mutate to lose any relation to the past? As for history, isn't it made necessary by the traces that constitute us and that do not necessarily have meaning in themselves?

The image of the crystal skin, or the semantic flotation linked to this expression, can help us address this paradox.

Crystal skin[3] is a technique used to smoothen the skin and purify it from all marks of finitude. The "crystal skin" trend aims to make

---

1   This article is part of the project Fondecyt 1210921, financed by the Ministry of Science in Chile. It has been translated from French to English by Lena Taub Robles. The original version in French did not use an inclusive writing, namely a writing that includes the feminine or form of referring to gender that escapes the opposition between masculine and feminine. Indeed, those changes in our habit of writing are necessary. However, they take time, they have to be considered differently in each language because each are singulars, and they require also decisions (for instance, does using a neutral pronoun in reference to God solve the violence of the use of the masculine? Does it help think that God has no gender? Does it on the contrary elude the history of violence that dwells into language?).
2   *La Peau fragile du monde* (Paris: Galilée, 2020), p. 29. This was translated as *The Fragile Skin of the World* (Cambridge: Polity, 2021), however, this quotation and subsequent ones in this article were translated by Lena Taub Robles.
3   The expression "peau de cristal," used in the original French text, may also be translated as "skin of glass." However, we wish to emphasize the "crystal skin" technique described here.

human being not in the image of God (the unknown) but in the image of himself, "himself" being none other than the being who is constituted in the control of his image and his being, a being that is not allogenic, but rather autogenic. The "crystal skin" trend further explains the kind of human that serves as a model for robots, for example. They do not have skin yet, but they are made in the image of a being with smooth skin, a skin that may not be a skin anymore. The "crystal skin" trend thus makes us look more like robots. It says something about the mutation of human beings into machines, which are made to resemble human beings who would no longer exist. Crystal skin thus seems to eliminate finitude and otherness.

But the expression "crystal skin" also implies a certain fragility. In Spanish, "piel de cristal" refers to a hypersensitive type of person. Now, it seems that this fragility has an aspect that is generational, and it is not unrelated to the pretention of emptying all otherness from the self. If the "crystal skin" trend seeks to show a self who is entirely master of itself, a sort of hyper-individualism without complex, this latter however has a shaky aspect that is terrifying. The autogenous dimension of the individual does not express as much the mastery of the self as it expresses solitude. It does not coincide as much with the liberation of finitude as with the fact of not being able to tolerate or love it anymore. It does not reveal as much the independence of subjects as it does the fact of not being able to count anymore on a "common," if not a story. The hypersensitivity that we attribute to new generations would be the opposite of hyper-individualism. Smooth skin is like a skin without a skin, without a protective layer, a skin that lies on the surface, without wrinkles, which are also channels, knowledge, markers of a history that one crosses and crosses again ceaselessly—without wrinkles and without the history that innervates and accompanies; without the past that opens up in each wrinkle, as if this generation were exposed solely and solitarily to the future, as if it were exposed to a future without the support, the innervation of a past, of a heritage. Thus, if this hyper-individualism that crystallizes on the skin seems to ignore the debt, the other, the finitude, it is also on the skin that something belonging to a different history seems to be written or said. In its smooth appearance, without flaws or signs of otherness, the skin is the place of a naked exposure to the future.

If we stick to this double ontology of the crystal skin, we could ask ourselves whether we are confronting a form of schizophrenia, where both a naïve penchant for freedom as mastery of the self (and thus without otherness), and a tension in front of the gap of a future that imposes itself without articulation with a past, simultaneously crystallize. Or if on the contrary, the crystal skin, in its double dimension, is a way of inhabiting this time of uncertainty and mutation, of paradoxically taking account of a certain mutation of the human being. Which is to say, of making history of this moment of transition beyond history. In other words, are we confronting a self-destruction of the human being who, mutating, must simply erase himself, or are we confronting a new articulation of his history?

*

Let's begin by asking ourselves what authorizes Nancy to speak about mutation. After all, isn't mutation relative to a way of observing a given object as exterior to a subject? If this is the case, isn't it structurally impossible to think the mutation as ours?[4]

To understand how Nancy confronts this paradox, it may be useful to draw a distinction between mutation and "the end of history." The thought of history pertains to the register of meaning. Mutation, on the other hand, has to do with the process of the formation of the living. We call a radical change the way in which the living constitutes himself and adapts by mutation to his environment. A historical change, on the other hand, is understood in terms of the world of meaning that each era configures or expresses. Thus, mutation belongs to the register of life and history belongs to that of meaning.

History and mutation, however, are not dissociable. History exists from certain mutations. If Nancy can speak about mutation and history at the same time, it is precisely because, in the upstream of history as we usually conceive it, as meaning, orientation or form, there are mutations that make possible the deployment of a history. In *The Fragile Skin of the World* and in the interview be-

---

4   In regards to this, Andrea Potestà points out in "Seul le permanent change" that: "On n'est probablement jamais vraiment à même d'isoler et de montrer du doigt une mutation *comme telle*." (We are probably never truly able to isolate and point out a mutation *as such*." *Les Cahiers philosophiques de Strasbourg*, no. 42 (2017), p. 139. (Translation by Lena Taub Robles).

tween Jean-Luc Nancy and Juan Manuel Garrido entitled "Phraser la mutation,"[5] Nancy is particularly interested in the West as a mutation from which man emerges mainly as self-producing and as constituting himself in relation to his finitude. Thus, we see that the very idea of history as ground for deployment of meaning or as an orientation vector of events requires at once both the production and the finitude. History understood in its rational dimension, as deployment of a meaning, thus depends on the mutation that constitutes the advent of the West.

If the mutation is what makes history possible, the difference between the "end of history" and a mutation is that the former consists of the accomplishment of meaning, whereas the latter, at least for Nancy, is what makes possible the history that cracks, that no longer holds. "That which exhausts itself, is the West itself,"[6] Nancy writes in *The Fragile Skin of the World*. And on the back of this book can be read: "Here we are, this old skin of the world cracks." History is understood in the horizon of sense or of non-sense—nihilism being, for example, the installation of non-sense—, the mutation in which we would find ourselves, on the other hand, is due to the fact that sense and non-sense would no longer be possible. There would be neither accomplishment nor negation of meaning.

However, what allows Nancy to speak about the end, or more precisely about exhaustion—and even of a "shortness of breath"[7] of the West? Isn't the end, by definition, what eludes us? Doesn't the idea of the end, or of mutation, finally come down to what Kant calls an "illusion of reason?"

In this regard, I think that, although they refer to different processes, "the end of history" and mutation are linked in Nancy's thought. If the West is running out of steam in its sense (this is to say in its history), it is because that which constitutes it in its structure, namely the mastery that technology makes possible, turns against itself. As Günther Anders already said in *The Obsolescence of Man*, the more man has the means to act, the more he is acted

---

5   Juan Manuel Garrido, "Phraser la mutation: entretien avec Jean-Luc Nancy," *Les Cahiers philosophiques de Strasbourg*, no. 42 (2017), pp. 5–25.

6   Nancy, *La Peau fragile du monde*, p. 37

7   Jean-Luc Nancy, "Être soufflé," *Lignes*, no. 68 (May 2022), pp. 245–254, here p. 254.

upon.[8] The atomic bomb represents this reversal of a mastery that has become a hold, and we could also say of a history transformed into destiny or of a history that reaches the conditions of its mutation. In other words, for Nancy, the mutation of the West has less to do with external actors—like climate change—that require new forms of adaptation, than with internal factors. If we mutate, it is because the world is cracking from within and not that the world forces new forms of adaptation. But then, does mutation also constitute the end of all thought, of all freedom? If mutation implies an end, what else is there for us to do but to passively wait for this end to be reached? But isn't it because the end is always inaccessible, outside of the realm of knowledge, structurally unthinkable, that precisely we have everything to do? Mutation seems to imply the refusal of our freedom, and thus of history; but it is also because the meaning of mutation—that is, its history—is out of reach, that our freedom is entirely at stake.

*

Let us return to the idea of a double ontology of the crystal skin. Whether it is conceived as a smooth skin or as extreme fragility, as the concept of an autogenous self or as pure exposure on the surface of the skin, an otherness of the future, crystal skin denotes hypersensitivity. The hyper individualism of the "crystal skin" would like to be rid of all finitude, all otherness of the self, but its condition of possibility is uniquely the technique. The self that has succeeded in exposing and constituting itself in a completely smooth skin is already other; it appears as other—for example, closer to the robot than to the human being. Therefore, as has been suggested, the smooth skin lies on the surface. Paradoxically, the elimination of finitude conceals an extreme fragility. Deviating from Nancy, one could say that the mutation that can be witnessed in this double ontology operates almost a metaphysical reversal: the sensitivity seems to have entirely taken the upper hand of reason to such a point that tactile relationships have become nearly impossible, since the skin is so sensitive, incapable of instituting limits. It is often said that the so-called "millennial" generation

---

8   Günther Anders, *Die Antiquiertheit des Menschen 1. Über die Seele im Zeitalter der zweiten industriellen Revolution*, C.H. Beck, Munich (1956).

does not tolerate pain. However, I take up a distinction made by Freud in *Why War?*: that this intolerance is not moral but rather aesthetic; it has to do with the way in which sensitivity takes over what would make possible its organization (understanding, for example). This inversion is characteristic of Freud's understanding of war in his correspondence with Einstein on the question of "Why war?" Freud, who saw in war an inescapable fact, inherent to the aggressive tendencies of the living being, suggests that this unavoidable characteristic of war could eventually be inverted by the development of sensitivity. Contrary to Kant, for whom history progresses by virtue of reason, for Freud, what evolves nearly to the point of self-destruction[10] is sensitivity. As Evelyne Grossman notes in *Éloge de l'hypersensible*,[11] human beings are increasingly allergic. In this sense, although for Freud war is inherent to instinct, the increase in sensitivity makes pain intolerable. This leads to an aesthetic and not a moral refusal of the violence of war. In a way, if it is possible to foresee an end to war, it is not because it may be considered an evil but because its atrocities may no longer be tolerated. Freud's argument—which, by the way, is only a brief proposition with no real development by which he concludes his letter to Einstein—is of course questionable. As sensitivity becomes more aware, thanks to technique—that is to say, as skin becomes more exposed—the techniques of war change, and we do not perceive violence. What is interesting, however, is that the reasons that can lead to the end of war are more aesthetic than moral. Thus, it is possible to think history freed from its rational orientation. There would therefore be an orientation of a sensitive order rather than a rational one.

This metaphysical reversal, in which we can see a primacy of the sensible rather than a primacy of reason, can however be reversed in its turn. More precisely, here it is not so much about opposing once again sensitivity and reason, but about seeing that reason emerges from the sensible. In fact, if we look at the crystal skin, at the extreme sensitivity of new generations, we can notice not only that this hypersensitivity is not irrational, but that above all it has heuristic virtues and that it is even hyperrational.

---

9   Albert Einstein, Sigmund Freud, *Why War?* (Paris: Rivages Poche, 2005).

10   Indeed, Freud suggests that intolerance to pain or what I call hypersensitivity could lead to the "extinction of mankind, for it impairs the sexual function in more than one respect" and thus the function of reproduction. Ibid., p. 65.

11   Evelyne Grossman, *Éloge de l'hypersensible* (Paris: Éditions de Minuit, 2017).

It suffices to think that it is from this hypersensitivity that political movements are formed in the face of global warming, for example. This hypersensitive generation can organize politically to demand, among other things, new forms of water rationing and exploitation of resources. It is important to note that this hypersensitivity is not natural. It is forged by science, by the techniques that allow more and more precision in calculation. We know, for example, the rate of CO_2 emissions that each human being on earth implicates. In turn, this new data develops new forms of reasoning that give place to new relationships with time. Let us think about the calculation that consists in preferring to not have children in order to reduce CO_2 emissions and thus "save the planet." From this precision in calculations and the reasoning that they induce are derived new mutations, since nowadays the decision to have or not children would no longer be based on a desire for transmission or a desire for freedom, but by virtue of a calculation whose object and whose semantic matrix no longer seem to have any human aspect (except perhaps the desire to preserve the species, but then again, one comes to imagine a species without new births).

The crystal skin seems to confine one either to a high-tech, dehumanized world, or to an extreme sensitivity, where one discovers oneself to be barely less vulnerable than a newborn. However, this smooth and hyper-exposed skin organizes the living in such a way as to forge new reasons, new political claims, and therefore new imaginaries. Here, sensitivity is neither a simple container in which the real is categorized and understood, nor is it pure spontaneity without designs. We will not oppose Kant to Bacon, for example. Here sensitivity reasons, calculates, to the point of balancing between preservation or extinction of the species and of life. It is forged by technology and by the new knowledge that it makes possible; it reasons and imposes its reasons through new political organizations. It thus creates a world even though it is believed to be infantile, self-centered, or reduced to extreme vulnerability. But if the crystal skin orders itself to new forms of rationality that it produces, can we truly speak of mutation? And can we affirm, as Nancy does, that while rational history ends, a new history begins? Is it not always in the same horizon of a reason at work, of an end that we wish to pursue, and of a human being who produces himself, that this double ontology of the crystal skin puts us? Ultimately, this hyperrationality of the hypersensitive points more than ever to a reason. Are we still prisoners of a teleological conception of history without knowing it?

*

I would like to respond to this last question by sketching out two different reflections. On one hand, I would like to show how this hypersensitivity, this sensitivity that is paradoxically hyper-tech, or this sensitivity made possible by a high-tech technology, that comes to define our appearances, our identities, and thus also our sensibilities, allows us to critically analyze the Jonassian idea of a responsibility for the future.[12] On this topic, the idea of responsibility for the future has no meaning if it does not proceed from an analysis of the present and of sensible structures that would make possible a point of contact between the present and the future. Furthermore, I would like to finish by sketching a reflection anchored in the place and moment where I write, that is in Chile, where there is an ongoing constituent process, this being a project to write the pillars and principles of a society. This constituent process has the particularity that it is developed in accordance with and in response to the uncertainty of the future more than as a guiding principle that would define its meaning. A reflection on this process would allow making sense of a possible articulation between mutation and history.

In *The Fragile Skin of the World*, Nancy reminds us that for Jonas, responsibility is measured to the future. To think the skin through rationalities and the political struggles that it makes possible would allow us to see a confirmation and a realization of the Jonassian proposition in the double ontology of the crystal skin. Now, this idea elaborated by Jonas in *The Imperative of Responsibility* is not so obvious. How to respond for something of which we have no idea? Either the future for which we must answer is a continuation of our present world, but in this case, it isn't a future, but simply a present that we would like to continue having and preserving; or the future is only the distant, the indeterminate. But in this case, we do not have to answer for it. Its indeterminacy is like a reassuring horizon that puts into perspective what science can predict. In both cases, we cannot think of a responsibility for the future. Responsibility is not something that can be established by a simple calculation, nor a relationship to the indeterminate, to what may come. To be called to respond, one must be destabilized in one's present.

---

12 Hans Jonas, *The Imperative of Responsibility* (Chicago: University of Chicago Press, 1984).

Responsibility comes from an invitation where the here and now are at stake. Therefore, the likelihood of the knowledge that science contributes to understanding what the state of the climate will be in a future time is not sufficient for changing our habits.

The double ontology of the crystal skin allows us to think the responsibility and the relationship to the future in a way different to that of conforming to the new knowledge that science makes possible. First, while sensitivity may reason or may be described in terms of hyperrationality, science in contrast traumatizes. The knowledge on global warming to which science contributes has the effect of confronting us with that for which we have no categories, that for which we are not prepared. Paradoxically, scientific knowledge confronts us with a radical non-knowledge that concerns the human being. Science makes progress in the knowledge of an object to come but puts us face-to-face with the non-knowledge of the subject of this future. This trauma has several effects. On one hand, it generates new subjective devices where the subjects are not so much constituted by the past but rather by this knowledge of the future. Far from bringing control, this knowledge destabilizes. Here indeed we are not faced with an object that we could apprehend in a continuous way, which already constitutes schemas, a rationality assured of itself. On the contrary, we are in front of the unknown that we are, in front of the impotence of science and the destitution to which the precision of knowledge exposes us. If history is conceived as rational orientation, but also as heritage and the necessity to reinterpret constantly this heritage is no longer the privileged ground of new political subjects, it is because knowledge exposes us with no return and without recourse to the future, to a future that is not placed in a temporal continuity with the present, but inversely, that leaves it bare. It is not therefore that science proves and guarantees that a responsibility for the future can be imaginable, but rather that it paradoxically constitutes us radically in non-knowledge. Here, if we can say that "another history begins," it is in the sense that science exposes us to the non-knowledge of the future. It poses the future like an unknown because it forces us to understand ourselves as unknown. The mutation expressed in the double ontology of the crystal skin is not resorbed in a new teleology or rational history. The hyperrationalism of new generations can reach in a burning way what alongside Nietzsche we can call "the ignorance of the future." The calculating attitude is destined to the incalculable.

So far, we can say that we are indeed mutating. This mutation generates new sensitivities that are also new forms of rationality. This hyper-rationalism, this excess in calculation that characterizes a generation that seems to twist the future that constitutes a new birth against the smallest CO_2 emission, is however traversed by the incalculable. It is perhaps in this articulation between the calculation and the incalculable that we can affirm with Nancy that although we are mutating, "a new history begins." The Constituent process that is currently taking place in Chile helps to illustrate this idea. It proceeds from a challenge that seems to me to be paradoxical because, in a way, it proposes to write the mutation. For example, the question of nature and environmental protection are approached in terms of the idea of a paradigm shift: it has to do with thinking nature in terms of itself and not in terms of the needs of human beings. It is a question of considering the right of nature, which is not the right of man. Here, and while exaggerating the objectives of this process, which is not homogeneous, given that its representatives are diverse, the challenge would paradoxically be that of writing a text where the human being is no longer either the center or the end of the articles proposed as principles constituting a political world. It would thus be a question of proposing a text that takes note of the fact that "man passes" or that "man passes man infinitely" as Foucault and Pascal write, cited by Nancy.[13] However, this is not without contradiction: is this text not the fruit of a work, of a reflection and of human political structures? Finally, isn't nature a human postulate, and the idea of a right of nature, isn't it technical throughout? To write a constitution is indeed a technical device that goes against an unaltered idea of nature.

These paradoxes do not constitute blockages but a possible articulation between mutation and history. Here the idea of a right of nature, no matter how paradoxical it may be, is not a romantic aspiration in search of a lost origin. Rather it affirms the limits of a humanity that has arrived at the awareness that if it is the technique that constitutes it, then the technique does not make it master of the world. On the contrary, it situates the human being at the center of the cracking of the world, in what Nancy calls "the fragile skin of the world." The constituent process is a human writing, which is developed from historical categories of law, while carrying them to certain limits. One can thus say that it takes note

---

13 Nancy, *La Peau fragile du monde*, pp. 20–21.

of a mutation that has already begun, even if it is impossible to circumscribe it. But it is precisely because it is impossible to circumscribe the mutation, that it is possible to articulate it in a history, which is to say, in a common or hybrid writing, a writing that tests the waters in a world—a world that is such only on the condition of looking for lineaments of a common project. In a way, this constituent process expresses above all the desire of a world and of the possibility of political action where everything seems to turn against the human being and against its vital element. Rather than passively accepting that "man passes," rather than passively accepting the idea of mutation, we seek to build a world again within this passage. We write the passage of man. Now, to write, is already to make history. It is to constitute this passage as trace or promise; as idea or failure; as imaginary or pitfall. Here, in this writing of the impossible, in the paradoxical project of a right that passes the right, mutation and history would be articulated. Where to pass does not mean to be surpassed but to inhabit the passage, to propose its lineaments and to make of these lineaments traces to be interpreted, confronted, to be replayed—as if, in this exposure of the skin's surface to the future, to a pure future of any past, it were necessary to build the past of a passage. Here history would consist in looking for a writing that, while not guaranteeing any knowledge, would allow us to be not so much the authors of the mutation, but its readers. In this way, without having any certainties, we do not remain passive in front of the mutation, and we respond to a future that we try to constitute as a trace.

Susanna Lindberg

Splendid Splintered Being

It is easy to notice that the words "splendid splintered being" of my title, while not exactly a translation, are nonetheless a nod to the word "éclat," which is one of Nancy's many signature words. What is *éclatant* is brilliant, radiant, shining, splendid in the sense of *splendor*. With Nancy, we do not seek the splendor of the sun outside of Plato's cave, but the brilliance of *éclats*, splinters like sparkles that spangle throughout the night. This splintering does not belong to high Romanticism's nocturnal visions. It belongs to the world *en* éclats, shattered, because originarily éclaté, which is not exactly exploded but dispersed and fragmented; such is "the space that is common to us all... at once as a distended, desolate extension—the 'desert that grows'—and as a broadly open, available extension."[1] In this paper, I would like to show that this éclat is also the mineral glare or sheen that lies in the bosom of the Earth and that signals Nancy's unheard-of *philosophy of nature*.

The title "splendid splintered being" translates l'être *en* éclats rather than l'être éclatant, and it thereby deliberately mimics the title of Nancy's wonderful article "Shattered Love" ("Amour en *éclats*"). Of course, splendid splintered being has everything to do with splendid splintered love, because the latter is fundamentally the love of being's splendor, that is, the hard and impenetrable core of philosophy, as explained in another article, "Le cœur des choses."[2] Being is what I will speak about. The question of being is at the heart of Nancy's thinking, for him it is the invisible core question of philosophy, its most splendid question, even after it has lost its once solid ground, has encountered the catastrophe of groundlessness, has been exploded and splintered by the force of nothingness. Ever since *The Experience of Freedom*, being is for Nancy the freedom that "bursts" and "shatters into splinters"

---

1   Jean-Luc Nancy, *Le sens du monde* (Paris: Galilée, 1993), p. 20. English translation: *The Sense of the World*, trans. Jeffrey S. Librett (Minneapolis: University of Minnesota Press, 1997), p. 9.

2   "Amour en éclats" and "Le cœur des choses" are both published in Jean-Luc Nancy, *Une pensée finie* (Paris: Galilée, 1990). As "Le cœur des choses" is not included in the English translation of *Une pensée finie—A Finite Thinking*, ed. Simon Sparks (Stanford: Stanford University Press, 2003)—I will refer to the French edition. The translations are my own.

("la liberté essentiellement s'éclate").[3] Freedom *is* the "archi-originary bursting of pure being" ("éclatement archi-originaire de l'être pur")[4] and its lightning-like irruption into existence ("Avec l'éclat—éclair et éclatement, éclatement d'un éclair—c'est le coup d'une *fois*, l'irruption existante de l'existence."[5])

Nancy works within the aftershock of the earthquake that was the crisis of metaphysics, a crisis which began to shatter philosophy in the early twentieth century and whose continuous quaking actually defines the field of "contemporary continental philosophy." Nancy works literally *right up against* phenomenology, *tout contre la phénoménologie*, which started, after all, explosively with the *epoche* of the question of being. Of course, instead of simply suppressing metaphysical questions, phenomenology sedimented, transmuted and decanted them, until Heidegger unearthed them in a rejuvenated form by posing his epoch-making "question of the sense of being." Nancy's thinking only makes sense right up against this question, through which Heidegger re-philosophizes phenomenology. Nancy comes right after the Heideggerian question of being and draws the energy of his work from his opposition to it, hence it makes sense for us to explain Nancy's thinking of being against Heidegger's.[6]

Nancy and Heidegger don't share the same metaphors: Heidegger does not invoke the question of being in terms of mineral or sidereal splendor. As soon as he asks what makes the luminous *Lichtung* possible, he starts to hearken to sounds and calls coming from the distance: For him, the darkness surrounding being is like a forest of audible echoes, not the firmament of visible sparkles. But these images are utterly secondary to the fact that Nancy and Heidegger share the same situation of thinking, namely, the necessity of starting with *being-in-the-world*. Heidegger describes it in terms of the *Dasein* (who is the place in which being becomes a question), and of *Being*, which is nothing substantive or substantial but the event of being (*Ereignis*) and the gift of being and time (*es gibt Sein, es gibt Zeit*). According to *Identität und Differenz*, the

---

3   Jean-Luc Nancy, *L'expérience de la liberté* (Paris: Galilée, 1988), p. 80. English translation: T*he Experience of Freedom*, trans. Bridget McDonald (Stanford: Stanford University Press, 1993), p. 57.

4   Ibid., p. 81 / 58.

5   Ibid., p. 110 / 82.

6   See Nancy, *Le sens du monde*, p. 32 / *The Sense of the World*, p. 17. I explain Nancy's relation to phenomenology in more detail in my "Pourquoi Jean-Luc Nancy n'est-il pas un phénoménologue?," *Lignes*, no. 68 (2022), pp. 225–232.

two are maintained in relation by their intimate correspondence—by the co-respondence in which one calls for the other, which is also the internal structure of the *Lichtung* of *aletheia*.

Now let us see, step by step, how Nancy deconstructs all the elements of this fundamental situation: the *Dasein*, the question of being, and the *Lichtung*. After that, we should be able to see how he digs into the Earth and discovers in its depths the glimmer of a mineral sidereal being.

1.
How does Nancy deconstruct Heidegger's *Dasein*?

It is well known that especially in *Being Singular Plural* he invites us to a redoing of the existential analytic from the point of view of being-with, such that the *Dasein* is rearticulated as *Mitsein*. Especially in *Corpus*, he also develops a thinking of bodies, *corpora*, that add weigh, sense, and even sensuality to existence. These are important moves in the direction of an originary ethics, but this is not my direction here.

This time I am interested in the *Dasein* only as the place of the question of being. When Heidegger speaks of the *Dasein* facing the event of being, he mostly appears to describe a call heard by a solitary thinker. In this moment the *Dasein* is alone, not radically alone as in being-towards-death, nonetheless apart from the tumultuous crowd. It (the *Dasein*, it feels silly to refer to it by the gendered pronouns "he" or "she" so I say "it")—*it* is not totally isolated because it is in dialogue with the few other thinkers and poets who have also heard the call of being, but these are never its contemporaries. These are either in its past, like Heraclitus and Hölderlin, or yet to come, but never here and now, *da*. Those who have heard the calling of being and who try to respond to it in their irremediably preparatory work are rare, separated, courageous, often tragic thinkers and poets who sometimes lapsed into folly. The subject of philosophy is not the abstract, nameless ego: It is a *Dasein* responsible for the question "who?". And although this is a question with no definitive answer, the "who?" is still a thinker or a poet whom we can *name* in our dialogues with him (never her).

Nancy turns totally against this heroism of thinking. (Actually it was Philippe Lacoue-Labarthe who had deconstructed the heroism of thinking, but Nancy presupposes his friend's work everywhere.) Nancy's thinking is anti-phenomenological insofar as it does not build on a first-person point of view nor does it even pose the question of the subject of philosophy: There is no ego, no self-consciousness, no transcendental ego nor even the *Dasein*. Nancy does not speak about the *thinker* but about *thinking*, *la pensée* (that must in his case be translated by *thinking* rather than *thought*, although both are linguistically correct). In this respect he is much closer to Hegel than to Heidegger.

What is this "thinking"? Nancy explains it concisely in "La surprise de l'*évènement*." Thinking has no subject—although a subject can sometimes result from thinking, as in the cases of Descartes, Kant and Hegel, whom Nancy studied in his first books. Instead of being a subject's *act*, thinking *happens*, it *takes place*. It surprises; it also surprises *itself* when it realizes that it does not know *who* thinks, *what* is thinking, and even *if* this is thinking. Thinking happens, it comes and surprises.[7]

Although thinking is not the subject's act, the surprise of thinking still happens *to us* and actually makes a *community* of us. Nancy emphasizes that thinking happens to a *plurality* (also practically: Nancy belongs to the rare philosophers who actually worked together with others, especially, but not only, with Lacoue-Labarthe). One does not think alone, thinking happens to more than one: Not to the *rare ones* described by Heidegger, the solitary heroes of being who stand always alone, each one marking an epoch of the history of being, but to *more than one* who share a need of thinking *here and now* and who therefore form something that Nancy calls a community, a generation, or an epoch.[8] This is not a fusional community of a common sense: Like Nietzsche's "we good Europeans" ("*nous autres bons européens*"), it is the community of stellar

---

7   In this, Nancy is momentarily close to the kind of phenomenology that developed the idea of *asubjective thinking* (especially Jan Patočka) but Nancy does not speak in negations (*a*-subjective, *non*-subjective) because as a good Hegelian he believes that negations conserve what they wish to overcome.

8   For example, Nancy notes that the task of rethinking concepts such as the *event* or the *worldliness of the world* was more than shared—undertaken together—by many thinkers at that time. See Nancy, *The Sense of the World*, note 19, p. 176; and Jean-Luc Nancy, *Être singulier pluriel* (Paris: Galilée, 1996), note 1, pp. 48–49, Jean-Luc Nancy, *Being Singular Plural*, trans. Robert D. Richardson and Anne O'Byrne (Stanford: Stanford University Press, 2000), note 32, p. 198. Following Nancy's idea, in a symposium and hopefully in this collective book too, I do not think, argue, and claim alone, but thinking might *take place*, *we* might be surprised by thinking. *We* think with Nancy and with one another, not because we say the same thing but because we share a common *cause* of thinking.

friends (*Sternenfreundschaft*) who do not need to agree in order to be with each other.

In *The Sense of the World* especially, Nancy shows why the question of thinking is also the question of *style*. "Thinking is surprised when the event happens." Style emerges from this surprise of thinking when it engages a work of sense. Style must be thought in a polemical relation to the idea of *method*. Method is the answer Modern philosophy gives when asked how it reaches truth and what makes it think that this truth can be shared by others. Rationalism, empiricism, dialectics, phenomenology, logical empiricism are methods in this sense: ways of exposing truth (e.g. as critique, as system...) that each time also determine the kind of subject that can reach this truth. Heidegger's description of the *path* of thinking (*Gang*) was already a deconstruction of the principle of the method, because a path is not a general tool of thinking but a *unique* trace of the experience of being. Nancy's idea of *style* rises from the same necessity for thinking to reflect upon its own gesture. However, for Nancy, the style is neither a universal method nor is it just the trace of a singular experience, for it also bears the trace of a *shared experience* that determines a certain *community* of thinking. For example, Nancy thinks that Heidegger and Badiou write in the style of truth, whereas Nancy and some others look for *another gesture* and "this different gesture is what is at stake in contemporary philosophical labor."[9] It looks for "another style, writing and exscription of philosophy" which does not think in the register of phenomenon anymore but in the register of "the dis-position (spacing, touching, contact, crossing)."[10] As Nancy explains in the chapter "Philosophical Style" in *The Sense of the World*, the other style that he is looking for keeps a distance from the splendor of appearing—éclat, again—that defines the phenomenological style as well as from the oracular-poetic style of late Heidegger. It needs to distinguish itself both from myth and from science; it is engaged in a debate with literature in order to find a certain *absence of style*; and it develops as a *sharing of voices*.[11] All

---

9 Nancy, *The Sense of the World*, p. 19.

10 Ibid., p. 176.

11 A style that corresponds to the ex-cription of the sense of the world must respect this world. *Ceterum censeo*: I believe that the style of writing expected of academic philosophers today, and that is taught to students, is totally without style and therefore incapable of enunciating the sense of the world. *When using it, we stop thinking.*

of this deserves to be explained in detail, but here it suffices to say that these considerations do not rise from "acoustic-decorative" aesthetic concerns but reflect the *ethos of thinking* that needs to correspond to its task, *making sense of the world*. Style results from thinking conceived as a praxis of sense.

2.
How does Nancy deconstruct Heidegger's *question of being*?

We know that especially in *Being Singular Plural,* Nancy counters the Heideggerian question of being by developing a thinking of singular plural being. Although the idea of singular plurality can also evoke a very different path to being than the one chosen by Heidegger—that chosen by Democritus, Lucretius, Spinoza, and Deleuze—its radicality comes to the fore when it is examined as a deconstruction of (Heideggerian) phenomenology.

The first element of this deconstruction is the destruction of the very form of the *question*—a work Derrida already started in *De l'esprit*. Nancy does not formulate a question of being coming from yonder and catching the thoughts of the *Dasein*. Thinking happens directly on things *because there are things*. Nancy exposes it in the most profound fashion in "Le cœur des choses" where he says: "At the heart of thinking there is something that defies all appropriation by thinking [...] this thinking is nothing else than the immanent immobility of things, *that there are* things."[12] The "there are," the *qu'il y a des choses*, is the weight and the gravity of things even before there is presence.[13] Like "the heart or the core of the stone exposes the stone to the elements," Nancy continues, things are there in that they are exposed to the element of their use and usury, so that "the event itself, the coming to presence of the thing, participates in this elementary essence." Furthermore, as soon as the thing is there and comes to presence, "it is already sense, it is in the element of sense."[14] This is how the anonymity of being is *exscripted* directly in things, so that it can eventually be further exscripted in whatever writing. I would love to show—but I can only mention it here—how this heavy, anonymous upheaval of things, this movement between their gravity and their exscription

---

12 Nancy, *Une pensée finie*, p. 199.

13 Ibid., pp. 200–201.

14 Ibid., pp. 202–203.

to presence, sense and writing, doubles the profound dialectics between gravity and light that is the core of Schelling's philosophy of nature. Neither Schelling nor Nancy begin the thinking of nature from the subject; both describe it as the upheaval of elemental being that is there, and then most surprisingly turns into thinking in the movement Schelling calls *light* and Nancy calls *exscription*. When Nancy describes the heavy movement of *being that is there*, he is also very close to Derrida's *khora*,[15] except that Nancy describes the core of things in terms of the heaviest possible materiality, whereas Derrida describes the origin of sense in terms of a fictive materiality without matter.

By thinking things insofar as they *are there* and *bring about* thinking, Nancy distances himself from the thinking of the *gift of being* developed by many later phenomenologists. It is true that he sometimes describes being in terms of the *offering* of *agathon*[16] or of the sublime offering at the limit of presentation.[17] In these examples, "offering" has a positive sense only insofar as it is opposed to the idea of the *gift* of being, because the latter tends to project a *giver*: The gift holds an echo of the ontotheological creator God even when it has been replaced by the neutral "*es*" of "*es gibt Sein*" and "*es gibt Zeit*." Being is not given *by* and it is not given *to*: Being *is* and this is why *we are*, too. In the article "L'amour en éclats," which is like the second section of the article "Le cœur des choses," Nancy proposes a thinking of *love* that oversteps the debate on economical vs. aneconomical *exchange* that haunts the discussion of the gift. As he says: "Love frustrates the simple opposition between economy and noneconomy. Love is precisely—when it is, when it is the act of a singular being, of a body, of a heart, of a thinking—that which brings an end to the dichotomy between the love in which I lose myself without reserve and the love in which I recuperate myself, to the opposition between gift and property."[18] Although love is all the singular sparkles of love (éclats *de l'amour*) that stud the world, the article aims at more than a human emotion: It aims at love as the ontological constitution of things. Nancy describes the coming to presence of beings as the love that bursts out in "outbursts of joy"—I would translate

---

15 Ibid., note 1, p. 208.
16 Nancy, *The Sense of the World*, p. 53.
17 Nancy, "The Sublime Offering," in Nancy, *A Finite Thinking*, p. 239.
18 Nancy, *A Finite Thinking*, p. 260.

éclats *de joie* by "sparkles of joy"—of being.[19] "There is this brilliant or shattering constitution of being [or sparkling constitution of being: *constitution* éclatante *de l'*être]. Love does not define it, but it names it, and obliges us to think about it."[20] The coming to presence of being is its love and thinking is the love of being.

As was said above, the second element of Nancy's deconstruction of the Heideggerian question of being is his opposition, in the name of its *plurality*, to the unity of being. He does not demonstrate the plurality of being but on the contrary posits it as the fundamental principle on which everything else rests: "*The plurality of beings is at the foundation [fondement] of being.* A single being is a contradiction in terms."[21] Nancy does not say that there *is being* but that there *are things*: "If there is something, there are several things, otherwise, there is nothing, no 'there is.'"[22]

Among the many consequences of the fundamental plurality of being, it suffices to mention two here. Firstly, it invites us to think finitude not as privation but as relation.[23] Finitude is conceived as privation above all by Heidegger, who thinks it as a relation to death or to nothingness. In order to think finitude as relation, it is not enough to conceive of it as a relation that stretches between already constituted beings, but one has to understand how *being happens by the spacing* or *by the distending* in which and from which things *result*. In other words, being is not an interiority that can also express itself to the outside. Instead, "the sense of being is existence, it is being-self-outside-of-self."[24] Being is être-*à*, *being-right-here* is also *being-towards*. Being is nothing else than being exposed to (être *exposé*) and being exscripted (être *excrit*). As we shall see in a while, because spacing is originary, sense emerges in the happening of space between things. Another important feature of the plurality of being is the eventlikeness of being. Things are not eternal like Lucretius's atoms, they are eventlike, they happen, and maybe they are just events. Their being is not a constant light, it flickers, twinkles, glitters, sparkles.

---

19 Ibid., p. 273.
20 Ibid.
21 Nancy, *Being Singular Plural*, p. 12.
22 Nancy, *The Sense of the World*, p. 58.
23 Ibid., pp. 29–30.
24 My translation from Nancy, *Être singulier pluriel*, p. 31. See Nancy, *Being Singular Plural*, p. 12.

3.
How does Nancy deconstruct Heidegger's *Lichtung*?

What Heidegger calls *Lichtung*, clearing, is being-in-the-world in the event of truth, *aletheia*. *Lichtung* is truth as the opening of the world in the light of being. Such an opening can take place because being gives itself as a question to the *Dasein*—who takes it upon itself to look for the sense of being. Heidegger also describes *Lichtung* in pseudo-poetic terms, the kitschy sound of which Nancy rejects, but which still belongs essentially to Heidegger's thinking. In such terms, *Lichtung* is the ray of light in the midst of obscurity and the deeper resonance in the midst of silence. It is also the domain of simplicity that can only be found when the noisy rustling of technological civilization is silenced, if only for a moment. However, it is not an Edenic state of nature: It is a historical place that is deployed in language when noisy everyday chatter gives way to poetry and thinking.

In *The Sense of the World*, Nancy says that the style of thinking that he is after distinguishes itself from such a style of truth and instead seeks the gesture of sense. For Nancy, truth is *being-such* (*l'être-tel*) whereas sense is *being-towards* (*l'être-à*).[25] Truth *punctures* whereas sense *connects* one to the other, *le sens enchaîne*, in the sense of relating, associating, linking.[26] Truth "punctures" because it takes place between being and the *Dasein*, who is struck as if by lightning by the question of the sense of being. The stroke of this question opens up the *Lichtung*. Sense *connects*, and what is most important is that it does not link being and thinking in mutual responsiveness, it connects things with one another. I like to think that sense not only connects human beings but all kinds of things: "*Some*thing is free to be stone, tree, ball, Pierre, nail, salt, Jacques, number, trace, female lion, daisy."[27] These open lists of very different things can be found in many of Nancy's texts and especially in *Corpus*, where they exemplify the unlimited plurality of things that are there.[28] Sense takes place as spacings between all kinds of

---

25 Nancy, *The Sense of the World*, p. 12.

26 Ibid., pp. 14, 176.

27 Nancy, *Une pensée finie*, p. 221.

28 Jean-Luc Nancy, *Corpus* (Paris: Métailié, 1992), English translation: "Corpus" in *Corpus*, trans. Richard A. Rand (New York: Fordham University Press, 2008), pp. 2–121. See also Nancy, *The Sense of the World*, p. 56: "It is a question of understanding the world not as man's object or field of action, but as the spatial

things and not only between humans. Sometimes the exscription of sense leads to thinking. But not all sense is philosophical nor is it necessarily human. Sometimes it is just the pressure of beings against one another, sometimes their practical use of one another, sometimes their sensitive touching, sometimes the intellectual signifying.

Another feature that differentiates Nancy's "sense" from phenomenological "truth" is the explicitly *technical* nature of sense. For him: "Sense is identical to the exercise of techne." Classical phenomenology tends to look for truth cleansed of the artifices of technics. Hence Heidegger's *Lichtung*—even though it must ultimately be articulated by language—is characterized by silent simplicity that can only be discerned if the technical framework of *Ge-stell* is removed. Analogically, Merleau-Ponty's flesh—although it is also revealed by art—is exemplified firstly and foremostly by carnal, sensitive touching. Nancy, on the contrary, defines the spacing of things in terms of technics—that is not just the way in which humans use nature but the way in which things relate to one another. In *The Sense of the World*:

> The world of technology, or the "technicized world", is not nature delivered up to rape and pillage. [...] It is the world becoming *world*, that is, neither "nature", nor "universe" nor "earth". [These are names for rationalized totalities.] World is the name of a gathering [*assemblage*] or being-together that arises from an *art*—a *tekne*—and the sense of which is identical with the very exercise of this art. [...] It is thus that a world is always a "creation": a *tekne* with neither principle nor end nor material other than itself. [...] But it is necessary to come to appreciate "technology" as the infinite of art that supplements a nature that never took place and will never take place. An ecology properly understood can be nothing else than a technology.[29]

In other words: Technics is not the way in which human beings use nonhuman beings. It is the way in which all things are together as world. Things do not just brush against one another like an impenetrable atom grazes another one. Things affect one another because their very being is being-to-the-other. This "to," this "à," is not just a neutral contact over the gap opened in the contact itself,

---

totality of the sense of existence, a totality that is itself *existent,* even if not in the mode of *Dasein.*"

29 Nancy, *The Sense of the World*, p. 41.

it is an active spacing in which things relate to each other *practically*. The *praxis* of things is neither a *theoria* nor a *poiesis*:[30] It is a *techne* and an art. We are used to speaking of human technics, but here technics characterizes everything that is. If one wants to distinguish a properly human *praxis*, then it would be the knotting of bonds, *nouage du lien*, and the tying of sense, *nouage du sens*,[31] that characterizes politics.

4.

At the beginning of this paper, I said that I would like to show you a glimpse of an unheard-of *philosophy of nature* that Nancy evokes and sketches but never completes. So: Does Nancy's singular plural being really imply a philosophy of nature, which he invokes several times but always in a conditional or future tense? (But also: Can contemporary philosophy of nature exist in any other tense, must it not always *tend towards* a natural science in perpetual becoming and work *with* it?)

Indeed, Nancy's philosophical work does not contain a fully-fledged philosophy of nature—no more, by the way, than it contains a fully-fledged philosophy of technics, either. However, he often points at the possibility of a philosophy of nature, at least at the time when he called his philosophy a materialism and an atheism,[32]—before he got caught in (what I consider to be) the ambiguous spiderweb of the deconstruction of Christianity.

What I call Nancy's philosophy of nature includes *all things there are*—"*some*thing is free to be stone, tree, ball, Pierre, nail…"—but it lingers on two exemplary types of beings: the stone (*pierre* without the capital letter) and the farthest reaches of outer space (*confins*). These examples belong to phenomenal nature and not to the mathematized image of nature constructed since early Modernity. In the framework of phenomenology, it is noteworthy that Nancy's examples belong to the *mineral* kingdom and not to the domain

---

30 "Technology is quite precisely that which is neither *theoria* nor *praxis*. […] *Tekne* makes coming get going, so to speak, where 'coming' refers to différance of presentation. *Tekne* thus withdraws from presentation the values of 'self' (on the side of the origin) and 'presence' (on the side of the end)." Nancy, *The Sense of the World*, pp. 40–41.

31 Ibid., pp. 103, 111.

32 "It will thus be a matter of 'atheism', but of an atheism where everything demands to be done," Nancy, *The Sense of the World*, note 54, p. 184.

of *life* that has stimulated many contemporary philosophers (after the German Romantics: Nietzsche, Heidegger, Derrida, Deleuze, Agamben...). Nancy links the stone to Heidegger's famous lecture course *Fundamental Concepts of Metaphysics*, in which the stone is defined as "worldless," whereas the animal and the human are defined as different *accesses* to the world. Against Heidegger, he asks why the "access" to the world should be defined in terms of identification and appropriation—"why could the world not also a priori consist in being-among, being-between and being-against? In remoteness [or in distancing: éloignement] and contact without 'access'?"[33] Here we find once again the move from truth to sense, from puncture to relation, and now from sensitive experience to the numbest contact. For the contact is the minimal condition of being. In "Le cœur des choses," the stone stands for the immobile inaccessible core of things (and not for their beating heart), for the fact of their *being there*, for the *gravity* of their being and also for the hard glimpse, éclat, of their presence to one another. The *stone* is the surprise of existence (or as Nancy said in *The Experience of Freedom*: "the stone is free"[34]). It can be captured by signification, like when it is the stone of Kaaba or Christ's gravestone,[35] but it does not need such a capture to be the surprise of being-there.

The simple mineral is also the first step of the philosophy of real nature in Hegel's philosophy of nature. In his systematic presentation, the stone stands for *gravity*, which is for him the first, albeit paradoxically *unliving*, phase of the *logic of life*, whose movement is conserved in a petrified form in the stone. Gravity is the fundamental law of heavenly mechanics, whose slow waltz appeared to the Moderns as the regular harmony of the closed solar system, but which has totally exploded, éclaté, in contemporary astronomy [following the soundtrack of Kubrick's *2001 Space Odyssey*, con-

---

33 Ibid., p. 59. Nancy also speaks about the stone in "Le cœur des choses," Nancy, *Une pensée finie*, pp. 202, 214–217.

34 Nancy, *The Experience of Freedom*, p. 159. Nancy continues: "In this sense, the stone is free. Which means that there is in the stone—or rather as it—this freedom of being that being is, in which freedom as a 'fact of reason' is what is put at stake according to co-belonging." Then he continues by emphasizing that this claim is above all a question and a provocation.

35 Nancy, *Une pensée finie*, pp. 207, 217. Christ's gravestone is central to Jean-Luc Nancy, *Noli me tangere* (Paris: Bayard, 2003). English translation: "*Noli me Tangere*," in *Noli me Tangere, on the Raising of the Body*, trans. Sarah Clift, Pascale-Anne Brault and Michael Naess (New York: Fordham University Press, 2008), pp. 3–56.

temporary celestial harmonies sound like György Ligeti rather than Johann Strauss[36]]. Nancy says that "In order to be understood as a world of sense—of 'absent sense' or exscribed sense—the world must also be understood in accordance with the cosmic opening of space that is coming towards us [...]."[37] "Today, if something like a 'philosophy of nature' is possible in a new way, it is as a philosophy of confines [*confins*: the farthest reaches of outer space]."[38] Such a philosophy of nature follows the movement of the explosion of classical celestial harmony, of the expansion of space truly *partes extra partes*, of the splendid splintered sparkling extension of infinite space. The obscure shining stones are the ontological measure of this space.

The mineral, sideral character of Nancy's "philosophy of nature" helps in understanding the particular kind of materialism he is after. Although he refers fondly to the ancient atomists, it is only in order to nod to the infinite plurality of things and to the indifference of star-gods, but not in order to embrace the idea of the ultimate components of the world. Matter is neither the unique substance of being nor the plurality of elementary substances: Nancy's materialism follows his ontology and is the thinking of plurality in terms of the *events* that take place *between* things. Because it thus thinks being in terms of the event of sense, Nancy's materialism is still a phenomenological materialism, if matter can be said to be a phenomenon, or a materialism which brings phenomenology to its extreme limits—where it can also be expressed in terms of a modal ontology, as Boyan Manchev shows in this volume. Heidegger loaded his word *Earth* with the phenomenological impossibility of thinking of matter or of thinking of it otherwise than as the limit of the world. Derrida reinterpreted the same impossibility in terms of *khora*, which is a thinking of materiality as the retreating of materiality, and a thinking of this dimension, not as a simple limit, but as an understanding that here thinking must rely on bastard reasoning, almost on fiction. Contrary to this, Nancy does not stop at the thinking of the limit of experience but oversteps it towards the thinking of the limit that a thing is to the other thing. He does not see the Earth as an impenetrable obscurity but he digs for the stones whose glare shows the extension of the obscurity;

---

36 Nancy refers to the film and its music in Nancy, *The Sense of the World*, pp. 38–39, but he only names Strauss.

37 Ibid., p. 37.

38 Ibid., p. 40.

he does not see the universe through the myth of an artisan god but through the planets and the stars. Like Hegel, he affirms the materiality of things and a material thinking of this materiality, and like Schelling, he shows how thinking is the way in which the gravity of matter itself turns into shards of presence that make the "brilliant or sparkling constitution of being (constitution éclatante de l'être)."

Boyan Manchev

La philosophie éclatante
or
Jean-Luc Nancy and the Struggle for the World

Jean-Luc Nancy, *La Philosophie en éclats*

Jean-Luc Nancy was one of the few contemporary philosophers who maintained in the firmest possible way the task of philosophy before the world. That is why today his philosophy, having set philosophy itself as a task, stands before us as a task. Therefore, our task—our duty and our desire—before it is a task before philosophy itself.

There is no doubt that Nancy's thought is among those which determine contemporary philosophy. We know out of experience that it provokes, mobilizes and even *ignites* thinking, but so far we still feel the need to imagine and decide on the *meta-concepts* to face its power—i.e., not simply to treat it as an object of the history of philosophy, but to further think it "from within," to think *with it*. Thinking with it, beyond idiosyncratic fascination or epigonous reproduction, remains our friendly duty towards Nancy's philosophy.

Empirical facts always run the risk of becoming fixed conventions with no heuristic potential. For instance, Nancy's early association with the method of deconstruction does not suffice to explain the originality and the crucial place of his philosophical work, especially in a moment when the history of contemporary thought itself has sunk into profound disorientation. Over the last year, when, as anticipated, the mourning of the singular subject of this philosophy enhanced the intensity of discourse in accord with the intensity of affective experience, we also witnessed the emergence of new powerful endeavors for synthetic expression of the singular phenomenon of this philosophy—themselves bearing witness to the incandescent power of Nancy's thought, of its irreducible, *living* force. In the present text I will in turn make an attempt to propose a perspective on the lines of force in his philosophy. Needless to say, it would be impossible to fully detach this attempt from my quarter of a century long dialogue with it—a dialogue that transformed our friendship into a true philosophical encounter. It is difficult to produce a *cold* synthesis out of it. Therefore, what follows is also an inevitable attempt to remobilize Nancy's philosophy in the perspective in which I have been trying to think and work *on* and *with* it: the perspective of *modal ontology*—a transformative dynamic reflection on the world and the subject.[1] That is why, in my attempt to strengthen this dialogue and intensify its continuity, I will hereby follow a line of force—that of materialist transformative ontology.

*

The first and perhaps major challenge that those approaching Nancy's thought will have to face is its unusual form. Neither systematic in the conventional sense, nor entirely fragmentary in the Pascalian or Romantic-Nietzschean traditions, its method resists the established meta-theoretical notions. We can therefore define Nancy's philosophy as *asystematic* instead of unsystematic. It is indeed fragmentary, but only in the sense of the Romantic writing in fragments, as it was defined by Friedrich Schlegel and interpreted by Lacoue-Labarthe and Nancy himself in *The Literary Absolute*. Nancy's method is therefore *asystematic*, but at the same time fos-

---

1 *Modal ontology* is an operational term that I introduced and developed along the way in my work over the last two decades. See for instance Boyan Manchev, *L'altération du monde. Pour une esthétique radicale* (Paris: Éditions Lignes, 2009) and Boyan Manchev, *Svoboda vypreki vsichko, t. 1: Svryhkritika i modalna ontologia* [*Freedom in Spite of Everything*, vol. 1: *Surcritique and Modal Ontology*] (in Bulgarian), (Sofia: Metheor, 2021). As a philosophical project, but also as a philosophical methodology, the *modal ontology* was an attempt to remobilize the line of "left Aristotelianism" (borrowing Ernst Bloch's term), which we can hypothetically trace from Aristotle through Avicenna, Averroes, Bruno and Spinoza to Schelling, Novalis, Bergson, Guillaume, and eventually Matheron, Deleuze and—why not?—Nancy. Broadly speaking, the modal ontology is based on the following general proposition: the existence of what exists or existence *as what exists* could only be conceived in the ways in which it expresses or manifests itself. If existence is the condition of expression, it always transcends itself, it steps through or beyond (the literal translation of *ex-sistere, ek-stasis*) its own condition—it *ex-sists* in every act of expression. In other words, modal ontology relates to the tradition of Aristotelian homonymy, while structurally transforming it: what exists has multiple and potentially irreducible modes; it is *co-incidental* to the multiplicity of the modes only in the very act (or acts) of the multiple expressions. Thus modal ontology affirms the principle of *ontological individuation*, unfolding the complex concept of existence from which it proceeds, contributing to overcome the millennial oblivion or reduction of existence.

tering a form of *intensive cohesion*: its consistency is not extensive but intensive.[2] Rather than being an explicitly articulated method, the cohesion of this philosophy is of the order of rhythm or tonality: a rhythm of direct affirmation. Accordingly, it constitutes a particular provocation both to the idea of philosophical form and the philosophical idea itself, to the extent that it emerges as philosophical form exemplifying the *formation of philosophical ideas*. Ultimately, this *intensive* modality of Nancy's philosophy could be described as *method-in-becoming*, which in this case stands for method-*of*-becoming. Undisputedly, this method is the expression of the affirmative power of his philosophy.

The Turn to the World

I will start with a provocative question, leastwise going against a certain doxa established in the history of contemporary thought in France: why is Nancy not a Heideggerian?[3] Undoubtedly, the shadow of Heidegger looms over Nancy's thought. Both Nancy and the friends from his youth recall the experience of his first encounter with the philosophy of Heidegger, particularly through the mediation of his "oldest friend," François Warin.[4] Nancy discovered Heidegger at a time when he was still profoundly and personally engrossed in the Christian philosophical tradition, even to the point of being a young Christian militant. Nancy's thought was thus paradoxically connected at the very onset with what Heideggerian

---

2   Intensive could even read as—why not?—*obsessive*. In the words of Nancy himself: "A collection is not a pure aggregation of different pieces. It builds a whole, if not a system (but, why not?), at least a coordination of themes. What perhaps is more, it makes sensible an insistence, if not an obsession (but, why not?), in a certain way of thinking." Jean-Luc Nancy, *The Birth to Presence*, trans. Brian Holmes et al. (Stanford: Stanford University Press, 1993), p. ix.

3   My question echoes Susanna Lindberg's recent attempt to detach Nancy's philosophy from the phenomenological tradition, and replicates the title of her powerful article "Pourquoi Jean-Luc Nancy n'est-il pas un phénoménologue?," sharing its unconventional proposal. See Susanna Lindberg, "Pourquoi Jean-Luc Nancy n'est-il pas un phénoménologue?," *Lignes*, no. 68 (2022), p. 225–232.

4   "François Warin [...] m'a fait lire la *Lettre sur l'humanisme*, parce qu'il avait été élève de Jean Beaufret, l'introducteur de Heidegger en France. Au début, ça m'a fait vraiment rire, le 'berger de l'Être' et tout ça, après j'ai compris que c'était beaucoup plus compliqué." Jean-Baptiste Marongiu, "Le partage, l'infini et le jardin. Entretien avec Jean-Luc Nancy," *Libération*, February 17, 2000.

philosophy pretended to overcome—the ontotheological tradition. In this sense, the struggle with this tradition from the inside and the singular attempt of turning it upside down enacted by the project of deconstructing Christianity could also be seen as an attempt to overturn the Heideggerian legacy. In personal terms, the shift in Nancy's attitude towards both the Christian tradition and Heidegger could be related to the decisive philosophical encounter in his life—the encounter with Philippe Lacoue-Labarthe. An unquestionable authority as (a radical) reader of Heidegger, from his *Typographies* to *Poetry as Experience* and *Heidegger, Art, and Politics: The Fiction of the Political*, Lacoue-Labarthe was undisputedly anti-Heideggerian in the decisive points and the overall orientation of his philosophy. Nancy largely adopted his line, especially after the turning point of the late 1980s and early 1990s (from the pantheist *Des lieux divins* [1987] and the seminal *L'Expérience de la liberté* [1988] to *Corpus* [1992, the year of the heart transplant surgery]), following Lacoue-Labarthe and even making a step beyond his intransigent and radical critical vein, in order to develop a singularly new proposal in philosophy. We may venture calling this shift of Nancy's direction in the late 1980s and 1990s a *turn to the world*. In fact, while the largest part of the early work of Nancy is dealing, broadly speaking, with the questions of subject, cogito, rationality, the production of meaning, voice and language, and with history of philosophy as field of forces, connected to the general line of the method of deconstruction, and proposing radical readings of philosophers and writers such as Descartes, Kant, Hegel, Marx, Nietzsche, Bataille and Lacan, from the late 1980s–early 1990s on Nancy engages with a perspective one might describe as ontological (although Nancy himself tends to avoid the term) and focuses on fundamental subjects and concepts—the *world* in the first place, closely related to the questions of being, sense, existence, body, thought, image, freedom, justice, as well as to the project for deconstruction of Christianity, adding a specific prism to the ontological horizon at stake.

Building upon Lacoue-Labarthe's critique of the ontopolitical premises of Heideggerian philosophy, the first elements of Nancy's departure from Heidegger are indeed ontological—they concern nothing less than the questions of existence and the world. Starting at any rate from the early 1990s with the break point of *Corpus*, one can observe a symptomatic trajectory in Nancy's oeuvre related to the substitution of the question of being with the question of the world. In fact, with regard to the 1990s we can rather speak of hesitation and oscillation between the two extremities—*Le sens du monde* (1990) on the one hand, and *Être singulier pluriel* (1996), on the other. Ostensibly, the latter—one of Nancy's momentous and philosophically emblematic works from this period—holds Being as a central concept. Yet, it stands as clearly detached from the Heideggerian perspective. "Being" is affirmed as *singular plural* (*singulier pluriel*), which in itself undermines the Heideggerian "capital" Being.[5] A decade later, in *The Creation of the World* (2002), the concept of the world had taken the place of Being. Nancy was therefore progressively displacing the Heideggerian focus on Being, *Dasein* and *aletheia*, and later, on *Ereignis*. What is certain is that "L'Être" [*Being, Sein*] strangely disappeared at some point from Nancy's work.

This transition was certainly not contingent. What is its profound meaning? Is this a substitution of one name for another? It is of course much more than that: the concept of *world* turns the onto-phenomenological structure of the relation *Sein / Dasein* upside down. One can risk describing the divergence between Nancy's idea of world and Heidegger's fundamental ontology as symmetrical to the opposition between Bataille's *excess* and Heidegger's *ekstasis*. In Nancy's view, Being does not reveal itself to consciousness, to the arrested gaze of Being's shepherd—instead, the world exceeds itself, as a "self." In opposition to the onto-phenomenological structure of the ecstatic revelation of Being *for* and *through* the existence (of) Dasein, Nancy sets the world, unorthodoxly, on the side of "subjectivity." The *World / Being* becomes the universal name of the irreducible multiplicity of singularities that appear in the mode of *being-for-each-other*; let me qualify their common appearance, their *comparution*, their *attitude* for one another, as *proto-subjective*. It is of crucial importance to emphasize the fact that in his most radical texts Nancy fosters the idea that these singularities could happen to be all forms of existence, even the nameless ones. Let me quote a stunning paragraph from *Le poids d'une pensée* (which also provides an explicit "retroactive" support to Susanna Lindberg's argument):

> It has been said that the watchword for all modern thought is "go to the things themselves". But in this "to the", we must discern all the necessary weight, all the heavy fall of thought necessary to make sense

---

5   See Lindberg, "Pourquoi Jean-Luc Nancy n'est-il pas un phénoménologue?"

weigh what exceeds sense, what opens it to the thing to which it is a question of giving, that is to say, in truth, of letting it give, of letting it deliver its sense: that which makes sense by excess over all sense. The existence of the smallest pebble is already exceeding; however light it may be, it already weighs all this excess weight.[6]

To sum up, the main points of Nancy's non-Heideggerian ontology (or philosophy of the world) could be synthesized as follows:

1) Existence:
– Existence is irreducible to Being: such is the principle of the radical philosophy of existence. The notion of existence is dissociated from its own hypostasis: the substantiated form of Being.

2) The world:
– The world is autopoietic and auto-transcending—it could not subsist without intrinsic difference and therefore multiplicity. The irreducible multiplicity of the world is the multiplicity of singularities irreducible to the hypostasis of the One—*Sein / Dasein*.

What Matter for the World?

My second provocative question: is Nancy's overcoming of phenomenology, including Heidegger's phenomenological ontology, an advance along the path of Spinozism?[7] Spinoza is rarely evoked by Nancy, though he was doubtless aware of the proximity of some of his own claims to Spinoza's conceptual vein. However, his attitude towards the Spinozist tradition remained as ambiguous as the rela-

---

6   Jean-Luc Nancy, "Le poids d'une pensée," in *Le poids d'une pensée, l'approche* (Strasbourg: La Phocide, 2008), p. 14 (translation mine, B.M.).
7   I have already raised this question in the past. The following paragraphs consist of a synthesis of the more detailed reading proposed in "Ontology of Creation," in *Re-treating Religion. Deconstructing Christianity with Jean-Luc Nancy*, ed. Alena Alexandrova, Laurens ten Kate et al. (New York: Fordham University Press, 2012), pp. 261–274. See also "Le désir du monde. Jean-Luc Nancy et l'Éros ontologique," in *Cahiers philosophiques de Strasbourg*, ed. Jérôme Lèbre and Jacob Rogozinski (October 2017), pp. 85–100. Nancy was himself changing his attitude to this association—from skeptical to approving. Parallel to my *Ontology of Creation* Anne O'Byrne proposed her own radically materialist reading of Nancy's ontology, see Anne O'Byrne, "Nancy's Materialist Ontology," in *Jean-Luc Nancy and Plural Thinking*, ed. Peter Gratton and Marie-Eve Morin (Albany: State University of New York Press, 2012), pp. 79–94.

tionship to the phenomenological one. To start with, it is quite obvious that the dogmatic "geometrical" form of Spinoza's philosophy is certainly alien to Nancy. Nancy hence seems to remain explicitly reserved about the radicality of Spinoza's ontology: "However," he writes in *The Creation of the World*, "the Spinozist's substance still keeps at a distance, or neutralizes, it seems to me, the question of the 'generosity' [the French term is *gratuité*] of the world as I wish to indicate it here."[8] Yet, this reservation, expressed ten years after the aforementioned "turn" of the early 1990s, is in fact in unison with the radicality of the affirmation conveyed in *Corpus*. Moreover, in a marginal note to "The Decision of Existence," which could also serve as a bridge for the somewhat adventurous transition from Heidegger to Spinoza, Nancy goes as far as suggesting "a 'Spinozan' reading, or rewriting, of *Being and Time*."[9]

Let me briefly revisit a paragraph in *Corpus*—the very turning point of Nancy's *turn-to-the-world*—whose conceptual stakes and consequences I have already attempted to address, and where the dynamics of excess is announced under the singular regime of *modalization*, in turn associating itself with the concept of *modal ontology*.[10] This is the chapter "Glorious Body," uniquely rich and powerful, but also enigmatic, a chapter that traces nothing less than a novel image of the creation of the world:

> That God created *limon*, and that he made the *body* out of *limon*, means that God modalized or modified himself, but that his *self* in itself is only the extension and indefinite expansion of modes. This means that "creation" isn't the production of a world from some unknown

---

8   Jean-Luc Nancy, *The Creation of the World or Globalization*, trans. and with an Introduction by François Raffoul and David Pettigrew (Albany: State University of New York Press, 2007), p.121, note 10.

9   Nancy, The Birth to Presence, p. 407.

10   I ventured introducing the term *modal ontology* in the beginning of the new century, drawing on the following passage from *Corpus*: "*Here*, in an essential, all-embracing and exclusive way, ontology is *modal*—or modifiable, or modifying. And the writing of this is a *corpus*," p. 51. ("Ici, l'ontologie est modale—ou modifiable et modifiante—de manière essentielle, entière et exclusive." Jean-Luc Nancy, *Corpus* [Paris: Métailié, 1992], p. 48.)

It is noteworthy that recently, in 2015, Giorgio Agamben published in his book *The Use of Bodies* a chapter entitled "Towards a Modal Ontology," a title repeating ten years later that of the program I directed at the International College of Philosophy, using the concept in a similar perspective, without mentioning its recent uses in a context quite similar to his own. See Giorgio Agamben, *The Use of Bodies* (Stanford: Stanford University Press, 2016).

matter of nothingness but consists in the fact that *the* matter (only that which there is) essentially *modifies itself:* it's not a substance, it's the extension and expansion of "modes" or, to put it more precisely, the exposition of what there is. Bodies are the exposition of God, and there is no other—to the extent that God exposes himself.[11]

The lecture "On the Soul," published in the second edition of *Corpus*, extends the argument of "Glorious Body" in an unexpected manner and with an explicit reference to Spinoza:

What's God for Spinoza? God is the unique substance. There's nothing else. The unique substance for Spinoza is not a mass, it is in itself double: it is thought and extension—the two being co-extensive and parallel to one another. And this very duality is God. Which is why, from that point on, we can forget God. Spinoza has been more than abundantly treated as an atheist, and, I think, rightly so. Let's forget God, then. The idea of the body is the idea, the vision and form of something that is both an expanse and an extension, insofar as this expanse or this extension is not merely exterior to the idea but visible or sensible in itself and as a form of itself.[12]

While Nancy thus progressively aligns himself with the theses on matter of the "Aristotelian left" (according to Ernst Bloch's formidable expression[13]), does the modal affirmation expressed in "Glorious Bodies" not also testify to his unconfessed Spinozism? Ostensibly, at least through the mediation of German Romanticism, but also through Kant,[14] Nancy tacitly moves closer and closer, even if unwillingly, to Spinoza. Hence, even if Nancy's relation to Spinoza is not unambiguous, his relation to the concepts of matter, existence, subject and world could be straightforwardly associated with radical Spinozism. In fact, the Spinozist tendency we identify in "Glorious Body" is one of radical, even paradoxical Spinozism: a Spinozism without the substance.

---

11 Nancy, *Corpus*, p. 61.
12 Ibid., p. 119.
13 Ernst Bloch, *Avicenna and the Aristotelian Left*, trans. Loren Goldman and Peter Thompson (New York: Columbia University Press, 2018).
14 See for instance the already quoted note 10 to "On Creation": "This is why one saw, following Kant, a flurry of Spinozisms," Nancy, *The Creation of the World*, p. 121.

God had made himself body, he had been extended and molded *ex limon terrae:* out of the fat, smooth, deformable extension of clay, the *raw* matter, consisting entirely of modalizing, or modification, rather than substance.[15]

Matter is not substance—it is conceived as "pure" modalization. Conversely, modalization—*metamorphosis*—would be the activity of matter without an external principle: as the very locus of metamorphosis, *"the body is the plastic material of spacing,* without form or Idea."[16]

But then again, what is substance? To sum up, the crucial point of Nancy's proximity to Spinoza is the idea of ontological immanence, namely creative power immanent in "substance," or, in Nancy's terms, *the creation of the world* immanent in the world. Nancy's principle of immanence, as announced in *Corpus*, is transformative. It is the principle of the modal ontology.

Transformative Ontology

As we can see, the modal moment is not only directly related to a new vision of creation—it is furthermore its only principle: the creation of the world is modalization and, consequently, the world is nothing but self-modalization. It is true that the "subject" or principle of self-modalization is designated as God, the most laden of all titles. Let us assume, however, that this designation has no other task than to affirm the irreducibility of the force, or rather the self-modalizing force, to a totalizing principle. It is affirmed as the force of a world that is absolutely immanent, but whose "absolute" immanence consists only in its unlimited excess over itself. Paradoxically, in the quoted paragraph God comes close to another term—*matter:* "That [...] means that God modalized or modified himself, but that his *self* in itself is only the extension and indefinite expansion of modes. [...] *the* matter (only that which there is) essentially *modifies itself:* it's not a substance, it's the extension and expansion of 'modes' or, to put it more precisely, the exposition of what there is."[17] This is a striking repetition or semantic resonance. The profound semantic structure of Nancy's

---

15 Nancy, *Corpus*, p. 61.
16 Ibid., p. 63.
17 Ibid., p. 61.

paragraph affirms: God is matter, matter is God. And indeed, truly so: long before being expelled by the one and only god of monotheism, the multiple gods of ancient times infinitely metamorphosed themselves, divine loci or singularities—modes irreducible and non-totalizable to a substance or to a sacred absolute principle. It is therefore not surprising to hear Nancy's radical proposal formulated a little further on: "Let's forget God, then."[18]

Does Nancy's *Corpus* then effectuate a return to the pre-scientific reflection on matter—the reflection on material modalization exemplified by Heraclitus or Anaximenes? Moreover, if modalization is another term for creation and if, consequently, modalization is *the only* matter, it follows that matter is itself creation. The concept of ontological modalization affirms the existence of matter not as a principle opposed to idea or form; it does not propose to reenact an ontological reduction, in order to explicate a whole and subordinate it to the determinism of necessity, ultimately fatalistic in the long run. On the contrary, modal thinking affirms matter not as subjugated substratum or as the solid mass of necessity, but as the possibility of the unbound emergence of the new, of the fermentation of the future—of *material freedom* as the only "substratum" of the world:

> [M]aterial freedom—matter as freedom—is not a freedom of gesture, still less of voluntary action, without also being the freedom of two shades of mica, of millions of dissimilar shells, and of the indefinite extension of the *principium individuationis,* such that individuals in themselves *never stop being individuated,* differing ever more from themselves, hence being ever more alike, interchangeable with themselves, but never reduced to substances, unless the substance, prior to sustaining something (self or other), comes to be exposed *here:* in the world.[19]

The chapter "Glorious Bodies" thus opens up a space of unknown relief and uncertain limits, a space of intense reflections in search of a proper name, a space of reflecting on the world to come—the reflection of the world-metamorphosis. By virtue of this paragraph, the question of the creation of the world can now be formulated as follows: *what is the matter of the world to come?*

---

18 Ibid., p. 119.
19 Ibid., p. 35.

The Singular Substance

"Form means that body is articulated, not in the sense of the articulation of members but as the relation to something other than itself. The body is a relation to another body—or a relation to itself."[20] A new displacement of the modal motif is underway at this point: the displacement or transformation of the modalizing movement into a reflexive movement. This displacement also affects the figure of God, who re-emerges only to be likewise transformed into a reflexive operation: "I'd say, very quickly, and using Spinoza's terms: God sees himself as *this* body, mine, yours. And, for Spinoza, God doesn't see himself as anything else. If God is the thought of extension, it's because he's the extension of thought."[21] This far-reaching transformation allows us to better understand the "reflexive" return to Spinoza's substance in *Corpus*. Substance would be nothing other than this capacity to relate, the *flexion* of the "*se*" [*se* voit— "sees himself"] which is at the same time the power of the "*ex*," of the *ex-tension* as the *exit* from oneself, and thus of metamorphosis. In a way, "substance" is nothing else but the self-reflexive moment of the body: of "extension" (and) of "thought."

Is the reflexion moment of Nancy's affirmation the Kantian transformative apostrophe to Spinoza? "On the Soul" again:

> Kant wrote, in a note to the *Prolegomena* (a note to paragraph 46), that the "self" is without substance and without concept, that it is "only sentiment of an existence" *(Gefühl eines Daseins)*. Furthermore, Kant doesn't put the article with *Gefühl*, he doesn't say a sentiment, or the sentiment, but "self" is sentiment of an existence. "Self" is sensing an existence. If we develop Kant's formula rigorously, sensing an existence does not mean that a self senses an existence outside itself, as of a table, say. Existence is what is sensed as existence. This does not mean that there is a little subject back behind, sensing itself as existence. There's no longer a subject "back behind." There's only a "self-sensing," as a relation to self as outside. And that's what being one's self is. Self being is necessarily being outside, on the outside, being exposed or extended."[22]

---

20 Jean-Luc Nancy, "On the Soul," in Nancy, *Corpus*, p. 127.

21 Ibid., p. 130.

22 Ibid., p. 132. I have sought to radicalize Nancy's proposal by fostering it in the perspective of a radical theory of the subject, exceeding phenomenology, which was the focal point of my philosophical efforts over the past few decades.

Yet, to relate, i.e. to *exit* oneself, to expose oneself or to be exposed, means to "individuate." Hence, substance—as freedom—is driven by a *principium individuationis*: "material freedom" is, as we have seen, that of "the indefinite extension of the *principium individuationis,* such that individuals in themselves *never stop being individuated,* differing ever more from themselves, hence being ever more alike, interchangeable with themselves, but never reduced to substances, unless the substance, prior to sustaining something (self or other), comes to be exposed *here:* in the world. [...] (One thing has to be admitted: if 'nature' is to be thought as the exposition of bodies, all of the 'philosophy of nature' has to be reworked.) (In other words: as freedom.)"[23] The most faithful description of "substance"-modalization will then be the dynamics of irreducible singularities, while *comparution, common emergence*, will be the term for the non-totalizable totality of relation-exposures. In the words of Bailly and Nancy: "The ontology of the 'common' and of 'sharing' would be nothing other than the ontology of 'being' radically subtracted from any ontology of substance, order and origin."[24]

If the extension of matter is always a movement of "individuation," and therefore of singularization, this would only confirm the hypothesis that the movement of metamorphosis—the pure force or activity of matter—coincides with the movement of appearance [*apparaître*]. In order to understand the effectivity of emergence, one would have to perform the following operation—to understand "the extension and expansion of the 'modes'," "the exposure of what there is," as the other term for the movement of the common emergence [*comparution*] of singularities. These two affirmations—or this double affirmation—also operate a double critique, the point of coincidence of the critique of the "metaphysics of presence" and consequently of the mechanics of appearance, in

---

I therefore claim that in the course of the transformative reflexive movement, i.e. the movement of the world's autopoietic excess, singularities obtain the intensity of a *subject*—an *agency*. As a result, Nancy's (figure of) the Subject emerges against (the background of) phenomenological consciousness (at this point, the anti-phenomenological drive of Nancy surprisingly acquires familiarity with the neutral ontology of his intermittent ally Alain Badiou: we can agree on Badiou's proposal that the subject is opposed to consciousness).

23   Ibid., pp. 35, 37.
24   "La comparution," in Jean-Christophe Bailly and Jean-Luc Nancy, *La comparution* (Paris: Christian Bourgois Éditeur, 1991), p. 57 (translation mine, B.M.).

other words, of the onto-phenomenological mode of being, and of the critique of the Aristotelian logic of the actualization of force.

The Revolutionary Creation, or the Struggle for the World

Thus the creation of the world according to both *Corpus* and *The Creation of the World* at the end appears as a *revolutionary creation*. In the "Metamorphosis of the World" Nancy answers my question about the desire of the world in the following way:

> *B.M.:* When you ask the question about the desire of the world: "we must ask ourselves afresh what the world wants from us" ["nous devons nous demander à nouveaux frais ce que le monde veut de nous"] (*La création du monde,* p. 18), we must apparently understand the world's desire as a *present* desire. The world is desire, and this desire is directed at us, it wants something from us. What does the world want from us now? Possible answer: the world wants its (re)subjectivation. [...] Does it give itself as this desire that wants (or that it wants) from us? What does it mean to respond to the world's desire? And also: can one respond to the desire of the world; and *who* would respond?

> *J.-L. N.:* If you ask: "What does the world want from us?" I think I would reply: it wants itself in us, like us, through us and all our worlds. But "it wants itself" is neither subjective nor voluntary. It might as well be said: "it pushes" [*il pousse*] (where "push" [*poussée*] can be understood in the sense of directional force and in the sense of biological growth). The push pushes itself: that is, it simply pushes.[25]

Surprisingly, we observe in this statement the same argumentative structure as in the paragraph on the reflexive seeing of God, but this time concerning the desire of the world. Therefore, the reflexive-modalizing seeing of God becomes or is transformed into the desire for the world. This is definitely not a question of a simple psychologizing reduction of the question of the world; on the contrary, this is a thesis on the matter of the world itself. This thesis does not simply seek to assert that the *push* or the drive

---

25 Jean-Luc Nancy and Boyan Manchev, "La métamorphose du monde," *Rue Descartes,* no. 64 (2009), pp. 84–85. This is, to my knowledge at least, the first English translation of a fragment of this conversation, which proposes a rare synthesis of Nancy's ontological concepts.

is the desire *of* matter (hence, to posit the matter as subject, or, in consequence, as self-affecting substance) but, conversely, that this desire, this drive, this push—this intensity, this energy—is the matter of the world itself. Matter is the transformation of the world immanent in the world, the only immanence of the world—the immanence of its unlimited excess beyond itself. It is therefore revolutionary: not a revolution of the concept of matter, but rather a matter-revolution; not revolutionary materialism but a revolution of materialism.

Modal ontology implies, I claim, the transition from a *necessary Being* to *being by necessity*. We have learned by Spinoza the name of this *being by necessity*: *freedom*.[26] We have ventured to radicalize Kant through Spinoza and Spinoza through Kant, claiming that modal ontology is the ontology of the world to come. The world-to-come is a *necessary world*, a world emerging out of an irreducible contingency and yet necessarily affirmed by its own power[27]—a power that must express itself, thus transforming the world *in* itself in a world *for* itself—by the free affirmation of the struggle *for* the world:

> *To create the world* means: immediately, without delay, reopening each possible struggle for a world, that is, for what must form the contrary of a global injustice against the background of general equivalence. [...] [T]o create as a struggle, which while struggling—consequently, by seeking power, by finding forces—does not seek the exercise of power—nor property—whether collective or individual, but seeks itself and its agitation, itself and the effervescence of its thought in act, itself and its creation of forms and signs, itself and its contagious communication as propagation of an enjoyment that, in turn, would not be a satisfaction acquired in a signification of the world, but the insatiable and infinitely finite exercise that is the being in act of meaning brought forth in the world [*mis au monde*].[28]

---

26 See Spinoza, First Part of the *Ethics: Of God*, "Definition 7. A thing is said to be free if it exists solely by the necessity of its own nature, and is determined to action by itself alone." Benedict de Spinoza, *Ethics Proved in Geometrical Order*, ed. Matthew J. Kisner, trans. Michael Silverthorne and Matthew J. Kisner (Cambridge and New York: Cambridge University Press, 2018), p. 4.

27 This is one of the fundamental theses of *Freedom in Spite of Everything* (2021), the object of our last exchange in 2021.

28 Nancy, The Creation of the World, pp. 54–55, last paragraphs of "Urbi et Orbi."

Thus Jean-Luc Nancy's philosophy of the world—the world as *sense*—extends the modal horizon of philosophy opened up by Kant, the Romantic philosophers, Marx and Nietzsche—and by Spinoza before them all: philosophy's task before the world is a task *for* the world—a desire and a struggle for the possibility of *a* world and for the necessity of *the* world. Jean-Luc Nancy persisted in this task with breathtaking imagination and exemplary courage, creating a body of philosophy as intense as the promise of the just world to come.

Michael Marder

A Non-Renewable Thinking: Meditations for Jean-Luc Nancy[1]

A finite energy: energy's finitude. Having emerged on the historical horizon, its specter quickly grows to unfathomable breadths and heights, displacing virtually all other concerns. Unlike the bloated specter, the energy that is finite in this sense has inflexible and nonnegotiable limits, putting it on the verge of being depleted and running out. It is finite as a resource, the object it has been reduced to and arrested within. Such an energy comes to an end without having even begun, without having had a chance to flow, to circulate, to be synergically shared, to be something other and something more (or less) than an object. And it hauls toward *their* ends—their termination without coming to term—entire worlds, a vast number of living beings and the finite material conditions of possibility for their existence.

A finite energy alludes to a finite thinking, which is the title of an essay and a book by Jean-Luc Nancy. The simple proximity of the two terms on a page tells us a great deal. What exactly? For instance, that there are different sorts of finitude with distinct relations to the possibilities of appropriation and of ending. The dividing lines pass not between energy and thinking, but between energy and thinking that are finite *in one way*, which I have barely sketched out, on the one hand, and energy and thinking that are finite *in another way*, yet to be outlined, on the other. The infinite is not panacea from resourcification, objectification, or substantivation. Other finitudes—of energy, of thinking, of being—should become prominent instead, as they already have, in part thanks to Nancy's body of work.

*

1   This text has benefited from the contribution of the project PID2021–126611NB-I00 Socioecos. Building sustainable society: Mobilization, participation and management of socio-ecological practices, supported by the Spanish Ministry of Science and Innovation.

As an object, finite energy is something to be acquired or squandered, gained or lost. (In effect, according to its spiraling dynamics exceeding those of dissipation in entropy, this odd object is lost *in* being gained—and much else along with it.) The irreversible, irrevocable loss of energy so conceived terrifies to the extent that this loss, specific and limited as it initially present itself, spells out the end of everything and everyone. Through the felt finitude of energy, finitude as such peers at us. But it is a finitude that does not exhaust the senses of the finite.

The political and environmental circumstances of the irreversible, irrevocable, and all-encompassing ebbing away are well-known. When French president Emmanuel Macron warns about the "end of abundance," just as the Russian supplies of natural gas to Europe are cut, the solid limits of energy (that is to say, of a certain *concept* of energy, regardless of the gasified or liquified state, in which combustible fossils are sold and bought) become all the more palpable. When the fossil sources of energy are rejected as non-renewable, regardless of the impact of their burning on the atmosphere and on global heating, a search for infinite (hence, infinitely renewable) energies commences.

In both instances—which are but the contemporary peaks of a tendency that began roughly half a century ago, though in truth it reaches back to the nineteenth century and what Nietzsche then diagnosed as the death of God—laments are voiced over *the end of infinity*, of what appeared to be infinite. Since, without any period of mourning, a new quest for renewables, for the infinitely suppliable and infinitely utilizable energy sources, is launched, we would be right to surmise that these laments have to do not with the infinite *per se* but with the appearance, the illusion that has been wrested away from us like a favorite toy from a child's hands. This realization, however, points beyond political and environmental circumstances and toward the philosophical frame for the ongoing and ever-deepening crisis of finitude.

*

There is a strong, if largely unremarked, psychological dissonance accompanying our economic, political, and environmental approaches to, and retreats from, energy. The ebbing away of finite energies is accompanied by an insatiable craving for infinitely renewable energy. The gap between these dissonant halves of our relation to energy keeps growing: the more acute the shortage and the sense of the end that subjectively corresponds to it, the more powerful and insistent the desire for the infinite. Does the non-acceptance of energy's finitude express a dissatisfaction with finite being as such, let alone with a finite thinking?

What the obsession with renewable energy shares with the use of fossil fuels is a lack of appreciation of the finite in its finitude, in its irreplaceability and singularity. Nancy's "finite thinking," for its part, spotlights the positive aspects of non-renewability. It is, in his own words, "not a thinking of relativity, which implies the Absolute, but a thinking of *absolute finitude:* absolutely detached from all infinite and senseless completion or achievement. [It is] not a thinking of limitation, which implies the unlimitedness of a beyond, but a thinking of the limit as that on which, infinitely finite, existence arises, and to which it is exposed."[2] A non-renewable thinking, one might say, which belongs together with the other (non-fossilized) non-renewability of energy.

The very first gesture in a preparation of and for non-renewable thinking—a gesture that is not at all theoretical and not even practical but affective, involving plenty of psychoanalytic work— is ridding oneself of the fear associated with the ultimacy of the end. As Nancy has noted more recently, "there is nothing alarmist or apocalyptic in thinking that existence as such can be brought before its own transience and finitude. It is precisely there that it takes on its infinite, unique, and unsubstitutable value."[3] The end is also the edge, where or when that which is ending may be touched, caressed, affirmed in its infinite uniqueness—the only infinity compatible with it. A finite thinking is a living thinking without the subterfuges of a "pure life," which would be unmixed with death. A finite energy is a living energy, the energy of this life and this thinking. To wish for its renewability is to disband everything that makes it unique, to render it anonymous and as good as dead in the very gesture of opposing entropy and death.

*

For Nancy, finitude is defiance, though not an outright negation. Like the divine *fiat*, which according to Schelling is the creative

---

2   Jean-Luc Nancy, "A Finite Thinking," in *A Finite Thinking*, ed. Simon Sparks (Stanford: Stanford University Press, 2003), p. 27.
3   Jean-Luc Nancy, "Overture," in *The Fragile Skin of the World* (London: Polity Press, 2021), pp. xiv–xv.

yes-no at the dawn of the world, finitude lends sense to being, while defying all programs of its reproduction (material, biological, social, political) along with possible or necessary reproducibility, renewability, recyclability... *"Finitude,"* he writes, "designates the 'essential' multiplicity and the 'essential' nonreabsorption of sense or of being."[4]

"Nonreabsorption" is key: the finite as finite cannot be taken up again into any system either in the guise of the same or in that of the other (who is, more often than not, the same merely othered). There is no economy of finitude, "of sense or of being" that are absolutely finite, unique, non-substitutable (not even by themselves), non-renewable. But this does not mean that finite senses, beings, energies are closed off, cut off from one another, utterly isolated as independent monads; on the contrary, one of Nancy's lifelong projects has been to demonstrate how community flourishes only in the sharing of the finite. What he, in a shorthand of sorts, denotes as "'essential' multiplicity" is being singular plural, in which singularity is, strictly speaking, irreplaceable. Nor does it mean that everything, including the world, is to be discarded after it has been thoroughly exhausted through use. Renewability should not be conflated with regenerability, the event of another arising that does not in the least aim to replace that which, or those who, preceded it. Strange as this may sound, regenerability depends on a certain non-renewability of finite existence.

Thanks to its nonreabsorption, finitude is neither digestible nor otherwise metabolizable, neither a return on an investment nor an assimilated element in the overall scheme of things. Although it is written off from the ledgers of being as a pure loss, it is not nothing, or, to repeat, not an outright negation. Similarly, a finite thinking is "not a thinking of the abyss and of nothingness, but a thinking of the un-grounding of being: of this 'being', the only one, whose *existence* exhausts all its substance and all its possibility."[5] With regard to the Kantian subcategories of modality, the merging of existence and possibility implies that there is no sense in searching for a more valuable remainder (including the remainder of sense) behind or above this singular being. The nonreabsorption of a being into a system has an obverse side: the thorough absorption of modal categories into one another and into this very being.

---

4   Nancy, "A Finite Thinking," p. 9.
5   Nancy, "A Finite Thinking," p. 27.

*

Were it not for time and space constraints, I could have cited and discussed every single line from Nancy's *A Finite Thinking*, both the book and the essay bearing this title, bringing to the fore the non-renewable energy of thinking and the other non-renewability, which has nothing in common with the fossilized remains of dinosaurs, whether the animals who lived and died millions of years ago or the more recent intellectual productions deserving such an appellation. Instead of mining the text for valuable fragments with the view to bolstering my argument (to be sure, I have not done this either, having merely skimmed the surface), an integral reading would have been a better approach, one that is more faithful to non-renewable thinking than the usual academic method. An excessively faithful hermeneutics, lingering with the text, refusing to leap over its passages, each of them leading to non-renewability—the non-renewability of thinking, being, energy—afresh.

After all, a body of thinking (Nancy's, above all) is *this being*, mutely demanding the acknowledgement of its absolute finitude, nonreabsorption into the economy of thought, unsubstitutability. It is not a resource, renewable despite all the mental extractivism it is subject to, but an energizing factor, energizing with its singularity, its uncategorizable being, irreducible to any of the existing or yet to be invented *-isms*. One of a kind, despite, also, some similarities to others (notably Derrida) in style and substance. A non-renewable thinking, which remains to be thought.

Sandrine Israel-Jost

How Does Nancy Pursue the Thought of the Milieu by Other Means?

I would like to suggest that Jean-Luc Nancy's thought, even if he has always distanced himself from using the notion of milieu (rather than using it in an eloquent silence, apart from very rare remarks, or rejecting it, or even making an unexplicit use of it, as an incident), proves to be very fruitful for understanding it. And yet, not only does Nancy use milieu very sparingly, as has been said, but also, some decisive movements in his thought appear to be completely set apart from what the notion of the milieu implies at first sight. How, then, can we bank on the relevance of Nancy's thought to examine the logic of the milieu in another way, another voice, and intonation? And all this in an affirmative style that would agree with what contemporary thinkers of the milieu have laid out.

This notion, whose relevance Canguilhem (who was one of the professors who influenced Nancy, according to his direct testimony[1]) firmly pointed out,[2] seems to be in direct opposition to some of Nancy's major philosophical stances. I will retain three of them: the first two, which directly correlate to one another, appear in dissonance with the classical elements of the thought of the milieu, while the third one clearly shows an affinity with it, opting for a difference in lexicon. But upon further examination, each one shows just as many opportunities for the thought of the milieu to grow from its evolution, by an uncertain nature, as are the adventures of the living—or of existence.

What are these three "stances," which describe at once a philosophical decision, but also a way to make a partition, to draw gestures of thought[3] from it, and to set it into movement? In a way, to

---

1 The first courses taught by the young Jean-Luc Nancy were courses on epistemology based on Canguilhem's teachings.

2 "The notion of milieu is in the process of becoming a universal and obligatory means of registering the experience and existence of living things, and one could almost speak of its constitution as a basic category of contemporary thought." Georges Canguilhem, "The Living and Its Milieu," trans. John Savage, *Grey Room*, no. 3 (2001), pp. 6–31.

3 By "gesture of thought," I refer to something that is neither an idea—a conceptual form—nor an argument or a demonstration, but rather an act of thought freed from provenance, coming from nothing, and destined to no result, caught

precisely make them act beyond simple philosophical stances, in directions that these stances carry without, however, containing or foreseeing them.

In the first place, the Nancyan thought of the outside, defined by openness and singularity, by sharing and emergence, appears in contrast to a milieu defined as closed and specific. In fact, the category of the milieu presupposes a subject that produces meaning according to its vital interests: a living being relates to the world insofar as it makes itself noticed and acts according to its needs. It is in this sense that it produces meaning. Now, for Nancy, meaning does not seem to come from a vital interest—and as such does not create a milieu for the existing being—but rather emerges *between* and *with* a "subject"—we will see very quickly why this is put in quotation marks. It is *between*, because a "subject" opens in itself an interval and a spacing through which it can precisely enter into communication *with* other "subjects," that exist, they themselves, from within their own spacing. Here we lose the essential feature of the subject as self-positioning, in favor of a "subject" that addresses other "subjects" in a relation of resonance, whose echoing strength depends precisely on its intervallic character. As such, a "subject" is not an autonomous individual, but rather a singular and moving point, that infinitely shares an exceeding movement with other singular points: "*In this sense*, we are never, each one next to the other, anything other than singular points in a general sending off that the sense makes of itself toward itself, and that begins and gets lost far below and beyond us, in its indefinitely open totality of the world."[4]

Opposed to the closed and specific milieu, is a totality understood not from its totalization, but as an opening that does not cease to take place. The outside has nothing to do with exteriority in relation to a subject, but quite differently, this opening moves from side to side, from the most intimate, a subject, in such a way as to make it come unhinged. As Shakespeare would say of time: a "subject" is in-itself-outside-of-itself. It in-itself is to be outside-of-the-self, carried above and beyond, and this is occurs indefinitely.

Therefore, touching on Nancy's second philosophical position, a thought of the outside leads to think of meaning independently of the position of an autonomous subject, and as such, a producer of meaning. Now, what is at stake in the category of the milieu is that

---

in its own movement, with no end. This does not mean that it is vanity, but on the contrary, absolute power—freed from an origin and a destination.

4   Jean-Luc Nancy, *La Pensée dérobée* (Paris: Galilée, 2001), p. 172.

it must consider the whole of the living animal as a subject that exists as a measuring center. Thus, it is from a theoretical and practical reconfiguration of the subject that it is defined as the agent of "a sense [which], from the biological and psychological point of view, is an appreciation of values in relation to a need. And for the one who experiences and lives it, a need is an irreducible, and thereby absolute, system of reference."[5]

Here we are in complete deviation from the idea of an overrun and overflowing "general sending." The thought of the outside naturally leads us to put the subject in quotation marks, it has become a trembling instance, and provisionally, its role will be seen throughout Nancy's work, held by "instances" that precisely thwart that of the subject. On one hand: *corpus*—not an individual body but spacing and place of existence; it is inorganic and made from an anarchic skin, an infinite opportunity for touch, exposing the existence, it itself breaks in. "The body is neither a 'signifier' nor a 'signified.' It's exposing/exposed: *ausgedehnt,* an extension of the breakthrough that existence is."[6] On the other hand: *self*—pushed without origin, "the push and press of existing," the taking place of an "it happens, it arrives."[7]

Finally, the third position, atypical in relation to the other two, seems more formal, without being reduced to a mere choice of lexicon. And it intervenes precisely where we can immediately identify a powerful proximity of Nancy's thought with the category of the milieu. Indeed, "milieu" states not a surrounding space, a simple environment, adapted to an organism, but rather the dynamic relationship that creates the signifying tension of a living being with their environment. Thus, perhaps the most solid and fruitful feature of such a category consists in positing the precedence of the relation over the terms at stake. Strictly speaking, there are no more terms—insofar as these would be ontologically extricable—but rather a renewed and plastic tying up of relations. If Nancy's philosophical position resonates immediately this time, with what the category of the milieu engages—the propositions giving the precedence of the "between" on what it pushes aside and holds

---

5   Canguilhem, *Knowledge of Life* (Paris: Vrin, 1998 (1965)), p. 120.
6   Jean-Luc Nancy, *Corpus* (New York: Fordham University Press, 2008), p. 25.
7   Jean-Luc Nancy, *Corpus III*: Cruor *and Other Writings*, trans. Jeff Fort et al. (New York: Fordham University Press, 2022), p. 22 and p. 12. *Cruor* is introduced by Nancy as a follow up to *Corpus*, in an expansion of the spawning in "the spaces of the 'between'" (p. 12) that *Corpus* had engaged.

together at the same time, are innumerable. The author of *The "there is" of the sexual relation* chooses the term "rapport" – and not "relation"—to describe it. In this regard, Nancy differs lexically from the tradition of the thought of the milieu, that is found in several ecologist-style philosophies,[8] but this does not mean that there should be a difference in the approach.

In what way, as we will see, does the Nancyan thought of the outside meet the "bubbles" that Jacob von Uexküll said illustrated the unnamable milieus that are juxtaposed in the same space, in an encounter that could very well burst these bubbles, without violence? How do *body* and *self* offset and implode a measuring subject that, by abandoning its consistency, invents another vitality, in vibration and intimate resonance with everything alive? Finally, what remains of the subject in a thought of the milieu pursued by other means? The path traced here conveniently borrows milestones that could have been otherwise distributed—thus the thought from the outside is immediately related with the recasting of subjectivity in the opposition body/self. The distinction between these two prisms has therefore something a bit artificial at first sight, but it has the challenge of showing how they are intertwined, despite instances of differentiated analyses. The third point being the one where we should have logically started—beginning with the rapport—Nancy—or the relation—the thought of the milieu. It does not have to do, however, with thoroughly deploying the thought of the milieu, but rather, on one hand, with evaluating the fruitfulness of Nancy's thought through the milieu, and on the other hand, with interrogating the becoming of the subject *via* the confrontation between one thought and another.

The continuation of this attempt will consist in putting Nancy's thought into perspective with classical elements of the category of the milieu according to these three entries, so as to create a tense dialogue, but hopefully it will produce fruitful agitations. It will have to do with pursuing this vis-à-vis its climate of différance, its quasi-chemical exchange times, its moments of distancing where one and the other divide in a new common point of departure, playing out in a score that is not necessarily concerted, but *still* playing together.

---

8   I refer to "ecologist-style philosophies" to point at the signature of thought that posits the primacy of the relationship. Among them there are many heterogenous references: for example Arne Naess and Gregory Bateson. For the present purpose, the reference to Gilbert Simondon, who in this regard is an heir of Gaston Bachelard, is central.

And here we already have a powerful meeting point between this "category of contemporary thought" and the general intonation of Nancy's philosophy: the idea that things play together without necessarily *going* together, in a new alloy, of that which does the *same*, infinitely different, indefinitely other in their sameness, and in a complicity that is diversely formalized by this sameness realized by otherness. An index, already, of a strong point of connection between the category of the milieu and the Nancyan way of making a category (category as for one and for the other formed as an opening decision, this one and that one being more of the order of the rhythm[9]—fluid form—than of that of the outline—fixed form): there is nothing dialectical there, so powerful seems to be the work of alienation in the other, as long as the passage to the other has nothing alienating, but also makes the fluidity adventurous. An also that precisely Nancy's thought, as the thought of the milieu, thinks from the heterogeneity of the singular, the fruitful alteration of the plural, and the general concertation—but never totalizing or unifying—of the singular and the plural.

The Thought of the Outside and the Logic of the Inside/Outside of the Milieu

In *Being Singular Plural*, Nancy says that "humanity is not 'in the world' as it would be in a milieu (why would the milieu be necessary?); it is *in* the world insofar as the world is its own exteriority, the proper space of its being-out-in-the-world."[10] We can read this affirmation in two different ways. In the most evident way, Nancy is against the idea that the world would respond subjectively to an organism, in a given intimate interaction, being a vital part of the existence of the organism. In this, Nancy is against the horizon of a given meaning, which, in the thought of the milieu, is developed from the living correlation between an organism and its milieu. Onthe contrary, the category of the milieu decisively breaks

---

9   Here I refer to the famous distinction made in "The Notion of 'Rhythm' in its Linguistic Expression" by Émile Benveniste. Generally, the thoughts on relation invest in the concept of rhythm. Nancy writes, among other instances: "Being, as the rhythm of bodies—bodies, as the rhythm of being. The thought-in-body is rhythmic, spacing, pulsing, giving the *time* of the dance, the *step* of the world." Nancy, *Corpus*, p. 100.

10   Nancy, *Being Singular Plural* (Stanford: Stanford University Press, 2000), p. 19.

with the idea of a space of the outside, in which subjects liable to their own interiorities and things juxtaposed beside each other would come to be lodged. The category of the milieu, so decisive for thought beginning in the twentieth century, emerges precisely from the idea of a homogenous space of coexistence of subjects and of things separated from each other. The first ones, because they are defined by their self-positioning, juxtaposed to each other, the second ones by their inert exteriority next to each other. The milieu articulates a living interaction, that precisely replays the physical deal of the interaction in a field that is quite different from that of a field of forces, namely of a field of meanings.

This inaugural conception of the milieu comes from biologist and ethnologist Jakob von Uexküll, and here we will hold onto a few elements that are useful to us. The milieu is not that which surrounds a being, but what maintains with it a "functional circle," whose starting point is the perceptive signs and whose end point is the actantial signs. The subjectivation of the surrounding space of the living animal that operates in Uexküll's biosemiotics theory has the effect of taking the subject out of a relationship of objectivation of that which surrounds it. This is precisely to the benefit of a theory of the specific sign: such a subjectivation precisely defines the milieu. A subject does not encounter objects in the world, but first exchanges with perceptive signs, that in their turn trigger a narrative sign.[11] A living being therefore has to do with signs that interest it vitally; that it perceives and agitates through the appropriate reaction. If for Uexküll a milieu appears to the subject as specific and closed, there is, however, a rhythmic or musical harmony that ensures the communication of these functional circles among each other.[12] The monadic characteristic of the milieu of such a species does not prevent a general partition of the living.

Canguilhem will expand the question of vital interest to include that of vital norm. Canguilhem's gesture consists in opening the

---

11 See the introduction to Jacob von Uexküll's *A Foray into the Worlds of Animals and Humans*, where one can find the famous analysis of the tick's milieu.
12 See Uexküll's *The Theory of Meaning*, specifically chapters 4, 10, and the conclusion, where one can read: "There are not only the manifolds of space and time in which things can be spread out. There is also the manifold of environments, in which things repeat themselves in always new forms. All these countless environments provide, in the third manifold, the clavier on which Nature plays her symphony of meaning beyond time and space." Jacob von Uexküll, *Theory of Meaning*, in *A Foray into the Worlds of Animals and Humans*, trans. Joseph D. O'Neill (Minneapolis: University of Minnesota Press, 2010), p. 208.

functional circle, precisely to prevent the vital interest from closing in on itself. The vital interest thus becomes the vital "norm,"
which is not established by the living being's mode of existence,
but expands in eccentric circles from the center, which is the subject as agent of vital adventures. Canguilhem thus defines the subject from its needs, making "absolute center," and if "the animal
finds it simpler to do what it privileges,"[13] it is precisely the state of
its health that allows it to reinvent the norms of its environment,
instead of constraining itself, which is the case when a pathology
affects it. But whether it has to do with an unhealthy or a healthy
subject, it is always a matter of a subject that makes an inside of
the outside from a procedure of vital evaluation, and conversely,
which makes of its inside the stake of a game of relation with that
which is "outside," and which is, however, intrinsically part of it.
No dialectic, therefore—no reappropriating passage in the crossing of alienation—but a relational game that constitutes both the
environment as well as the living being, both shaping the "inside/
outside" of the environmental logic.

Let's see how to link the movement with Nancy's apparent hostil-
ity toward the milieu. In Nancy, the outside in the quotation above
is formulated in a double oxymoron: "its own exteriority," on one
hand, "the proper space of its being-out-in-the-world," on the other
hand. There are numerous statements in his writing that unfold
such a contraction of opposites. It is that the "own" in Nancy is not
a given interiority, but rather a push and a thrust, without origin
or destination, and being in favor of an otherwise powerful tension—whose power does not take its impulse from an initial motive
nor from an aimed at goal. This "own" asserts the extension of the
outside, an extension from a within, which is no more thought of as
interiority than the outside is external to its existence. It is precisely
the dimension of opening, the expansion and extension that makes
the outside a movement from the inside—the power of the outside
invaginates itself in the inside to makes itself dis-enclosure.

The dis-enclosure—one of Nancy's titles—states this general
movement from the outside, whose address opens onto a distancing
"[t]hat removes the possibility of designating points, subjects, objects,
or distances. Distancing simply distances those who are close, those
who are the closest, and thus opens the incommensurable."[14] A way

---

13 Canguilhem, *Knowledge of Life*, p. 113.
14 Jean-Luc Nancy, *Adoration* (New York: Fordham University Press 2013), p. 87.

of saying the dimension of the inside, that takes no part in the stable position of a given interiority, but on the contrary designates the defeat of any insurance linked to an internal mooring: "This outside of the outside envelopes an 'interior'; where expectations are disarmed, knowledge disconcerted, as also certitudes and doubts."[15] The outside affirms the movement that takes off outside from the outside, in the incommensurable, which Nancy says is "inside," an inside that is itself infinitely distant, for it is "an inside more interior than the extreme interior, that is, more interior than the *intimacy* of the world and the intimacy that belongs to each 'me.'"[16] Nancy borrows, thus, the simultaneous movement from an inside/outside of the logic of the milieu, but at a distance from the position of the semiotic subject (Uexküll) or the measuring subject (Canguilhem). Consequently, this sinking of an inside/outside passes any evaluation of a need, to the benefit of an impulsive drive losing itself in its passion, and also finding itself in it.

Canguilhem writes that "[o]nly a living being, infra-human, can coordinate a milieu. To explain the center by the environment would thus seem to be a paradox."[17] A measuring center, in the thought of the milieu, is literally defined by the outside, that is inside. Nancy, in turn, is in an opposition that is at once both strict and asymmetrical to this position. The outside is not that of a specific inside, but of an inside whose intimacy is lost in the extension of the being. Such intimacy is being-with. But the being-with—and it is in this that Nancy joins the logic of the milieu, from its generic and unspecific dimension—is not essentially of individuals, one another, but of the simultaneity of the inside and the outside, from the "general sending" of meaning.

It is the logic of the milieu that makes it fully understood that "'[w]ith' is the sharing of time space; it is the at the same time in the same place as itself, and itself, shattered. It is the instant scaling back of the principle of identity: Being is at the same time in the same place only on the condition of the spacing of an indefinite plurality of singularities. Being is Being; it does not ever recover itself, but it is near to itself, beside itself, in touch with itself, its very self, in the paradox of that proximity where distancing [*éloignement*] and strangeness are revealed. We are each time an other, each time

---

15 Jean-Luc Nancy, *Dis-Enclosure* (New York: Fordham University Press, 2013), p. 78.

16 Nancy, *Being Singular Plural*, p. 11.

17 Canguilhem, *Knowledge of Life*, p. 70.

with others. 'With' does not indicate the sharing of a common situation any more than the juxtaposition of pure exteriority does."[18] The logic of the milieu allows understanding the *simultaneity* of the inside and outside in Nancy, and by this, the formulation of the with, which does not consist in phenomenologically linking one to another, but in thinking an original simultaneity, saying the being's own otherness in privacy, which spaces out infinitely.

The second way of reading the proposition according to which humankind is not in the world as in a milieu consists consequently in avoiding the specific characteristic of the logic of a measuring inside/outside, to keep only the logic brought to the general dimension of the being. And to posit that "[i]nner experience is the experience of what places me outside of the outside of the equivalence of values, even of the valence of values in general, and thus outside of all subjectivity as of all property, whether this be the property of mercantile goods or of spiritual goods (competences or virtues)."[19] The logic of the milieu as an affirmed simultaneity of the inside and the outside becomes for Nancy the starting point of a thought where the subject disappears, insofar as the measuring instance no longer has a place. The measuring animal becomes immeasurable, and thus an intimate and active rapport with the immeasurable in general. A new neuralgic point of the milieu—no longer central, but infinitely in contact.

Body and Self: The Eccentricity of the Milieu as Spacing and the "Palpitating Push of Life"

The immeasurable is in no way solipsistic—its absolute is not isolated—but on the contrary holds onto countless bodies. Each one absolutely singular, each one absolutely milieu with-itself-with-others. In *Corpus*, Nancy considers such an environment by way of dawn: "Dawn is the drawing of a line, a presentation of place. Dawn is the sole medium for bodies, which subsists neither in fire nor in ice (solar thinking sacrifices bodies, lunar thinking phantasmagorizes them: taken together, they compose the Aztec-Austrian System—in a word, Metaphysics) [...] The dawn is just: it stretches equally from one edge to another. Its half-tone is not a chiaroscuro

---

18 Nancy, *Being Singular Plural*, p. 35.

19 *Nancy, Dis-Enclosure*, p. 78.

of contrast or contradiction. It's a complicity of places to be opened up and extended. It's a common condition: not of measured spaces, though all spacings are equal, all in the same light."[20]

This is one of the very rare mentions of the category of the milieu in Nancy's work, and here it specifies—localizes—its use. In a manner of agreeing with the thought of the milieu—which is a strong thought of space as place, insofar as space is no longer a homogenous field, but rather a space of specifically vital places—, Nancy develops a thought that extends it toward the idea of an equality. Such an equality does not have anything precisely homogenizing but says that what exists is accomplice in the singular spacing of the being. Such complicity does not state the harmony of a totality (Uexküll), but rather the same gesture opening each spacing infinitely different. This is not the same idea of partition from both authors. In Uexküll's thought of the milieu, it tunes independent melodies in a general concert of nature, while for Nancy, it is the equality of dawn that makes its ontological softness—the being being withdrawn from the violence of measuring, away from the frost or the fire of separatist or hierarchical metaphysics.

The unmeasurable has to do with what Nancy calls "spacing." Spacing states the immeasurable extension of the "inside-outside, upside-down."[21] And it is a body—always already body-to-body—that launches this meaning and makes room for such a spacing: it *is* such a spacing. It is for this reason that the body is "the being of existence" and that such an ontology is of/from the "place of existence, or the *local existence.*"[22] This environmental way of recasting ontology has no hold on the classical local/global distinction, since the ontology of the body is also an ontology of the world. Existence is local because [it is] spacing: extension from the breaking point of existence in the smallest parcel of body or drifting from one end to the other of the globe, from body to body.

The ontology of the body is environmental insofar as it affirms that there is no space, but rather place, articulated by a/from the body, by a/from the world—and there is no other world than the world of bodies, yet another affirmation following an environmental style. It is an articulation that is meeting and encounter—an encounter does not have a place *in* spacing, but it is spacing in itself: *a body is the spacing of that which it encounters.* Finally, we

---

20 Nancy, *Corpus*, pp. 47–49.
21 Ibid., p. 31.
22 Ibid., p. 15.

will note another environmental-style affirmation in what sense is for Nancy, even in senses,[23] whose last straw is "the sense of the spacing of senses."[24] Sense itself spaces in the way of a sense. "But a sense *open* as 'sensory' senses are—or rather, opened *by* their opening, exposing their being-extended—a significance, itself spacing, of spacing."[25] To feel is sense in its own spacing, in the middle of the extension of a *with* following the order of a shared feeling. The sense results, not as a production of a subject, but from this sensitive thrust of the being, infinitely shared, infinitely spread out.

If *Corpus* already indicates major features likely to follow an open environmental thought beyond the biosemiotics of a subject or the measuring invention of a living being, we will find, in its late follow-up, *Cruor*, something to make the movement more complex and denser. *Cruor*, in fact, takes up *Corpus* from a greater affinity with the thought of the milieu insofar as it makes central to its reflection the question of a vital drive—that, if it is not mistaken with the vital interest, nevertheless makes explicit the instance of emergence, the *self*, at once "the motor and the effect of the push,"[26] signaling to Uexküll's "functional circle," but from the bottomlessness of the original absence and end. Be it a thought of the milieu taken to the abysmal excess of the thought of the outside.

Cruor was published almost thirty years after the first edition of *Corpus*. From the outset, the introduction sets the threshold from where to take up the topic: "Space-time, the grappling of bodies or the body-to-body [*le corps-à-corps*], contact, all the ways of being outside and, even more, of being an outside."[27] Nancy states the new beginning: "In a single leap, 'me and you' allowed a transition from the interval or between-two to the between-us, without any preparation for this leap: it seemed necessary, long after, to account for the *between* insofar as it stretches from one body to others, even as it stretches and tenses within each one something like its own drive, which is what makes it a body and makes each and all of us body-to-body."[28] A way of saying that the logic of the *with* could eliminate what connects or pulls one to another,

---

23 Here, it would be fruitful to compare Nancy's philosophical affirmations with Erwin Straus's great work *The Sense of the Senses*.

24 Nancy, *Corpus*, p. 31.

25 Ibid., p. 83.

26 Nancy, *Cruor*, p. 23.

27 Ibid., p. 3.

28 Ibid.

giving the inside/outside as a general method, which leaves intact the question of the point of impulse of such movements—and of the vitality of the drive in general. At stake, here, is the question of community and the question of the instance that designates an impulsive singularity, and this in the way that they make a partition – the ways in which they share and resonate in each other.

The hypothesis pursued here is precisely that Nancy borrows more decisively the logic of the milieu to fill this theoretical gap. At the end of the book, we can indeed read these lines, that precisely cite a philosopher of environmental individuality: "Affectivity, as we have said, does not happen to the subject: it stirs him and therefore moves him. As Simondon wrote: "Affectivity-emotivity is a movement between the naturally indeterminate and the *hic et nunc* of present existence." Existence which is therefore seen as "incorporated in the collective," since "the individual as experiencer is a connected being." At this point, we must agree with Lacan's assertion: "The collective is nothing other than the *subject* of the individual." This must, of course, be understood based on the nature of the Lacanian subject, whose "existence is that of an 'in-between,' he belongs to a *mesology*." The collective is at the same time what we might call the natural milieu of the individual, and the relational space in which individuals form relations with each other. They mutually experience each other as long as they are moved: no matter how small the emotion, it is what sets in motion the egos *between them*.[29]

I will comment on this passage in a pointed reflection of what precedes, and which concerns the *self*, which is the conceptual center of the book. The *self* is immediately related to life, this is an unstable and provisional result of "the palpitating push of life,"[30] so that life finds there its infinitely resonant singularity, from oneself to another self, but also from the bottom without background on an original spacing. This means, on one hand, the communication and contagion of emotions *between oneself*, and that in an expression contrary to it, consecrated, 'as between-self.' And in this sense, the self has no other stability than as communication and contagion. This directly refers *self to body*, such that it comes close in *Corpus*. But the most notable dynamic, on the other hand, in this last book, and its robust references to life, is the dynamic

29 Jean-Luc Nancy, "Longing for the Father," *Corpus III*, trans. Agnès Jacob, pp. 54–55.
30 Nancy, *Cruor*, p. 9.

that is proper to the self, in a vital formalization of the outside that precisely prepares the passage previously quoted.

It isn't the *self* that is explained through life, such an instance expressing itself vitally, but life that implies the self, such that the self is the absolutely contingent result, and it is absolutely in contact. The self is thus life insofar as its push and its restraint, its pulsation that has nothing automatic, but proceeds from a repetition that is vital insistence or persistence. Thus, the *self* is the agent and the stake of a movement of a push that can also very well want to be followed or not followed: "Life death," as Nancy says, referencing one of Derrida's seminars. But what is at stake here is not the continuation or the cessation of life, but rather its end without end, which precisely makes life and death indistinct. This phrase, in Nancy, states the distinct indistinction of the being whose self is echoed. "Everything happens in a kind of overflow of nothing or in a superabundance of non-being that makes up the sole substance of what we have endeavored to call 'being.'"[31] The self is thus the push that makes being "more than being, living more than living."[32] The *self* thus bears its improper provenance, but insofar as "The self signals (like every living unity), but it relates and reports this signal to itself: it signifies itself."[33] We could therefore risk arguing that Nancy takes up Uexküll's functional circle from the space of being. This allows Nancy to qualify the distancing of the being, and to make an ecology of its ontology. And it is precisely the bottomlessness of the self that allows designating it according to an environmental dynamic: "Its 'in itself' is not at all an entity suspended in a hinter-world; it is a push, a pulsive drive, whose dynamic mobilizes the world and being-in-the-world."[34]

If the self is a relation, it isn't in the manner of a subject as relation to self. *Self* signals toward an environmental subject whose consistency is the *between*, and thus distinguishes itself radically from an idealistic subject as relation to self, to relate to any interesting strangeness[35] that presupposes its vitality. From here, Nancy

---

31 Ibid., p. 12.
32 Ibid., p. 8.
33 Ibid., p. 11.
34 Ibid., p. 21.
35 For Nancy, the vital interest is precisely the one that deals with the foreignness perceived in the self. "Where does it come from ? 'Self,' is what happens when there is foreignness. In this sense, 'self' is quite the opposite of 'to oneself' or 'in oneself': it is not a given property, it is given as improper, foreign." Ibid., p. 26.

takes on this psychoanalytically charged term (Klein, who he cites, but also Winnicott, whose vital and existential *self* at the same time could have contributed to his last book), itself spread between the scansion of a self that returns to itself in the manner of a vital rhythm, with all the randomness and the unforeseen that this presupposes, and the drive of existence that Nancy defines, faithful to his thought of the outside, but this time it is explicitly taken up from the question of the milieu: "Not in the midst of something else because there is nothing else: but as the midst or medium, the midway of all ways. Each instance of *self* [*chaque coup de soi*], whatever *it* may be, is an unprecedented taking-place. *It happens, it arrives.* In this point, physics and metaphysics merge: impulse and alterity, each one conditions the other."[36] It is in this sense that Nancy bursts Uexküll's mesological bubbles, whether by being a pulsation whose vitality is spacing, or through such an implosion/explosion: "What is extended does not pass from inside to outside but is amplified, spread out, distended, disposed, or even dislocated: it is to itself its own matter and form, according to a plasticity, an elasticity, or a ductility that makes up its very being."[37] A *self*—whichever one—is a general milieu, this qualifier is evidently not meant to be understood in the vague general sense, but in the sense of singular/plural rhythmicity of spacing, a vital dynamic. In this regard, it would be necessary to show how, in the environmental thought, the "subject" (organism, individual, body, self, etc.) makes milieu: it is the center and the circumference, or, for Nancy, the infinite opening. From one to the other, there is this same distinct indistinction.

Conclusion:
"The Relation-Between" as an Element
for an Environmental Thought

To conclude with a stealthy incursion into *The "there is" of the Sexual Relation*, may seem to constitute a step backwards. Not because it is a book that predates *Cruor,* but because it engages precisely the most vivid of his reflections on both the coupling of the two, what *Cruor* precisely proposes to expand in latitude, if one may say

---

36 Ibid., p. 12.
37 Ibid., p. 21.

so—what happens between more than two—and in longitude—to dig up the between itself. I will limit myself to outlining what, from the analysis of the relation in this work, signals to an environmental style thought that will discreetly amplify throughout the years. First, it is in this book that Nancy explains himself in a problematic way on the choice of the term relation. It is problematic, in the first place, because the philosopher refers precisely to the Kantian category of relation to approach its features. In second place, Nancy notes the differences in accent between the *relation* (pointing toward the sexual) and the *relationship* (coloring rather a romance), suggesting that the term relation is only privileged in the beginning of the work, namely in a free analysis of the Lacanian statement.

Nonetheless, we will be attentive to a moment of analysis of the *between* that sends us back literally to milieu as "category of contemporary thought." Nancy writes: "But what is between two is not either one of the two: it is the void—or space, or time (including, once again, simultaneous time), or sense—which relates without resembling, or resembles without uniting, or unites without finishing, or finishes without carrying to its end. (This is why the 'without- relation' of relation has become an almost obsessive preoccupation for contemporary thought, to the point where this relation itself needs to be turned around: if without-relation opens relation, relation in turn clears the way for without-relation.)"[38] Did Nancy have in mind Canguilhem's words referring to the category of the milieu? Indeed, the "without-relation" is none other than the relation thought environmentally—the relation, in Simondon's sense, that precisely at the end of his last book, *Cruor*, Nancy makes meet with Lacan.

---

38 *"The 'there is' of the Sexual Relation,"* in Jean-Luc Nancy, *Corpus II: Writings on Sexuality*, trans. Anne O'Byrne (New York: Fordham University Press, 2013), p. 8.

Ian James

Thinking Heteropoiesis with Nancy and after History

When I first met Jean-Luc Nancy in Strasbourg in 2003, we spoke at some length about what it might mean to write a book "on" his philosophy. I was then preparing a monograph that was later published in 2006, *The Fragmentary Demand*.[1] We discussed the difficulty of approaching or addressing the singularity and movement of a thinking that was always in movement in its ceaseless passage to the limit of thought, and that would suffer greatly from being pinned down, reduced, or fixed into a unified corpus or philosophical doctrine. Nancy himself was typically open, generous, and encouraging, though perhaps also and understandably a little skeptical and wary. Anyway, I think I persuaded him that the project was worthwhile and after some very rich discussion about a number of things he allowed me to plunder his archive and take what I wanted from his store of off-prints and, in the following days, sent me attachments of as yet unpublished material. Apart from a sense of his extraordinary openness and generosity, one thing I took away from that first meeting was a strong feeling that Nancy wanted far less to be written "on" or "about" and far more to engage in a shared thinking with his interlocutors. It has been such a privilege to spend so much of my career thinking with Nancy, as well as writing, yes, both on and about him. Above all he taught me that when we think, we think out of our relations with others, alongside them, and with them. It is this that has led me to try to recast the concept of "heteropoiesis" in the context of thinking both with Nancy and with biological theory.

In what follows I treat Nancy's philosophy and the biological theories of Maturana, Varela, and Robert Rosen as different techniques of thought that, in their own different or similar ways, attempt to think the presencing, presentation, or production of entities, organisms, and, finally, of cultural forms.[2] It is out of the

---

1   Ian James, *The Fragmentary Demand: An Introduction to the Philosophy of Jean-Luc Nancy* (Stanford: Stanford University Press, 2006).
2   My use of the term "technique of thought" builds upon the philosophical perspectives developed in previous work arguing that we should understand philosophical, scientific, aesthetic, and other knowledge forms as specific techniques that, in their different ways, respond to, are determined by, and thereby

differences and similarities discerned between these fragments that I try to recast the concept of "heteropoiesis." Heteropoiesis thought in a mapping of philosophical and biological theory onto each other, without any assumption of an absolute identity between them, will emerge as a base-line concept, a kind of mapping and modelling tool that will open the way for a novel naturalist and re-alist understanding of narrative and other fictional forms. The key point to be made here is that heteropoiesis may be used to describe the production of biological organisms and entities, of the worlds and world-forms experienced by living beings in general and as such, and, finally, the production of the symbolic forms of human culture. Heteropoiesis is, above all, a concept that describes com-ing into form in *relational terms*. Forms are born in and out of the "hetero-": the other of the relations to, but also of, an alterity or an outside, as opposed to the "auto-" of the self-organization of a closed system.

I. Beyond History

In an essay published in the year before his death, entitled "Un avenir sans passé ni future," Jean-Luc Nancy begins with an in-dication that we might be tempted to view our contemporaneity as a time that has been shorn of any confidence in both the past and the future.[3] Nancy, here, is not simply repeating a central and recurrent theme of post-modernity, the failure of grand narratives, but is pointing, I think, to a different way of understanding and responding to the eclipse of linear and teleological history. Nor, in speaking of a "time to come without past or future," is he repeating the Hegelian/Kojèvian motif of "The End of History." We are not at the end, or in the "post-" of a period after, but rather in a differ-ent space located outside of any linear history, in whose ascend-ing line things would get better while inching towards its ultimate end, its moment of fulfilment. "C'est en fait, l'histoire elle-même

---

model, a plural real whilst not at any point, either as a singularity or in their plurality, totalizing or giving a representation of the real. See Ian James, *The Technique of Thought: Nancy, Laruelle, Malabou and Stiegler After Naturalism* (Minneapolis: Minnesota University Press, 2019); for a complementary yet dis-tinct and comprehensive account of how philosophy might renew its techniques in the light of philosophies of technology see Susanna Lindberg, *Techniques en philosophie* (Paris: Hermann, 2020).

3   Jean-Luc Nancy, *La Peau fragile du monde* (Paris: Galilée, 2020), pp. 23–42.

qui s'est fragilisée jusqu'à s'évanouir et à nous laisser orphelins du progrès et avec lui de la 'bonne vie'./Ce deuil, nous le portons mal et difficilement."[4]

This mourning, and the disorientation that comes with it, has led us perhaps, Nancy thinks, to seek refuge in presentism, in an exclusive preoccupation with the presence of the present. But then we are still no less in mourning and no less beholden to the idea of history as centered on the human, and on human progress. It is just that the "good life" towards which we have hitherto been striving is now to be located in a commitment to the present. "Il est donc nécessaire," Nancy suggests, "de nous dégager aussi bien du deuil que de la représentation dont nous portons le deuil: celle de l'histoire maîtrisée."[5]

Yet, for Nancy, this would not entail an abandonment of the present but rather a certain cultivation of it, the need to "en recevoir [le don] comme allogène au temps."[6] It would be a question of cultivating a different kind of future that arises from elsewhere, a future which, as the title of his essay indicates, is not linked to a past (that of linear historical progression) nor to a future (that of an end to come), but which surges as a future "de l'approche et de la survenue d'un inconnu dont ni passé ni futur ne peuvent nous *éviter* le surgissement."[7] Nancy evokes here an alterity that is perhaps *both* behind and ahead as an "elsewhere" of the present, one that is both harbored within it, yet "at the same time" in turn harbors and exposes the present as such. We need, he notes, to detach ourselves entirely from any pathos of originary beginning and ultimate end and to turn towards this *à-venir* that is without past or future: "au lieu de vouloir détecter et décoder les messages de l'origine et de la fin, nous devons nous faire au silence et à l'obscurité qui sont au cœur de tout soubresaut et de tout surgissement." We need, he suggests, citing Clarice Lispector, to come to terms with "l'inconscience creative du monde."[8] The "elsewhere" is a *worldly* affair even as it is somehow anterior to the manifestation of any given world as such. And *as such*, I would argue, it is also an affair of relation and relations, the relations of what Nancy would call sense, of the sense of the world, relations

---

4   Ibid., p. 24.
5   Ibid., p. 26.
6   Ibid., p. 25.
7   Ibid., p. 27.
8   Ibid., p. 28.

spaced out in that silent and obscure elsewhere, far behind and ahead of the present, shorn of the past and future of linear history, but giving the present in its futural emergence, its arrival, its exposure. And this is not to say that the past as we know it historically, a past of (amongst other things) oppression and exploitation, enslavement and annihilation, expropriation and colonization, is abandoned or elided by thought and therefore forgotten. For, as Faulkner famously wrote, "The past is never dead. It's not even past," and no doubt all those relations of sense that produced the historical worlds of violent oppression are no less at play in that silent and obscure elsewhere that emerges in and as the present, as our present.[9]

Nancy directs thought, in the time after linear historical time, to that which comes in the emergence of our world, from that elsewhere which is as real as it gets: ungraspable, unthinkable, excessive, yet no less real for all that in its arrival, its opening, its surging into presence.

II. Closure

As is well known, Maturana and Varela's theory of "autopoiesis" was an attempt to define life in terms of the self-production, self-organization, and self-maintenance of biological systems. It also had an influence well beyond biology, in, for instance, Niklas Luhmann's systems theory. It has been noted that the concept of "autopoiesis" was born out of a constructivist approach and from the experimental results of empirical research into the neurobiology of visual perception.[10] As a theoretical understanding and technique, then, it combines the empirical investigation of biological organisms with the philosophical assumption that any reality seemingly independent of them will be a construct of their internal coding and perceptual organization. As the editors of Maturana and Varela's seminal work, *Autopoiesis and Cognition,* put it in their introduction, a living, autopoietic system is formed in: "a topology in which elements and their relations constitute a closed system, or more radically still, one which from the 'point of view' of the

---

9 William Faulkner, *Requiem for a Nun* (London: Vintage, 2015 [1996]), p. 85.
10 Juan Carlos Letelier, Gonzalo Marın, Jorge Mpodozis, "Autopoietic and (M, R) systems," *Journal of Theoretical Biology* 222 (2003), pp. 261–272, p. 268.

system itself, is entirely self-referential and has no 'outside'."[11] The ability of living organisms to self-produce and reproduce, to self-organize and self-maintain, is predicated on an internal circularity of relations to relations that specify the functional components of a biological system and give it its form. As Maturana puts it in the essay "Biology of Cognition": "this circular organisation con-stitutes a homeo-static system whose function is to produce and maintain this very same circular organisation by determining that the *components* that specify it be those whose synthesis or main-tenance it secures."[12]

In this way the theory of autopoiesis affirms a constructivist non-realism. Maturana again: "For every living system its particular case of self-referring circular organisation specifies a closed domain of interactions that is its cognitive domain, and no interaction is possible which is not prescribed by the organization."[13] This non-realism is confirmed by claims that: "reality as a universe of inde-pendent entities about which we can talk is, necessarily, a fiction," or in comments made by both Maturana and Varela in *The Tree of Knowledge*: "We do not see what we do not see, and what we do not see does not exist."[14] Yet this does not mean that biological organ-isms are somehow solipsistically imprisoned in their own worlds and held within some kind of neurobiological subjective idealism. Maturana and Varela make a distinction between the organisation and structure of autopoietic systems and carefully emphasize that although such systems are *organizationally* closed, they are also *structurally* open.[15] Again, as their editors put it: "perception should not be viewed as a grasping of an external reality, but rather as the specification of one."[16] The external world is still "out there" but it becomes a question of what each organism specifies as existing in a certain way and in such a way as to permit the continuation of life. So, the relations of the system to its outside are entirely specified by the internal coding and organization of the system.

---

11 Humberto Maturana & Francisco Varela, *Autopoiesis and Cognition: The Realization of the Living* (Dordrecht: Reidel, 1980), p. vi.

12 Ibid., p. 9.

13 Ibid., p. 49.

14 Ibid., p. 52; Humberto Maturana & Francisco Varela, *The Tree of Knowledge* (Boston: Shambhala, 1988), p. 242.

15 On this see Cary Wolf, *Critical Environments: Postmodern Theory and the Pragmatics of the Outside* (Minneapolis: Minnesota University Press, 1998), p. 59.

16 Maturana & Varela, *Autopoiesis and Cognition*, p. xv.

III. Openness

The closure of autopoietic living systems, as understood by Maturana and Varela, is also very saliently signaled in the way they understand the boundaries of organisms. As Maturana puts it: "The organism ends at the boundary that its self-referring organisation defines in the maintenance of its identity."[17] This contrasts starkly, I would argue, with the understanding of the living and of its organization that was developed by the theoretical biologist Robert Rosen. Rosen understands living organisms as metabolic repair systems, or (M, R)-systems. These are systems whose functional components and their interrelations have the property of being able to repair and reproduce themselves. The metabolism of a living organism thus has a circular causality and a certain closure with respect to its self-maintenance and propagation. It is, as Rosen himself puts it, "closed to efficient causes." Within a living organism "all efficient causes are produced inside the organism whenever we pull a fabricator inside a system by putting it together with what it fabricates, the result is necessarily an (M, R)-system."[18] On the face of it Rosen's (M, R)-systems and Maturana and Varela's autopoietic systems may appear to be very similar to each other. Both share a circularity of organization that entails a closure of the system upon itself enabling it to self-maintain and self-reproduce.[19]

Yet there is also a key difference between them, one which pertains to the question of the boundaries of the living system in question and the nature of the relations that are maintained to the world exterior to the organism. It might be worth noting at this point that Rosen's relational biology is a theoretical approach that deploys mathematics, and specifically the mathematics of category theory, to understand the organization of living systems in concrete and real terms. Organization here becomes a thing that is just as real, if not more so, than anything that might be identified as physical substance or matter with regard to the materiality of living beings.

---

17 Ibid., p. 20.

18 Robert Rosen, *Life Itself: A Comprehensive Inquiry into the Nature, Origin, and Fabrication of Life* (New York: Columbia University Press, 1991), p. 252. See also Letelier et al., "Autopoietic and (M, R) systems," p. 265.

19 The is the central point made by Letelier et al. in "Autopoietic and (M, R) systems." They do not, however, foreground the difference between the two accounts in the way that has been done here.

The approach taken, then, is one in which the seemingly abstract formalism of category theory and its diagrammatic thinking is deployed as a technique to discern a more complete and concrete reality of biological existence, that of its organizational specificity that marks it out as living.

In this, Rosen's theory gives us something approximating a relational ontology that is at the same time a relational realism. In this context, the relation of the organism to its environment is decisively different from that of the constructivist perspective that orientates the theory of autopoiesis. Rosen writes: "we find a *natural system* Ω, embedded in its environment. In general, this system will be *open*. Hence, the environment will be the seat of a variety of influences determining the behaviour of the system Ω."[20] In contradistinction to autopoietic organization, (M, R)-systems are open, and the relations that they maintain with their environment are relations of influence: the influence from the environment determines the organism rather than the organism specifying the environment.

As has been noted by others, what an (M, R)-system lacks "is the generation of its own border and the internal topology that Autopoiesis implies."[21] Where, for Maturana and Varela, an "organism ends at the boundary that its self-referring organisation defines," in Rosen's theory there is no such marking of a separation or discreteness between the living system and its surrounding world. The (M, R)-system may be closed to efficient causes and have a circular organization that allows it to endure and reproduce but "it has only the property of circular cellular organization and lacks spatial confinement."[22] This constitutive openness arguably results from the relational ontology that Rosen's use of category theory implies. In particular, it may result from his understanding of functions and components as fundamental units of biological organization: "the notion of *component* is tied to that of *function*, and this in turn is dependent upon the larger system of which the component is a part."[23] This gives us a model according to which biological components are always determined in their function according to the environment of the surrounding organizational system. The components of the cell are given their functions by the needs of

---

20 Rosen, *Life Itself*, p. 122.
21 Letelier et al., "Autopoietic and (M,R) systems," p. 268.
22 Ibid., p. 271.
23 Rosen, *Life Itself*, p. 121.

the cell, those of the cell by those of the organ or system of organs that form the organism. There is nothing closed in the structure of the component itself which will determine the function. With regard to function: "its description changes as the system to which it belongs changes."[24]

The most decisive and important point to note here is that, given the absence of spatial confinement in (M, R)-systems, what is true for the component of a cell in relation to the cell, or of the cell as a component of an organ and organism, is equally true for the organism itself in relation to its surrounding world. In Rosen's theoretical biology: "Organisation [...] inherently involves *functions* and their interrelations," but these do not begin or end at the boundaries of the individual organism. If an organism is taken as a component of its surrounding environment its function will be determined by and change according to the shifting organization of that environment. The openness of (M, R)-systems yields a fully-fledged relational vision of the natural world. This has been put very well by Nathaniel Laurent in a recent paper. Relational biology "is particularly in agreement with a network perspective about biological systems. More precisely, the class of (M, R)-systems described by Robert Rosen gives us a formal picture of an autonomous life form composed of a relational network between functional components. Necessarily, the realization of such a universal formalism of life gives rise to a diversity of interacting natural systems."[25]

IV. Narrative

We are no doubt still a long way from a theory of narrative and of literature. Yet heteropoiesis, as derived from this contrast between the autopoietic and relational-biological understanding of living systems, will serve as a base-line concept that will allow for a mapping of the functional relations of Rosen's theory onto the relations of trans-immanent sense and of the coming to presence of the present as thought by Nancy. This mapping does not assume that Rosen's theory and Nancy's philosophy can, by bringing them into

---

24 Ibid.
25 Nathan Laurent, "Biological networks from the relational biology perspective," in *Biological Systems from a Network Perspective*, ed. Timoteo Carletti, Roland Cazalis and Ron Cottam (Namur: Presses Universitaires de Namur, 2019), pp. 147–168, p. 12.

a relation of analogy for instance, be said thereby also to be in a relation of identity each with the other. Rather, it opens up the possibility of discerning at least some degree of structural isomorphism
between them and of attributing a quality of sense and meaning to
Rosen's biological relations (insofar as functional components are
endowed with a kind of purposive finality that necessarily implies
meaning) whilst at the same time locating the Nancean dimension
of "sens" in excess of any human taking in hand of being and as
an articulation of a broader cosmological and biological vision.[26]
In this way, both Nancy's ontology and that of Rosen can be said
to describe the production of organisms, entities, and forms out of
the "hetero-" of relations that articulate a non-bounded field of alterity or otherness. If autopoiesis is the closed self-production and
self-maintenance of a living organism or form, then heteropoiesis
would refer to the way in which forms and their production result
from, or are constructed out of, the interacting relations, and the
relations to relations, that constitute the wider field within which
those forms come to exist as such.

So what this mapping of Nancean *sense* onto relational biology
gives is the first step in an understanding of the natural world in
which living systems are already articulations of sense and meaning. As open relational systems geared toward the meaning finality
of functions, they are liable to build orders of sense and meaning from the simplest interactions of cells through to those of the
ever more increasingly complex living organisms and their diverse
modes of interaction with their surrounding environments. In this
perspective the human order of sense, meaning, and symbolic
forms find their precondition in the preceding non-human orders
of sense and mean articulated within biological life. They also find

---

26 I argue for the alignment of Nancy's thinking with a non-reductive naturalist
vision at much greater length in a mapping of his thinking onto the relational
biology of Georges Canguilhem. Canguilhem explicitly attributes the quality of
"sens" to biological organisms and their (inter-)relations and develops a theory
similar in certain key respects to that of Rosen. It is interesting to note that both
Canguilhem and Rosen at various points in the development of their respective
theories were influenced by cybernetics and that Nancy was personally and significantly influenced by Canguilhem, having been taught by him at the Sorbonne
in the early 1960s and, under Canguilhem's influence, having undertaken a year
of biological study as part of his preparation for the *aggrégation de philosophie.*
See James, *The Technique of Thought*, pp. 75–90; on Nancy's debt to Canguilhem see Ian James, "Affectivity, Sense, and Affects: emotions as an articulation
of biological life," *Angelaki* 26, no. 3–4 (2021), pp. 155–161.

their precondition within the structural operation of heteropoiesis, where any given form is formed out of systemic relations as a unit or component of another more complex set of forms and systems which are themselves formed out of relations and so on.[27]

For now though, and by way of conclusion, I want to underline the way in which the concept of heteropoiesis can work as a formal tool that allows the relations as thought by different relational theories to be mapped onto each other (according to degrees of structural isomorphism) or constructed out of each other (according to the relational understanding of production "from" an outside). This will open the way for the elaboration of a novel naturalist, and realist, theory of literature that responds to the imperative articulated by Nancy that we cultivate the present and "receive it(s gift) as allogenic to time." Other theories will come into play in this mapping and construction of the relationality of sense and meaning out of and after biological life: one might cite von Uexküll's *Umwelttheorie*, Juri Lotman's conception of the semiosphere, Gregory Bateson's systems theory, Terrence Deacon's thinking of the human as a symbolic species, and also biosemiotic theory as developed by figures such as Jesper Hoffmeyer and Claus Emmeche, and taken over into the cultural sphere by Wendy Wheeler. From this perspective, narrative form and literary space cannot be perceived autopoietically as closed or autonomous. Rather they are fabricated and produced out of the relations of sense and meaning, sign relations, textual and symbolic networks which make them possible as such. But these relations are real relations, or more specifically they are relations that are both to and of the real, that "unconscious of the world" that is, as Nancy put it, the obscure elsewhere from which the present surges and presences, and from which any form will take form. Narrative here is no mere constructivist construction of codes and signifiers but rather is formed of sign-relations, of their relations to other relations, which are articulated in a regression of signs into deep, biological non-human life. So, this relational world is not bound by the human order of language or of symbolic figuration but rather extends into the realm of the zoological and the biological. To think heteropoiesis after life, then, and to think narrative in terms of heteropoiesis, is

---

27 I have begun to sketch this out elsewhere and expect to develop this much more in future: see Ian James, "Narrative Voice, Heteropoiesis, and the Outside," in *Perspectives on the Self – Reflexivity in the Humanities*, ed. Tereza Matejckova & Vojtech Kolman (Berlin: De Gruyter, 2022), pp. 155–173.

to affirm that the stories we tell ourselves today, now, in a time outside of the linear time of teleological history, will be stories that are of the real, from the real, and that this real is not just that of the worlds that we live and have lived in but is also and irreducibly a natural and biological real in which we as human are embedded, in which we come to presence, and from which our form or forms are produced.

Georgios Tsagdis

Drawing Life:
Freedom and Form in Jean-Luc Nancy

> Life is the autonomy in the phenomenon;
> it is the scheme (*Schema*) of freedom
> Schelling[1]

Freedom, form, life: no sooner are the words invoked, than the figure connecting them is drawn and set in motion, triangulating in a kaleidoscope of possibilities. Out of all possible constellations, this essay pursues one of the most obvious, but arguably not least propitious, tracing, through a close reading, Nancy's major exposition of *freedom* in *The Experience of Freedom* (1988) up to the point where it touches on the minor theme of *form* in *The Pleasure in Drawing* (2009).

What this tracing effects is not only to indicate—despite shifts of emphasis and terminological prerogatives—a vector of continuity in Nancy's work across decades and domains, but importantly, to draw on life, in order to draw life in the wake of Jean-Luc Nancy's passing, which took place amidst an entrenched and often embittered contestation of life and freedom, that is, of life against freedom and freedom against life.

To make sense of the two, in the thick of the cacophony of their touts, Nancy's indifference towards the "sense" of "freedom" makes for a most conducive beginning.[2] He writes: "Freedom is also wild freedom, the freedom of indifference, the freedom of choice, availability, the free game, freedom of comportment, of air, of love, or of a free time where time begins again. It frees each of these possibilities, each of these notions of freedom, like so many

---

1   Friedrich Wilhelm Joseph Schelling, *Sämmtliche Werke*, I, ed. K. F. A. Schelling (Stuttgart: Cotta, 1856–1861), p. 249. Friedrich Wilhelm Joseph Schelling, "New Deduction of Natural Right," in *The Unconditional in Human Knowledge: Four Early Essays (1794–1796)*, trans. Fritz Marti (London: Bucknell University Press, 1980), pp. 221–247, p. 222.
2   Jean-Luc Nancy, *The Experience of Freedom*, trans. Bridget McDonald (Stanford: Stanford University Press, 1993), p. 154.

freedoms of freedom—and it is freed from these."[3] Nancy will call for the same freedom, the same annulment of privilege with regard to the senses of love, the senses of sense and one should say with him, the senses of life: for there are indeed the lives of humans and viruses, as much as the afterlives of the living, the lives of ideas, precarious and bare lives, lives unlived and lives relieved of the burden of life—life leads numerous lives.

I. Of Freedom

To begin then with freedom. A task as foreboding today as it was more than three decades ago, when Jean-Luc Nancy took it up, venturing to think freedom for the first time since Heidegger, not as a merely historic, but as a "guiding" theme. For Nancy, Heidegger constitutes the last in a lineage of thinkers running through Spinoza, Kant, Schelling and Hegel, who recognized freedom as "the fundamental question of philosophy, in which even the question of being has its root."[4] Importantly, as last in this line, Heidegger marks also its interruption, so that Nancy understands his own task as a meditation on an *inherited interruption*; an exploration of the "space left free by Heidegger."[5]

Retracing this exploration, one first encounters Nancy's encounter with Kant. This sets the stakes of the Heideggerian inheritance under the rubric of three major counter-premises, three major refutations. Firstly, contrary to his explicit postulation, Nancy claims, Kant already gleaned that freedom is not an "Idea."[6] Freedom is instead an "essential fact" of existence and of its meaning: the fact of being abandoned to being-in-the-world, and one without which existence is reduced to (the fact of) mere survival.[7] As such, freedom is—if anything—"the force of resistance to the Concept or Idea of Freedom";[8] by default withdrawing when enveloped in an "Idea."[9] This disarticulation of freedom from its Idea is particularly

---

3   Ibid., pp. 56–57.
4   Ibid., p. 33.
5   Ibid.
6   Ibid., pp. 10–11.
7   Ibid., p. 2.
8   Ibid., p. 35.
9   Ibid., p. 47.

significant for Nancy, as is its postulation as an actual force, not least, the force that effects precisely this disarticulation.

Secondly, contrary to the Kantian free will that wills to constitute itself as both the represented object and representing subject,[10] becoming thereby the most essential property of the subject, Nancy labors to extirpate or ex-propriate freedom from the subject.[11] Nancy finds in Hegel the first gesture of this ex-propriation, which shows freedom as the finite exposure to the "infinite separation of essence as existence."[12] This expropriation, prepared by Schelling and carried forward by Heidegger, becomes in Nancy equivalent to the subject's originary exposure to infinite difference. Ultimately, Nancy will proclaim freedom as having *"the exact structure of the subject."*[13] What is equated in this emergent merging of subject and freedom, is the self-construction and self-appearance of the subject. This is not a vindication of Hegel: the subject makes itself in appearing to itself precisely *as incapable of making itself*, and vice versa, it appears to itself as making itself in a way that *must remain opaque.*[14] There is no dialectic and no synthesis here: this *subjectum sive libertas* (i.e. subject or freedom) does not produce a mastery of meaning or sense, but remains naked no-thingness.

Thirdly, Nancy opposes the equation of freedom with causality or necessity, effected by Kant and most of the subsequent tradition. Nancy notes that by laying freedom as the "keystone" of the architectonic of pure reason,[15] Kant made it impossible to prove the fact of its existence from within the logic of this architectonic.[16] The short-circuiting of this logic becomes accordingly apparent in the emergence of freedom as the non-physical cause that inserts itself surreptitiously into a chain of physical causality.

From 1929 onwards, Heidegger attempted to extract the notion of freedom from causality, an effort culminating in his 1936 course on Schelling's "On the Essence of Human Freedom," where freedom was cast as archi-foundation—the *"Abgrund* of human reality."[17] In Schelling, Heidegger discovered the fact of freedom as necessary to human essence, but soon went on to abandon

---

10 Ibid., p. 4.
11 Ibid., p. 7.
12 Ibid., p. 33.
13 Ibid., p. 90. Emphasis in the original.
14 Ibid.
15 Ibid., p. 21.
16 Ibid., p. 25.
17 Ibid., pp. 35–36.

the Schellingian paradigm on account of its failure to consider this freedom as "nothing," that is, as a finitude, which an infinite being cannot found.[18] Shortly after, with very little explanation, Heidegger would abandon the theme of freedom altogether. In a 1943 seminar note, he offered the scant explanation: "'Freedom' forfeited its role originally in the history of Being, for Being is more original than beingness and subjectivity."[19] Causality and subjectivity—if they still mattered at all—were absorbed by beingness.[20]

This is the interruption that Nancy and with him we, today still, inherit. Its lineaments amount to the dissociation of freedom from its Idea, its expropriation from the subject and its release from causality. This triple freeing of freedom is not merely negative: freedom is acclaimed as the force of things, the force of existence as act.[21] Freedom is acclaimed as co-originary with the subject, as the subject's self-difference, or as Nancy would say a few years later, its "singular plurality." Finally, freedom is acclaimed as the nothingness that founds and supports every act, the effects of which may vary "depending on the linking of forces," but which is itself, as *thing*, always the same, an absolute intensity.[22]

As might already be clear, Nancy does not merely pick up where Heidegger left off. The effected interruption is not incidental, but is anticipated by aporias which are integral not only to this interruption, but also already to the logic of freedom that animated a tradition that led up to its own exhaustion. The entwinement, if not identification, of freedom and causality informs one of these aporias. For Kant and much of post-Kantian philosophy, freedom was understood as the enigma of causality that postulated the free will as the cause of its own representation.[23] As caused, the will is here the object of absolute self-knowledge, yet as cause, it is the absolutely incomprehensible, that is, absolutely free subject of self-legislation. The necessary, if inexplicable coincidence of this refraction of the will corresponds to the necessity of the Idea. And since the Idea is itself a (re)presentation of necessity, the law of freedom becomes equivalent to the necessity of necessity.[24] This

---

18   Ibid., p. 37.
19   Ibid., p. 38.
20   Ibid., pp. 38–39.
21   Ibid., p. 102.
22   Ibid., p. 104.
23   Ibid., p. 45.
24   Ibid., p. 46.

configuration of freedom as redoubled necessity constitutes for Nancy an expression of theoretical and practical powerlessness.[25]

From Rousseau and Kant to Marx and Heidegger, the escape from this double impotence consisted in doubling the stakes on the side of *praxis*, by "stretching out" freedom, construing it as a passage from *theoria* to *praxis*.[26] Despite aligning with and advancing the three aforementioned refutations, Heidegger, in postulating freedom as the most fundamental ontological determination, retained *praxis* as its domain. Even as he replaced the Kantian pure will as the subject's "form of legislation" with "the duty of existence,"[27] Heidegger remained within the orbit of practical necessity, occluding, according to Nancy, the "an-archy" of existence, its de-liverance from every law unto the fact of freedom.[28] Moreover, and indeed more importantly, this ontologization of *praxis* under the aegis of freedom, a recoil, as it were, of the "practical" into the theoretical, amounted for Nancy to a suppression of the distinction of freedom from truth, where this distinction would have to be maintained in order to think—in Nancy's words—"*together* and *in the same originarity*, the withdrawal of freedom's being and its singular factuality."[29] In another idiom, if one might still employ these words without blushing, what would have to remain free is the relation of freedom's essence or quiddity to its existence or haecceity, the relation of freedom to itself, its auto-affection.

Thus, Nancy will pursue the Heideggerian interruption, which at the very moment of freedom's nearly silent discrediting and abandonment, inserted, surreptitiously, the "free" (*das Freie*).[30] Rejecting the word "freedom," Heidegger preserved and promoted its semantic root in order to account for the groundlessness of being and the leap of thought it calls forth.[31] The "free" became thus the "existing opening" wherein freedom takes place; it became Heidegger's way of saying: "*chōra*."

The *chōra* of freedom is for Nancy the space of experience. Nancy recalls the origin of the word "experience" in *peirā* and in *ex-periri*, which bespeak a lack of foundation that calls for an act of

---

25 Ibid.

26 For Hegel this was a passage of realization, one that transformed comprehension to self-comprehension. Ibid., pp. 50–51.

27 Rendering "*das Sollen des Da-seins*"; ibid., p. 26.

28 Ibid., p. 30.

29 Ibid., p. 42.

30 Ibid., p. 40.

31 Ibid., pp. 42–43.

founding on the basis of perilous experimentation by a subject not in royal command, but undergoing a trial or passion, "exposed like the pirate (*peirātēs*) who freely tries his luck on the high seas"; for freedom cannot be appropriated but only "pirated," illegitimately seized.[32] Nancy asserts that the experience of founding is the essence of experience in general, yet the foundation laid "is more or less the *nothing* itself, this ungraspable *chorā*, carried to the incandescent intensity of a decision."[33] Said differently, the foundational act decides existence through a piracy that "pirates the im-propriety and formlessness of a *chorā*,"[34] the *chōra* of freedom. It is in this sense, that freedom is the experience of the limit, of *peras*: the limit one can never reach, yet nonetheless must hold on to.

This is then where the inherited interruption, or perhaps the interrupted inheritance of freedom, has led Nancy: the fact of freedom consists in a self-founding, not by *causing* itself, but by undergoing the experience of an exposure to one's own limit, that is, to the nothingness of one's own existence. Importantly, in this regard, the self does not have the experience *of* existence; rather the experience it has *is* existence.[35]

Understanding freedom as an experience of limits, or as liminal existence, is what invites an examination of form. For form is precisely the limit where the formed and the formless mutually touch. As Nancy exclaims, "the fever of drawing, the fever of art in general, is born of the frenzied desire to push form right to the limit, to make contact with the formless, as an erotic fever pushes bodies to the limits of their own forms."[36]

II. Of Form

To continue then with form. Nancy turns to drawing as a principal practice of form, for in drawing the form remains open: initiated and incomplete, forever beginning and without closure.[37] The character of drawing as incessant beginning is decisive for Nancy and

---

32 Ibid., p. 20.
33 Ibid., p. 84.
34 Ibid., p. 85.
35 Ibid., p. 89.
36 Jean-Luc Nancy, *The Pleasure in Drawing*, trans. Philip Armstrong (Stanford: Stanford University Press, 2013), p. 78.
37 Ibid., p. 92.

it is this character that carries into the aesthetic domain, that is, the domain of truth on the surface of sense and affect, the theme of freedom. Recalling the distinction of power and freedom in *The Experience of Freedom*, makes the purview of drawing, and thus of form, clearer: "power has an origin, freedom is a beginning. Freedom does not cause coming-to-being, it is *an initiality of being.*"[38] The drawing of a form *is* freedom insofar as it *initiates being.*

Nancy takes on the objection that drawing initiates a simulacrum, rather than being itself, by appropriating and undoing Platonism at once. He commits to an understanding of drawing as the *designation of the Idea*, precisely in a Platonic sense: the Idea as the intelligible model of the real, the "visible form" of the thing, visible however only to the intellect.[39] Drawing "proceeds from the desire to show this form" and in this sense, it "designates, presents, monstrates, or ostentates" the Idea.[40]

However, this presentation of the Idea is never mere (re)production. It consists, rather, in an excess of *intention*, "a tension that allows the form to open itself to its own formation."[41] In drawing, the form draws freedom, it draws life to form itself. Accordingly, Platonic mimesis is also adopted and adapted, as what takes hold of and makes evident "the formative and rousing force of the Idea, the ostention and emotion of truth."[42] Mimesis does not (re)present the Idea, rather it manifests its force. This vouches for the provocation that mimesis is "without model," since the forms it procures conform to and make visible the model of the Idea only in the sense of truth, which inflects knowledge into pleasure,[43] carrying forth and playing out the formative, rather than the formed form: *forma formans*, rather than *forma formata.*[44]

As force, form is *dynamis*, yet, contrary to the Aristotelian definition of the distinction between *physis* and *technē*, in which *physis* has its forming principle within itself, as entelechy, whereas *technē* receives this principle from the craftsman, form is here a *self-forming* force.[45] Nancy calls this metastable process a *state of formation* (*status formandi*) or *birth* (*status nascendi*): a state in

---

38 Nancy, *The Experience of Freedom*, p. 78.
39 Nancy, *The Pleasure in Drawing*, p. 5.
40 Ibid., p. 10.
41 Ibid., p. 39.
42 Ibid., p. 20.
43 Ibid., p. 61.
44 Ibid., p. 21.
45 Ibid., p. 12.

which the form as formation of the Idea precedes and extends itself beyond itself, beyond what allows its identification in the present of its presentation. Thus, whereas "formed form summons a new formation; the Idea makes demands on itself beyond its identifications […]."[46] Drawing accordingly "designs to designate" "the nascent form whose form is nowhere given in advance."[47] In turn, the forms that drawing and more broadly *technē* develop constitute a mimesis or "imitation of nature" only in the sense "of the inimitable forming force of a germination or of a reproduction and growth presumed without art, in other words, without artifice and thus without search or effort."[48] Freedom is, one must premise, without search or effort.

All the same, a "practice of forms" does not know its limits in advance—if it is able to give form to the formless, to make the one touch the other, it is because it touches, by surprise, its own limit.[49] As such, the freedom of the forming form is without search only in the sense that it does not undertake a programmatic search of a pre-established discovery; the force of the forming form is rather itself constituted as an incessant search of what cannot be known, or imagined, what in fact cannot exist before it is "found." Ultimately, it is not about showing what does not show or showing that it does not show, but rather showing "the infinity of becoming visible."[50] As with freedom, this is the actualization of an infinitude, the actual "infiniteness *of the finite as finite*."[51]

III. Of Life

To close with life. Or rather, perhaps, to open with life. In the brief sketch above, the drawing of form was understood as a practice of freedom, one in which the formative force of things reaches its limits and thus forms itself. In that regard, drawing imitates nature: not by representing nature, but by becoming-nature, becoming self-forming freedom.

---

46 Ibid., p. 25.
47 Ibid., p. 22.
48 Ibid., p. 33.
49 Ibid., p. 75.
50 Ibid., p. 92.
51 Nancy, *The Experience of Freedom*, p. 172.

Nancy asks himself: "Would I say that all things are free?" He responds immediately: "Yes, if I knew how to understand this. But at least I know that it would have to be understood."[52] For it becomes soon apparent that unless nature, that is, *everything*, is free, humans cannot be free either. If nature is delivered to causality, Kantianism is bound to return.

However, the proclamation that all is free, is reached only late in *The Experience of Freedom*. Earlier in the work, freedom is directly connected to existence, which is consistently understood as thought. "[...] The *life* of the existent is identically its *thought*,"[53] writes Nancy, making it difficult to escape the elision of the "existent" with *Dasein*. In turn, it is thinking that "trembles with freedom,"[54] since freedom is a leap and a burst into existence, a leap "in which existence is discovered as such"; "this discovery *is* thinking."[55] Adjoining the preceding, it appears that *the life of the existent which is thought, consists in existence discovering itself*; or in other words: thought discovering itself, thought thinking itself— a prime mover, forever actual, forever alive.

This classical recoil is however recuperated by an "internal" inflection of thought, which amounts, in truth, to thought's self-deconstruction. Nancy calls the burst of freedom "the *other* thought of all thought"—"not the Other of thought, nor the thought of the Other, but that *by which* thought thinks."[56] Nancy continues: "this other thinking, which frees all thought as such, is not restricted to any definite form of thought—it is perhaps the form-lessness of all thought and is accordingly not restricted by that which goes by the name of 'philosophy'."[57] Freedom is ultimately thought only in the sense of the discovery of the *chōra* of thought, of the nothingness that conditions it. This nothingness is—*not only* to the existent, but *to all being*—life.

In closing this brief exploration, which attempted a cut across three very complex domains, it is worth rehearsing one last time the tension and stakes at hand. Early in *The Experience of Freedom* a line appears that might, again, have come from Heidegger's hand: "human beings are not born free in the same way that they

---

52 Ibid., p. 158.
53 Ibid., p. 104.
54 Ibid., p. 59.
55 Ibid., p. 58. Added emphasis.
56 Ibid., p. 59. Added emphasis.
57 Ibid., p. 60.

are born with a brain; yet they are born, infinitely, to freedom."[58] The choice of the brain is not accidental: not even the most intimate material substratum of thought is born to freedom—only thought, the life of the existent, is. The discourse of neuroplasticity was in its infancy at the time of *The Experience of Freedom*'s composition, the adult brain being thought as a finished product; but this is not decisive here.

What seems decisive, is that thought, under the name of existence, makes a "something" out of a "thing," allowing it to be one among many possible singularities that break with the necessary, self-enclosed repletion of a material universe.[59] In this sense Nancy claims: "phenomena are necessary, the very existence of the thing is free."[60] For it is in thought where the gift of freedom is given, the opening of the world takes place, the simple "there is" appears. Thus, for Nancy freedom is not an essence, but "the *being-free of being*, where its being is expended. It is its very life, if life is understood as originary auto-affection. But being is not a living being and is not 'affected' by its freedom: being is only what it is insofar as it is in freedom and as freedom, the being of a bursting of being that delivers being to existence."[61] At this pole, being becomes itself, which means "something," only in freedom, *eo ipso*, in thought.

However, as mentioned, the attraction of a second pole becomes stronger as the book progresses. Nancy retracts: "I have tried to say that 'we are the freedom of all things' and perhaps this expression should not be kept. It does not mean that we represent the entire world in our freedom, but rather that freedom of being puts itself at stake as the free existence of the world and as our ex-istence *to* this freedom—which also means that we are responsible for the freedom of the world."[62] From the onto-epistemological condition of the thing's freedom, the existent becomes its guardian or shepherd. Thus, if anything altogether appears, as a phenomenon or to itself as subject, it is not through reason, but through its own free coming.[63] If freedom is the *other* thought of thought, as well as its condition, it is already free and already being, perhaps already life.

---

58   Ibid., p. 32.
59   Ibid., p. 53.
60   Ibid.
61   Ibid., p. 57.
62   Ibid., p. 160.
63   Ibid., p. 94.

Accordingly, one can see existence taking place "on the surface of things," decided by a clinamen, which is not chance, but the free opening of the *"there is"* in general, that is, "each time."[64] And thus Nancy can write: "In this sense, the stone is free. Which means that there is in the stone—or rather, *as* it—this freedom of being that being is, in which freedom as a 'fact of reason' is what is put at stake according to co-belonging."[65]

"The stone is free": the enigma of this utterance is the profound inheritance of Nancy's meditations on freedom. If, as Nancy writes: "we are born and we die *to nothing other than freedom*,"[66] we share in this freedom with what is not born and does not die, yet emerges and vanishes, we share in "this incandescence of nothingness in which every cause withdraws into the thing."[67]

---

64 Ibid., p. 159.
65 Ibid., pp. 159–160.
66 Ibid., p. 119.
67 Ibid., p. 105.

Nidesh Lawtoo

Shared Voices: Lacoue-Nancy's Mimetic *Methexis*[1]

Le partage répond à ceci: ce que la communauté me révèle, en me présentant ma naissance et ma mort, c'est mon existence hors de moi.
Jean-Luc Nancy, *La Communauté désœuvrée*

Il faut *distribuer les rôles—ou partager les voix*, si j'ose dire.
Philippe Lacoue-Labarthe, *Scène*

What's in a voice? And if the echoes a voice generates are neither singular nor plural, but singular plural, what shared voices animate Jean-Luc Nancy's untimely reflections on subjectivity, community, and being in common? The answers to such questions are necessarily multiple and do not conform to univocal interpretations restricted to the logic of identity that constitute the metaphysics of the Same. On the contrary, they are animated by a voice that gave a singular tone, timbre, and relational touch to ontologies of difference that dominated the French philosophical scene from the 1970s to the 1990s, and whose echoes reach well into the present—remaining to be mediated in the future as well.

These echoes are particularly strong when it comes to the question of community, and for a reason that is at least double. First, because Nancy urged future generations of philosophers and artists to think and rethink the shared experience of being in common in a neoliberal, globalized, and mass-mediatized age prey to the Scylla of atomistic isolation, and the Charybdis of new fascist fusions. He did so in a number of influential texts over three decades that started with an article for a special issue of the journal *Aléa* titled, "La Communauté, le nombre" (1983). Nancy's article, already titled "La Communauté désoeuvrée," took Georges Bataille's theory of communication as a starting point to rethink a community that is neither based on a fusional organism nor on an atomistic subject but, rather, on a space of "sharing [*partage*]" that reveals

---

1   This project has received funding from the European Research Council (ERC) under the European Union's Horizon 2020 research and innovation program (grant agreement n°716181; *Homo Mimeticus*).

"my existence outside myself [*hors de moi*],"[2] as Nancy puts it. The article quickly turned into a book, sparking an interminable debate, or *entretien*, with Maurice Blanchot that Nancy pursued in a number of essays that spanned over thirty years: from *The Inoperative Community* (1983) to the still untranslated *La Communaute affrontée* (2001) to the *Disavowed Community* (2016),[3] among other texts that posited the "communal character of our existence"[4] at the heart of contemporary philosophical debates. Second, because Nancy was sensitive to the fact that "'loss' is constitutive of 'community' itself."[5] Hence, like Bataille before him, Nancy often stressed death as the inner experience that reveals a communal existence also exposing us to our shared finitude. Or, as he put it: "Death is indissociable from community, for it is through death that the community reveals itself—and reciprocally."[6]

Animated by a feeling of loss shared by a community of thinkers that each entertained a unique rapport with Jean-Luc, I welcome this volume's timely invitation not only to reflect *on* Nancy but *with* him, for it is in the experience of relationality, or rapport, that his thought on community emerged in the first place.[7] In an affirmative Nietzschean spirit we also shared, I do so by recalling that Nancy was as much sensitive to the affirmative counterpart of death as to a constitutive experience that belongs to the shared foundations of community. Hence, he equally stressed that "only community can present me my birth,"[8] by which he meant the birth of a singular plural being who is not confined to an atomistic, autonomous subject, or *ipse*, who would preexist others perceived

---

2   Jean-Luc Nancy, "La Communauté désoeuvrée," *Aléa.* no. 4 (1983), p. 34 (my translation).

3   Jean-Luc Nancy, *The Inoperative Community*, ed. Peter Connor, trans. Peter Connor et al. (Minneapolis: University of Minnesota Press, 1991), hereafter *IC* in the body of the text; *La Communauté affrontée* (Paris: Galilée, 2001); *La Communauté désavouée* (Paris: Galilée, 2014).

4   Nancy, *La Communauté désavouée*, p. 11 (my translation).

5   Nancy, *The Inoperative Community*, p. 12.

6   Ibid., p. 14. I traced the continuities between Nancy's and Bataille's concept of community in Nidesh Lawtoo, *(New) Fascism: Contagion, Community, Myth* (East Lansing: Michigan State University Press, 2019), pp. 53–128.

7   The "original" starting point of Nancy's reflections on the "inoperative community" bore the traces of the experience of a life in common as it was dedicated to the members of this community: "Anne, Claire, Emmanuel, Francine, … Mathieu, Philippe," including the names of the cats as well. Nancy, "La Communauté désoeuvrée," p. 11.

8   Nancy, *The Inoperative Community*, p. 15.

outside from a distance. On the contrary, it entails a birth of a relational subject that is already other from the inside, for it co-appears, or "compears [*com-paraît*],"[9] with the other via a mysterious form of affective communication that transgresses the boundaries of individuation generating forms of *ek-stasis*. This non-linguistic, perhaps sovereign, and certainly contagious communication is at the palpitating heart of an experience of sharing, or *partage*, that both divides and unites self and other, alter and ego, along paradoxical lines that Nancy sums up via a syntactically compressed affirmation as follows: "you shares me ['*toi partage moi*']."[10]

It is this *partage* that both connects and disconnects self and other, *toi* and *moi*, but also *pathos* and *logos*, philosophy and literature, that I would like to interrogate in what follows. I shall do so via a concept that may not have been "proper" to Nancy but that plays an important and rarely noted role in the emergence of not only his philosophical but also his literary thought on community, and on the sharing it entails nonetheless.

The Partage of Mimesis

Le *logos* est un partage, notre partage…
Ce partage est aussi celui de la philosophie et de la poésie.
Nancy, *Le Partage des voix*

How, then, does this partage operate? And wherein lies its affective power of contagious communication? Furthering a recent *re*-turn of attention to mimesis, or "mimetic turn,"[11] I suggest that despite the singularity of Nancy's plural thought, or perhaps because of it, the inner experience of a mimesis without a model is always already shared. For Nancy and others of his generation, mimesis cannot be reduced to a mirroring representation or copy of ideal Forms restricted to the metaphysical logic of the Same. On the contrary, since at least the 1970s, a different thought on mimesis has emerged

---

9   Ibid., p. 28.
10   Ibid., p. 29.
11   Jean-Luc Nancy and Nidesh Lawtoo, "The *CounterText* Interview: Jean-Luc Nancy. Mimesis: A Singular-Plural Concept," *CounterText* 8, no. 1 (2022), p. 23, pp. 23–45. In addition to Nancy, contributors to the mimetic turn included areas as diverse as literary theory (J. Hillis Miller), feminist philosophy (Adriana Cavarero), political theory (William Connolly), new materialism (Jane Bennett), posthuman studies (Katherine Hayles), among others, see www.homomimeticus.eu.

that troubles metaphysical binaries (copy/original, appearance/re-ality, self/other, etc.), thereby providing alternative, more destabi-lizing, immanent, and affirmative foundations to rethink the prob-lematic of mimesis from the angle of difference.[12] It is this mimetic tradition at the margins of philosophy that needs to be rethought today via a genealogical perspective that looks back to the shared origins of philosophy and literature in order to look ahead to future developments in the transdisciplinary field of "mimetic studies."[13]

The genealogy of this ancient concept is, of course, far from new. At least since Plato, in fact, mimesis has been endowed with an af-fective power of participation, or *methexis*, that troubles the onto-logical distinctions Plato appears to set up. Mimesis in fact passes like a magnetic current across the traditionally opposed yet mirror-ing discourses that still tend to be grouped under the agonistic ru-brics of literature and philosophy, or, to use more classical terms, *muthos* and *logos,* including dialogues on the mimetic power of *muthos*. Perhaps, then, this affective mimesis, constitutive of a subject without proper identity that I call *homo mimeticus*, even animates the communal experience of a sharing, or partage, from the inside-out. In its genealogical process of emergence, mimesis also generates a double movement of receptivity to *pathos* on one side and *distance* from it on the other that is at the palpitating heart of Nancy's syncopated meditations on a "singular plural being" (*être singulier pluriel*).[14] That is, a shared being who "com-pears" with the other, via a relation of communication with another who is already internal not only to what the ego is (*ego sum*) but to its process of becoming other (*ego sum alterum*).[15] You will have guessed it: my hypothesis is that Nancy's untimely reflections on the sharing of the subject constitutive of being in common, or community, finds its clearest manifestation not only in the shared exposure to finitude and death but also in a biographical relation-ship of mimetic communication. In fact, Nancy's communal reflec-tions cannot be dissociated from his *life* in common with a singular thinker who made the problematic of the mimetic subject its guid-

---

12 Sylviane Agacinsky et al., *Mimesis des articulations* (Paris: Aubier-Flammar-ion, 1975).

13 See Nidesh Lawtoo, *Homo Mimeticus: A New Theory of Imitation* (Leuven: Leuven University Press, 2022).

14 Jean-Luc Nancy, *Being Singular Plural*, trans. Robert D. Richardson and Anne E. O'Byrne (Stanford: Stanford University Press, 2000).

15 See Jean-Luc Nancy, *Ego Sum* (Paris: Flammarion, 1979).

ing thread, or *fil conducteur*: namely, the French philosopher, poet, man of the theater, literary critic and Nancy's life-long collaborator, friend, and sharer of communities, Philippe Lacoue-Labarthe.[16]

Nancy's friendship with Lacoue-Labarthe is truly singular in the history of philosophy. It is not only based on a community of interests but also on what in an interview Nancy calls a "sharing [*partage*] of our personal lives, which was then translated into a community of life [*communauté de vie*] of almost twenty years."[17] If the exceptional degree of intellectual partage can find some contemporary analogues in experimental thinkers who, during the same period, also opened up philosophy to the "outside" (Deleuze and Guattari come to mind), the singular plural case of the Lacoue-Nancy duo—to echo the Janus-faced appellation that was common among their shared students in Strasbourg—is, to use a phrase of a third philosopher-friend they had in common, "fascinating, admirable, and enigmatic."[18] Another term Jacques Derrida adds to account for this "writing *à deux*" is "impossible," alluding to another precursor the "three musketeers"[19] of deconstruction share, namely Georges Bataille. And Derrida's allusion to Bataille is all the more relevant insofar as the Lacoue-Nancy duo was redoubled by a more secret, inner, yet no less communicative dimension entangled with what Derrida calls "the ties of familial community,"[20] whose narration, as Nancy recently suggested, is best mediated via the register of "myth."[21]

Not unlike the community of the Jena Romantics they analyzed early in their careers, this community of life, or life in common, will take a long time to be properly evaluated, for it concerns the coappearance of entangled affects and concepts internal to not only

---

16   For a special issue on the role mimesis plays in Lacoue-Labarthe's thought, including contributions by Alain Badiou and Jean-Luc Nancy, among others, see *Poetics and Politics: with Lacoue-Labarthe*, ed. Nidesh Lawtoo, *MLN* 132, no. 5 (2017).

17   Philippe Choulet and Jean-Luc Nancy, "D'une mimesis sans modèle: entretien avec Philippe Choulet au sujet de Philippe Lacoue-Labarthe," *L'Animal: Littératures, Arts et Philosophies* no. 19–20 (2008), p. 107 (my translation).

18   Jacques Derrida, *For Strasbourg: Conversations of Friendship and Philosophy*, ed. Pascale-Anne Brault and Michael Naas (New York: Fordham University Press, 2014), p. 9.

19   Ibid., pp. 9, 10.

20   Ibid., p. 9.

21   For Nancy's autobiographical reflection on "life in myth" at play in his collaboration with Lacoue-Labarthe, see Mathilde Girard and Jean-Luc Nancy, *Proprement Dit: Entretien sur le mythe* (Paris: Lignes, 2015).

shared literary-philosophical but also to political, psychoanalytical, and ontological discourses, or *logoi*. In fact, it is relatively well-known that Nancy and Lacoue-Labarthe's intellectual careers find a shared staring point in a number of co-authored books that go from their philosophical interpretation of Lacan in *The Title of the Letter* (1973) to their genealogy of Romanticism in *The Literary Absolute* (1978), from their account of the mimetic logic, or mimetology, of Nazism in *The Nazi Myth* (1981) to the edited volume on *Retreating the Political* (1981, 1983), among other texts in common.

However, a systemic account of this shared literary-philosophical starting point is still missing in the voluminous secondary literature on Nancy that has been expanding over the past decades. More important for us, and less known, is that this shared experience of thought, or *logos*, is redoubled by a less visible, more private, and intimate, yet no less shared experiential affect, or *pathos*, whose conjunction provides perhaps a *coup d'envoi* that will set these singularly unique, yet shared philosophical-literary careers in motion. My contention is that the shared experience of a mimesis without a model located at the juncture where literary *pathos* meets philosophical *logos* plays a key role in the singular plural com-pearance of Nancy's corpus. If only because it channels an affective participation, or, to use one of Nancy's terms, a "participatory mimesis [*mimesis participative*]"[22] whose will to power of communication contributes to his singular plural thought on community, being in common, and related subjects.

The haunting presence of a different thought of mimesis that in-*forms* (gives form to) Nancy's never-ending dialogue with Lacoue-Labarthe and the redoubled "dialogue on dialogue" it entails is explicitly staged in *Scène* (2013).[23] Part of an agonistic confrontation on the Aristotelian concept of *opsis* (mise-en-scène or spectacle) that pivots around the problematic of mimesis and related concepts (figure, type, representation, mime, etc.), *Scène* stages on one side Lacoue-Labarthe's career-long suspicion of the theater's spectacular properties—predicated on the logic of representation—

---

22   Jean-Luc Nancy, *Le Partage des voix* (Paris: Galilée, 1982), p. 64 (my translation).
23   Philippe Lacoue-Labarthe and Jean-Luc Nancy, *Scène. Suivi par Dialogue sur le dialogue* (Paris: Christian Bourgois, 2013). Interestingly, the first dialogue, "Scène," is followed by a second dialogue, titled "Dialogue on Dialogue," which was originally titled: "Dialoguer: un nouveau partage des voix." This is a confirmation that *Le Partage des voix*, published three decades earlier than *Scène*, plays a pivotal role in Lacoue-Nancy's shared genealogy. Hence my focus on that text.

in favor of the sobriety of voice, and on the other Nancy's more baroque appreciation of visual figurations. This *differend* on mimesis (voice contra spectacle, echo contra figure, sobriety contra effusion etc.) should not be underestimated, for it has broader aesthetic and, especially, political and ontological implications constitutive of Lacoue-Labarthe's ontotypology, which culminate in his critique of fascist and Nazi figures—a critique he shares with Nancy.[24]

The agon on mimesis is thus not clear-cut, for it is predicated on a mirroring logic that requires a hermeneutical effort in order to be foregrounded. A close reading of *Scène* would in fact reveal that the visible agon they stage is predicated on a more imperceptible but, in my view, more fundamentally shared communication in which Nancy echoes Lacoue-Labarthe on mimetic *lexis*, for instance, while the latter corrects his echo's different repetition, and so on.[25] Predictably, this dialogue generates a spiraling regress that brings the contenders to the verge of "making a scene [*faire une scène*]," triggered by what Lacoue-Labarthe, thinking of René Girard, calls "the suffocating economy of rivalry."[26] Still, such a scene never spectacularly appears in the dialogue, despite, or rather because of, the shared mimetic *dia-logic* of the agon at play. As Derrida jokingly put it in the context of another, more playfully tragic dialogue in his final scene of *adieu* to Strasbourg and his friends, when Lacoue-Nancy restart the dialogue, one can only say: "Ok, here we go... [*c'est parti*]."[27]

Short of reconstructing the unending conversation between Nancy and Lacoue-Labarthe on a plurality of mimetic subjects, I continue a dialogue with Nancy that was interrupted by his death by taking some additional steps on the path of an ongoing genealogy of *homo mimeticus* that Nancy actively contributed to in his last years.[28]

---

24 On the relation between mimesis, politics, and myth in both Lacoue-Labarthe and Nancy, see Jean-Luc Nancy and Philippe Lacoue-Labarthe, "The Nazi Myth," *Critical Inquiry* 16, no. 2 (1990), pp. 291–312; Jean-Luc Nancy, "For Philippe: The Conversation Resumed (Ten Years Later)," *MLN* 132, no. 5 (2017), pp. 1140–1150; and Nidesh Lawtoo, "The Power of Myth (Reloaded): From Nazism to New Fascism," *L'Ésprit Créateur* 57, no. 4 (2017), pp. 64–82.

25 Lacoue-Labarthe and Nancy, *Scène*, pp. 70–75.

26 Ibid., p. 44.

27 Derrida, *For Strasbourg*, p. 18.

28 To minimally contextualize my dialogues with Nancy, I should say they started orally at KU Leuven as part of the *Homo Mimeticus* project. The first took place in December 2018 in the context of a conference devoted to Nancy's work on myth titled "HOM Workshop *à partir du Mythe Nazi*." For the "original" audiovisual recording, see Lawtoo, *HOM Videos ep. 5. Philosophy and Mimesis:*

I shall thus be strategically selective in my genealogical perspective. I take a starting point that is double, as it stages the shared problematic of mimetic methexis from both the side of affective experience or *pathos* and the one of conceptual thought or *logos*—without setting up a binary between these mirroring perspectives. After all, *pathos* and *logos* are part of the same Janus-faced argument about the mimetic experience of communal methexis.

Schematically put, on the side of *pathos*, I briefly recall that in our dialogue Jean-Luc reflected on the role of affective participation, or methexis, at play in his life in common with Philippe. He considered it vital for the development of his own communal thought, which is also a thought on a community among singular plural subjects. Nancy, in fact, stated that "he didn't think much about it [a shared, communal subject] before"[29] his encounter and *partage de ... vie personnelles* with Lacoue-Labarthe. He then proceeded to articulate the centrality of this affective partage for his relational account of the subject, community, and literature, in both written and oral communications. On the side of *logos*, I now supplement this perspective by turning to a short but this time more ancient and well-known Platonic dialogue titled *Ion* in which the problematic of mimetic methexis first enters the philosophical scene. In the process, this dialogue, which Nancy brilliantly analyzes in *Le Partage des voix,* generates a "sharing of voices" that is broader in scope and is constitutive of the agonistic relation between Plato and Homer, staging philosophy contra literature in general. At one remove, this game of mirroring dialogues may also reveal what I call a mimetic agon between Nancy and Lacoue-Labarthe. I hasten to add that mimetic agon cannot be reduced to the logic of mimetic rivalry.[30] If only because instead of generating ressentiment, violence, and sad passions, it affirms a joyful, re-*productive*, and creative mimetic communication that animates Nancy's untimely reflections on being-in-common.

Jean-Luc Nancy, 2021, https://www.youtube.com/watch?v = 7je_FSOQDYU (accessed May 8, 2022); for the French written version, see Jean-Luc Nancy and Nidesh Lawtoo, "Mimesis: Concept singulier pluriel. Entretien avec Jean-Luc Nancy," *L'Ésprit Créateur* 61, no. 2 (2021), pp. 147–167. I here refer to the English translation in *CounterText*. See also note 64 for the sequel to this dialogue.
29 Nancy and Lawtoo, "Mimesis: A Singular-Plural Concept," p. 33.
30 I discuss the difference between René Girard's theory of mimetic rivalry and mimetic agonism in Nidesh Lawtoo, *Violence and the Mimetic Unconscious: vol. 1: The Catharsis Hypothesis* (East Lansing: Michigan State University Press, 2023), pp. 45–57.

As we turn to see, and perhaps hear, these mimetic reflections, which are also reflections on mimesis, are as much on the side of philosophy as on the side of literature. They rely on both *logos* and *pathos*, and they are equally at play in written traces and experiential bonds—all of which are constitutive of the singular plural voice of a communal methexis at play in *homo mimeticus*.

Shared Enthusiasm: Socrates Contra Ion

Chez Platon, une compétition s'instaure
entre le philo*sophe* et un autre.
Nancy, *Le Partage des voix*

In *Le Partage des voix* (1982), Nancy reloads the ancient quarrel between philosophy and poetry via an interpretation of a short Platonic dialogue, titled *Ion*, on the nature of literary inspiration.[31] Ion is, in fact, a rhapsode, that is, a professional reciter of oral poetry who is specialized in dramatizing and thus interpreting Homer; he just won a contest, or agon, at the festival of Asclepius.[32] In the context of this theatrical-philosophical scene, Plato, under the mask of Socrates, admits to Ion at the outset that he is "often envious of you rhapsodists" (530b); and putting this envy to productive use via what Friedrich Nietzsche, echoing Hesiod, calls "good Eris," Plato redoubles the agon as he sets out to "assume the place of the overthrown poet and inherit his fame."[33]

The stage for what I call a mimetic agon, in which the envied model leads to a desire not to suppress but to surpass him or her in thought or *logos* is thus clearly set. Ion, in fact, serves as Plato's antagonist for a philosophical-literary contest that stages Socrates

---

31 Plato, *Ion*, trans. Lane Cooper, *The Collected Dialogues of Plato*, ed. Edith Hamilton and Huntington Cairns (New York: Pantheon Books, 1961), pp. 215–228; hereafter *Ion* followed by in-text line number.

32 On agon in Greek culture, see Jakob Burkhardt, *The Greeks and Greek Civilization*, ed. Oswyn Murray, trans. Sheila Stern (New York: St Martin's Press, 1998), pp. 160–213; and Friedrich Nietzsche, "Homer's Contest," trans. Christa Davis Acampora, *Nietzscheana* no. 5 (1996), pp. 1–8.

33 Nietzsche, "Homer's Contest," p. 5. Nietzsche specifies: "We do not understand the strength of Xenophanes', and later Plato's, attack on the national hero of poetry if we do not also think of the monstrous desire at the root of these attacks" (p. 4); a desire, or rather mimetic drive, that is not simply driven by jealousy and ressentiment (bad Eris) but by the drive to excel (good Eris).

contra the representative of a Homeric culture that was central to the education of the Greeks and that Plato seeks to overturn and re-place.[34] How? By staging a mirroring contest confronting Socrates's dialectical *logos* contra Ion's oral practices of "dramatic 'imitation' or 'impersonation'" that operate on the emotional register of *pathos*, a mimetic *pathos* that, as Erik Havelock also shows, trigger a "personal identification by which the audience sympathizes with the performance."[35] Contra this oral literary tradition, Socrates argues that Ion, and at one remove Homer, is dispossessed of any "knowledge [*epistēmē*]" (*Ion* 532c); he even lacks mastery of a poetic "art [*tekhnē*] of poetry" (532c). Instead, if Ion can interpret and impersonate Homer (and only Homer) so well, it is because he is driven by a "power divine" (533d) that renders him "divinely inspired" and "enthusiastic" (533e)—that is, *en-theos*, in the god. According to this mythic reconstruction of the origins of poetic inspiration that will cast a long shadow on romantic theories of ge-nial originality, Plato suggests that when Ion is reciting Homer, he is participating in the god of music, Apollo. He is thus possessed by a mysterious power divine that passes and communicates through him, reaching the audience as well—hence his success on the ago-nistic literary stage.

How does such a contagious communication work? Within the dialogue itself, to account for this contagious power, Socrates con-vokes the allegorical trope of a "magnet" or "Stone of Heraclea" (533d) that "does not simply attract iron rings" but "also imparts to the rings a force enabling them to do the same thing as the stone itself" (533d). Hence, the magnet forms a long chain that goes from Apollo to the Muses to the poet (Homer) to the rhapsode (Ion), reaching to affect the audience in the theater and generating a form of enthusiastic intoxication Plato compares to the Dionysian mae-nads.[36] Thus reframed, Ion turns out to be a "middle ring" (536a), a medium, or *passeur*. As Nancy puts it in his penetrating interpre-tation of this Platonic dialogue, Ion is both held and possessed by a contagious power of inspiration that ensures what he calls "the

34 Plato's *Ion*, trans. Andrew Miller (Cambridge, Mass.: Hackett, 2018).
35 Eric Havelock, *Preface to Plato* (Cambridge, Mass.: Harvard University Press, 1963), pp. 21, 26.
36 I first discussed *Ion* in relation to Dionysian mimesis in Nidesh Lawtoo, *The Phantom of the Ego: Modernism and the Mimetic Unconscious* (East Lansing: Michigan State University Press, 2013), pp. 58–64; for readings of *Ion* in line with *Homo Mimeticus*, see also Niki Hadikoesoemo, "Altering Bodies: Thinking of Intervention through Impersonation," *Performance Philosophy* 5, no. 2 (2020).

passage of communication"[37] whose primary characteristic is to be shared—or as Nancy will later say, in common.

Written in 1982, at a transitional moment of passage from a period of intense work in common with Lacoue-Labarthe to Nancy's work on community based on the paradoxical logic of partage, *Le Partage des voix* is a singular plural text that operates on more than one level. There is, indeed, more than one voice that is shared between the lines calling for a discerning interpretation, or *hermeneia*. Of course, the sharing that gives the title to Nancy's essay is, first and foremost, the one of Ion, the rhapsode, who gives voice to Homer, interprets him for the audience, and makes Socrates' conjure the mysterious trope of the magnet to account for an interpretation that is not one, for it is not based on any art or *techne*. Confronted with this "riddle" (532c), Nancy takes the Platonic/Socratic metaphor of magnetism literally as he notes that "the characteristic of magnetism ... is that it communicates its force."[38] This is a communicative force, or power, that passes through a "sharing of voices" that is first and foremost poetic as it connects and disconnects the rings in the poetic chain that are, to be specific, "unchained" [*dechaînés*].[39] In fact, the rings are not chained into one another but, rather, adjacent to each other, each singular in their poetic powers but magnetized by the same force they share and that shares them.[40] At one remove, Nancy also notes that the partage goes beyond poetic principles for it passes across the literature-philosophy divide. As he puts it, as often in Plato's dialogues, a "competition" or agon is playfully staged "between the philosopher and another."[41] This agon, then, does not simply oppose the *pathos* of poetry to the *logos* of philosophy in order to submit the former to the latter. On the contrary, Nancy specifies that it is a question of "showing that the philosopher is better *in the domain of the other* [i.e., poetry], or that he is the

---

37 Nancy, *Le Partage des voix*, p. 75.

38 Ibid., p. 61.

39 Ibid.

40 For a compelling account of *Ion* inspired by Nancy and attentive to both the mimetic agon between Plato and Homer and the uniqueness of poetic voices, see Adriana Cavarero, "The Envied Muse: Plato versus Homer," in *Cultivating the Muse: Struggles for Power and Inspiration in Classical Greece*, ed. Efrossini Spenzou and Don Fowlers (Oxford: Oxford University Press, 2002), pp. 47–67. I join Cavarero's and Nancy's interpretations of *Ion* to give an account of Plato's critique of the *vita mimetica* in Lawtoo, *Homo Mimeticus*, chapter 2.

41 Nancy, *Le Partage des voix*, p. 59.

truth of the other."[42] And Nancy adds that Socrates "envies not so much the prize but the art of the rhapsode himself."[43] There is thus a mirroring agonistic relation characteristic of mimetic agonism between Socrates and Ion, the philosopher and the poetic "other" that Nancy designates as playing the "role of a rival—or a double."[44] That is, a figure who is also characterized by a strange "dispossession or depropriation" of identity, for as Nancy specifies in a revealing phrase, "he has nothing proper", yet his competence remains "singular"[45] nonetheless.

The mythic scene of the mimetic agon is beginning to delineate itself; the echoes can be heard. Beneath the agonistic division between Socrates and Ion and, at one remove, Plato and Homer, also lies a contemporary sharing of voices between literary-philosophical doppelgängers that are singular plural. Nancy, for one, notes that what "Ion" (and we should now be suspicious of univocal identifications) stages in this scene of "partage" is "an originary difference of poetic genres or voices—and maybe underhand, a sharing [*partage*] of poetic and philosophical genres."[46] This is indeed a partage in the double sense that it both divides and connects along paradoxical lines constitutive of mimetic agonism, if only because "Plato" partakes in the power he seeks to oppose via the mimetic genre of the dialogue. Thus, Nancy adds: "It is not an accident if Plato plays the poet."[47] There is, in fact, an ambivalent relation that continues to tie philosophy to literature in the very medium of their opposition. Or, as Nancy puts it elsewhere: "philosophy, literature, each mourning and desiring the other (the other as such, the other as same [*l'autre même*]), but each also competing with the other in fulfilling mourning and desire."[48] This relationship is, indeed, a classical scene of competition, which does not mean that it is necessarily an Oedipal, rivalrous scene nor that this scene of mirroring agon between philosophy and literature is disconnected from the present.

Rather than framing this competition within a familial triangle, let us return to the paradigmatic example of *Ion* to ask a more

---

42 Ibid.
43 Ibid., p. 55.
44 Ibid.
45 Ibid., pp. 66, 60.
46 Ibid., p. 66.
47 Ibid., p. 65.
48 Jean-Luc Nancy, *Expectation: Philosophy, Literature*, trans. Roberto Bononno (New York: Fordham University Press, 2017), pp. 27–28.

general literary-philosophical question: What force allows for such a *partage des voix, the partage* that is as much a *participation* in the same flow of magnetic contagion as a *division* via uniquely separately connected rings. This is the same *con*-division that, in the same years, will become central to Nancy's thought on singular plural beings and communities as well.

The Impropriety of Mimesis: Nancy avec Lacoue

Protée peut prendre tous les rôles,
dans la philosophie et dans la poésie
Nancy, *Le Partage des voix*

The answer, which should be clear to readers familiar with this classical yet always new mythic scene of contestation between philosophy and literature, should not come as a surprise. This contagious force endowed with the power of partage is not proper to Ion alone, for its defining characteristic is to be shared. This force is constitutive of a *"partage* of poetic and philosophical genres"[49] that are both divided and shared, shared-divided (*partagées*), and is nothing less and nothing more than the improper question of "mimesis." As Nancy puts it: "one must conclude that the rhapsode is here the representative of the singularly complex problematic of *mimesis.*"[50] This is not a mimesis that passively copies the original poet via the visual schema of representation predicated on the logic of the same long familiar from the myth of the cave and the idealist metaphysics Plato articulates via the trope of the mirror in book ten of the *Republic*. Rather, it is a complex poetic mimesis animated by a magnetic transitive "force" or *pathos* of "participation" (*methexis*). First staged and theorized in *Ion*, this *pathos* is essential to grasp the contagious powers of mimesis that go from Plato to Nietzsche to Bataille, and beyond.[51]

Bringing this tradition into the present and closer to home, Nancy specifies that this type of mimesis is characterized less by a "figuration" than by a paradoxical "receptivity that gives rise to an

---

49 Nancy, *Le Partage des voix*, p. 66.
50 Ibid., p. 70.
51 On the links between Plato's *Ion* and modernists like Nietzsche and Bataille, see Lawtoo, *The Phantom of the Ego*, pp. 52–68.

activity."[52] And in a passage that is worth quoting, he qualifies this mimetic paradox as follows:

> [It is] an active creative, or re-creative mimesis, or alternatively, it is a mimetic creation, but effectuated via a *mimesis* that proceeds from *methexis*, from a participation itself due to the communication of enthusiasm—unless mimesis is not the condition of this participation.[53]

There is thus an undecidable, paradoxical, and above all re-*productive* mimesis at play in this ancient agon between philosophy and poetry. Be it Plato contra Homer, Socrates contra Ion, or closer to home and between the lines, Nancy contra Lacoue-Labarthe, this agon is mimetic because it is not only based on simple opposition but also continuity, not only on distance but also on proximity, generating a sharing of voices that exceeds the logic of mimetic rivalry.[54] In fact, this partage between philosophical and poetic voices does not lead to any violence, let alone sacrificial exclusions of the poet as a *pharmakos*, as is already the case at the end of the *Republic*. Rather, in *Ion*, the magnetic force sets in motion a productive form of sharing that oscillates from *logos* to *pathos* and back. This playful oscillation is not simply generative of pathologies but of what I call patho-*logies* that is, critical *logoi* on *pathos* that are already constitutive of Platonic dialogues themselves. The genre of the Socratic dialogue, in fact, partakes in the mimetic register that Plato opposes in theory but relies on in dramatic practice. And he does so to generate with and contra Ion/Homer a protean discourse characterized by mythic allegories, exemplary heroes, dramatic contests among other literary-philosophical devices that are constitutive of the birth of philosophy itself.

Thus reframed, mimesis is not only an ancient concept internal to Platonic dialogues. It is also a modern concept internal to contemporary dialogues on a mythic dialogue. Now is the moment to register explicitly what has remained implicit so far: the *partage des voix* Nancy theorizes within his interpretation of the dialogue *Ion* is already redoubled by a shared mimetic experience of partage between literature and philosophy that operates in his own

---

52 Nancy, *Le Partage des voix*, p. 62.
53 Ibid., p. 71.
54 For Nancy's reflections on how he and Lacoue-Labarthe put this mimetic agon to productive philosophical use, see Nancy and Lawtoo, "Mimesis: A Singular-Plural Concept," pp. 31–33.

communal experience of thought and life with Lacoue-Labarthe. In foundational works like *Typographie* (1975), *Le Sujet de la philosophie: Typographies I* (1979) and *L'Imitation des modernes: Typographies II* (1981),[55] as well as in the works in common with Nancy already mentioned, Lacoue-Labarthe, in fact, made an original interpretation of mimesis without proper models the guiding thread of his entire literary-philosophical career. Lacoue-Labarthe's account of the "impropriety" of the mimetic subject, its "plastic" malleability, and the "paradoxical" ability of the actor to turn a "restricted" (or passive) mimesis into a productive, "general" (or active) mimesis characteristic of Denis Diderot's "paradox of the actor" in particular and of the "imitation of the moderns" in general, finds in Plato's theory of mimesis a key genealogical starting point.[56] As Lacoue-Labarthe sums it up, "Plato, in his way, knew this very well: the mimeticians are the worst possible breed because they are no one, pure mask or pure hypocrisy, and as such unassignable, unidentifiable, impossible to place."[57] And yet, at the same time, and without contradiction, "theatrical mimesis" also "provides the model for a general mimesis" that "reproduces nothing given" but entails "an imitation of *phusis* as a productive force, or as *poesis*"[58] that is of Aristotelian inspiration and that Lacoue-Labarthe finds in Denis Diderot's *Le Paradoxe du comédien*, the matrix text for the imitation of the moderns.

All this and more is clearly echoed in Nancy's interpretation of "Plato's rhapsode," a protean character that "enchanted Philippe," as Nancy puts it, precisely for its anticipation of the modern insight that "the actor has nothing proper to itself."[59] It is thus no genealogical accident that Nancy not only quotes Lacoue-Labarthe's account of "Diderot's Paradox" a few pages later;[60] he also leans on this paradox to give mimetic specificity to his genealogy of shared voices.

---

55 Lacoue-Labarthe's theorizations of mimesis are regrettably not available in their entirety in English as yet, but the essential texts are collected in Philippe Lacoue-Labarthe, *The Subject of Philosophy*, ed. Thomas Trezise, trans. Thomas Trezise et al. (Minneapolis: University of Minnesota Press, 1993); and, especially, in Philippe Lacoue-Labarthe, *Typography: Mimesis, Philosophy, Politics*, ed. Christopher Fynsk, trans. Christopher Fynsk et al. (Stanford: Stanford University Press, 1989).

56 See Lacoue-Labarthe, *Typography*, pp. 96–138.

57 Ibid., p. 259.

58 Ibid., pp. 257, 255–256.

59 Choulet and Nancy, "D'une mimesis sans modèle," p. 111.

60 Nancy, *Le Partage des voix*, p. 72, n 52.

Nancy, in fact, tells us that this dispossessed subject has "nothing proper [*rien en propre*]"[61] to itself. And paradoxically, precisely because of this "absence of proper capacity" or "*dépropriation*,"[62] this (dis)possessed figure enters into an enthusiastic state of creative receptivity that is both passive and active, restricted to copying a model (Homer) and reproductive of a magnetic spell that generates (Dionysian) bonds. In the passage I just quoted, Nancy even opens up the hypothesis that "mimesis could be the condition of this participation"[63] in the first place, thereby entangling mimesis and methexis in the sharing of voices he performs both philosophically and poetically.[64]

It would be useless to deny it. There is, indeed, an echo of the subject, or a mimetic phantom, animating the paradoxical voice (passive/active, dispossessed/possessed, copying/creative, reproducing/producing, etc.) of that *mime de rien* who is masked as Ion: a "Proteus," Nancy specifies, "who can assume all roles, in philosophy and in poetry."[65] At this stage, the identity masked under this protean figure appears unmasked. Still, at a closer interpretation its identity is actually undecidable. For instance, our *hermeneia* makes us wonder: Is this virtuous play of poetic and philosophical roles "proper" to Lacoue-Labarthe's mimetology, as Nancy's implicit yet numerous and unmistakable references to the paradox of mimesis suggest? Or is it "proper" to Nancy, whose mimetic agonism has led him to aspire, in a mirroring move of "appropriation," to be better in the domain of the other by "exappropriating"[66] this mimetic thought in writing? Or a shared intermixture of both?

---

61 Ibid. p. 66.

62 Ibid.

63 Ibid., p. 71.

64 Ibid. The full passage establishes a link between hermeneutics and rhapsody via the link of a "'knowledgeable' [*savante*] mimesis" (p. 78) and reads as follows: "*Hermeneia* is *mimesis*, but an active *mimesis*, creative or re-creative, or again it is a mimetic creation, but effectuated by a mimesis that proceeds from *methexis*, of a participation itself due to enthusiasm—unless mimes is not the condition of this participation" (p. 71). See also Nancy, "The Image: Mimesis and Methexis," trans. Adrienne Janus, in *Nancy and Visual Culture*, eds. Carrie Giunta and Adrienne Janus (Edinburgh: Edinburgh University Press, 2016), pp. 73–92.

65 Nancy, *Le Partage des voix*, p. 84.

66 To add the voice of a middle man who informs both Lacoue-Labarthe and Nancy on the improper logic of mimesis, Derrida, in dialogue with both, elaborates on the logic of "exapppropriation" as follows: "What I wished to say with exappropriation is that in the gesture of appropriating something for oneself, and thus of being able to keep in one's name, to mark with one's name, to leave in

These, as Lacoue-Labarthe would put it, are improper questions, if only because the logic of mimesis is itself based on a logic of impropriety. Later, in *Scène*, for instance, Nancy speaks of a "mimesis" that pleases them both ("la *mimèsis* qui nous 'réjouit'") in terms of a "participation in or by a sharing [*partage*]" whose characteristic is to put the subject "outside of itself [*hors de soi*]— identical and different, or neither simply identical nor simply different."[67] The echoes with Ion are strong, the doublings of identity visible; yet no univocal identifications are tenable when both the thought and experience of mimesis are so intimately shared. As Lacoue-Labarthe prefigures in the second epigraph to this essay, "*distributing* [distribuer] *of roles*"—say, between the philosopher and the poet—can only lead to "*sharing* [partage] *of voices*."[68] What we can tentatively say, then, is that this magnetic interplay of sameness and difference, philosophy and rhapsody, *logos* and *pathos*, is not destructive but productive, not based on a mimetic rivalry but on a mimetic agon. As I tried to show elsewhere, this mimetic agon reloads a patho-*logical* paradox of mimesis that— via a long chain of thinkers that goes from Plato to Nietzsche, Derrida to Girard, Lacoue-Labarthe to Nancy, Adriana Cavarero to Catherine Malabou among others—continues to channel a magnetized mimetic *pathos* that reaches into the present.[69] Under different masks and a conceptual persona characteristic of a *homo mimeticus* that is returning to haunt the philosophical and artistic scene, this paradox, in fact, directly informs the mimetic turn to a different, more embodied, and participatory theory of mimesis already prefigured—between lines still in need of interpretation or *hermeneia*—in Plato's untimely dialogue.

In the end, after focusing the attention on the immanent fact that all affects are mimetic and contagious (or mimetic *pathos*), Ion equally registers an oscillation toward / away from mimesis that I group under the rubric of *pathos* of distance and locate at the palpitating heart of *homo mimeticus*. Ion's recitation of Homer is, in fact, both unique, and *pace* Socrates, based on a poetic *techne* after all, for he can control the mimetic *pathos* he triggers in spectators from a *distance*. Thus, Ion specifies that he gives spectators

---

one's name, as a testament or an inheritance, one must expropriate this thing, separate oneself from it." Derrida, *For Strasbourg*, p. 24.

67 Lacoue-Labarthe and Nancy, *Scène*, p. 32.

68 Ibid., p. 76.

69 See Lawtoo, *Homo Mimeticus*.

"very close attention," adding, "for if I set them weeping, I myself shall laugh when I get my money" (535e). And yet, at the same time, and without contradiction, Ion is thoroughly possessed by a magnetic power that is not proper to him and dispossesses him of his "proper" identity, generating a magnetizing *pathos* that is shared via communal forms of con-division. At the heart of mimetic, participatory matters, there is thus a *pathos* of distance at play in mimetic subjects. As Nancy also notes "[Ion] is capable of 'participation' and of simultaneously keeping at distance, and this singular capacity of doubling proceeds itself from the absence of proper capacity"[70]—and this *pathos* of distance, or partage, is also constitutive of a singular plural ego that is not one, for it is a phantom ego exposed to being in common.[71]

This inner experience, I could only begin to show, is constitutive of the life in common Lacoue-Nancy affirmed together with many others in Strasbourg at the twilight of the last century. It is also the palpitating heart of a new protean theory of mimesis vital to facing shared communal catastrophes at the dawn of the twenty-first century. If the myth of the singular plural origins of community are only now beginning to be told by drawing on the oral tradition of the dialogue,[72] their philosophical relevance to account for Nancy's *logos* on community, and mimetic studies more generally, still needs to be followed up.

Within the limit of this essay, I wanted to show that in the alternation of voices at play in a pivotal text like *Le Partage des voix*, it is indeed no longer clear *who* exactly speaks: the philosopher or the poet, the specialist of the *logos* or the technician of *pathos,* Nancy or Lacoue-Labarthe? Or, perhaps, a *passeur* shuttling back and forth between the two? What is certain is that Lacoue-Nancy's intimately shared mimetic *methexis* blurs the very line dividing

---

70 Nancy, *Le Partage des voix*, p. 74.

71 On the genealogical link between the phantom of the ego and community this article furthers, see Lawtoo, *The Phantom of the Ego*, pp. 295–304.

72 After conducting the 2018 interview on mimesis, Nancy and I agreed to return to the personal side of his life in common with Lacoue-Labarthe and the sharing it entails via "a different medium." Nancy and Lawtoo, "Mimesis: A Singular-Plural Concept," p. 44, n 2. We did so in the summer of 2020, in between pandemic lockdowns during a two-day video interview with Nancy, while also adding the voices of Claire Nancy, Jean-Christophe Bailly, Michel Deutsch, among others. For a prelude of this still inedited video, see Nidesh Lawtoo, "Jean-Luc Nancy: The Community of Strasbourg (A Prelude)," https://www. youtube.com/watch?v = wZhbbWS3tdA&t = 25s (accessed August 7, 2022).

concepts from affects, *logos* from *pathos*, philosophy from rhapsody. As Nancy concisely puts it in a chiastic mirroring phrase that sums up the paradox of shared voices not only at play in Plato's dialogues but also in his unending dialogues with Lacoue-Labarthe, "a philosophical rhapsody allows for a philosophy of rhapsody."[73] And what is Nancy's unclassifiable thought if not *also* a philosophy of rhapsodies, on the muses, intoxication, love, the body, and the arts more generally?

In their process of their mimetic communication, Lacoue-Nancy's duet generated a long chain that goes not only from the Muses to the community of spectators. It also connects, like a magnetic flow, singular plural beings at the heart of an inoperative-cooperative community of thought that, as this volume shows, continues to be passed on in the present—inspiring, and perhaps magnetizing, future generations as well.

---

73 Nancy, *Le Partage des voix*, p. 79.

Jérôme Lèbre

L'espace toujours laissé libre

C'est une invitation plus qu'une demande, formulée par les éditrices et éditeurs de cet ouvrage collectif : que nous écrivions moins *sur* Jean-Luc Nancy qu'*avec* lui, dans ce rapport sans rapport qu'est l'entretien indéfiniment continué avec un disparu. Cela doit être possible ; autrement dit, un impératif catégorique plane sur l'invitation : sois libre, dégage-toi un peu de la pensée de l'autre, montre que les livres que tu connais t'ont laissé un espace de liberté, et ainsi *sois fidèle* ; car c'était aussi la demande constante de Nancy, que l'on parle d'autre chose que de lui. Celles et ceux qui ont organisé un colloque « sur » lui le savent bien ; et surtout, il était, il est toujours le penseur de *l'avec*, pas du *sur* (qui, en l'occurrence, devient vite le *sous* du commentaire asservi) ; il suffit de le lire pour se rendre compte qu'il se tournait, se tourne encore, autant ou plus vers la pluralité et la singularité des êtres que vers celles des philosophes, et qu'il aimait aussi le faire en écrivant avec d'autres, pas forcément philosophes.

Cependant l'invitation se mue immédiatement en injonction contradictoire, formulée à la fois comme un impératif venant de l'autre et de soi-même. « Sois libre ! » commande une liberté rendue impossible par le commandement, déterminée et circonscrite par lui, si bien que toute émancipation (celle de l'enfant vis-à-vis des parents, de l'esclave ou du disciple vis-à-vis du maître) garde de cette manière la main sur celle ou celui qu'elle émancipe, lui impose une configuration non-libre de la liberté. Il faudrait donc que tout commence ou recommence par soi-même. Mais « le pouvoir de commencer par son propre chef » tente de faire coïncider deux incompatibles, soi et la cause originaire, autrement dit la chose différente de moi et qui serait la véritable origine de ma pensée (*Ur-sache*) : et c'est là « l'auto-illusion essentielle » de la métaphysique. On aura compris que ce n'est pas moi qui le dis, et plus précisément c'est Heidegger. Il en découle selon ce dernier que penser vraiment, c'est être en relation à autre chose de plus originaire que soi, l'être même, qui me précède toujours.

Commentant ce passage dans un texte intitulé « L'espace laissé libre par Heidegger »[1], Jean-Luc Nancy y voit une autre contradiction : il faudrait d'un côté abandonner l'idée même de liberté, au profit d'une autre pensée qui serait véritablement pensée d'un autre, et donc ouverture à l'être, lequel est ce dehors qui m'appelle sans cesse, me sort de moi-même. Mais d'un autre côté cet abandon n'a de sens que s'il est la voie vers une autre liberté, plus authentique, celle de l'être lui-même : car le propre de l'être est de laisser être tout ce qui est. Autrement dit, Heidegger ne peut vraiment abandonner la liberté, mais seulement la définir comme abandon de la pensée à la donation originaire de l'être : c'est-à-dire comme vérité. « La primauté ontologique revient donc en fin de compte à la vérité »[2], la liberté s'est retirée en elle. Le raisonnement est assez abstrait, on le comprendra sans doute mieux en soulignant que ce retrait de la liberté prend la forme d'un destin ; le site de notre époque est en effet celui où l'être se voile et se dévoile comme technique : asservissement de la nature et de l'homme lui-même à ce qui devait être la maîtrise de la nature par l'homme. S'ouvrir à cette vérité destinale, donc la pensée, devrait nous en libérer, mais il est bien difficile de voir comment, surtout quand Heidegger rajoute que seul un Dieu peut nous sauver…

Je m'interromps (ou j'interromps Nancy ?) pour constater avec celles et ceux qui auront bien voulu me suivre jusqu'à ce point que je fais exactement l'inverse de ce que l'on m'a invité à faire, et même l'inverse de ce que je dis. Il s'agissait de penser librement avec Nancy et me voici en train de réfléchir sur lui, de commenter un de ses textes sur la liberté, où lui-même parle d'un autre philosophe, Heidegger. Et ni lui ni moi ne répondons à cet appel de Heidegger, qui n'a de sens que s'il ouvre à cet autre appel, celui de l'être même : il nous faudrait penser ce qui à chaque fois, dans tout ce qui apparaît, voile et dévoile en même temps l'origine de toute apparition, il nous faudrait sans cesse être dehors – en dehors de soi et en dehors des textes. Mais peut-être est-il impossible de penser l'être, non seulement par soi-même, mais aussi sans citer des textes masquant ou dévoilant le sens de l'être (toute la pensée de Heidegger, qui serait plus que l'exemple de cette impossibilité), peut-être est-il impossible de répondre à la demande ou à l'invitation de nos éditeurs et éditrices, de distinguer entre penser *avec*

---

1   Jean-Luc Nancy, *L'Expérience de la liberté*, Paris, Galilée, 1988, p. 57 *sq.*
2   *Ibid.*, p. 60.

et penser *sur* ; peut-être même y a-t-il quelque texte de Nancy qui nous dirait déjà que c'est impossible, et qu'il nous suffirait de commenter…

Celui-ci par exemple, dans *Demande* : « Le Livre est là […] il faut écrire sur lui, le faire palimpseste, le surcharger, brouiller ses pages de lignes rajoutées… »[3]. Nancy cite alors, volontairement sans guillemets, La Bruyère : Tout est dit, et l'on vient trop tard, depuis plus de sept mille ans qu'il y a des hommes et qui pensent. Mais Nancy précise tout de suite que cette phrase commence de nouveaux *Caractères*, de nouveaux signes dans une nouvelle forme (et qui ne cesseront, rajoutons-le, de se rajouter à eux-mêmes, au point de devenir l'œuvre inachevée d'une vie). Tout texte ouvre ainsi l'espace indéfini de sa traduction, de son commentaire ou de sa reprise sous une autre forme : ainsi « Nul lieu ne sera libre de livres », et cela même sous l'aspect des pages blanches, celles que l'on trouve déjà dans *Tristram Shandy* ; et tout aussi bien « Aucun livre ne sera libre de livres »[4]. On ne se libère pas en faisant sem-blant d'avoir renoncé à tous les livres pour tout recommencer à partir de soi (Descartes), mais tout au contraire en écrivant à la fois sur et avec, dans l'interstice entre les deux homonymes latins du livre et du libre (*liber / liber*) ; ou encore, « il faut écrire sur le livre *pour une délivrance* »[5], et c'est donc maintenant ainsi que nous entendons la demande des éditeurs et éditrices de cet ouvrage, tout comme cette phrase de Malebranche que Nancy disait avoir médité pendant cinquante-cinq ans, et toujours cité de mémoire, c'est-à-dire toujours inexactement (s'écartant du texte de *La Recherche de la vérit*é par l'ajout d'un « avec eux ») : « Il ne faut croire ni Aristote ni Descartes mais méditer avec eux, comme ils ont fait »[6].

Reprenons à partir de là ce que Nancy nous dit de l'espace laissé libre par Heidegger. Ce dernier semble avoir soumis l'idée même de liberté à celle de vérité. Mais celle-ci ne se présente pas pour au-tant comme un principe ou comme un dogme : bien au contraire, comme l'écrit Heidegger dans *Le Principe de raison*, la raison est fondamentalement absence de raison et de fondement. L'être est sans pourquoi, et c'est ainsi que même quand il se donne comme domination de la technique, cette domination est ce qu'elle est,

---

3   Jean-Luc Nancy, *Demande*, Paris, Galilée, 2015, p. 47.

4   *Ibid.*, p. 50.

5   *Ibid.*, p. 47. C'est l'auteur qui souligne.

6   Jean-Luc Nancy, *in* Jérôme Lèbre et Jean-Luc Nancy, *Signaux sensibles*, Montrouge, Bayard, 2017, p. 21.

simple vérité indissociable d'un véritable oubli qui a décidé du destin de l'Occident puis de la mondialisation : l'oubli de l'être, qui n'est en tant que tel pas domination mais donation de tout ce qui est. Le destin qui nous domine encore aujourd'hui étant de tout dominer, y compris nous-mêmes, nous sommes incapables de simplement laisser être, et telle est la vérité, sans fondement. Cette pensée du sans pourquoi est selon Heidegger « la région où réside l'essence de la liberté » : non pas de la liberté « comme pouvoir en quelque sens que ce soit », précise Nancy, mais comme « un nouvel espace de jeu »[7]. Ainsi Heidegger en libérant la vérité de tout fondement a « gardé un espace libre pour la liberté », tout en estimant que seule la liberté le refermait toujours, que seule la vérité était en mesure de l'ouvrir.

C'est bien tout le problème, et dans toutes ses dimensions (philosophique, éthique, politique) : *garder* un espace libre, ce n'est pas encore le *laisser* libre. Ce problème est d'abord celui que nous avons signalé plus haut en parlant d'émancipation : toute liberté accordée par une autorité (parents, maîtres, Etat) est toujours préconfigurée autoritairement, comme espace délimité de la liberté : au-delà de cette limite, votre ticket n'est plus valable, disait Romain Gary... C'est donc aussi le problème du droit : les libertés accordées sont des libertés surveillées, et c'est ainsi que les droits se convertissent en devoirs (de travailler, de voter, d'obéir aux lois et aux réglementations, etc.) ; autrement dit ces libertés « dessinent les contours de leur concept commun – la liberté – comme les bords d'un espace vide, vacant, et dont la vacance pourrait bien en définitive être le seul trait qu'il faille retenir pour pertinent »[8]. C'est ainsi le problème de toute philosophie, ou même de la philosophie, en tant qu'elle resserre le lien entre liberté, vérité, et pouvoir politique : ainsi la souveraineté chez Rousseau s'érige « à la fois en compréhension absolue de sa propre liberté et en contrainte absolue sur soi-même et sur chacun des membres du corps souverain », de même que la morale kantienne a pour matrice « l'identité de la liberté et de la loi »[9] ; et c'est alors bien encore cette souveraineté contraignante qui devient chez Heidegger celle de l'être même.

Et pourtant, à chaque fois, la ou les philosophie(s) indiquent un au-delà de leur clôture : le contrat qui oblige chacun à être libre et fonde la souveraineté n'est formulé nulle part, l'acte par lequel

---

7 Nancy, *L'Expérience de la liberté, op. cit.*, p. 62–63.
8 *Ibid.*, p. 42.
9 *Ibid.*, p. 65.

un peuple est un peuple n'est autre que le fait du peuple comme pluralité de singularités co-existantes ; la loi morale est l'au-delà de toute vérité et même de toute loi formulable, donc aussi de tout droit institué, elle est l'impératif adressé à chacun d'extraire la vérité d'elle-même et de se libérer de toute vision conforme de la liberté ; Quant à l'être, il se dissémine dans l'espace de ces êtres pluriels qui coexistent librement, au-delà de toute loi, de tout pouvoir ou de toute vérité institués ou accomplis.

Il en découle que le problème de la liberté n'en est pas vraiment un, ou même c'est « tout sauf un problème », c'est bien plutôt « un fait, ou un don, ou une tâche »[10], autrement dit une demande : chaque philosophie (et la philosophie) diffère de l'Etat, qu'elle n'a cessé en même temps de vouloir comprendre et fonder, en tant qu'elle ne garde pas simplement l'espace qu'elle libère, mais libère aussi l'espace qu'elle garde, ou plutôt demande toujours (c'est son seul impératif, sa seule loi) à s'extraire de sa vérité pour que l'espace qu'elle laisse libre soit véritablement libéré. S'il est une philosophie de Nancy, c'est alors bien celle qui parvient à formuler cette demande, et qui s'engouffre dans l'espace laissé libre par Heidegger (et au-delà, par toute la philosophie) pour y répondre, en devenant tout entière une pensée de l'espace libre, ou de la liberté spatialisée.

L'espace est alors celui de la comparution d'une pluralité indéfinie d'êtres libres, ou plutôt délivrés : « Quand il y a l'existant, il n'y a ni essence, ni loi, et c'est dans cette anarchie que l'existence se décide. Elle se livre à elle-même, elle se dé-livre pour soi ou bien elle se délivre de soi. *Le fait de la liberté est cette dé-livrance de l'existence de toute loi et à elle-même en tant que loi* »[11]. Être ainsi délivré de soi, c'est alors immédiatement être avec l'autre, la singularité se redonnant et se libérant à chaque fois *avec* les autres, et n'existant que dans cet avec. Autrement dit, la liberté est partagée et n'existe que dans ce partage entre êtres délivrés de tout, et se communiquant cette délivrance : « le partage ontologique, ou la singularité de l'être, ouvre l'espace que seule la liberté peut, non pas «remplir», mais proprement espacer », si bien que la « forme originaire de la liberté » est « celle d'un libre-espace de déplacements et de rencontres », une « composition extérieure de trajectoires et d'allures »[12]. Même ce que nous nommons décision

---

10 *Ibid.*, p. 85.
11 *Ibid.*, p. 37.
12 *Ibid.*, p. 96 et p. 100.

n'est pas de l'ordre de la disposition intérieure ou « individuelle », mais de l'exposition d'une singularité libre en rapport à d'autres : la décision est donc à chaque fois ce qui laisse les êtres singuliers être ce qu'ils sont, « ce qui signifie que la décision est essentiellement «ouvrante» ou «spatialisante» »[13].

Tel est donc l'espace laissé libre par Nancy, qui est l'espace libre en tant que tel, éclaté dans l'être-avec de singularités libres : donc à la fois l'espace que nous habitons et qui reste entre nous, dans cet écart qui est indissociable de notre coexistence. On voit dès lors ce qu'il y aurait d'incongru à parler de « la philosophie de l'espace chez Nancy » : car cet espace n'est pas chez lui, et il n'est même pas circonscrit par la philosophie, il est littéralement laissé ou offert à chaque être singulier, décidant du sens qu'il donne à son existence avec d'autres. Mais, et c'est là que la liberté redevient un problème, un espace définitivement libéré est-il vraiment laissé libre ? Ou pour le dire plus simplement : est-ce que nous ne venons pas trop tard, est-ce que tout n'a pas été dit sur la singularité et la liberté ? Il nous resterait certes à expérimenter cette liberté, à exister singulièrement, c'est-à-dire aussi démocratiquement, et même dans l'anarchie – hors de tout principe et de toute vérité instituée, à commencer par celle des institutions. Mais ce serait bien la fin de la philosophie.

Il va cependant de soi que ce n'est pas ici ni ainsi que la philosophie finit. S'il y a bien, selon l'un des derniers textes de Nancy, une fin de la philosophie[14], elle est inscrite dès l'origine dans son programme, qui était justement de n'ouvrir sur la liberté qu'en la refermant sur une vérité : donc de se réaliser elle-même, de s'auto-accomplir. Or non seulement ce programme s'est réalisé dans chaque pensée rendue dogmatique (par son auteur, plutôt masculin, ou par ses disciples) mais aussi hors de la pensée : c'est-dire à la fois comme politique occidentale et comme technique occidentale. L'Occident s'est auto-réalisé en occupant tout l'espace du monde par la colonisation et la « mondialisation » ; la technique est la procédure même de cet auto-accomplissement resserrant en permanence sa domination sur toutes les sphères de l'existence. S'il existe alors et encore une possibilité de relance de la pensée, elle se trouve dans ce que la philosophie a toujours elle-même pensé

---

13 *Ibid.*, p. 185–186.
14 Cf. Jean-Luc Nancy, « La Fin de la philosophie et la tâche de la pensée », en ligne : https://www.philosophy-world-democracy.org/other-beginning/la-fin-de-la-philosophie [consulté le 07 mars 2023].

comme l'autre de l'autoréalisation et de l'autonomie, c'est-à-dire qui est radicalement l'autre (*allo* et pas seulement *hétéro*). Entendons alors par là non seulement l'espace libre gardé par la philosophie, mais celui qui se trouve *hors d'elle*. Ce ne sont pas que des mots : Nancy a toujours pratiqué cette *allotropie* dont il parle, qui se tourne avant tout vers la littérature et l'art. Il s'agissait alors pour lui (et il s'agit toujours pour nous) d'éviter le risque évident d'une philosophie de la littérature et de l'art qui s'approprie son objet et pense pour lui, mais aussi celui, moins évident, d'une philosophie qui, consciente que son accomplissement est par définition insuffisant, demande à la littérature ou à l'art de lui offrir une dimension d'inaccomplissement. La voie est donc plus étroite qu'on ne pense : il s'agit de « passer la limite de l'interrompu et de l'ininterrompu »[15], de se trouver un passage singulier qui repasse sans cesse et dans tous les sens de la philosophie à l'art et à la littérature. Entendons que l'immensité de l'espace laissé libre devient toujours pour chacun et chacune d'entre nous (philosophes, écrivains, artistes) la voie étroite de ce passage ; c'est bien ce que dit Celan à propos de la poésie : « Elargir l'art ? Non. Mais va vers l'art, dans le resserrement qui t'est le plus propre. Et rends-toi libre »[16].

C'est bien de cela qu'il s'agissait dans le livre à propos des arts que nous avons écrit à quatre mains : « vous ne pouvez pas trouver une seule œuvre d'art qui ne se tienne – tendue, fragile, vibrante, dans l'équilibre furtif d'un passer »[17], disait-il. Cet équilibre, c'est évidemment celui qui fait que tout le passé se trouve de nouveaux passages, ou si l'on veut, une trace qui est aussi un tracer, une trace à venir : « la philosophie cherche des traces et des indices. L'art donne des vestiges : ça s'est passé, c'est passé, c'est infiniment dans le passage et le *passer*. »[18] Et cela peut être aussi tenu ou resserré qu'un trait qui dans le même mouvement coupe une page blanche et dessine un contour, commence et s'arrête librement tout en se continuant virtuellement à l'infini. Le trait (graphique, mais aussi bien musical ou gestuel, ou tout simplement artistique et à chaque fois différent dans chaque art et chaque œuvre, donc toujours singulier) est ainsi l'autre de la philosophie comme de la littérature, qui ne connaissent qu'une technique, celle de l'écriture, qu'un tracé, celui des caractères linéaires. La philosophie risque

---

15 Nancy, *Demande, op. cit.*, p. 13.
16 Cité par Nancy *in L'Expérience de la liberté, op. cit.*, p. 54.
17 *In* Lèbre et Nancy, *Signaux sensibles, op. cit.*, p. 147.
18 *Ibid.*, p. 146.

ainsi toujours de partager avec la technique la tentative d'achever l'infini (chaque système court ce risque au nom de la vérité
et chaque réseau d'appareils au nom de l'efficacité) ; la littérature délivre le texte en le livrant à un inaccomplissement infini ;
quant à l'art, il est à chaque fois « l'accomplissement fini de l'infini inaccomplissement ». Toutes ces définitions qui ne cessent de
s'indéfinir traduisent l'exposition irréductiblement hétérogène de
la vérité, et font que « pour parler de l'art il faut tendanciellement
aller vers la littérature : raconter l'œuvre, raconter ce qui *se passe*
dans la peinture de Rembrandt ou le cinéma de Kiarostami. Le
raconter sans prétendre interpréter, épuiser une réserve de sens ».
C'est bien ainsi que Nancy écrivait sur les artistes ou avec eux :
« il s'agit moins de parler sur l'art que de lui parler, voire de le
laisser se dire. Et cela suppose que l'art le demande... » Jamais
« l'art » ni l'artiste n'a demandé que le philosophe épuise le sens de
son œuvre : mais bien plutôt qu'il l'expose, le dissémine, le fasse
éclater, livre des éclats de vérité qui sont aussi des écarts, et par là
même des passages.

Finalement j'aurai bien plus écrit ici « sur » Nancy qu'avec lui,
même en citant ce livre écrit avec lui. Mais comment faire autrement, du moins ici et maintenant ? La mort d'un philosophe important laisse une évidence qui est aussi un désert (un espace évidé)
en lequel il faut beaucoup errer pour se trouver des passages, ou
même (ce serait une définition possible de l'écriture) se trouver
un passer (qui n'est pas que le sien, ni celui de l'autre, bien plutôt
un passer *entre* soi et les autres). J'indique cependant dans le peu
d'espace que je me suis laissé trois passages possibles.

Le premier est d'autant plus large qu'il suppose un abandon radical de ce que Nancy (ou Derrida) ont pu nous dire : il est celui
d'une repolitisation de la philosophie, *après* sa fin, qui fait de l'espace public tout l'espace, sans tenir compte de l'espace *laissé libre*
par les structures de domination ; on ne compte plus en effet les
politiques du couple, de l'art, de la littérature, etc.

Le second passage, bien plus étroit, est celui d'une redéfinition
de notre *ethos* : cette tâche est commune à Nancy, Foucault, et bien
d'autres, à ceci près que cet *ethos* se situe *d'après* Nancy au-delà
du politique, qu'il est simplement « ouverture d'espace », donc espacement ou « mise en liberté des lieux »[19]. Ces lieux ne sauraient
alors être libres de livres, et l'une des questions que l'on peut se

---

19 Nancy, *L'Expérience de la liberté, op. cit.*, p. 188 et p. 186.

poser à leur propos est de savoir pourquoi Nancy comme Foucault et bien d'autres respectent l'interdit heideggérien de traduire *ethos* par *caractère*. La raison avancée par Heidegger avant d'être globalement acceptée est que cette traduction serait « moderne et psychologique »[20] : elle dissimulerait donc ce que les Grecs entendait encore dans le mot *ethos*, à savoir le séjour de l'homme sur Terre et en relation à l'être. Il n'a pas fallu plus que cette affirmation brutale pour que la philosophie contemporaine se masque toute une histoire des textes dont la principale « caractéristique » est de déborder la philosophie[21]. De fait il revient à Théophraste, disciple d'Aristote, d'avoir traduit à l'intérieur du Grec les *ethoi* de son maître, en les nommant *kharakteres*. Il est impossible de savoir si l'écrit qui porte ce nom appartient à une éthique, une poétique et une rhétorique, mais ce qui est sûr est qu'il n'appartient pas à la psychologie. C'est ainsi que les *Caractères* de Théophraste ont joué un rôle fondamental pour le théâtre pendant des siècles et dans toute l'Europe, servant de substitut aux pages perdues qu'Aristote a consacré à la comédie dans sa poétique. C'est ainsi également qu'à partir du XVIIe siècle, le même texte participe à la naissance refoulée de la littérature européenne : par exemple en France, La Bruyère, cet auteur négligé, presque impossible à citer, a vu que la possibilité de cerner l'homme par ses *marques* ouvrait celle de continuer indéfiniment des « remarques » sur l'homme, donc de le suivre dans la pente constante qui l'éloignait de son essence : il en découle que chaque être singulier devient également être d'écriture et de fiction, personnage (*character* en anglais, *charakter* en allemand). On comprend dès lors la stratégie de Heidegger : non pas lutter contre l'aspect « psychologique » du caractère, mais fermer violemment, sous un prétexte historiquement faux, cet espace du personnage, qui est aussi celui du théâtre, de la littérature et de la fiction : il n'est pas question pour lui que l'homme puisse séjourner ne serait-ce qu'une seconde de plus dans des textes qui le remarquent, mais qui aussi le marquent et le constituent, puisqu'il doit séjourner auprès de l'être. Ceux qui n'ont pas lu Heidegger ont continué à vivre dans cet espace, à commencer par Freud, chez qui le caractère est le condensé d'une histoire singulière, à la frontière entre la fiction et le réel, qui structure le moi et le protège. Ainsi,

---

20 Martin Heidegger, *Heraklit*, Gesamtausgabe, Bd. 55, Klostermann, Frankfurt am Main, 1976, p. 349 ; cf. « Lettre sur l'humanisme », trad. R. Munier *in Questions III et* IV, Paris, Gallimard, 1990, p. 115.

21 Cf. sur ce point J. Lèbre, *Les Caractères impossibles*, Paris, Bayard, 2014.

faire du caractère le séjour de l'homme, *inscrire* celui-ci dans un espacement qui est à la fois celui de l'écriture et celui des êtres, c'est continuer ce débordement de la philosophie qui occupait Nancy dans un espace qu'il a laissé libre.

Le troisième passage est au plus proche du second : que l'on se souvienne de ce moment où les sciences humaines naissent au cœur de ce qui se nommait « histoire naturelle » : c'est alors le caractère de l'humain qui s'inscrivait dans cette nature, au même titre que celui des animaux ou des configurations géologiques et géographiques : tout avait un *caractère*, tout pouvait se décrire et se raconter. Foucault instaure dès *Les Mots et les choses* et encore plus par la suite une rupture jamais justifiée (sinon par l'autorité de Heidegger) entre cette caractéristique et l'*ethos* de la modernité. Le propre des sciences humaines est peut-être justement d'avoir passé outre cette rupture (à ceci près qu'il faudrait revisiter ce que Bourdieu nomme *ethos*) et d'avoir continué à caractériser l'humain tout en l'inscrivant dans un espace qui le débordait de toute part. Il faut ici donner toute sa place à la science (en partie) humaine qui est restée longtemps la plus éloignée de la philosophie, à savoir la géographie : longtemps freinée par le vieux dualisme entre « géographie physique » et « géographie humaine » qui hantait l'histoire naturelle, elle a trouvé récemment dans la phénoménologie l'ouverture d'un nouveau champ : celui d'une Terre qui précède l'homme et d'une humanité qui la reconfigure, sans jamais pouvoir la réduire à ses projets et ses représentations. Autrement dit, la géographie s'est ouverte à l'ontologie, et l'ontologie gagnerait tout autant à s'ouvrir à la géographie[22]. Cette voie étroite ouvre un immense espace : celui de tous les êtres qui sont autrement que libres ou autrement libres, celui qui élargit vraiment la communauté des êtres libres à tous ceux qui sont *avec* eux : animaux, forêts, montagnes, fleuves, océans, et déserts, tous à chaque fois *singuliers,* tous à chaque fois descriptibles. On notera que ce champ géographique est aussi celui de la littérature, comme des récits non-occidentaux ; il est temps que la philosophie y trouve son passage ; cet espace laissé libre par Nancy et bien d'autres est en effet *aussi* « composition extérieure de trajectoires et d'allures », « libre-espace de déplacements et de rencontres »[23].

---

22 Cf. Augustin Berque, *Ecoumène. Introduction à l'étude des milieux humains,* Paris, Belin, 2009, Introduction.
23 *Ibid.*, p. 96 et p. 100.

Ginette Michaud

Demande de Jean-Luc Nancy, ou
Comment rephraser la « philolittérature »

> Entre littérature et philosophie manque cet enlacement,
> cet embrassement [...]. Leur distinction en est exactement
> le désenlacement, le désembrassement. La mêlée ainsi dé-
> mêlée est partagée par la plus tranchante des lames : mais
> la coupure même porte à jamais les adhérences de l'em-
> mêlement. Entre les deux, il y a de l'indémêlable.[1]
>
> Jean-Luc Nancy, « *Un jour, les dieux se retirent...* »

I

Si l'essentiel du travail de Jean-Luc Nancy n'est pas consacré à la
littérature, il est incontestable que le philosophe a été si souvent
conduit à réfléchir sur des questions littéraires que la littérature est
dans sa pensée une basse continue. Dans son « Introduction » à la
traduction en anglais de *Demande* (qu'il n'hésite pas à qualifier
de « *summa poetica* »), Jean-Michel Rabaté souligne que « *[f]or the
first time* [...] *Nancy takes his stand both as a philosopher and as a
poet facing* [...] *the loaded, enigmatic, and tantalizing interactions
between poetic form and abstract thought* »[2]. Il note aussi que, dans
la tradition française, seul le nom de Paul Valéry vient à l'esprit
comme ayant traité de la littérature tant dans ses aspects concrets
que théoriques. Isabelle Alfandary écrit pour sa part qu'il y a dans
Demande « un souci de la lettre et de son faire propre, son *poeïn,*
un soin porté à la langue, à sa *technè,* à son travail singulier. Ce
souci ne se rencontre pas couramment dans un discours philosophique, sous la plume d'un philosophe »[3]. On ne peut donc qu'être

---

1   Jean-Luc Nancy, *Demande. Philosophie, littérature,* textes réunis avec la collaboration de Ginette Michaud, Paris, Galilée, 2015, p. 38.
2   Jean-Michel Rabaté, « "Wet the Ropes !" : Poetics of Sense, from Paul Valéry
to Jean-Luc Nancy », dans Nancy, *Expectation : Philosophy, Literature,* trad.
anglaise Robert Bononno, New York, Fordham University Press, 2018, p. ix.
3   Isabelle Alfandary, « "*[L]'ars poetica* en tant que tel" : de quelques enjeux
philosophiques de la poésie pour elle-même », *Les Cahiers philosophiques de
Strasbourg,* « Jean-Luc Nancy : penser la mutation », n° 42, 2017, p. 205.

d'accord avec Rabaté lorsqu'il affirme : « *[i]t is now time to reco-gnize that the work of Jean-Luc Nancy* [...] *cannot be reduced to an offshoot, albeit a highly creative one, of deconstruction, even if we know the complicity that links him with Derrida* »[4]. Si Nancy par-tage le point de vue de Derrida concernant la répression de l'écri-ture par le discours philosophique – critique que Rabaté résume en ces termes : « *first, philosophy breaks with the illusion of transpa-rency condensed in the wish to hear oneself speak; then philosophy has to reckon with form, which should lead to a study of the formal practices and programs offered to philosophers ; finally, philosophy can never be fully regulated by the law of pure thinking* »[5] –, leur approche respective des enjeux relatifs à l'écriture diffère néan-moins. Nancy insiste plus que Derrida sur les traits techniques et formels dans ses propres « *exercises as a close reader*[6] » de la poésie d'Hölderlin, par exemple, ou dans son exploration de différents genres littéraires, souvent sous le mode de la dérision ou du pas-tiche (il adopte en effet souvent un ton sérieusement parodique).

Reprenant l'ancien dialogue entre la philosophie et la littérature dans lequel « *the two domains* [...] *act as sparring partners, each attempting to stare the other down* »[7], Nancy déplace cette confron-tation de toujours sur un autre terrain où poésie et pensée « sont envisagées dans la tradition schlegelienne depuis leurs affinités électives »[8]. On pensera bien entendu à *L'absolu littéraire*, cet ou-vrage sur la théorie de la littérature des romantiques allemands qui a fait date depuis sa parution en 1978, et même au *Titre de la lettre*, paru cinq ans plus tôt et également co-écrit avec Philippe Lacoue-Labarthe, qui marquait déjà leur intérêt commun pour la « "philolittérature" »[9], ce rapport de « voisinage intime, complexe, conflictuel, séducteur et captateur à la fois »[10] qui fait toujours l'ob-jet « d'un partage extrêmement complexe et lui-même toujours en

---

4   Rabaté, « "Wet the Ropes !" : Poetics of Sense, from Paul Valéry to Jean-Luc Nancy », *in Expectation*, *op. cit.*.

5   *Ibid.*, p. xvii.

6   *Ibid.*, p. xix.

7   *Ibid.*, p. x.

8   Alfandary, « *"[L]'ars poetica* en tant que tel" : de quelques enjeux philoso-phiques de la poésie pour elle-même », *loc. cit.*, p. 210.

9   Jean-Luc Nancy, « D'une *"mimesis* sans modèle". Entretien avec Philippe Choulet au sujet de Philippe Lacoue-Labarthe », *L'Animal*, Cahier « Philippe Lacoue-Labarthe », n° 19–20, hiver 2008, p. 109.

10   Nancy, « Compter avec la poésie », *in Demande*, *op. cit.*, p. 154.

transformation »[11], comme le note Nancy dans *L'Adoration*. Dans un texte intitulé « Pensée psalmodiée », il revient sur ce partage ou partition entre la philosophie et la littérature, définissant la poésie comme « une pensée continue, la reprise obstinée d'une même pensée sans monotonie puisqu'elle n'est assurée de rien et ne forme pas de concepts. / Elle n'en forme pas car elle est tout occupée de sa propre insistance sans assurance. C'est là peut-être une des définitions possibles de la poésie (la philosophie serait alors l'insistance d'une assurance) »[12].

Si cette question fut au cœur des travaux menés conjointement par les deux amis philosophes, l'un et l'autre emprunteront après *L'absolu littéraire* des voies assez différentes, Lacoue-Labarthe s'engageant dans la grande question de la *mimêsis* (imitation sans modèle des Modernes) et de son « ontotypologie » qu'il repère dans la métaphysique et tout particulièrement dans le « national-esthé-tisme » de Heidegger, tandis que Nancy se tourne plutôt, dans le sillage de Bataille et de Blanchot, vers des motifs qu'il décrit lui-même comme « ontologiques et communautaires (ou bien : de communauté ontologique)[13] ». Le « *cum* », cette pensée de l'« avec » laissée en suspens dans le *Mitsein* et le *Mitdasein* heideggériens, la question de l'être-en-commun se retrouveront ainsi au fondement de sa pensée de l'écriture.

La réflexion de Nancy au sujet de la littérature s'est ainsi pour-suivie de manière intense depuis les années soixante-dix, comme le montre *Demande* qui rassemble ses textes sur une période de près de quarante ans. La littérature occupe dans ce corpus philoso-phique une place déterminante, et souvent là où on ne l'attendait pas, qu'on pense notamment à sa reformulation de la question de la création *ex nihilo* dans *La création du monde ou la mondialisa-tion* où, comme le note Michel Lisse, « *[i]nterestingly, Nancy does not consider artistic or poetic creation to be creation in the weak sense, but rather creation in the strongest sense* », « *taking the con-cept of creation understood as God's act of creation to be the least*

---

11 Jean-Luc Nancy, *L'Adoration (Déconstruction du christianisme 2)*, Paris, Galilée, 2010, p. 62.

12 Jean-Luc Nancy, « Pensée psalmodiée », *Lettres françaises* (supplément à *L'Hu-manité*), nº 160, 17 mai 2018), p. VII, en ligne : https://www.humanite.fr/sites/default/files/les-lettres-francaises-17-mai-2018.pdf [consulté le 20 mai 2022].

13 Nancy, « D'une "*mimesis* sans modèle". Entretien avec Philippe Choulet au sujet de Philippe Lacoue-Labarthe », *loc. cit.*, p. 109.

bad analogy for the process of literary writing »[14]. On pensera également à ses essais sur Blanchot qu'il inscrit au cœur du dispositif de *La Déclosion*, à ces multiples citations de Rimbaud, Faulkner, Lowry et Coetzee dans *L'Adoration*, ou encore à *Sexistence* où il convoque encore de manière très révélatrice la littérature, déclarant qu'il « fer[a] désormais appel, en contrepoint, à différents textes, surtout littéraires, témoins de ce à quoi le discours ne peut suffire »[15] :

À l'instar de cette citation, des inclusions ou des intrusions littéraires, narratives ou poétiques, se produiront au long de mon propos comme relais, des allusions ou des suppléments tournés vers ce que le seul discours ne suffit pas à énoncer ou plutôt à annoncer. Tout ici est suspendu à un désir de dire ce que le désir exprime ou éprouve outre les mots.[16]

« Désir de dire [...] outre les mots » : ce serait déjà une définition de la « littérature » ou de ce qui se tient sous ce nom pour Nancy, qui dit ainsi nommer « moins quelque chose qu'un au-delà de toute chose » :

> Je nomme une sorte de chose-en-soi ou de parousie, de présence absolue, de plérôme ou de pléthore – plénitude, comble, rassasiement infini, principe de plaisir illimité. Le plaisir se révèle dans sa plénitude de désir : il est moins ce qui charme et séduit que ce qui s'excite soi-même à se poursuivre, à ne pas cesser de s'intensifier.[17]

II

Avant de décrire le genre de fiction qui fascine Nancy par son « excédence de sens[18] », je voudrais brièvement revenir à cet ouvrage fondamental qu'est *L'absolu littéraire*, où deux aspects marquent pour lui le concept de *Literatur* tel que l'élaborent les romantiques d'Iéna : d'une part, le retrait qu'opère la littérature par rapport au mythe ; d'autre part, la notion de *poiesis*, c'est-à-dire d'un acte qui

---

14 Michel Lisse, « Literary Creation, Creation ex Nihilo », trad. anglaise John McKeane, *in* Alena Alexandrova, Ignaas Devisch, Laurens ten Kate et Aukje van Rooden (dir.), *Re-treating Religion : Deconstructing Christianity with Jean-Luc Nancy*, New York, Fordham University Press, 2012, p. 207–208.

15 Jean-Luc Nancy, *Sexistence*, Paris, Galilée, 2017, p. 46, note 1.

16 *Ibid.*, p. 25, note 1.

17 *Ibid.*, p. 21.

18 *Ibid.*, p. 180.

« se donne sa figure, son allure », « [q]ui ne demande donc qu'à se dire : à dire ce qui ne se dit pas mais se fait, à faire donc ce qui ne peut se limiter à dire, à dire-faire ou faire-dire »[19], ainsi qu'il l'écrit encore au sujet de la fiction dans *Sexistence*. Comme le voit bien Aukje van Rooden, la littérature serait donc, aux yeux de Nancy, ce qui

> would displace mythology, or rather [...] this displacement itself is literature. Literature and poetry mark, in other words, the retreat of an original foundational sense ; they echo the interruption of myth. More specifically, literature and poetry do not provide a fixed and accomplished sense, a full presence, but are the expression of a creative and transgressive force, a force that resists presence. Following the early Romantics, Nancy thus proposes to understand literature or poetry not as a specific artistic genre but as the expression of the very act of creating: as poiesis.[20]

Tout autant que l'interruption du mythe, cette notion de *poiesis* est donc capitale pour saisir le rapport essentiel qu'entretient la fiction au monde, non pas en tant que sa représentation mais bien en tant que création *effective* du monde. Dans *L'Adoration*, Nancy explicite l'importance de ces deux traits en les reliant à la question de l'« avec » et du partage des voix :

> C'est aussi pourquoi notre monde est celui de la littérature : ce que ce terme désigne d'une manière dangereusement insuffisante, décorative et oisive, n'est pas autre chose que le frayage des voix de l'« avec ». Là où ce que nous nommons le mythe donnait voix à l'origine, la littérature capte les voix innombrables de notre partage. Nous partageons le retrait de l'origine et la littérature parle à partir de l'interruption du mythe et en quelque sorte en elle : c'est dans cette interruption qu'elle fait, que nous faisons du sens. Ce sens est de fiction : c'est-à-dire qu'il n'est ni mythique ni scientifique, mais il se donne dans la création, dans le façonnement (*fingo, fictum*) des formes elles-mêmes mobiles, plastiques, ductiles, selon lesquelles l'« avec » se configure indéfiniment.[21]

---

19 *Ibid.*, p. 170.
20 Aukje van Rooden, « Intermezzo », *in Re-treating Religion*, *op. cit.*, p. 186.
21 Nancy, *L'Adoration*, *op. cit.*, p. 62.

On ne saurait par conséquent trop insister sur la portée de cette notion puisque c'est la *poiesis* qui, je cite de nouveau Aukje van Rooden,

> *provides Nancy with a specific view not only of creation but also of community, of our being together in the world. According to Nancy, our idea of being together has always been characterized by a mythological search for a common figure or narrative with which we can identify. By contrast, Nancy tries to understand our being together as an act, a* praxis, *rather than as a fulfilled work or a closed figure* [...]. *This original co-existence of beings does not correspond to a common figure but is in itself figurative, or poetic. Our co-existence, in other words, can be conceived of as a form of co-*poiesis.[22]

Je ne peux évidemment pas retracer ici la genèse du concept de *Literatur* chez les premiers romantiques allemands[23]. Selon cette conception dont Nancy hérite, « la littérature [est] considérée comme l'essence de l'art », ce qui implique que, désormais, « [c]'est l'intention poétique qui fait le Poème », qui ne se limite nullement à la *technè* poétique « tenue pour pratiquement ornementale »[24]. Or Nancy va, au contraire, accorder une attention extrême à tous ces enjeux prosodiques et rythmiques (rime, mètre, syncope), relevant de ce qu'Isabelle Alfandary appelle le « pré-sentir » dans son étude sur l'*ars poetica* nancéen. Non entièrement « réductible au pressentiment romantique ni à l'émotion hyperbolique », ce *pré-sentir* « loge au cœur de l'expérience de la poésie, de l'expérience que constitue la poésie pour la pensée »[25], et c'est dans cette voie que s'engagera la poétique – la poématique, pour être plus précise – de Nancy dès *Les Muses* (1994) où, comme le note Alfandary, il fait preuve d'une « sensibilité aiguë » à « "l'essence sensible" de la production du sens » en poésie, « nécessité tensionnelle »[26] qui marquera toute sa conception poétique : « Cette analyse de la pro-duction du sens propre à la poésie, cette protension intenable du sens entre touchant et touché, cet "en-avant" entre sensation

---

22   van Rooden, « Intermezzo », *loc. cit.*, p. 187.
23   Sur cette question, voir Cosmin Toma, *Neutraliser l'absolu. Blanchot, Beckett et la chose littéraire*, Paris, Hermann, 2019, p. 32 *sq.*
24   Alfandary, « "[L]'ars poetica en tant que tel" : de quelques enjeux philoso-phiques de la poésie pour elle-même », *loc. cit.*, p. 211.
25   *Ibid.*, p. 200.
26   *Ibid.*, p. 201.

et sens rendent compte philosophiquement du procès du sens à
l'œuvre dans le poème »[27].

On ne saurait donc assez marquer ce legs théorique du romantisme allemand pour la littérature en tant que *question* chez Nancy,
de même que sa dette envers Bataille, Blanchot, Benjamin et Derrida
en ce qui concerne, entre autres, le « refus de toute croyance en un
langage transparent et transitif »[28], l'autonomie de l'œuvre d'art et
la remise en question de la représentation au profit de la présentation ou *Darstellung*. Comme le rappelle Benjamin, « [d]epuis le romantisme seulement, l'idée s'est imposée qu'une *œuvre* d'art pourrait être saisie dans sa nature véritable dès lors qu'on la contemple
pour elle-même, indépendamment de son rapport à la théorie ou à
la morale, et qu'elle pourrait se suffire de ce regard »[29].

Car c'est bien là ce que nous avons appris des romantiques, dit
Nancy : l'œuvre comme « *opus operans* »[30], comme « infinition »[31],
« non pas son accomplissement mais son opération, non pas sa fin
mais son infinité, non pas son entéléchie mais son énergie comme
acte d'une dynamique qui ne résorbe pas dans un produit[32] ». Cette
thèse autonomiste de l'absolu littéraire (autoproduction et auto-
critique) ne doit toutefois pas faire oublier que la dissolution en
est aussi la contrepartie (si *absolvo* signifie « achever », il signifie
également « séparer, détacher »). Il s'agit donc tout autant pour la
littérature de s'absolutiser que de renoncer à tout absolu (rassem-
blement, totalisation, achèvement).

Enfin, dernière remarque liminaire : si dans *L'absolu littéraire*,
Lacoue-Labarthe et Nancy gardent « à la notion d'"absolu" sa part
de mystère, rappelant par là sa complicité avec la théologie[33] », il
faut souligner que « Le mystère dans les lettres », pour emprunter
ce titre à Mallarmé, ne saurait pour Nancy « se poursuivre par des
voies exclusivement solitaires ; il doit impérativement mettre le
cap sur le dehors, consentir à la parution et à l'extériorisation »[34],
voire à ce que Jean-Luc Nancy appelle la « comparution », d'où son

---

27 *Ibid.*
28 Toma, *Neutraliser l'absolu, op. cit.*, p. 25.
29 Walter Benjamin, « Lettre à Gershom Scholem du 30 mars 1918 », *in* Theo-
dor W. Adorno et Gershom Scholem (éds.), *Correspondance*, vol. 1 : 1910–1928,
trad. française Guy Petitdemange, Paris, Aubier Montaigne, 1978, p. 166.
30 Nancy, « De l'œuvre et des œuvres », *in Demande, op. cit.*, p. 92.
31 *Ibid.*, p. 90.
32 *Ibid.*, p. 91.
33 Toma, *Neutraliser l'absolu, op. cit.*, p. 52.
34 *Ibid.*, p. 120.

insistance particulière sur l'écriture en tant que « la communauté de l'écriture, l'écriture de la communauté »[35], selon ce chiasme qui marque de nouveau sa dette envers Blanchot.

III

Quelles lignes de force peut-on dégager de l'approche nancéenne de la « littérature » ? Je me limiterai à trois points. On retiendra d'abord que la réflexion de Nancy est placée sous le signe conjoint, non sans paradoxe, d'un commencement radical et d'une répétition originaire, ce qu'il appelle avec Blanchot « l'immémorial », ce qui ne veut pas dire ici l'ancien, le primitif ou le premier, pas plus que le dehors n'est extérieur. La « fiction » désigne pour Nancy une « figuration de l'infigurable »[36] : l'écriture « se consacre à considérer l'événement qui n'a pas eu lieu ou dont l'avoir-lieu ne peut que rester conjectural tant il est reculé en deçà de tout vestige, de toute trace qu'on en pourrait trouver »[37]. Écrire ne consiste donc pas, du point de vue nancéen, « à transcrire des données préalables – des événements, des situations, des objets, leurs significations – mais à inscrire des possibilités de sens non données, non disponibles, ouvertes par l'écriture elle-même »[38]. Isabelle Alfandary a raison de suggérer que « [c]ette proposition critique n'est pas une proposition parmi d'autres : la singularité que l'écriture signifie et qu'elle acte […] procède d'une dislocation entre littérature et événement, d'une disjonction entre écriture et avoir-lieu »[39].

Deuxième point : les écrits de Nancy sont traversés de manière insistante par les motifs de l'oralité, de la profération/énonciation, du « partage des voix ». On ne s'en étonnera pas puisque, dès *Le Discours de la syncope* (1976), les notions d'interruption et de suspens se sont révélées cardinales. Or ce « *sun* » grec, c'est aussi ce que traduit le « *cum* » latin, ou l'« avec », soit la séparation et la conjonction, la conjonction disjoignante qui ne cesse de s'opérer – de s'*apérer* – dans toute la pensée nancéenne. La « syncope »

---

35 Jean-Luc Nancy, *La communauté désœuvrée*, Paris, Christian Bourgois éditeur, 1999, p. 104.

36 Nancy, « La raison demande la poésie », *in Demande, op. cit.*, p. 169.

37 Nancy, « […] devrait être un roman […] », *in Demande, op. cit.*, p. 82.

38 *Ibid.*

39 Alfandary, « "[L]'*ars poetica* en tant que tel" : de quelques enjeux philosophiques de la poésie pour elle-même », *loc. cit.*, p. 203.

ouvre toute synthèse en son cœur même, comme il le déclare dans « La raison demande la poésie ». Rappelons que cet « avec », « constitutif de l'existant », doit être ici « non de façon catégoriale, mais existentiale »[40]. Dans *Sexistence*, Nancy précise de nouveau que « [l]'"avec" n'est jamais une chose, une substance ni un sujet. Il est l'élément du seul sens, dans tous ses sens, c'est-à-dire de toutes les façons du sentir, recevoir ou repousser un dehors, n'être jamais "dedans" sans ce dehors qui vient et qui s'écarte »[41]. Cet « avec » – qui peut être désigné de plusieurs noms : entre-deux, venue, ab-sens – a partie liée avec la question du dehors qui se fait, dans cette poétique de l'exscription, également primordiale. En effet, dans la littérature ou la poésie, ce qui intéresse surtout Nancy, c'est ce qui vient « de très loin et s'enlèv[e], se soulèv[e] vers le plus lointain »[42] : « la présence pour se présenter doit *venir*. Et pour venir elle doit être envoyée, adressée, expédiée. C'est ce qu'on appelle l'existence : la venue de tout à tout »[43], affirme-t-il dans *Sexistence*. Ce qui lui importe avant tout ici, c'est donc « cet envoi – cet envol, cette levée – [qui] s'expédie lui-même toujours hors de soi »[44].

Troisième point : l'interaction entre le corps et le sens. S'appuyant sur une conception de la littérature qui est fondée (mais est-ce un fondement ?) sur la « *creative division of the speaker* », la « *demotion of the domineering Author* » et un « *newly enfranchised Reader* »[45], la littérature ne répond pour Nancy d'aucune utilité ni fonction : elle est échange, passage, *trans*-formation des formes, sans donnée préalable. Peut-être sa spécificité, tout comme celle de l'art, tiendrait-elle pour lui dans cette formule, à savoir qu'elle ne fait pas sens (*meaning*) mais bien *sense* (en gardant le mot lui-même entre les langues, comme le suggère Jean-Michel Rabaté[46]) :

---

40 Jean-Luc Nancy, « Mit-Sinn », *in* Elke Bippus, Jörg Huber et Dorothee Richter (dir.), *Mit-Sein*, Zurich, Voldemeer, 2010, p. 21–32 ; inédit en français, 2010, p. 1. Je cite ici la version française que m'avait communiquée Jean-Luc Nancy.

41 Nancy, *Sexistence, op. cit.*, p. 51.

42 *Ibid.*, p. 49.

43 *Ibid.*, p. 50.

44 *Ibid.*, p. 51.

45 Rabaté, « "Wet the Ropes !" : Poetics of Sense, from Paul Valéry to Jean-Luc Nancy », *in Expectation, op. cit.*, p. xviii.

46 « *Following Nancy's use, one should translate* sens *as "sense," for in recurrent phenomenological explorations that are not limited to poetry and include the substance of the world, Nancy insists upon the interaction between the body and meaning, between flesh and words.* », *Ibid.*, p. xvii.

« Cela se nomme une sensation : telle est la première allure du sens »[47]. La littérature, c'est ce qui est sensible à la possibilité du sens ; c'est ce qui « est toujours susceptible de "faire", du moins de suggérer du sens »[48]. *Du* sens, *des* sens, et non pas *le* sens ; signifiance, significabilité, et non pas signification. Comme il le demandera très tôt au sujet du *Witz*, « [l]a question qui s'impose est dès lors extrêmement simple : comment l'insignifiant peut-il prendre une telle importance, et qu'est-ce que cette opération engage ? »[49] Dans la littérature ou l'art, ce qui est désigné (ou dessiné), ce n'est donc pas le « plein de sens »[50] mais le rapport à la chose même. La littérature est ainsi le lieu d'approche, sans appropriation possible, de la chose, l'« approche d'une intimité inimaginable »[51] qui s'offre en se retirant, captant de manière sensible ce retrait où le toucher, la touche, ne peut advenir que par écartement, espacement, renvoi à l'autre. La littérature – le poème, le chant, l'art ou toute autre forme naissante – fraye un accès privilégié en ce qu'elle « se » fait sens dans le débordement du sens, par excès et intensification. Ce que cet *ars poetica* donne à penser/sentir comme rapport au monde, Nancy le condense en ces termes :

> Dans le sentiment tel que nous le comprenons (en tant qu'affect, émotion, trouble) [...], il n'y a rien d'autre que le développement de ce sentiment de soi qui fait le monde : s'ouvrir et se recevoir de sa propre ouverture comme autant de touches indéfiniment multipliées et relayées de choses en choses, de pressions en saisies, de capteurs en réflecteurs, d'actions en réactions.[52]

Il ne s'agit donc plus simplement pour cette poétique de l'exscription de reconnaître que l'œuvre d'art entretient un rapport au monde, mais bien que le monde vient en elle pour s'y former. Mieux : une forme qui « rejoue et relance le *ex nihilo* qui est [le] partage »[53] du monde. Ainsi, la littérature n'est pas « réponse à une question », à une demande, mais « réponse à un appel »[54].

---

47 Nancy, « Mit-Sinn », *loc. cit.*, p. 3.
48 *Ibid.*, p. 2.
49 Nancy, « En guise de prologue », *in Demande, op. cit.*, p. 17.
50 Nancy, « Mit-Sinn », *loc. cit.*, p. 2.
51 *Ibid.*, p. 3.
52 *Ibid.*, p. 5.
53 Nancy, *L'Adoration, op. cit.*, p. 61.
54 Nancy, « Les raisons d'écrire », *in Demande, op. cit.*, p. 48.

IV

Je voudrais maintenant dire un mot au sujet de la poésie puisque c'est surtout elle qui porte la pointe la plus aiguë du rapport au langage et qui offre par conséquent la plus grande « résistance » pour Nancy. Dans un entretien où il commentait la triple mutation en cours (« capitalisme, technique, démocratie »), il déclarait que, si « nous ne savons pas ce que "penser" veut dire »,

> [e]n revanche, nous savons – ou peut-être faut-il dire nous éprouvons – autre chose : la même parole qui dépose ses significations fragiles, usées ou vidées ne cesse pourtant pas de se relancer elle-même en tant qu'appel et échange, exhortation ou émotion, désir inextinguible de sens et passage incessant à la limite du sens, ou bien au sens comme limite… Cela résonne plus du côté de la poésie que de la philosophie mais aucune culture, aucune configuration d'humanité n'a jamais été exempte de ce que le mot « poésie » désigne si mal et si bien (lui aussi déchiré comme l'infini).[55]

Si, donc, la « poésie », tout en étant un nom inadéquat à ce qu'elle désigne, nous interpelle toujours, c'est parce qu'elle reste chevillée à ce « désir inextinguible de sens ». Mais que signifie au juste « poésie » pour Nancy ? Touche de langage, parole naissante ou « forme intimante »[56], « poésie » est essentiellement (mot évidemment piégé) pour lui envoi, adresse, allure, ton et timbre d'une voix. D'une voix très singulière, car elle n'est ni celle du poète dans sa « subjectivité » au sens courant du terme ni même celle du poème, mais ce qui émane du langage, « du devenir-voix du langage »[57], comme le dit Jean-Christophe Bailly dans *L'élargissement du poème*. Cette venue de la voix, dictante ou récitante, ancienne et inouïe, tient à un dire plutôt qu'à un dit, à « une diction, une scansion, une récitation dans laquelle le plus ancien et toujours déjà disparu […] affleure et se donne à sentir, se prête à une jouissance qui n'est pas de signification ni de satisfaction, mais de touche et

---

55 Juan Manuel Garrido Wainer, « Phraser la mutation : entretien avec Jean-Luc Nancy », *Mediapart*, 13 octobre 2015, en ligne : http://blogs.mediapart.fr/blog/juan-manuel-garrido-wainer/121015/phraser-la-mutation-entretien-avec-jean-luc-nancy [consulté le 20 mai 2022] ; repris in *Les Cahiers philosophiques de Strasbourg, op. cit.*, p. 119–125.

56 Jean-Christophe Bailly, *L'élargissement du poème*, Paris, Christian Bourgois éditeur, 2015, p. 109.

57 *Ibid.*, p. 58.

de tact – une cadence de lecture et le visage intact de l'ami de mille ans »[58], comme l'écrit Nancy au sujet de Pascal Quignard.

Ces lignes disent déjà comment la « littérature » entretient un rapport particulier, peut-être unique, à la question du mythe. Dans *Proprement dit*, Nancy reprend cette question qu'il complexifie encore :

> Mais revenons au mythe ou plutôt à ce qui pouvait en rester – puisqu'au fond la question est : que reste-t-il après l'« interruption » ? ou bien : qu'est-ce qui s'entend encore ? qu'est-ce qui traverse encore sourdement la cloison qui est venue interrompre ?
> Reste… la littérature (et la question de la littérature pour/dans la philosophie) […].[59]

Reste la littérature, donc, et le poème en tant que cet « ouvert », sans majuscule, qui « excède la seule question de son genre »[60], l'élargissant, l'étendant au-delà de lui-même : l'ouvert « comme le nom générique de ce qui ne se ferme pas sur soi, de ce qui se déprend de la pulsion d'enclore, qui est encore, malgré tant d'efforts faits pour la réduire, absolument dominante »[61].

Le poème nancéen par excellence serait donc celui qui, loin de « la déclamation ou [de] la pose poétique en général »[62], s'impose par sa *retenue* précisément, « *ne se déclarant qu'à peine en tant que telle. Rien qui touche à ce que ce mot évoque d'emphase. Des envois brefs, fugitifs, presque laconiques. Rien qui confine à l'hymne ni même à ce qu'on appelle "lyrisme"*[63] ». S'il est attentif à ce retentissement en ses multiples tonalités, il est particulièrement sensible à un certain timbre qui est avant tout celui « *d'une parole parlée plus que chantée, et plutôt brève, rapide, parfois murmurée, et ainsi adressée. La sonorité vient par là, avec le timbre et les rythmes de ce* parlando[64]. » C'est cette vocalité qui attire Nancy par sa « vérité

58 Jean-Luc Nancy, « Jadis, jamais, bientôt (l'amour) », *in* Philippe Bonnefis et Dolorès Lyotard (dir.), *Pascal Quignard. Figures d'un lettré*, Paris, Galilée, 2005, p. 384.
59 Jean-Luc Nancy, *Proprement dit. Entretien sur le mythe*, avec Mathilde Girard, Paris, Lignes, 2015, p. 33.
60 Bailly, *L'élargissement du poème*, op. cit., p. 8.
61 *Ibid.*, p. 9.
62 Nancy, « Deguy l'an neuf ! », *in* Yves Charnet (dir.), *Le poète que je cherche à être. Cahier Michel Deguy*, Paris, La Table Ronde et Éditions Belin, 1996, p. 168.
63 Jean-Luc Nancy, préface à Gérard Haller, *Météoriques*, Paris, Seghers, 2001, p. 10. Les italiques sont dans le texte.
64 *Ibid.*

matérielle »[65] dans des vers qui sont « *mesures de souffle de pensée. Souffles plus ou moins courts, tendus, retenus, exhalés, soufflés. Des phrases aussi : des énoncés, des prononcés* »[66]. C'est pourquoi la scansion du souffle porte toujours ici un enjeu important, une question vitale en quelque sorte : « Comment, en d'autres termes, s'accorder à un monde désaccordé, ou comment trouver un souffle sans inspiration ni expiration (une apnée, en somme) ? »[67] Le vers procède ainsi à une « nécessaire désubjectivation de la poésie », et « désubjectiver veut dire : reprendre la mesure du monde »[68], rien de moins. Une telle définition justifierait à elle seule qu'on accorde plus d'attention à cette question du poétique, d'autant que, plus et mieux que d'autres formes de pensée peut-être, elle résiste. Mais ce salut à la poésie, ce désir de littérature, est toujours aussi chez Nancy, il est important de le souligner, un adieu :

> Il est possible que cet adieu soit encore à prononcer envers la poésie. [...] Dire adieu c'est se tenir sur la barque qui dérive, et regarder à la fois l'image qui s'éloigne (le mythe, la scène d'origine) et *la suivante encore invisible*.
>
> Dire adieu veut dire : savoir regarder l'invisible. Le regarder à nouveau et le regarder nouveau.
>
> C'est ce que fait le poème : il s'éloigne du poème, les yeux tournés vers lui, mais tourné aussi vers l'invisible d'une forme à venir, ou peut-être seulement d'un trait, d'un battement. La poésie comme cadence d'une venue plutôt que comme scansion d'un cycle d'origine et de fin.[69]

« [R]egarder à la fois l'image qui s'éloigne [...] et *la suivante encore invisible* » : s'agit-il ici de la figure d'un mythe ou de son congédiement, ou encore d'un poème qui commence lui-même à se distendre, à s'étendre, à se tourner « vers l'invisible d'une forme à venir » ? Tombeau ou naissance ? Deuil ou désir ? Un commencement, une fin ? Les deux à la fois ? Dans « Pensée psalmodiée », Nancy rappelle que « la poétique immanente des langues fait résonner "psaume" et "spasme", comme Paul Celan a su en faire usage » et que, même s'il est maintenant impossible pour le poème d'en rester à « l'implo-

---

65 Jean-Luc Nancy, « Vers endurci », postface à Philippe Beck, *Dernière Mode familiale*, Paris, Flammarion, 2000, p. 210.
66 Nancy, préface à Haller, *Météoriques*, *op. cit.*, p. 13.
67 Nancy, « Vers endurci », *loc. cit.*, p. 204–205.
68 *Ibid.*, p. 205.
69 Nancy, « Poème de l'adieu au poème : Bailly », *loc. cit.*, p. 61–62.

ration », il doit malgré tout trouver les ressources pour « implorer dans un chant singulier, doux-amer et vibrant-accablé »[70].

La littérature ou l'« art » valent donc en ceci qu'ils échangent « du sens hors de la signification »[71] : « ils ne signifient pas : ils emportent les significations dans un autre régime, où les signes renvoient à l'infini »[72]. Ce n'est pas par hasard si, dans *L'Adoration*, Nancy a recours à ce qu'il nomme une « cadence finale », citant une brève scène érotique d'Élizabeth Costello de Coetzee qui figure, peut-être mieux que tout discours, ce qui est en jeu dans l'adoration même. La littérature est cette figure de l'infini qui donne accès à une parole sans laquelle « nous n'entrerions même pas dans la sphère du sens, c'est-à-dire d'abord dans celle du langage »[73]. Ces convocations de la littérature passent outre la raison, la parole poétique faisant « venir le très ailleurs comme ailleurs, et en le gardant ailleurs[74] ». Car n'est-ce pas cela que fait la poésie : revenir « une fois de plus du plus lointain, du plus ancien, comme le plus ancien, le très ailleurs, *ici même ailleurs* »[75] ?

C'est en ce sens que la poésie se fait exscription. Le poème tente d'étendre, d'élargir (tenue, étendue, tension, attention, attente, tentation : nul hasard non plus si c'est cette chaîne lexicale qui revient dès qu'il est question de la littérature dans ces textes), il réclame un dépassement des limites, une expansion, une sortie hors d'elles-mêmes, au dehors, au monde. Ce qui est visé dans le dire poétique, c'est le monde lui-même, jamais des « objets » et pas non plus des « sujets », mais « des choses : c'est-à-dire des présences. Les présences sont mystérieuses, elles se dérobent à l'approche, bien qu'en même temps nous puissions parvenir dans leur proximité »[76]. Telle est alors la force – force fragile, précaire, toujours incertaine – de ces « formes où le texte avec sa prosodie, d'une part, la musique avec ses couleurs, d'autre part, gardent à chacun leur autonomie » : les poèmes « scandent, ils cadencent une pensée qui ne conçoit ni ne conclut, mais qui éprouve un monde »[77].

———

70 Nancy, « Pensée psalmodiée », *loc. cit.*, p. VII.
71 Nancy, *L'Adoration, op. cit.*, p. 62.
72 *Ibid.*, p. 63.
73 *Ibid.*, p. 90.
74 Nancy, « Deguy l'an neuf ! », *loc. cit.*, p. 168.
75 *Ibid.*, p. 169.
76 Nancy, « Il fervore della parola », préface à Nancy, *Narrazioni del fervore. Il desiderio, il sapere, il fuoco*, trad. italienne Alberto Panaro, avec un essai de Flavio Ermini, Bergame, Moretti & Vitali, 2007, p. 9. Ma traduction.
77 Nancy, « Pensée psalmodiée », *loc. cit.*, p. VII.

Ainsi, ce que nous nommons du nom ancien et pourtant toujours renouvelé de « poésie », n'a rien d'un état d'âme, de la nostalgie ou de l'imprécation. Si le poème importe, c'est parce qu'il ne se conforme à aucune « précédence idéale »[78], à rien de donné, qu'il est attention au « tout-venant ». Si le poème survit et déjoue les mythes des origines et des fins, ce n'est pas parce qu'il serait évasion ou supplément d'âme, mais parce qu'il est cette offre sans demande et qu'il ne « tombe » jamais sous le sens.

Comment dès lors penser ce mot, « littérature » ou « poésie » ? Garde-t-il une pertinence ? Le poème, disait plus haut Nancy, est « désir inextinguible de sens et passage incessant à la limite du sens, ou bien au sens comme limite ». Reste, donc, oui, le poème. C'est en tout cas sur cette question, sans phrasé encore, que se clôt cet entretien alors qu'il se demande s'il ne faut pas « [a]ujourd'hui redevenir délibérément poètes… qu'est-ce que cela voudrait dire ? » :

Chacun est dans le réel, n'est que là… immergé dedans, se débrouillant à sa manière avec l'opacité et le poids du réel…

Mais bien sûr cela demande de dire à nouveau le « réel », de le phraser, de le nommer, de l'éprouver et de dire cette épreuve. Et alors on retrouve l'aiguillon d'une attente d'écriture, d'expression, de mots où le réel puisse respirer ou transpirer…

[…]

Rien que je sois capable de nommer – mais au moins savoir que nous sommes dans cet élément-là.[79]

---

78 Bailly, *L'élargissement du poème, op. cit.*, p. 102.
79 Nancy, « Phraser la mutation », *loc. cit.*

Peter Szendy

Rumémoration

Jean-Luc aura rarement écrit – littéralement inscrit – le mot « rumeur ». Mais si l'on y prête l'oreille, on l'entend bruire un peu partout. Comme un bruit indistinct qui n'affleurerait pas – si ce n'est exceptionnellement – à la surface vigile de ses textes, tout en grondant en continu, quoique sourdement, quelque part derrière. La rumeur n'est jamais bien loin lorsqu'il y va de l'être-avec, du *cum* de la communauté : peut-être est-elle même le fond sans fond depuis lequel tout être-ensemble s'enlève.

Les seules pages que Jean-Luc a explicitement consacrées à la rumeur, sous ce nom et sous ce titre, sont une réponse à l'invitation du critique d'art Hans-Ulrich Obrist, qui lui avait demandé de contribuer à une collection de textes sur ce qu'on appelle parfois des « légendes urbaines » *(urban rumors)*. « Rumoration », titre de la réponse de Jean-Luc, a été repris dix ans plus tard, en 2011, dans le recueil intitulé *La Ville au loin*[1]. On y tombe certes sur la question la plus frontale, la plus directe qui soit au sujet de la rumeur (« Qu'est-ce que la rumeur ? »), mais celle-ci refuse pourtant de se laisser saisir, de se laisser arrêter dans une phrase, dans un énoncé stable. À peine est-elle dite ou désignée qu'elle change aussitôt d'aspect ou de consistance, comme si elle se transformait *avant même d'avoir eu le temps de prendre forme.*

« Rumoration » s'ouvre en effet, *in medias res,* à la manière d'un travelling, d'un mouvement ambulatoire où la rumeur est emportée (p. 125) : « Je marche dans la rue cherchant une phrase. Pour ouvrir un texte, que je dois écrire, il me faut cette phrase. Le texte doit parler de la rumeur. Qu'est-ce que la rumeur ? Je pense à l'air de la calomnie du *Barbiere di Siviglia.* J'entends la musique, elle se joue dans ma tête... *incomincia a sussurrar... piano piano, terra terra, sotto voce...* » À peine nommée pour être interrogée dans son essence (« qu'est-ce que la rumeur ? »), la rumeur donne le change et devient un air chanté venu de l'opéra de Rossini. Mais, ne pouvant pas plus s'installer dans le médium de la musique que dans

---

1   « Rumoration » a d'abord paru – avec quantité d'autres réponses d'artistes, architectes, sociologues ou philosophes – dans « Urban Rumors : A Project Curated by Hans Ulrich Obrist », *Mutations,* Bordeaux, ACTAR, 2001 ; puis dans Jean-Luc Nancy, *La Ville au loin,* Paris, La Phocide, 2011, p. 125–127.

celui du langage, elle tend déjà à revenir vers celui-ci, à redevenir un début de discours articulé : « *piano piano, terra terra, sotto voce...* Je marche en cherchant à faire venir une phrase au rythme de la musique ou de mes pas. Je cherche à utiliser la marche et la familiarité usée de la ville pour m'isoler dans ma tête et profiter de la marche pour avancer mon travail. » La rumeur oscille ainsi, elle balance ou chancelle dans son cours entre énonciation et énoncé, entre dire et dit, entre pur bruissement et parole à l'œuvre en quête d'un sens.

Or, cette vacillation inchoative que rien ne stabilise encore, voilà qu'elle passe maintenant d'une langue à une autre (du français à l'anglais à l'italien et retour) : « Je cherche à [...] profiter de la marche pour avancer mon travail. Je perds ma question, je pense à autre chose. Le sens français de "rumeur" (anglais de *rumor)* s'est perdu dans le sens italien de *rumore,* qui désigne le bruit. Mais en français, "rumeur" désigne aussi le murmure ou le grondement. » Le temps de repasser un instant par la musique de l'air de Rossini (« la musique orchestre les bruits de la rue... *e le teste ed i cervelli fa stordire, e fa gonfiar...* »), la rumeur semble maintenant cristalliser en une image devant les yeux du marcheur ou flâneur : « Une affiche accroche mon regard, sur la paroi d'une halte d'autobus. »

Un demi-siècle plus tôt, en temps de guerre, l'affiche en question aurait pu être l'une de celles que l'on trouvait placardées pour avertir le public – le passant, le quidam, ces sujets par excellence de la rumeur (ou mieux : à la rumeur) – des dangers que font courir les bruits qui courent. « Écoute », « quelqu'un m'a dit », « et j'ai vu », « j'entends que », pouvait-on lire sur telle affiche conservée à la Library of Congress : imprimée entre 1941 et 1945, elle était diffusée, comme tant d'autres du même genre, afin de prévenir la propagation de rumeurs dangereuses pour la sécurité nationale. C'était l'époque des *rumor clinics,* ces rubriques qui se sont multipliées dans les quotidiens (la première est apparue en 1942 dans le *Boston Herald)* pour désamorcer les rumeurs en les analysant et en les soumettant à l'épreuves des faits (on y reconnaîtra les précurseurs des *fact checks* du *New York Times,* des « décodeurs » du *Monde* ou du service « Désintox » de *Libé*ration). Ces « cliniques de la rumeur » côtoyaient d'ailleurs parfois des publicités, comme ce fut notamment le cas dans les pages du magazine *Life,* où l'explication de leur fonctionnement fait écho en colonne de droite à l'annonce d'une promotion sur une brassière[2].

L'affiche qui ponctue la déambulation rumoreuse de Jean-Luc dans « Rumoration » appartient à ce même genre : « Une affiche accroche mon regard, sur la paroi d'une halte d'autobus. C'est [...] une publicité pour de la lingerie. » Et c'est cette affiche qui, d'une part, reconduit le marcheur vers ce qui aimantait sa quête (la rumeur) ; mais c'est elle aussi qui, d'autre part et en même temps, le détourne, le séduit ou l'éconduit à nouveau, refusant à la rumeur polymorphe le statut, la station ou la stance d'un « sujet » au sens plein et stable du terme : « L'image est accompagnée d'une légende qui énonce : "Apprenez-lui la méditation." Je pense que je suis justement en train d'essayer de méditer la formation d'une phrase. Je reviens à mon sujet. Peut-être n'en ai-je même pas encore fait mon sujet. C'est juste un murmure dans ma tête. Je pense que la rumeur est le plus souvent malveillante, médisante ou calomnieuse. »[3]

Dans cette promenade ou flânerie en quête d'une phrase qu'est « Rumoration » (« je marche dans la rue cherchant une phrase »), dans ces phrases qui elles-mêmes se suivent en déambulant à la rencontre d'une phrase à venir, la rumeur est fuyante et fluante, elle se lève, elle rumore (le verbe « rumorer » est attesté en moyen français comme signifiant « faire du bruit »), elle bruisse à chaque instant et pourtant elle ne cesse d'échapper, elle qui résiste à se laisser assujettir, à devenir l'objet d'un discours, son thème, ce sur

---

2   Sur les *rumor clinics,* voir Gordon W. Allport et Leo Postman, *The Psychology of Rumors,* New York, Henry Holt and Company, 1947, p. 18 *sq.* La publicité côtoyant les images desdites « cliniques de la rumeur » est tirée du magazine *Life,* 12 octobre 1942, p. 94.

3   L'affiche en question fait probablement partie d'une campagne de publicité pour la marque de lingerie Aubade, en 2000 ; la photo en noir et blanc d'un corps de femme, agenouillée et vêtue de ladite lingerie (la tête se trouve hors cadre), est accompagnée de la légende suivante : « Leçon n° 32 : L'inciter à méditer. »

quoi porterait l'interrogation du penseur ou de la pensée en marche
(« peut-être n'en ai-je même pas encore fait mon sujet »). La rumeur rumore, en somme, mais sa rumoration rumoreuse passe
d'un médium à l'autre, elle se déforme sans cesse, déjouant toute
prise de forme, comme si elle consistait ou insistait précisément
dans l'entre-formes. Car la rumeur est un défi à la pensée : son
lexique, ses noms (colportage, calomnie, commérage, ragots, on-
dit, fausses nouvelles ou *fake news,* bruit public, légende urbaine,
théorie du complot…) ne cessent de déborder ou de déplacer les
limites que l'on voudrait lui assigner. Si bien que le concept-de-ru-
meur est toujours sur le point de basculer en un concept-rumeur,
comme si le concept lui-même faisait du bruit, son extension mou-
vante brouillant son intension, introduisant un effet de bougé dans
sa compréhension.

Et c'est pourquoi, bien souvent, on en minimise la puissance,
on la balaye d'un revers de la main, on la considère comme né-
gligeable, comme indigne que la pensée s'y arrête. Jean-Luc, au
moins une fois, aura lui aussi cédé à cette tentation. À une question qu'on lui posait en 2018 sur « une espèce de régime de mensonge qui s'installerait avec la multiplication des *fake news* par
exemple, ou le mensonge utilisé comme arme dans les élections
américaines », il aura répondu[4] : « Je ne crois pas trop à ça. Je vois
bien que cela se répand beaucoup […]. Les fausses nouvelles ont
toujours existé. Je comprends même mal pourquoi on se focalise
sur cette ébullition des fausses nouvelles. Nous sommes bien sûr
dans un monde où une telle quantité d'informations se propage
à tout moment que sans arrêt il circule absolument tout et son
contraire. De ce point de vue-là, les réseaux sociaux sont autant
mauvais que bons. Ils permettent une communication instantanée
très rapide et en même temps ils diffusent n'importe quoi. »

Serait-ce donc une simple question de quantité, d'échelle, de
masse ? Entre le *logopoios* (celui qui met en circulation des fausses
nouvelles, qui les fabrique grâce à « une composition [*sunthesis*]
de propos et de faits fictifs [*pseudōn logōn kai praxeōn*] ») tel qu'on
le trouve décrit dans les *Caractères* de Théophraste (rédigés probablement vers la fin du IVe siècle avant notre ère) et les tweets ou

---

4   Jean-Luc Nancy, *La Vérité du mensonge,* Paris, Bayard, « Les petites conférences », 2021, p. 60 (il s'agit d'une conférence pour un public d'enfants prononcée en avril 2018).

posts conspirationnistes d'aujourd'hui, est-ce juste une affaire de nombre, de portée dans la diffusion ?[5]

« Je ne crois pas trop à ça », dit Jean-Luc. L'importance des rumeurs, sous les formes qu'elles prennent aujourd'hui, serait elle-même presque de l'ordre d'une rumeur (« cela se répand beaucoup »). Comme si la rumeur était vouée à sécréter de la rumeur, sans fin et depuis toujours.

Si, en 2018, Jean-Luc a donc l'air de mettre sur un même plan toutes les *fake news* qui auraient circulé de Platon jusqu'à nos jours (« les fausses nouvelles ont toujours existé »), il semble bien que dans « Rumoration », en revanche, la rumeur dont il parle et à laquelle il prête l'oreille appartient à la ville moderne, à ce qu'il appelle lui-même « un remuement sonore des rues », propre sans doute à une époque où, dans les rues, on peut se demander comme il le fait : « Quel est le bruit de cette photo ? »[6] Car le bruit qui court et se métamorphose en air chanté ou en affiche ou en phrase, ce bruit relève de la « parole quotidienne » dont Blanchot, dans *L'Entretien infini,* identifiait l'espace propre comme étant celui de « la rue », là où « la dense présence des grandes agglomérations urbaines » laisse croître l'un de « ces admirables déserts que sont les villes mondiales »[7].

Difficile de dire, pourtant, comment la rue rumoreuse qu'évoque Blanchot se différencie de l'agora, du portique *(stoa)* ou de la boutique *(ergastērion)* où le *logopoios* décrit par Théophraste passe toute sa journée *(enēmereuousin)* à inventer des légendes urbaines. Difficile de dire aussi ce qui la différencierait, cette rue de la ville moderne, des agoras virtuelles – des forums de discussion – où se répandent les fausses nouvelles d'aujourd'hui. Il est tentant de penser que la rumeur grecque circulait dans des rues qui, comme celles où « l'orgueilleux » caractérisé par Théophraste rend ses arbitrages, appartenaient à un monde désormais oublié, un monde que Marc Bloch avait cru voir revivre dans « la marche que suivaient presque toujours les fausses nouvelles » au sein des tranchées de la première guerre mondiale : « le soldat du front », se souvient-il en 1921, aura été ramené « aux moyens d'information et à l'état d'esprit des vieux âges, avant le journal, avant la feuille

5   Voir Théophraste, *Caractères,* VIII, 4 ; traduction française d'Octave Navarre, Paris, Les Belles lettres, 1920, p. 25.

6   Nancy, *La Ville au loin, op. cit.,* p. 126–127.

7   Maurice Blanchot, « La parole quotidienne », dans *L'Entretien infini,* Paris, Gallimard, 1969, p. 362.

de nouvelles imprimées », condamné à un anachronique isolement d'avant les médias de masse.[8]

Ce qu'on entend bruire dans la rue rumoreuse de Blanchot – la même, peut-être, que celle où Jean-Luc marchait en 2001 –, c'est ce qui n'a pas encore cristallisé ou pris forme. C'est une simple propagation qui n'est pas encore propagande : « l'irresponsabilité de la rumeur – là où tout est dit, tout est entendu, incessamment et interminablement, sans que rien s'affirme, sans qu'il y ait réponse à rien – s'appesantit rapidement en donnant lieu à "l'opinion publique", mais seulement dans la mesure où ce qui se propage devient (avec quelle facilité) mouvement de propagande, c'est-à-dire par le passage de la rue au journal, du quotidien en perpétuel devenir au quotidien transcrit [...], informé, stabilisé »[9]. Ce que l'antique *fama* confondait en un même mot, Blanchot le sépare ici, le distingue. Et peut-être cette distinction pourrait-elle éclairer, aujourd'hui encore, la manière dont, sur les réseaux sociaux, l'anonymat du bruit qui court se précipite (au sens chimique du terme) en un discours politicien (la tristement célèbre mouvance d'extrême droite connue sous le nom de QAnon en témoigne, elle qui semble avoir commencé par un message anonyme signé « Q » sur le forum 4chan, avant d'être régulièrement présente dans les messages retweetés par Donald Trump).

Mais, même si le passage qu'observe Blanchot du quotidien informe au quotidien imprimé – du journalier au journal – pourrait le donner à penser, on aurait tort de croire que la configuration, la conformation discursive qui se saisit des rumeurs courant les rues pour les modeler serait leur devenir médiatique, à savoir la médiatisation d'un immédiat. Car la rumeur est déjà médiale. Il faudrait dire, plus exactement, que la rumeur, c'est une pure médiateté qui médiatise absolument – « mouvement neutre où le rapport semble réduit à sa pure essence, pur rapport de personne et de rien », écrit Blanchot dans un passage qu'il faut lire de près[10]. « La puissance de la rumeur », en effet, n'est pas dans la teneur ou le contenu

---

8   Théophraste, *Caractères*, VIII, 4 et XXIV, 4, *op. cit.*, p. 26 et p. 57 ; Marc Bloch, « Réflexions d'un historien sur les fausses nouvelles de la guerre », *Revue de synthèse historique*, tome XXXIII, n° 97–99, 1921, p. 32–33.

9   Blanchot, « La parole quotidienne », *in L'Entretien infini, op. cit.*, p. 363 ; voir aussi p. 362 : « ce qui est publié dans le rue n'est pourtant pas réellement divulgué : on le dit, mais cet "on dit" n'est porté par aucune parole réellement prononcée, de même que les rumeurs se rapportent sans que personne les transmette et parce que celui qui les transmet accepte de n'être personne ».

10   Blanchot, « La question la plus profonde », *in L'Entretien infini, op. cit.*, p. 26.

de ce qu'elle charrie, elle « n'est pas dans la force de ce qu'elle dit » : elle émane plutôt de « ce qui *se* rapporte » (on est tenté de mettre l'accent, dans la tournure passive qu'emploie Blanchot, sur le pronom réfléchi : la rumeur ne rapporte ou ne met en rapport rien d'autre qu'elle-même avec elle-même) et dont la « seule vérité, incontestable, c'est d'être rapporté », précisément.

En ce sens, la rumeur n'est autre que la pure rumoration du médium en tant tel, comme le donne à entendre Blanchot lorsqu'il prête l'oreille à ce qui bruit ainsi de soi et pour soi à travers les médias[11] : « Combien de personnes mettent en marche leur poste de radio et quittent la pièce, satisfaites de ce bruit lointain et suffisant. Cela est absurde ? Nullement. L'essentiel, ce n'est pas que tel homme s'exprime et tel autre entende, mais que, personne en particulier ne parlant et personne en particulier n'écoutant, il y ait cependant de la parole et comme une promesse indéfinie de communiquer, garantie par le va-et-vient incessant de mots solitaires. » C'est de ce caractère archimédial de la rumeur rumorante que témoigne aussi l'expression « téléphone arabe », dont Frantz Fanon rappelait que « les Européens » l'utilisaient « dans les pays du Maghreb » pour désigner « la rapidité relative avec laquelle, de bouche à oreille, les nouvelles sont diffusées dans la société autochtone »[12].

La question du rapport, voire de la complicité ou de la collusion de la rumeur et des médias se complique donc irrémédiablement. Faut-il voir dans lesdits médias quelque chose comme des voiries informationnelles, comme des canaux, comme des infrastructures propices à la propagation des rumeurs ? Et si oui, faut-il y inclure la rue comme infrastructure médiatique ? Ou l'agora, qu'elle soit réelle ou virtuelle, ou encore le forum (de discussions) ? Ou bien faut-il penser que la rumeur est elle-même une infrastructure (voire sa propre infrastructure), ce que l'on pourrait entendre de deux manières au moins, selon deux inflexions ou portées du préfixe *infra-* : d'une part, qu'elle serait un soubassement, un fondement pour l'être-avec ou l'être-ensemble de celles et ceux qui partagent un dire plutôt qu'un dit ; mais d'autre part, qu'elle serait aussi et en même temps une structure « inframince »[13], à savoir imperceptible

---

11   Blanchot, « La parole quotidienne », *in L'Entretien infini, op. cit.,* p. 358.
12   Frantz Fanon, « "Ici la voix de l'Algérie" », dans *Sociologie d'une révolution (L'An V de la révolution algérienne),* Paris, Maspéro, 1972, p. 61.
13   À Denis de Rougemont, Marcel Duchamp disait : « Le bruit ou la musique que fait un pantalon de velours côtelé comme celui-ci, quand on bouge, relève de l'infra-mince. Le creux dans le papier, entre le recto et le verso d'une feuille

ou insaisissable, échappant à toute thématisation ou représentation objectivante (« peut-être n'en ai-je même pas encore fait mon sujet », confiait Jean-Luc dans « Rumoration », tandis qu'il tentait de prêter l'oreille à ce qui « est juste un murmure dans ma tête »).

La rumeur, en somme, serait une archistructure et une anarchistructure à la fois.

Si sa « seule vérité », comme l'écrit Blanchot, est le fait « d'être rapporté », c'est que la rumeur est pur rapport à soi en tant que différence d'avec soi – Jean-Luc dirait sans doute : pur renvoi. Difficile, dès lors, de ne pas laisser se surimprimer l'un sur l'autre ou l'une sur l'un la rumeur et le mythe qui, « immédiat-médiat », est « le murmure » ou « la parole de ce qui se dit soi-même et ne dit que soi » : le mythe comme ce que j'appellerai ici, en mémoire de Jean-Luc (et de ce que fut notre amitié parfois troublée de quelque rumeur), une *rumémoration*. « Le mythe », dit-il encore, « fait – il fait en disant, il feint – l'*avant* qui jamais n'a précédé »[14].

La rumeur mythifiante (Jean-Luc dirait aussi *mythante)* produit ou sécrète donc son antécédent, son préalable qui pourtant, en tant qu'il est à faire, reste à venir. Et c'est en ce sens que la rumoration mythopoïétique a une texture où s'entrelacent ce qu'on peut décrire comme un mouvement anaphorique et un mouvement cataphorique.

Qu'est-ce à dire ?

Dans ses *Caractères*, Théophraste fait reposer l'autorité ou la créance du facteur de rumeur sur une série de garanties qui alternent, se relaient ou réfèrent l'une à l'autre, sans que l'on puisse jamais vérifier ou attester leur validité, l'établir de manière stable et définitive : « Et alors, ou bien c'est d'un tel, soldat, qu'il tient la chose, ou bien d'un esclave d'Astéios, le joueur de flûte, ou bien de Lycon, l'entrepreneur [...]. Dans ses histoires, il a toujours ainsi

---

mince... » (« Marcel Duchamp mine de rien », *Preuves,* n° 204, 1968). Dans ses *Notes* (Paris, Flammarion, 1999, p. 24), il avait recours à la comparaison suivante : « Quand la fumée de tabac sent aussi de la bouche qui l'exhale, les 2 odeurs s'épousent par infra mince ».

14   Je viens de citer *La Communauté désœuvrée* (Paris, Christian Bourgois, 1986 [2004], p. 125) et *Proprement dit. Entretien sur le mythe* (Paris, Lignes, 2015, p. 53, p. 68 et p. 72). Voir aussi *À l'écoute* (Paris, Galilée, 2002, p. 25), où Jean-Luc parle de « la forme » ou de « la structure du *soi* en tant que tel » comme « mouvement d'un renvoi infini puisqu'il renvoie à ce (lui) qui n'est rien hors du renvoi ».

des garants [*anaphorai*] qu'on ne saurait atteindre »[15]. La rumeur, en somme, ne fait qu'*imiter* la testimonialité en la différant infiniment. Mais précisément, c'est en cela que la rumeur révèle aussi ce qui, dans tout témoignage sans doute, reste toujours en souffrance, à venir.

Il faut s'arrêter un instant sur le terme grec qu'utilise Théophraste pour désigner ceux qui apparaissent comme les témoins introuvables auxquels la rumeur, chaque fois, prétend attacher ou accrocher sa véridicité, à savoir : *anaphorai*. Ce sont, littéralement, ceux auxquels on peut se référer *(anapherō)*, ceux qui accréditent, en étant censés l'arrêter, le mouvement *(phora)* de ce qu'il faut bien appeler la *référance*[16].

Mais l'*anaphora*, ce n'est pas seulement le recours à quelqu'un ou quelque chose qui puisse garantir l'autorité. Dans le traité sur la syntaxe *(peri suntaxeōs)* du grammairien grec Apollonius Dyscole, le mot désigne aussi le renvoi à un nom qui, en amont dans le discours, a déjà été utilisé, qui est donc déjà connu (« c'est en tant qu'il remplace un [nom] mentionné antérieurement que le pronom deviendra anaphorique, puisque le propre de l'anaphore [*idiōma anaphoras*], c'est la connaissance seconde [*deutera gnōsis*] d'une personne mentionnée antérieurement [*prokateilegmenou prosōpou*] »[17]). Parmi tant d'exemples possibles d'anaphore, en voici un qui pourrait avoir été entendu, attrapé au vol dans une conversation rumoreuse : « on *le lui* avait pourtant bien dit » (les pronoms *le* et *lui,* que je souligne, renvoient respectivement à l'énoncé antérieur de ladite rumeur et à son destinataire précédent). En d'autres

---

15 La Bruyère, qui a traduit Théophraste en 1688 (ses propres *Caractères* étaient originellement une sorte de commentaire ou de postface), propose pour cette phrase : « il allègue pour témoins de ce qu'il avance des hommes obscurs qu'on ne peut trouver pour le convaincre de fausseté » *(Les Caractères de Théophraste traduits du grec avec Les Caractères ou Les Mœurs de ce siècle par La Bruyère,* Paris, Bourdilliat et Cie, 1861, p. 84).

16 Le verbe *fero* (dont l'infinitif est *ferre* tandis que le supin, utilisé pour construire le participe, est *latum)* est l'équivalent latin du grec *pherō.* Dans « Préjugés – devant la loi » *(La Faculté de juger,* Paris, Minuit, 1985, p. 122), Jacques Derrida propose le terme de *férance* pour dire « le rapport, la relation, la référence ». Et dans *Donner le temps, 1. La fausse monnaie* (Paris, Galilée, 1991, p. 164), il écrit : « *Fero* signifie aussi "je rapporte", au sens de raconter, au sens de la *relation (latum,* participe de *ferre),* de la relation comme récit [...] Est-il nécessaire de souligner que cette problématique [...] nous porte et reporte sans cesse au cœur des grandes questions de la référence et de la différence ? »

17 Apollonius Dyscole, *De la construction,* II, 10 ; traduction française de Jean Lallot, Paris, Vrin, 1997, p. 150.

termes, comme le notait Émile Benveniste, « [l]'anaphorique [...] ne renvoie pas à la chose, mais à la notion antérieurement formulée de cette chose », si bien qu'« [i]l est le signe d'un signe »[18].

Le fait que ce sens grammatical ou syntaxique soit apparu bien plus tard que l'époque de Théophraste (Apollonius Dyscole était actif à Alexandrie au IIe siècle de notre ère) ne doit pas nous détourner de l'essentiel : à savoir que la structure autodéictique du discours (désignant son cours antécédant) et la structure autotestimoniale de la rumeur (témoignant d'elle-même) partagent la même anaphoricité fondamentale.

Mais, comme l'écrit Blanchot, « la puissance de la rumeur » – on pourrait dire aussi bien : du mythe – réside également « en ceci : qu'elle appartient à l'espace où tout ce qui se dit a toujours déjà été dit, *continue d'être dit, ne cessera d'être dit* »[19]. L'anaphore rumoreuse se double donc nécessairement de ce que, en empruntant à nouveau au lexique des linguistes, on pourrait décrire comme une *cataphore,* à savoir un report ou une férance en avant [20].

La formule anacataphorique par excellence de la rumeur ressemblerait à ceci : « Oui, je le sais, je l'ai entendu, c'est incroyable, mais croyez-moi, je vais vous le dire... » C'est ainsi que se meut la rumeur, c'est ainsi qu'elle se rumémore sans cesse en arrière et en avant d'elle-même.

---

18   Émile Benveniste, « L'anaphorique prussien *din* et le système des démonstratifs indo-européens », *Studi Baltici,* n° 3, 1933, p. 124.

19   Blanchot, « La question la plus profonde », dans *L'Entretien infini, op. cit.,* p. 26 (je souligne).

20   Voir le remarquable article de Michel Maillard, « Anaphores et cataphores » (*Communications,* n°19, 1972, p. 94) : « [L]e lien référentiel porte le nom d'anaphore lorsque le référé précède le référant et celui de *cataphore* lorsque le référé suit le référant sur la chaîne discursive. [...] Dans la cataphore, il faut "descendre" au fil du discours pour trouver la détermination attendue. »

Rodolphe Burger

Jean-Luc's Voice

Writing on a voice. Better: making it heard. Painting a portrait through it. Or rather: painting the portrait of this voice. A musician's gamble. And the beginning of a series of columns to be read aloud.

Jean-Luc Nancy is not only one of the great voices of philosophy today (accentuate the *is*). Jean-Luc Nancy has (accentuate the *has*) a voice. To make his portrait would be first to make his voice heard. Everybody knows that such a task is impossible. A voice, any voice, is indescribable. It is more singular than the face (here, cue the voice of Jean-Luc quoting Deleuze, *La voix est très en avance sur le visage, très en avant... [The voice is far ahead of the face, far before...]*), than the look, than the fingerprints (as he says in *"Vox clamans in deserto"*), it is impossible to capture a voice, there's no adjective capable of catching it (not even "somber" which would suit him well and which Littré opposes to "clear").

It is nevertheless the case that a voice is heard/hears itself. For almost thirty years, Jean-Luc's voice has resounded in me as the voice of philosophy, and if I dared, I would sing his praise, if I could, I would deliver his panegyric, I would say how I hear it, for example and in particular when he speaks of the voice:

(Here loop – *It is not enough to make a discourse on the voice. One must know with which voice to pronounce it. Which voice speaks of the voice?* – press "play.")

A philosophical calling always determines itself from a singular voice. In my case, it was not Jean-Luc's, who was never really *my* professor. The voice that made me hear philosophy, I want to name it, was that of Gilbert Rémy (here cue a recording of Gilbert's voice pronouncing the word *"philosophie,"* with his curious emphasis on the *"phie,"* so that it sounded almost like *"philosophille"* [philo-girl]). Jean-Luc was the second philosophical voice that I heard in Strasbourg. Simultaneous with that of Philippe Lacoue-Labarthe. During those years, their two voices combined as one, shared, and their dialogue was like an extraordinary stereophony of thought. Since then, I have never heard Jean-Luc's voice ("solo") without perceiving an echo of this sharing and of this stereophony.

(Here, simultaneously cue the voice of Philippe reading *The Echo of the Subject* and that of Jean-Luc reading *Sharing Voices*, or a passage from *Ventriloque*, or another from *Ascoltando: Undoubtedly, sonority is more than a privileged model of the sending back [renvoi] that precedes and forms any sending [envoi] of the subject, of a sensing being* (emphasize *sensing*) *in general. Sonority resonates* (accentuate *resonates*) *essentially: it is in itself resonance. One could say that the echo belongs to sound, to its immanence —*

... Resonance is in the sound itself: a sound is its own echo chamber...)
This stereophony has become (or was it always?) internal (accentuate *internal*).
The voice of Jean-Luc is as if redoubled in itself.

It is not only deep, profound, ample, and warm, as is evident. It gives the permanent resonance of harmonic bass, medium bass (Baryton-Martin?), which appears to double, or more exactly to underpin the "other" voice, the "philosophical," the clear and distinct (clarity of elocution, distinction, pronunciation). A *basso continuo* forms the sensible counterpoint to the high and intelligible voice that it makes heard. One might believe it is a special effect (here cue an example of a voice passed through a "harmonizer"), or some miracle inspired by the vocal techniques of the Pygmees or Mongols (here, with appropriate software, compare the specters of the voices of Jean-Luc and a "poly-harmonic" singer).

But the real miracle is the total absence of miracle, the perfect naturalness of this voice which simply makes one hear the voice in the voice, that is to say, and here I let him speak: *A voice that is unspeakable because it is anterior to speech, an infant speech that can be heard beyond any speech and even in speaking itself: for even if the voice is infinitely more archaic than speech, there is no speech that would not already be heard through a voice.*

I would say that Jean-Luc's voice material-ly [*matériel-lement*] performs, in its very grain (here, cue Barthes' voice describing the voice of Panzera), the same logic of retroactive anteriority that he makes us hear in any voice. There is no hidden voice because there are no hidden thoughts (A. whispers this truth to me about Jean-Luc: he is a man who can think everything because he is absolutely without any hidden thoughts—perhaps even without consciousness), no voice to be heard other than the one that speaks (without speaking) *with-in* [à même] every voice.

This is why it is so calm. This voice tranquilly says (emphasize *tranquilly* like Augustin's voice on the phone) that one can stay here, in this very immanence–transcendence of the voice that one *is* when one *has* it. "The voice of his being" could be the perfect slogan for this new way of speaking/thinking with one's voice.

This is why it dialogues so easily, this is why it is so open towards other voices, the voices of the entire history of thinking and non-thinking. Hence its tone, so soft and firm even in *polemos*, its total absence of warlike pathos, intellectual resentment, philosophical phobia. He seems to say that everything can be thought, and that care can become the best weapon, perhaps the most terrible for the enemies of thinking (here, cue Ponge's voice on Groethuysen, and Granel's on Derrida).

This voice is its own tuning fork [*diapason*]. In fact, it is in this way that he reformulates the so-called "question of the subject": *The subject, a tuning fork? Every subject a differently tuned tuning fork? Tuned to itself—but without known frequency?*

New translation for *Dasein* [être-là]: the being-tone [*l'être-la*] as the being that gives itself the tone [*l'être-la comme l'être qui se donne à lui-même le la*]. But this tone without measure that *Dasein* gives to itself is also one that it receives. And the "there" [*là*] (accentuate the accent [à] on the la) of *Dasein* says nothing else than the equivalence between a giving and a receiving. This tuning fork with unknown frequency that is the subject must be made to resonate with this, the world: *A world... a web of references to this maintenance [tenue]. In this sense it resembles a subject...*It only resembles it: *the world is not presupposed: it is only coextensive with its worldly extension, with the spacing of the places between which resonances play.*

It is in the maintaining of the voice that the question of maintenance [*tenue*] in general resonates—the question of "maintaining oneself" in the world, of maintaining the note from which all correctness, as well as all justice, can be rethought.

How can a voice make its own resonance be heard? For this, it must practice restraint. There's no resonance without restraint. (Here, cue the silence: a brief gap, period, that always precedes Jean-Luc's speaking). Speaking gets into swing, it doesn't start without first puffing itself up a bit. Or else it uses small archi-rhythmic gimmicks which precede the pronunciation of a thought (here, cue Jean-Luc's gimmicks, the "well"'s and the "so then"'s that syncopate his speaking, and mix them with Lacan's "mm"'s and "eh"'s, with Deleuze's "uh, yes"'s and "well there"'s, and add some of Derrida's rises to high pitches). These effects are not just for show, but are absolutely necessary. With them, a thinking gives itself its tempo, its unique timing. This is how it puts itself into motion (here cue Jean-Luc quoting Montaigne: *Le branle mesme de ma voix tire plus de mon esprit que je n'y trouve lors que je le sonde et employe à part moy* [*the very vibration of my voice draws far more out of my spirit, than what I find when I try to sound and use it myself*]. The voice that machines itself (Deleuze) opens the space-time, the very spacing of thought. In Jean-Luc's case, it is the *festina lente* of intuition that holds itself and imposes its rhythms on its becoming-concept. In Miles Davis' case, it is sometimes a long silence before the first phrase that opens the concert, and sometimes the brief trumpet phrase that notes a coming change of speed for his musical vessel. Such gestures are archi-rhythmic because they precede the rhythm and make it possible as such, as the always unique time that one must give oneself to think/play.

Once the tone is set and the tempo indicated, one can hear the calm, regular, almost monodic voice, and Nancy-thinking starts. This thinking can use any resource. It does not fear any objects, it likes to play without missing a beat (but it regulates the metronome). It is not by chance that pure tautology is its horizon. And if it was nothing other than this? To re-pronounce, refreshed, with a new rhythm and tone, all of the names of philosophy and all concepts without exception (and if you look at them carefully, perhaps there are no bad ones as long as they are pronounced properly?). This thinking, this voice, polishes again the words that are the heaviest and most unusable (creation, sense, freedom, and, while we're at it, all of the names of God... which other voice could do this?), and does the whole journey over again with tranquil joy. All of these analyses, all of this philology, all of this history and this geography, all of these readings, quotations, and recitations, all of this aims at the most simple result: producing each time again, and each time differently, the A = A which is entirely contained in what it says.

Throughout this text I have taken the liberty of calling Jean-Luc by his first name. It should not be heard as me being overfamiliar with him, even though I feel an immense friendship towards him.

It is the voice that goes by its first name. And the general operation of this voice could be described as a pre-nominalization of everything that it states and pronounces. The speaking voice brings all contours to fade: it raises all things as if calling them by their first name.

Post-scriptum

This text was first published, in French, in a special issue of *L'Animal* (no.14–15, summer 2003) dedicated to Jean-Luc Nancy, and then in *Vacarme* 26 (2 January 2004).

Translation Susanna Lindberg
and Donovan Stewart

Jean-Christophe Bailly

Die fortwährende Überraschung des Sinns

zu Jean-Luc Nancy

Die beiden Teile dieses Textes entsprechen zwei Vorträgen, die ich im Abstand von einer Woche gehalten habe. Den ersten am 15. Januar 2022 in der Maison de la poésie in Paris, anlässlich eines von Marc Goldschmit und Isabelle Alfandary organisierten Nachmittages zu Ehren Jean-Luc Nancys; den zweiten am 22. Januar im Rahmen einer von Jérôme Lèbre, Divya Dwiwedi, Shaj Mohan und François Warin initiierten Konferenz am Centre Pompidou. In beiden Fällen legitimieren die Form der Hommage und die Dringlichkeit der Texte zumindest teilweise ihre verknappte Gestalt. Immer wieder überkam mich, beim Schreiben wie beim Sprechen, die Angst davor, letztlich nichts anderes zu tun, als Denkbewegungen Jean-Luc Nancys verkürzend zusammenzufassen oder übermäßig zu kondensieren. Doch selbst wenn dies der Fall sein sollte, hätte ein solches Resümee – als Schwelle dann – vielleicht durchaus seinen Platz.

I

Als ich unmittelbar nach dem Tod Jean-Luc Nancys eilig auf die Bitte um eine schriftliche Würdigung reagieren wollte, die ich natürlich nicht abschlagen konnte, wurde mir ein bisschen schwindelig. Jenseits der Schwierigkeit, die diese Art von Übung ohnehin mit sich bringt, hatte ich nämlich einen wirklich beachtlichen Bücherhorizont vor mir – oder vielmehr hinter mir, in manchen Fällen sogar ziemlich weit weg. Zu meinem Glück, wenn ich das so sagen darf, befand ich mich zu jener Zeit auf dem Land und folglich in materieller Distanz zu diesem außerordentlichen Sinnreservoir. Da ich also nichts nachschlagen konnte, musste ich mich mit meinem Gedächtnis und den Zitaten zufriedengeben, die in Texten auf meinem Computer vorkamen – ein Umstand, der sich als rettend erweisen sollte. Jetzt aber, da ich den Büchern leibhaftig gegenüberstehe – ich habe zwar nicht alle, aber dennoch ziemlich viele –, gerate ich in eine Verlegenheit, die vermutlich all jene verspüren, die gebeten worden sind, über sein Werk zu sprechen, zumal eher allgemein als unter einem besonderen Aspekt. Zugegeben: Angesichts eines solchen Überflusses ergreift einen zuallererst die Freude, und sie ist umso größer, als sich dieses Werk keineswegs als Masse darbietet, nicht einmal als eine Masse, die man in mehr oder minder distinkte Sektionen unterteilt hätte. Von welcher Seite man sich ihm auch nähert – das Werk erscheint im Modus der Dissemination, und zwar so sehr, dass man mit Fug und Recht sagen könnte, die unendliche Dissemination, die zu den wirksamsten Denkmustern dieses Werkes gehört, zeichne auch seine grundlegende Verfahrensweise aus. Mag die Quantität (verschiedener Zeichen, Seiten, Vorträge, Bücher und Aufsätze) auch ein Kennzeichen des Nancy'schen Werks sein, es bildet doch nie einen Block: Nicht im Geringsten stellt es von sich aus Monumente auf; nicht einmal ansatzweise legt es über oder neben sich einen Aussichtspunkt fest, von dem aus es zu betrachten und zu resümieren wäre – wodurch man es im Übrigen zwangsläufig verfehlte. Vielmehr bleibt es gerade dadurch sich selbst treu, dass es sich in entkoppelten Stücken auf Wege begibt, die es selbst bahnend öffnet – und es ist kein Zufall, wenn der französische Begriff für das Freischlagen eines Weges, *frayage*, der klanglich mit der *fraie*, dem Laichen von Wassertieren und folglich mit dem lebensweltlichen Bereich der Fischerei in Verbindung steht, in Jean-Luc Nancys Schreiben so häufig wiederkehrt. Unter seiner Feder bedeutet *le frayage* eine Weise, die Welt zu lesen, eine intuitive Wissenschaft des *kairos*, oder auch die endlos wiederaufzunehmende Strategie eines Erfassens, das an sich immer schon den Anlass einer weiteren Wiederaufnahme bildet. Jede einzelne der somit verfolgten und gebahnten Fährten zeigt dem Leser einen Weg auf, den er sodann selbst beschreiten darf – auf den Spuren seines gleichermaßen konzentrierten wie amüsierten Reiseführers. Wer jemals einem oder mehreren dieser Wege gefolgt ist, weiß aus eigener Erfahrung, dass sie mitnichten ein bekanntes und abgestecktes Territorium durchlaufen, sondern vielmehr selbst ein anderes, neues umschreiben, das sich nur in stetiger Ausdehnung und als immerfort sich ausdifferenzierendes Firmament zu sehen gibt, und dessen Kohärenz umso überraschender ist, als sie keines Bindemittels bedarf.

Nun sind die meisten dieser Wege zunächst Hinweise, denen Nancy folgte, weil man ihn dazu eingeladen hatte. Zu Beginn von *Signaux sensibles*, dem Gesprächsband mit Jérôme Lèbre, erzählt er, wie beispielsweise seine Auseinandersetzung mit dem Porträt aus einem »zufälligen Grund« entstand, »der von anderswo, von

jemand anderem her« kam.[1] Dies sei »übrigens bei einem Groß-
teil der Themen und Gegenstände«[2], mit denen er sich beschäftigt
habe, der Fall, mit Ausnahme von drei Problemfeldern: dem Sinn,
dem Christentum und dem Geschlecht. Ich denke, man könnte
hier noch ein viertes Feld hinzufügen, ein politisches nämlich, das
sich um die Frage der Gemeinschaft oder der Möglichkeit eines uns
benennenden und ernennenden »Wir« dreht. Dieser Beschreibung
zufolge gäbe es also auf der einen Seite eine Art kontinentalen
Sockel, der seinerseits in drei – oder vier – Richtungen fortstrebte,
auf der anderen Seite stets latent auftauchende Halbinseln und Ar-
chipele. Doch eine solche Aufteilung zwischen einem eher zentri-
petalen begrifflichen Grundstock einerseits und zentrifugalen Vor-
stößen andererseits wäre auch nur bedingt gültig, da wir es ja mit
einer Verschachtelung von Begriffen, Denkfiguren, Wissens- und
Erfahrungsbereichen zu tun haben, die sich selbst in einem perma-
nenten Werden befindet. Mit all seinen Kollisionen, Leitmotiven,
Varianten, Wiederholungen und Wiederaufnahmen wird dieses
Werden keineswegs durch das, was uns heute seiner Ausdehnung
beraubt, unterbrochen, sondern vielmehr durch jede einzelne Lektüre wachgehalten und wiedergeweckt. Sogar der unscheinbarste
Streifzug durch dieses Werk setzt die gesamte Lexik des *Mit* in Bewegung. Als *work in progress* arbeitet das Werk unermüdlich über
das, was es nun scheinbar abschließt, in Wirklichkeit aber öffnet,
hinaus; und das, was man im Prinzip von jedem der Interpretation
offenstehenden Werk sagen könnte, zeigt sich bei Jean-Luc Nancy
als singulärer Neuanfang, als ein Fortwähren, das jedes Lesen neu
entdeckt. Trotz seiner großen körperlichen Erschöpfung und der
zunehmend erdrückenden Last unserer Zeit hat es bei Nancy bis
zum Schluss einen Enthusiasmus des Denkens gegeben, der un-
gemein ansteckend war. Der »Aufriss«, der seine Laufbahn vorzeichnet – ich denke, Jean-Luc hätte es mir nicht übelgenommen,
dass ich diesen Ausdruck hier bei Heidegger leihe – der Aufriss,
der seine Laufbahn vorzeichnet und somit nicht zuletzt auch den
Weg des Lesers ausleuchtet, ist selbst Resultat eines Elans:

> »Philosophieren geht nicht ohne Elan, und der muss sogar ziemlich hef-
> tig sein. Er muss das Denken nach vorne katapultieren und dabei von
> etwas losreißen: vom abgelagerten, sedimentierten, halb zerfallenen

---

1   Jean-Luc Nancy und Jérôme Lèbre: *Signaux sensibles. Entretien à propos des
arts,* Montrouge 2017. Übers. L.S.
2   Ebd. Übers. L.S.

Sinn nämlich, um es dem möglichen Sinn in die Arme zu werfen, dem Sinn, der nicht gegeben, nicht verfügbar ist, dem man auflauern muss und den es in seinem unvorhersehbaren, nie einfachen, nie eindeutigen Kommen zu überraschen gilt.«[3]

Genau diese Art, zum Sinn zu kommen, indem man ihn, der nicht gegeben ist, kommen lässt, ist das Bahnen, Öffnen, Erkämpfen – *le frayage*: eine Arbeit, eine ausgeführte Handlung, eine Untersuchung und eine Suche, ein *progress* oder ein *process*, der aber nur möglich ist, weil der Sinn selbst äußere oder innere Bewegung ist [une motion ou une émotion]: »Die Wahrheit punktiert, der Sinn verkettet.«[4] Diese Formulierung ist rein deskriptiv und als solche zu verstehen. Sie beschreibt die Existenzweise des Sinns: Er existiert, indem er Wahrheitspunkte [points de vérité] miteinander verkettet und zum Ausdruck bringt. Diese Wahrheitspunkte sind fest, können sich aber in Fragezeichen [points d'interrogation] verwandeln: »Die Wahrheit wird ein Fluchtpunkt, der sich allmählich in ein Fragezeichen umformt. Die Wahrheit wird: Was ist Wahrheit?«[5] Von einem Punkt, von einem Abgrund zum anderen eilt [trace] und schreibt sich [se trace] der Sinn, bahnt er sich Wege [fraye] und flieht [fuit]. Jeder Punkt kann als Ruf vernommen werden – verstanden und gehört: Die Philosophie antwortet auf diesen Ruf; ihre Gegenwart oder Rolle ist nichts anderes als die Antwort auf diesen Ruf, den sie über sich selbst hinaus weiterschickt, in einer endlosen Bewegung: »Es kann sein, dass man auf diesen Ruf nur durch die Wiederholung des Rufs antwortet«, heißt es in *Les raisons d'écrire*[6], und die Wiederholung wird mit einer Kette von Rufen (oder Antworten) verglichen, wie sie des Nachts von einem Posten zum nächsten über die Stadtmauern eilen. Als ich diese Beschreibung in einem durch die Nacht rasenden Zug las, spürte ich, wie etwas Präzises sich darin zeigte, als hätte der Flügel von Minervas Eule mich kurz und leicht berührt. Vor allem aber hatte ich den Eindruck, ein Echo dessen zu vernehmen, wonach sich der Wächter in Aischylos' *Agamemnon* sehnt, wenn er in der Er-

---

3   Jean-Luc Nancy: »Un jour, les dieux se retirent …«. (*littérature, philosophie: entre deux*), Bordeaux 2002, wieder aufgenommen in Jean-Luc Nancy: *Demande. Littérature et philosophie*, Paris 2015. Übers. L.S.
4   Jean-Luc Nancy: *Der Sinn der Welt*, übers. von Esther von der Osten, Berlin 2020, S. 27.
5   Nancy: »Un jour, les dieux se retirent …«, a.a.O., S. 39. Übers. L.S.
6   Jean-Luc Nancy: »Les raisons d'écrire«, in: Nancy: *Demande*, a.a.O., S. 45–58, hier S. 48. Übers. L.S.

öffnungspassage der *Orestie* (Aufriss oder Anschnitt der gesamten abendländischen Theatergeschichte) die lange nächtliche Stille beschreibt, in der schließlich das erlösende Signal erklingen wird (»Die Götter bitt' ich um ein Ende dieser Müh'n: / Ein langes Jahr nun lieg' ich auf dem Dach hier / Des Atreushauses, lagernd wie ein Wächterhund. / Der Sterne nächtliche Versammlung kenn' ich jetzt«[7]). Dabei wartet dieser Wächter nicht nur auf die Nachricht über das Ende des Krieges von Troja und auf das, was sie für ihn bedeutet. Er wartet zunächst und in erster Linie darauf, dass eine Reihe von Signalen sichtbar wird; darauf, dass sich ein Feuer nach dem anderen entzündet und die Signalreihe sich von Bergkamm zu Bergkamm bis zu ihm hin durchschlägt. Anders gesagt wartet er auf die reine Bewegung eines kommenden Sinns – oder auf seine sichtbare Allegorie, auf das Kommen selbst. Auf das Kommen dieses Sinns, der laut Jean-Luc Nancy den Tatsachen »weder hinzugefügt noch vorausgesetzt«[8] wird, sondern eben ihr *Ankommen*, ihr *Kommen* selbst ist. Durch dieses unablässige Kommen wird der Sinn endlos freigesetzt und fortgeschrieben. Von Ruf zu Ruf setzt die Weitergabe das Geschehen komplett neu aufs Spiel, was bedeutet, dass es sich die ganze Zeit ändert, und dass es folglich keine andere Gabe gibt, als die des Sinns, und zwar gerade, weil er nicht gegeben ist, sondern kommt. Auch wenn Jean-Luc Nancy diese Begrifflichkeiten meines Wissens nicht verwendet hat, könnte man sagen, dass seiner Art und Weise, das Kommen zu beschreiben, eine Kraft der Desubstantivierung innewohnt, durch die die infinite Verbform – *ankommen, kommen, werden* und sogar, natürlich, *sein* – besonders geeignet wirkt, um Geschehendes zu bezeichnen und dabei vor jener Form der Sinnablagerung zu bewahren, die unter der totemistischen Aufsicht der Nomen und Namen allzu oft entsteht.

An wiederholter Stelle und insbesondere in *Zum Gehör* hat Nancy das sinnliche Register des Klanglichen bemüht, um das Kommen zu beschreiben. Tatsächlich wirkt es beim Klang ja so, als ereignete sich in jedem klanglichen Ereignis die gesamte Ausdehnung von Punkt zu Fluchtpunkt, vom Moment des Erscheinens bis zu dem des Verschwindens. Als wäre die Form des Klangs, entschieden unentscheidbar zwischen Sendung und Empfang, zwischen

---

7   Aischylus: *Die Tragödien*, übertragen von Johann Gustav Droysen, durchgesehen von Walter Nestle, Stuttgart 2016, S. 149.
8   Jean-Luc Nancy: »Récit, récitation, récitatif«, in: Nancy: *Demande*, a.a.O., S. 59–77, hier S. 70. Übers. L.S.

Ausstrahlung und Hörerfahrung, nichts anderes als ein Vorübergehen, eine ausgedehnte Ankunft. »[D]ie klangliche Präsenz *kommt
an*«[9], und diese Ankunft weist die Präsenz, die sie gleichsam unter-
zeichnet, als eine fortwährende Herkunft aus, als exakte Überlagerung dessen, was sich entfaltet, und dessen, was erlischt. Präsenz
gibt es nur als etwas, das aufkommt, in Gang ist, und die Spezifik
der klanglichen Präsenz ist die sinnliche Form, in der sich das Sein
des Sinns entbirgt. Der Sinn, der »direkt auf der Welt«[10] ist, zeigt
sich dort nur, insofern er erklingt, und dieses Erklingen hat stets
die dehnbare Länge eines Vorübergehens oder eines Sprungs, der
irgendwann endet. Doch vor dem Verklingen gibt es den Ruf, und
so weiter, ohne Ende. Derart wahrgenommen und verstanden, vermischt sich Sinn zwangsläufig mit Fülle; er ist jene Fülle, durch die
sich die Welt ausbreitet, indem sie sich unendlich fragmentiert. Die
Unendlichkeit der Fragmentierung und die Fülle des Sinns sind ein
und dieselbe Sache. Es ist verblüffend, wie ruhig Jean-Luc Nancy
diese Beschreibung hinnimmt. Er benennt »diese Fragmentierung
von Sinn, die die Existenz *ist*«[11], um innerhalb der Zerstreuung
selbst eine Art unteilbare Einheit anzuzeigen, die durch das »il y
a« verbürgt ist: »es gibt es-gibt – und eben das macht Sinn, und
nichts außerdem macht Sinn«.[12] In der Unanimität des es-gibt wird
die Singularität jeder Existenzspitze freigesetzt. Dennoch ist dieses
»es gibt«, in das alles hineinpasst oder hineingehen kann, kein Be-
hältnis [contenant] und noch weniger ein Kontinent [continent]:
Die Entfaltung geschieht nie in Form eines Er- oder Ausfüllens,
und es gibt kein *Eines,* kein kleines *ein,* das einem großen, vor-
gängigen *Einen* nachzutrauern hätte oder von ihm abhängig wäre.
Die unmittelbarste Konsequenz des es-gibt ist, dass es keine Vor-
gängigkeit gibt, und erst recht keinen Ursprung. In *Cruor,* das
traurigerweise Jean-Luc Nancys letztes Buch gewesen sein wird,
findet sich eine verblüffende Formulierung, die diese Flucht aus
der Gerichtsbarkeit des Einen zusammenfasst und verdichtet: »Der
bang ist nicht einheitlich.«[13] Die Nähe des Endes mag das Buch von
vorne bis hinten säumen, doch geht es in erster Linie stets um die

9 Jean-Luc Nancy: *Zum Gehör,* übers. von Esther von der Osten, Berlin 2020,
S. 23.
10 Nancy: *Der Sinn der Welt,* a.a.O., S. 29.
11 Ebd., S. 192.
12 Ebd., S. 83.
13 Jean-Luc Nancy: *Cruor,* übers. von Alexander García Düttmann, Zürich
2022, S. 56. [Gemeint ist der *big bang,* der Urknall, *A.d.Ü.*]

Universalität des Drängens, um die unendliche Ausdehnung eines jeden Anfangs, eines jeden Spannungsverhältnisses, das ein Selbst mit sich selbst und dem pflegt, was über es hinausgeht – es geht um die Beharrlichkeit [persévérance[14]] eines jeden Dings in seinem Sein. Es ist bezeichnend, dass sodann das Ding und das Selbst des Dings auf absolut konkrete Weise gekennzeichnet werden, durch Formen des Einen nämlich, die dem entliehen sind, was man früher die drei Reiche nannte: »So erhält sich jedes Ding in seinem Sein, das selber nichts anderes ist als diese Erhaltung. Die Erhaltung eines Glimmers, eines Blatts oder eines Bären.«[15] Durch die Wahl dieser Begriffe – eine Wahl, die vielleicht überrascht, sicher aber erfreut – öffnet sich die Punktgenauigkeit dessen, was sich jedem generischen Zugriff entzieht, die *Exaktheit*, die (im quasi musikalischen Sinn) der Kontrapunkt der Fülle ist. Mit der Wahl dieser drei Nomen oder Namen eines Minerals, einer Pflanze und eines Tiers verlassen wir – selbst wenn sie, und das ist sicherlich kein Zufall, auf eine gewisse romantische Tradition hindeuten (schließlich verdanken wir Jean-Luc Nancy und Philippe Lacoue-Labarthe mit *Das Literarisch Absolute* die erste nennenswerte philosophische Studie zur deutschen Romantik in Frankreich) – nicht jene Alltäglichkeit des Sinns, von der es schon in *Der Sinn der Welt* hieß, dass wir sie nicht als »trüben Gegensatz zum Glanz« zu denken haben, »sondern als die Größe der Einfachheit, worin der Sinn über sich hinausgeht.«[16]

Wir befinden uns hier mitten in der Kontaktzone, in der die Philosophie mit der Poesie verkehrt oder sich ihr anschließt, und zwar freilich nicht so sehr in ihren Werken, als vielmehr gemäß der Spannung, durch die letztere die Sprache aufwirbelt. Ist Poesie »die umfassende Handlung der Sinnbereitschaft«[17], dann kann ihr Verhältnis zur Philosophie, ihrerseits als »Praxis des Sinns« definiert, nur das einer Nähe sein. Diese Nähe, die weder versiegelt werden kann, noch versiegelt werden darf, kommt aus der Beschäftigung mit denselben Anliegen, oder auch, präziser, und selbst wenn es sich hierbei um einen religiösen Begriff handelt: aus derselben Observanz. Definiert man Observanz als strenge Hochachtung für das Kommen als solches, kann man, glaube ich, verschiedene Techni-

---

14 [A. G. Düttmann übersetzt »persévérance« im folgenden Zitat mit »Erhaltung«, *A.d.Ü.*]
15 Ebd., S. 56.
16 Nancy: *Der Sinn der Welt*, a.a.O., S. 33.
17 Jean-Luc Nancy: *Résistance de la poésie*, Bordeaux 1997, S. 12.

ken der Observanz ausmachen, die nur dann zusammenarbeiten oder zusammenwirken können, wenn sie auch distinkt bleiben. Philosophie und Poesie – oder vielleicht präziser noch philosophische Rede und Gedicht – hören einander zu, hören die jeweilige Weise, mit der sich die jeweils andere dem Sinn nähert und ihn konfiguriert. Der Sinn, dessen Praxis die Philosophie ist, wird durch das Gedicht abgetastet, skandiert (»Poesie operiert als Skanner des Sinnes«, sagt Jean-Luc in *Kalkül des Dichters*[18]), was bedeutet, dass das es-gibt gleichermaßen als solches gedacht wie in jedem einzelnen seiner Punkte sondiert wird (werden muss). Das es-gibt ist die Immanenzebene, auf der sich *singulär plural sein* verwirklicht. Dabei ist diese Verwirklichung das Gegenteil einer Stapelung, und was Jean-Luc Nancy im ersten Band von *Dekonstruktion des Christentums* am Beispiel eines Baumes[19] zeigt, gilt für alle Dinge auf der Welt. Der Baum wird dort als »Zugehörigkeitseinheit« beschrieben, die in eine unendliche Vielfalt simultaner, jederzeit miteinander in Bezug stehender Existenzen zerfällt. Die »Bezugskraft« [»puissance de rapport«], die das Subjekt auszeichnet, ist die entscheidende Akteurin: Die Welt hat nur insofern statt, als sie sich unter ihrem Drängen entfaltet, in der akuten Unendlichkeit einer großen Geste, eines langen Lieds, derer wir weder Ursprung noch Ende kennen. Besser: Nur, indem das Werden sich aus der doppelten Vormundschaft von Ursprung und Ende befreit, kommt es zu sich selbst. In diesem Prozess ist jeder Punkt, jedes Eine, nicht als feste Einheit zu verstehen, sondern als das, was die »Schließung oder Totalisierung des Netzes [unterläuft]«[20]. Als beruhte alles gewissermaßen auf der Qualität der Individuation, die in unmittelbarer Nähe zur Bezugskraft steht.

Es ist faszinierend, wie vollkommen, wie vollkommen produktiv sich hier die ontologische Seite von Nancys Denken mit dem überlagert, was in diesem Denken zum Politischen gehört – ohne dass diese Überlagerung jemals systematisch würde. Denn was ist die von ihm vorgestellte »Politik des unendlichen Bezugs« [»politique du lien infini«] anderes als die menschliche Umsetzung besagter Nähe von Singularität und Bezugskraft? Als die für eine Gemeinschaft denkbare Konsequenz gemeinsamer Observanz dessen, was

---

18 Jean-Luc Nancy: *Kalkül des Dichters. Nach Hölderlins Maß*, übers. von Gisela Febel und Jutta Legueil, Stuttgart 1997, S. 20.

19 Jean-Luc Nancy: *Dekonstruktion des Christentums*, übers. von Esther von der Osten, Berlin 2020, S. 126.

20 Nancy: *Der Sinn der Welt*, a.a.O., S. 160.

ihr widerfährt, wenn sie versteht, dass das, was ihr widerfährt, das ist, was in jedem einzelnen ihrer Punkte freigesetzt wird? So gesehen beruht der unendliche Bezug nicht nur darauf, dass man gemeinsam dem Gemeinsamen ausgesetzt ist, sondern auch auf der Differenz, die in jeder Form der Exposition erfahren wird. So wie kein Bestandteil des Baums auf seine Zugehörigkeit zu der Einheit, an die er gebunden ist, reduziert werden kann, so ist ein Subjekt nie nur eine beliebige Stichprobe der Menschheit, die als solche unendlich austauschbar und ersetzlich wäre. Ohne ein Denken der Unersetzlichkeit ist eine Politik des unendlichen Bezugs weder denkbar noch möglich. Damit das Unersetzliche stattfinden kann, braucht es ein nicht geschlossenes Netz, in dem alle Differenzen freiwerden können. Die Stimme, insofern sie zugleich die Signatur des Individuums und das ist, was die Möglichkeit eines Austauschs eröffnet, ist das Organ dieser Differenz. Die Mit-Teilung der Stimmen kann man auch jenseits des Dialogischen vernehmen, jenseits dieses Raums einer immergleichen Szene, in der das Durcheinander der Stimmen, jede in ihrem eigenen Tonfall, die chorische Möglichkeit kapert und sie auf seine eigene Nostalgie des Einen reduziert. Das letzte Kapitel des (meiner Meinung nach viel zu wenig gelesenen) Buches, das Nancy über Hegel geschrieben hat, ist dem »Wir« gewidmet, das heißt jenem Pronomen, das sowohl die Möglichkeit des Diversen als auch das Risiko verkörpert, diese Möglichkeit in einer künstlichen Einheit zu verzehren. Am Ende gründet oder verankert Nancy dieses Wir – und er hat immer wieder betont, dass damit »wir alle« gemeint sind, und nicht eine bestimmte Untergruppe der Menschheit – am Ende verankert er es in einer Gemeinschaft, und zwar einer Gemeinschaft der Beunruhigung, der Unruhe: »In dieser Unruhe, *die wir sind*«[21], sagt er, und ich sehe in diesen grandiosen Zeilen, in denen ganz nebenbei das Absolute in seiner Bedeutung und Schlagkraft von Grund auf neu ins Spiel gebracht wird, den Schatten oder Widerhall dessen, was wir bezüglich desselben Wir und seiner Möglichkeit zur Disposition stellen wollten, als wir *La Comparution* verfassten. Damals hatte gerade der sogenannte Fall des Kommunismus stattgefunden, vor inzwischen dreißig Jahren schon.

---

21 Jean-Luc Nancy: *Hegel*, übers. von Jörn Etzold und Thomas Laugstien, Zürich 2011, S. 238. [Etzold und Laugstien übersetzen »dans ce non repos que nous sommes« mit »in dieser Unruhe, *in der wir sind*«. A.d.Ü.]

Über die Idee, aus der dieser Text entstand, und über die Art, wie er geschrieben wurde, hätte ich gerne noch einmal gesprochen[22] – vor allem deswegen, weil mich diese Erfahrung Jean-Lucs lächelnder Hartnäckigkeit und seiner entwaffnenden Ruhe ganz nah gebracht hat. Aber sowohl sein beeindruckendes Engagement als auch seine Großzügigkeit sind Eigenschaften, die ich hier nur am Rande erwähnen kann, zum Abschluss dieses viel zu kurzen und viel zu summarischen Versuchs, etwas zu rekapitulieren. Was ich vor allem sehe, ist all das, was ihm nicht gerecht wird, was dieser Versuch beiseitelässt, all die Punkte, von denen ich nicht oder zu wenig gesprochen habe, zum Beispiel unser langes und immer wieder unterbrochenes Gespräch über den Atheismus. Es wird der rote Faden unserer oft so freudvollen Unterhaltungen gewesen sein, die mir nunmehr so sehr fehlen.

II

Die berühmt gewordene Formulierung des 2014 verstorbenen Landschaftsgestalters Michel Corajoud, Landschaft sei »der Ort, an dem Himmel und Erde sich berühren«, hat eine durch und durch philosophische Konsistenz. Diese Berührung, die feine Kommissur, die wir stets vor uns haben, ist zwar absolut konkret, wird aber durch ihre Entfernung und durch ihre Permanenz zu einer sichtbaren Allegorie der Idealität. Ich war äußerst überrascht, als ich bei der erneuten Lektüre von *Dekonstruktion des Christentums* auf die Figur einer Öffnung stieß, die den Gedanken Corajouds (den Jean-Luc Nancy, glaube ich, gar nicht kannte) widerhallen lässt und dabei die Resonanz verstärkt, die das wesentlich unzertrennliche und dabei absolut getrennte Paar Erde/Himmel in und für uns auslöst.

Ausgehend von dieser recht kurzen Passage möchte ich (heute, an diesem Tag zu Ehren Jean-Luc Nancys und in der entsprechend gebotenen Kürze) die Intensität des Denkens hervorheben, seine inspirierte Bewegtheit, die sofort zutage tritt, wenn man sich auch nur auf einen einzigen Moment im unendlichen Linienspiel dieses Werkes konzentriert. Da ist eine Zeichnung – und Nancy hat bekanntermaßen viel über das Abenteuer der Zeichnung nachgedacht, über die Art und Weise, wie sie das Linie-Werden eines

---

22 Einmal habe ich es bereits getan, und zwar in Jean-Christophe Bailly: »Retour sur *La Comparution*«, in: Gisèle Berkman und Danielle Cohen-Lévinas (Hg.): *Figures du dehors. Autour de Jean-Luc Nancy*, Nantes 2012, S. 127–133.

jeden Punktes behandelt, darstellt und vervielfältigt[23] – und man greift nur ein einziges Segment heraus, wobei die Logik weniger die der Stichprobe, als vielmehr die der Großaufnahme oder der Zeitlupe ist. Beim Lesen muss man – selbst dort, wo der Text ein bisschen schwierig oder technisch wird – eher schnell vorgehen, um folgen zu können, wobei »folgen« die Handlung bezeichnen soll, durch die sich der Sinn entfaltet. Doch wer sich auf die Reise macht, verpasst zwangsläufig auch etwas auf dem Weg, und unter all dem, was man verpasst, findet sich zunächst das Knäuel der Abzweigungen, die der Text zwar selbst nicht genommen hat, aber als solche anzeigt. In Nancys Texten gibt es häufig – und das hat mit der Energie zu tun, von der sie getragen werden – eine hohe Intensität des Verweisens, eine Art Schaulaufen möglicher Abzweige.

Wir befinden uns also – und damit komme ich zu besagter Textpassage[24] – auf Erden, vor der Falte. Nach einer umfassenden Auseinandersetzung mit den Dingen, ihrer Beziehung zum Ganzen und zum Raum kommt es plötzlich, nachdem anhand eines einfachen Gebäudes die aporetische Natur jeder Beschreibung veranschaulicht wurde, zu einem Bruch. Ganz oben, dort, wo das Gebäude aufhört, greift etwas ein: »*das* Weite und *das* Lichte von keinem Ding – was man ›den Himmel‹ nennt« (124). In Bezug auf die Wahrnehmungsensembles, die das Gebäude oder seine Umgebung bilden – die Bäume, die am Straßenrand geparkten Autos und so weiter – wird der Himmel als »das paradigmatische Nicht-Ding« (125) definiert. Als solches ist er der lateinische *Dies*, Tag, Tageslicht, die Bedingung jeder Unterscheidung [de tout discernement possible]. Weit geöffnet vollzieht der Himmel, Nicht-Ding, die Aufteilung des Sichtbaren zwischen seinem ununterscheidbaren [incernable] Raum und dem Bereich des Unterschiedenen [cerné], »eine[r] Erde-der-Dinge« (125). Aus der Nacht herausgetreten (und die gestirnte Nacht Kants ist hier unterschwellig präsent), verrichtet das Licht sein Tagwerk – es erhellt. Durch das Licht kommen

---

23 Namentlich in *Die Lust an der Zeichnung*, dem Begleittext einer Ausstellung im Musée des Beaux-Arts in Lyon, mit deren Kuration Museumsdirektorin Sylvie Ramond Jean-Luc Nancy betraut hatte. [Der Text erschien zunächst im Ausstellungskatalog (Sylvie Lecoq-Ramond und Éric Pagliano (Hg.): *Le plaisir au dessin. Catalogue officiel de l'exposition organisée par le Musée des Beaux-Arts de Lyon, du 12 octobre 2007 au 14 janvier 2008*, Paris 2007) und wurde anschließend bei Gallimard verlegt. Dt. Fassung: Jean-Luc Nancy: *Die Lust an der Zeichnung*, übers. von Paul Maercker, Wien 2013. A.d.Ü.]

24 Nancy: *Dekonstruktion des Christentums*, a.a.O., S. 123–129. [Seitenbelege im Folgenden in runden Klammern nach dem Zitat, A.d.Ü.]

die Dinge, und Nancy wählt dafür das direkteste, einfachste Beispiel, den Baum: eine Existenzform, die als Nahtstelle zwischen
Erde und Himmel fungiert – zwischen der ERDE-der-Dinge und dem
Nicht-Ding der endlosen Verräumlichung. Dennoch ist es nicht
möglich, den Baum, einen Baum in der Existenzordnung des Dings
zu verorten – und genau deswegen wird er hier auch aufgerufen:

> »Die Zugehörigkeitseinheit, von der die Spendung des Sinnlichen stets
> herrührt, hat sogar nur selten ›dinglichen‹ Stil. Der Baum beispiels-
> weise, den das Licht des Tages erstrahlen lässt, indem es sich in ihm
> bricht, behauptet vor unseren Augen die Einheit einer Fülle. Diese sta-
> pelt evidentermaßen nicht übereinander erst ein ›Ding‹, das der Stamm
> wäre, dann andere ›Dinge‹, die Äste wären, dann die Zweige, bis hin zu
> der beweglichen und schillernden Vielfalt der kleinen-Blätter-Dinge.«
> (125f.)

Um diesen Austritt aus dem »dinglichen« Modus, für den die pflanz-
liche Fülle nur ein Beispiel unter vielen ist, noch eingehender und
konkreter zu beschreiben, lässt Nancy uns in die Weite stürzen
und richtet den Blick auf zwei weitere Zugehörigkeitseinheiten (so
lautet der gewählte Begriff), die beide dem Bereich entstammen,
den man für gewöhnlich ›Landschaft‹ nennt. Erstens »die Einheit
der Erstreckung eines Hangs« (126), zweitens »die zwei Arten der
Vorbeigehens-Einheit, ein Vorbeigehen-das-bleibt (der Fluss), und
ein Vorbeigehen, das selbst vorbeigeht (der Vogelflug)« (126).
Hier sollte man, da es sich ja nicht zuletzt um einen Spaziergang
handelt, um einen Ausflug der Philosophie außerhalb ihres Rah-
mens, kurz innehalten. Was mit dem Hang, dem Fluss oder dem
Vogelflug kommt, ist nicht das »Land« im Sinne Heideggers, dem
zugeschrieben wird, in sich selbst und gemäß der hierarchisierten
Weise einer Aufteilung vom Weltlosen über das Weltarme zum
Weltbildenden zu ruhen – es ist die Welt, wie sie sich entfaltet,
wie die sichtbaren Idealitäten (des Baums, des Hügels, des Vorbei-
gehens) sie zugleich anwesend und unbegreiflich machen. Dieses
Weltganze, das sich in distinkte, aber ineinander geschachtelte Zugehörigkeitseinheiten zerlegen lässt, ist das Zahlreiche, was nicht
die Zahl, sondern die Quantität als solche ist, gemäß ihres mal
nüchternen, mal immensen, in jedem Fall aber unberechenbaren
Überflusses. Das »Zahlreich-Sein« ist von Natur aus eine »Heraus-
forderung an die Deskription« (127), und zwar in erster Linie, weil
das Zahlreich-Sein nicht gegeben ist, sondern sich mit dem vermischt, was ankommt, das heißt mit dem, was in den Büchern

Nancys als *Kommen* immer wieder gleichsam als Leitmotiv wie-derkehrt. Das Kommen ist nicht die Zeit, sondern das, was sie ausliefert [livre], oder freisetzt [délivre], wobei die Weisen und Stile des Freisetzens selbst zahlreich sind. Wie wir gerade gese-hen haben, bestimmt Nancy derer zwei – zwei Weisen des Vorbei-gehens. Ohne viel Aufhebens, im Handumdrehen oder eben im Vorbeigehen treten wir in eine Analytik der Zeit ein: Die beiden Weisen, die Nancy in einem Text aus *Die fragile Haut der Welt*[25] an-hand des Gegensatzes zwischen Zufall und Jahreszeit beschreibt, werden hier durch den Fluss und den Vogelflug ausgestaltet. Der Fluss (und es ist bemerkenswert, dass Nancy hier das französische Wort *rivière* benutzt, und nicht etwa das metaphysisch aufgela-dene *fleuve*) ist die Seite jener merkwürdigen Permanenz, die es erlaubt hat, aus dem Wasserlauf das plastische Äquivalent der Zeit zu machen, da er ja tatsächlich, während und solange man ihn be-obachtet, vorbeigeht *und* bleibt, wie ein endlos vorüberziehendes Band. Wenn hier plötzlich Vogel und Vogelflug (wobei man, um den Einschlag des Zahlreichen zu betonen, hier vielleicht besser sagen sollte: Vögel und Vogelflüge, gibt es derer doch so viele ver-schiedene …) im philosophischen Text auftauchen (dessen Rück-bezüge auf die Geschichte der Philosophie, namentlich auf Kant und Husserl, ich hier gewiss ein bisschen zu freimütig auslasse), dann, um die reine Form des Dahingehens zu bedeuten, unter der die Möglichkeit aufscheint, dass es letztlich nur Vorbeigehen gibt und dass die sichtbaren Idealitäten beziehungsweise die in Trau-ben von Zugehörigkeitseinheiten versammelten oder dissoziierten Dinge die Erscheinung dieses Vorübergehens selbst sind oder viel-leicht auch sein Schmuck.[26]

Als Nancy auf diese »Idealitäten des Sichtbaren« zu sprechen kommt, »die wir erkennen, ohne überhaupt daran denken zu müs-sen« (126), behauptet er, keine Philosophie habe sie je zu sagen gewusst. Stimmt das? Ich weiß es nicht, aber ich bin mir sicher,

---

25 Jean-Luc Nancy: *Die fragile Haut der Welt. Mit einem Beitrag von Manuel Garrido und Versen von Jean-Christophe Bailly,* übers. von Thomas Laugstien, Zürich 2021 Darin »Was an der Zeit ist« [frz. »L'accident et la saison«, A.d.Ü.], S. 103–118.

26 »Die Form des Erscheinens zu verfolgen – die erscheinende Form und das Erscheinen der Form – bedeutet, das zu verfolgen, was sich in der Erscheinung zeigt oder entzieht« / »Poursuivre la forme du paraître – la forme paraissante et le paraître de la forme – revient à poursuivre ce qui se dérobe ou se qui se retire dans l'apparition«, ist im Ausstellungskatalog von *Le Plaisir au dessin* zu lesen, a.a.O., S. 40. Übers. L.S.

dass auch andere Formen der Auseinandersetzung, angefangen bei der Poesie, nicht unbedingt vor diesem Manko gefeit sind. Kurz gesagt: Das fällt jedem schwer. Man sieht förmlich, wie sich an dieser Stelle eine Diskussion mit Jean-Luc Nancy öffnet, in der man ihn gerne fragen würde: Wie kann man sich dem, was du als das »Beharren der Substanz, […] uns in ihren Banden zu halten«[27], beschreibst, entziehen? Da fällt mir plötzlich auf, dass die Denkbewegung Nancys selbst dieser Art von Entzug in vielen Momenten Konsistenz verleiht. Die soeben kommentierte Passage steht exemplarisch für ein Denken, das sich selbst als Vorübergehen anerkennt: ein Berühren, ja, wie es gesagt worden ist, doch steht diese Berührung eben der Flüchtigkeit nahe und nicht dem, was sich aufdrängt, einprägt oder einschreibt; sie ist das Gegenteil von dem, was Philippe Lacoue-Labarthe – in diesem Fall ohne Jean-Lucs Beteiligung, aber ganz in der Nähe seines Freundes – als Kennzeichnen des Typs und der Figur beschrieben hat. Dieser ihnen gemeinsame Traum von einer leichten, flüchtig berührenden Typografie und von einer durch diese Typografie ermöglichten Begegnung mit der sinnlichen Welt, die es nur als sprechende gibt und die stets dicht über dem spricht, was sich unablässig jeder Vereinnahmung entzieht; dieser Traum, der in den Worten Jean-Luc Nancys der Traum eines grenzenlosen Bahnens ist, ist der Traum eines von jedem Vollendungswillen befreiten Sinns. Es gibt »die fragile Haut der Welt«, sie ist tätowiert, und wenn die Hand der Zeit über sie geht, dann zittert sie leicht.

Aus dem Französischen von Laura Strack

---

27 Nancy: *Dekonstruktion des Christentums*, a.a.O., S. 113.

Martta Heikkilä

Jean-Luc Nancy: Life

Philosopher Jean-Luc Nancy passed away in Strasbourg on the 23rd of August 2021, succumbing to long-term illnesses. Nancy can be considered as one of the most prominent philosophers of the present, both in France and internationally. His extensive work has most often been attributed to movements such as postmodernism, poststructuralism, deconstruction and post-phenomenology, although his thinking extends beyond the conventional limits of these categories.

Nancy made most of his life's work at the University of Strasbourg in the east of France, where he held the professorship of philosophy from 1988 to 2002. Nancy's œuvre includes more than seventy books, hundreds of scholarly articles and other writings, and innumerable contributions to philosophical debates, politics, art, technology, theology and globalization, among other themes.

His writings span a period of more than fifty years, from the 1960s until the end of his life. Among Nancy's last works are *La Peau fragile du monde* (2020), *Un trop humain virus* (2020) and *Mascarons de Macron* (2021). His posthumously published books include so far *Cruor* (2021), *La vérité du mensonge* (2021) and *La haine des Juifs: Entretiens avec Danielle Cohen-Levinas* (2022).

Jean-Luc Nancy was born on the 26th of July 1940 in Caudéran, a municipality in the district of Gironde in the south-west of France. Nowadays, Caudéran forms a part of the city of Bordeaux. Nancy's father worked as an engineer in the French army's department of propellants, and after the Second World War he was assigned to serve in the occupation forces in Germany. During 1945–1950, the Nancy family lived in Baden-Baden in the south of Germany. While living there, Jean-Luc Nancy learned the German language as a child. After those years, the family returned to live in Bordeaux. Nancy first took an interest in philosophical questions at school age, which led him later to study philosophy and theology and prepared the ground for a decades-long career in philosophy.

Nancy's youth around the mid-1950s was marked with participation in various organizations, such as a short-time membership in the JEC (Christian Student Youth), where he discovered non-communist left-wing politics especially on the occasion of the Algerian

War (1954–1962).[1] As a student, he participated in political action in several organizations, such as the National Union of Students of France (UNEF), the French Democratic Confederation of Labor (CFDT) and, for a brief period in the early 1960s, the Unified Socialist Party (PSU). During this time, he published philosophical articles in the *Esprit* journal. In 1967, he began philosophical and political co-operation with writers Daniel Joubert and Paul Kobisch and artist Théo Frey. Together they participated in various events and actions associated with Marxism and Situationism.

Nancy has described the events of 1968 as crucial to his thinking. Although he was not directly involved in subversive or anarchist activities, he regards the significance of the year 1968 as a watershed: social movements exposed the crisis that existed within established institutions and their structures. "The crazy year" of Europe offered Nancy an insight into the history that happens to us at a particular moment, but whose truth we cannot determine.

Nancy studied philosophy first at the University of Toulouse (1958–1959). From there, he moved to Paris and received his bachelor's degree (*licence*) under the supervision of Georges Canguilhem and Paul Ricœur at the Sorbonne in 1962. His thesis dealt with G. W. F. Hegel's philosophy of religion. He then received his master's degree in philosophy (*diplôme d'études supérieures*) in 1963 and *agrégation*[2] in 1964, both at the Sorbonne. In 1964, Nancy began studies at the faculty of theology in Strasbourg, but quickly interrupted them and moved to nearby Colmar in the east of France to teach philosophy during the years 1964–1968. After this, he worked as an assistant at the department of philosophy in Strasbourg while writing his doctoral dissertation on Immanuel Kant's philosophy, *Le Discours analogique de Kant*, again under the supervision of Paul Ricœur. Around the same time, Nancy became acquainted with Philippe Lacoue-Labarthe (1940–2007), with whom he studied the writings of, for example, Claude Lévi-Strauss, Gilles Deleuze and Jacques Derrida. Nancy's meeting with Lacoue-Labarthe meant the beginning of their long-time intellectual and professional collaboration in Strasbourg. Nancy's interest in Derrida's philosophy was first aroused when he followed

---

1 Léon Strauss, "Nancy, Jean-Luc," (2013/2022), https://maitron.fr/spip.php?-article145672 (accessed August 4, 2022).
2 The *agrégation* is a competitive examination for civil service that is required to teach in the French public education system.

Derrida's lectures at the Sorbonne and read his interpretations of Martin Heidegger's thinking in the 1960s.

After finishing his dissertation in 1973, the University of Human Sciences of Strasbourg appointed Nancy as *maître de conférences*, equivalent of lecturer or associate professor. In this position, he taught philosophy in Strasbourg until 1988; in the 1970s, he lectured frequently also at the École Normale Supérieure in Paris. During these years, he began publishing philosophical works in rapid succession.

In his first books, Nancy addresses the critique of the metaphysics of presence and the concept of the subject. These approaches provide him perspectives on the classics of philosophy—Lacan (*Le titre de la lettre*, 1973, with Lacoue-Labarthe),[3] Hegel (*La remarque spéculative (Un bon mot de Hegel)*, 1973),[4] Kant (*Le Discours de la syncope*, 1976)[5] and Descartes (*Ego sum*, 1979),[6] as well as the literary tradition of German Romanticism (*L'Absolu littéraire*, 1978).[7] These monographs may, in a broad sense, be called commentaries, but Nancy also "deconstructs" the philosophers in question and develops a practice and style of deconstruction that differs from Derrida's.

Nancy prepared his *habilitation* (the second doctorate) under Gérard Granel's supervision. He defended his thesis *L'Expérience de la liberté* in 1987 at the University of Toulouse Le Mirail, which brought him the title of *docteur d'Etat*.[8] The dissertation, translated in English as *The Experience of Freedom* (1994), is a study

---

3   Jean-Luc Nancy and Philippe Lacoue-Labarthe, *Le titre de la lettre: Une lecture de Lacan* (Paris: Galilée, 1973), translated as *The Title of the Letter: A Reading of Lacan*, trans. François Raffoul and David Pettigrew (Albany: State University of New York Press, 1992).

4   Jean-Luc Nancy, *La remarque spéculative (Un bon mot de Hegel)* (Auvers-sur-Oise: Galilée, 1973), translated as *The Speculative Remark (One of Hegel's Bons Mots)*, trans. Céline Surprenant (Stanford: Stanford University Press, 2002).

5   Jean-Luc Nancy, *Le Discours de la syncope* (Paris: Flammarion, 1976), translated as *The Discourse of the Syncope*, trans. Saul Anton (Stanford: Stanford University Press, 2008).

6   Jean-Luc Nancy, *Ego sum* (Paris: Flammarion, 1979), translated as *Ego Sum: Corpus, Anima, Fabula*, trans. Marie-Eve Morin (New York: Fordham University Press, 2016).

7   Jean-Luc Nancy and Philippe Lacoue-Labarthe, *L'Absolu littéraire: Théorie de la littérature du romantisme allemand* (Paris: Seuil, 1978), translated as *The Literary Absolute: The Theory of Literature in German Romanticism*, trans. Philip Barnard and Cheryl Lester (Albany: State University of New York Press, 1988).

8   The jury of Nancy's thesis included Lucien Braun, Jacques Derrida, Jean-Toussaint Desanti, Gérard Granel, Jean-François Lyotard and Georges Mailhos.

concerning the question of freedom in the philosophy of Kant, F. W. J. Schelling and Hegel.[9] In 1988, the year of the French publication of his thesis, Nancy was appointed as professor of philosophy at the University of Human Sciences of Strasbourg.

In addition to his positions in French universities, Nancy worked as a visiting professor and researcher at universities across the world in the 1970s and 1980s, for example at the University of California at Irvine, San Diego and Berkeley, as well as the Freie Universität in Berlin. At the invitation of the French Foreign Ministry, Nancy gave lectures in Europe and the United States, in addition to holding numerous positions of trust and expertise, such as the Georg Wilhelm Friedrich Hegel Chair and professorship of philosophy at The European Graduate School in Switzerland.

From the early 1970s until the 1990s, Nancy wrote several books and essays together with his longtime associate and collaborator Philippe Lacoue-Labarthe.[10] In 1974, Nancy, Derrida, Lacoue-Labarthe and Sarah Kofman established the collection "La philosophie en effet" (Philosophy at work) at the publishing house Galilée in Paris.[11] The series is still in existence, and in the dissemination of poststructuralist thinking its importance has been remarkable.

At Derrida's suggestion, Nancy and Lacoue-Labarthe founded the Centre de recherches philosophiques sur le politique (Centre for Philosophical Research of the Political) in 1980 at the École Normale Supérieure in Paris. The aim of the institute was to explore the connections between philosophy and political thought, and it brought together many important researchers until its closing in 1984.[12] The operation of the Centre produced two collective

---

9   Jean-Luc Nancy, *L'Expérience de la liberté* (Paris: Galilée, 1988), translated as *The Experience of Freedom*, trans. Bridget McDonald (Stanford: Stanford University Press, 1993).

10   Among books that Nancy has co-authored with Philippe Lacoue-Labarthe are *Le titre de la lettre* (1973), *L'Absolu littéraire* (1978), *Le mythe nazi* (1991), English collection *Retreating the Political* (ed. Simon Sparks, 1997), and several shorter essays. Like Nancy, Lacoue-Labarthe held a professorship in philosophy at the University of Strasbourg.

11   The first publication in the "La philosophie en effet" collection was Jacques Derrida's *Glas* (Paris: Galilée, 1974).

12   Among the philosophers associated with the Centre de recherches philosophiques sur le politique were Alain Badiou, Etienne Balibar, Luc Ferry, Denis Kambouchner, Sarah Kofman, Claude Lefort, Jacques Rancière and Jacob Rogozinski.

volumes, *Rejouer le politique* (1981) and *Le Retrait du politique* (1982).[13]

Nancy's works began to attract worldwide interest in the 1980s, when their English translations were first published. The concepts of "the political" (*le politique*) and the radical rethinking of Heidegger's notion of "being-with" (*être-avec*; *Mitsein*) gained increasing importance in Nancy's philosophy and acquired him broader attention. In this respect, the publication of *La Communauté désœuvrée* in 1986 was especially important.[14] In the debate on community, central background figures were Maurice Blanchot and Georges Bataille. Nancy wrote *La Communauté désœuvrée* in response to Blanchot's book *La Communauté inavouable*.[15] A few years later, Giorgio Agamben, in turn, replied to both Blanchot and Nancy by writing *La comunità che viene* in 1990.[16]

At the end of the 1980s, Nancy's health deteriorated. He underwent a heart transplant in the early 1990s and his recovery was retarded by cancer diagnosed at the same time. Due to the illnesses, he was forced to suspend his teaching activities and other duties, but he continued to write, and several of his best-known books were published in the 1990s. Nancy describes the thoughts and philosophical questions raised by heart transplantation in *L'Intrus* (2000), translated as *Intruder*.[17] It may be said that, especially for a wider audience, *L'Intrus* and *Corpus* (1992),[18] works spawned by personal experiences, form the core of Nancy's production with their thinking of corporeality and illness. His essay *L'Intrus* inspired also the film of the same name, directed by Claire Denis (France, 2004).

After Nancy's health had improved, he continued his work in the post of professor until 2002, and even in retirement, he published

---

13 Both *Rejouer le politique* (Paris: Galilée, 1981) and *Le Retrait du politique* (Paris: Galilée, 1982) were edited by Nancy and Lacoue-Labarthe.

14 Jean-Luc Nancy, *La Communauté désœuvrée* (Paris: Bourgois, 1986), translated as *The Inoperative Community*, ed. Peter Connor, trans. Peter Connor et al. (Minneapolis: University of Minnesota Press, 1991).

15 Maurice Blanchot, *La Communauté inavouable* (Paris: Minuit, 1983), translated as *The Unavowable Community*, trans. Pierre Joris (New York: Station Hill, 1988).

16 Giorgio Agamben, *La comunità che viene* (Torino: Einaudi, 1990), translated as *The Coming Community*, trans. Michael Hardt (Minneapolis: University of Minnesota Press, 1993).

17 The English translation of "Intruder" is included in Nancy's *Corpus*, trans. Richard A. Rand (New York: Fordham University Press, 2008), pp. 161–170.

18 Jean-Luc Nancy, *Corpus* (Paris: Métailié, 1992).

philosophical works continuously, even several of them annually, in addition to articles and other writings. Nancy was likely the longest-lived person in France to have undergone a heart transplant.

The philosophical style of Nancy's studies of, among others, Kant and Hegel in the 1970s already anticipated his writings of the 1980s and 1990s, when he began to work with topics that form the core of his production: community, freedom, corporeality and ontology. Nancy's thinking of ontology focuses on the finitude of existence, being-in-the-world and the fragmentation of being that he treats in his methodological books *Une pensée finie* (1990),[19] *Le Sens du monde* (1993)[20] and *Être singulier pluriel* (1996).[21] In the early 2000s, he undertook an examination of Christianity, especially what he called its "deconstruction" (*La Déclosion*, 2005, and *L'Adoration*, 2010).[22] Concurrently, he had a keen interest in arts and literature, and in *Les Muses* (1994)[23] and *Au fond des images* (2003)[24] he provides his most profound discussion of the ontology of art and the image. In his numerous publications on arts, he also approaches literature (*Demande*, 2015),[25] the different varieties of visual art, such as drawing (*Le Plaisir au dessin*, 2009)[26] and painting (*Portrait*,

---

19 Jean-Luc Nancy, *Une pensée finie* (Paris: Galilée, 1990), partly translated as *A Finite Thinking*, ed. Simon Sparks, trans. Simon Sparks et al. (Stanford: Stanford University Press, 2003).

20 Jean-Luc Nancy, *Le Sens du monde* (Paris: Galilée, 1993), translated as *The Sense of the World*, trans. Jeffrey S. Librett (Minneapolis: The University of Minnesota Press, 1997).

21 Jean-Luc Nancy, *Être singulier pluriel* (Paris: Galilée, 1996/2013), translated as *Being Singular Plural*, trans. Robert D. Richardson and Anne E. O'Byrne (Stanford: Stanford University Press, 2000).

22 Jean-Luc Nancy, *La Déclosion (Déconstruction du christianisme, 1)* (Paris: Galilée, 2005), translated as *Dis-Enclosure: The Deconstruction of Christianity*, trans. Bettina Bergo, Gabriel Malenfant and Michael B. Smith (Stanford: Stanford University Press, 2008); *L'Adoration (Déconstruction du christianisme, 2)* (Paris: Galilée, 2010), translated as *Adoration: The Deconstruction of Christianity II*, trans. John McKeane (Stanford: Stanford University Press, 2013).

23 Jean-Luc Nancy, *Les Muses* (Paris: Galilée, 1994/2001), translated as *The Muses*, trans. Peggy Kamuf (Stanford: Stanford University Press, 1996).

24 Jean-Luc Nancy, *Au fond des images* (Paris: Galilée, 2003), translated as *The Ground of the Image*, trans. Jeff Fort (New York: Fordham University Press, 2005).

25 Jean-Luc Nancy, *Demande: Littérature et philosophie* (Paris: Galilée, 2015).

26 Jean-Luc Nancy, *Le Plaisir au dessin* (Paris: Galilée, 2009), translated as *The Pleasure in Drawing*, trans. Philip Armstrong (New York: Fordham University Press, 2013).

2018),[27] film (*L'Évidence du film: Abbas Kiarostami*)[28] and music (*À l'écoute*, 2002).[29] In his last publications, Nancy dealt with topics such as the body, politics, Jewish and Christian faith and the history of philosophy. These works, along with his many contributions to public debate, display the diversity of Nancy's philosophical subjects that remained in effect until the end of his life.

---

27 Jean-Luc Nancy, *Portrait*, trans. Sarah Clift and Simon Sparks (New York: Fordham University Press, 2018). The English collection *Portrait* includes Nancy's books *The Look of the Portrait* (*Le Regard du portrait*, Paris: Galilée, 2000) and *The Other Portrait* (*L'Autre portrait*, Paris: Galilée, 2014).
28 Jean-Luc Nancy, *L'Évidence du film: Abbas Kiarostami / The Evidence of Film* (Bruxelles: Yves Gevaert, 2001, bilingual edition, trans. Christine Irizarry and Verena Andermatt Conley).
29 Jean-Luc Nancy, *À l'écoute* (Paris: Galilée, 2002), translated as *Listening*, trans. Charlotte Mandell (New York: Fordham University Press, 2007).

The Authors

Jean-Christophe Bailly was born in 1949 in Paris. He is a writer who experimented in all genres except the novel. His relationship to philosophy, based on an active reading into early German Romanticism, has intensified since the 1980s when he met J.-L. Nancy and P. Lacoue-Labarthe. He published, together with Nancy, *La Comparution* (1991). Among his numerous works are: *Panoramiques* (Bourgois, 2000), *Le Champ mimétique* (Seuil, 2005), *Le Versant animal* (Bayard, 2007), *L'Élargissement du poème* (Bourgois, 2016) ou *L'Imagement* (Seuil, 2020). His most famous book is *Le Dépaysement* (Seuil, 2011).

Rodolphe Burger is a French composer, guitarist and singer. Founder of the rock group *Kat Onoma* (1986–2002), he currently pursues a solo career through his label *Last Band* and the *Rodolphe Burger Company*, often via numerous collaborations with other artists. He is also the founder of the festival "C'est dans la vallée."

Marcia Sá Cavalcante Schuback is Professor of Philosophy at the Södertörn University in Sweden. She is the author of several articles and monographs in the fields of Hermeneutics, Phenomenology, German Idealism, French contemporary Philosophy and aesthetics. She has also translated philosophical works into Portuguese. Among others are: Martin Heidegger's *Being and Time*. Some of her latest publications are *Time in Exile: In Conversation with Heidegger, Blanchot and Clarice Lispector* (SUNY, 2020), *Ex-Brasilis, brev från Pandemin* (Faethon, 2021), *The Fascism of Ambiguity: a Conceptual Essay* (Bloomsbury, 2022). *Atrás do pensamento: a filosofia de Clarice Lispector* (2022).

Marcus Coelen works as a psychoanalyst in New York and Berlin; teaches literature and literary theory at the Ludwig-Maximilian University, Munich. He is a translator, author, and an editor, of the book series "Neue Subjektile" with Turia + Kant, Vienna, among others.

Alexander García Düttmann teaches philosophy at the University of the Arts in Berlin. His most recent book publications include *In Praise of Youth* (diaphanes: Zurich 2021) and *Anarchy and Refusal* (Mudito & co: Barcelona 2023). In 2022, his translation of Jean-Luc Nancy's last book, *Cruor*, was published in Germany (diaphanes: Zurich 2022).

Juan Manuel Garrido is Professor of Philosophy at Universidad Alberto Hurtado in Santiago de Chile.

Martta Heikkilä is Adjunct Professor in Aesthetics at the University of Helsinki, Finland. She lectures and publishes on the theory of contemporary art and aesthetics in the context of Modern continental philosophy, particularly phenomenology and poststructuralism. Her current research project concerns the concept of the work of art and its philosophical contexts during the past few decades. She is the author of *Deconstruction of the Work of Art: Visual Arts and Their Critique in Contemporary French Thought* (Lexington Books / Rowman & Littlefield, 2021), *At the Limits of Presentation: Coming-into-Presence and Its Aesthetic Relevance in Jean-Luc Nancy's Philosophy* (Peter Lang, 2008) and the editor and coauthor of *Introduction to Art Criticism* (in Finnish; Gaudeamus, 2012) and *Analyzing Darkness and Light: Dystopias and Beyond* (Brill, 2023), among others.

Erich Hörl is the Chair of Media Culture and Media Philosophy at Leuphana University of Lüneburg and Co-Director of Leuphana Institute for Advanced Studies in Culture and Society. He is concerned with questions of a general ecology and a critique of Environmentality. He also works on the problem of the Disruptive Condition. His publications include *The Sacred Channels. The Archaic Illusion of Communication* (Amsterdam University Press 2018, with a preface by Jean-Luc Nancy), programmatic collections such as *Die technologische Bedingung* (Suhrkamp 2011), *General Ecology. The New Ecological Paradigm* (Bloomsbury Academics 2017), *Critique and the Digital* (with N. Y. Pinkrah, L. Warnsholdt, diaphanes 2021), and an edition of texts by Gérard Granel, *Die totale Produktion. Technik, Kapital und die Logik der Unendlichkeit* (Turia + Kant 2020).

Valentin Husson est philosophe, docteur, et chargé de cours à l'Université de Strasbourg. Il est l'auteur de nombreux articles sur le thème de l'écologie et de l'alimentation. Il a par ailleurs publié *Vivre(s). Malaise dans la culture alimentaire* en 2018 chez les Contemporains favoris, et en 2021 chez diaphanes *L'Écologique de l'Histoire*, préfacé par Jean-Luc Nancy. Son prochain ouvrage, *L'art des vivres*, paraîtra en 2023 aux PUF.

Sandrine Israel-Jost teaches philosophy at the HEAR (Haute École des Arts du Rhin), in Strasbourg. She was the student and doctoral student of Jean-Luc Nancy. She is the author of a doctoral thesis in philosophy on the concept of contingency which she tries, starting from a dialogue between Aristotle and Nietzsche, to think about the present and not the future. She has published articles focusing mainly on the links between literature and philosophy or between art, aesthetics and ecology/ecosophy. A work on the problem of "milieu", based on Hippocrates and D.W. Winnicott, is in preparation. She is an associate member of Crephac (Centre de recherche en philosophie allemande et contemporaine, Strasbourg), and is Vice-President of ARPPS (Association pour les rencontres Philosophie-Psychanalyse, Strasbourg).

Ian James completed his doctoral research on the fictional and theoretical writings of Pierre Klossowski at the University of Warwick in 1996. He is a Fellow of Downing College and Professor of Modern French Philosophy and Literature in the Faculty of Modern and Medieval Languages and Linguistics at the University of Cambridge. He is the author of *Pierre Klossowski: The Persistence of a Name* (Oxford: Legenda, 2000), *The Fragmentary Demand: An Introduction to the Philosophy of Jean-Luc Nancy* (Stanford: Stanford University Press, 2006), *Paul Virilio* (London: Routledge, 2007), *The New French Philosophy* (Cambridge: Polity, 2012) and *The Technique of Thought: Nancy, Laruelle, Malabou and Stiegler after Naturalism* (Minneapolis: Minnesota University Press, 2019).

Apostolos Lampropoulos is Professor of Comparative Literature at the University Bordeaux Montaigne. In 2022 he was Visiting Fellow at the Cluster *Temporal Communities: Doing Literature in a Global Perspective* of the Free University of Berlin. He has published the monograph *Le Pari de la description* (2002), while another one, entitled *Gastrotopies: Athens 1990–2010* (in Greek), is forthcoming. He has co-edited the special issues "Configurations of Cultural Amnesia" (*Synthesis*, 2010) and "Learning from documenta" (*FIELD*, 2021), and the volumes *States of Theory* (2010; in Greek), *AutoBioPhagies* (2011), and *Textual Layering* (2017). He has translated J. Derrida's *Circumfession* (2019) and co-curated the exhibition *Intimacy: New Queer Art from Berlin and Beyond* (2020–2021) at the *Schwules Museum* of Berlin.

Nidesh Lawtoo teaches philosophy and literature at KU Leuven where he leads the ERC project, *Homo Mimeticus*. His work revisits the aesthetic, philosophical, and political implications of mimesis. Lawtoo is the editor of *Conrad's* Heart of Darkness *and Contemporary Thought: Revisiting the Horror with Lacoue-Labarthe* (2012), and the author of *The Phantom of the Ego: Modernism and the Mimetic Unconscious* (2013), *Conrad's Shadow: Catastrophe, Mimesis, Theory* (2016) and *(New) Fascism: Contagion, Community, Myth* (2019). His next books are a diptych on *Violence and the Unconscious*, vols., I, II (2023) and a volume that sets new foundations for mimetic studies titled, *Homo Mimeticus: A New Theory of Imitation* (2022). He also conducted an interview with Nancy, titled "Mimesis: A Singular Plural Concept" *CounterText* 8.1 (2022).

Jérôme Lèbre is Professor of Philosophy, khâgne, Lycée Louis-le-Grand. Last published works: with Jean-Luc Nancy, *Signaux* sensibles (Paris, 2017); Eloge *de l'immobilité* (Paris, 2018); *Scandales et démocratie* (Paris, 2019); forthcoming in 2023 : *Les Travers du monde, méditations sur l'obstacle.*

Susanna Lindberg is a Professor of Continental Philosophy at the University of Leiden, Netherlands. She is a specialist in German idealism, phenomenology, and contemporary French philosophy. In recent years, her research has focused on the question of technics. After earning a PhD at the University of Strasbourg and a *habilitation* at the Université Paris Ouest Nanterre, she has worked as a researcher at the University of Helsinki and at the Université Paris Ouest Nanterre; as a lecturer and professor at the University of Tampere, and as a core fellow at the Collegium for Advanced Studies of the University of Helsinki. Her publications include *From Technological Humanity to Bio-Technical Existence* (forthcoming with SUNY Press, 2023), *Techniques en philosophie* (Hermann, 2020), *Le monde défait. L'être au monde aujourd'hui* (Hermann, 2016), *Heidegger contre Hegel: Les irréconciliables*, and *Entre Heidegger et Hegel: L'éclosion et vie de l'être* (L'Harmattan, 2010). She has also edited several collected volumes, notably *The Ethos of Digital Environments. Technology, Literary Theory and Philosophy* (with Hanna-Riikka Roine, Routledge, 2021), *The End of the World* (with Marcia Sá Cavalcante Schuback, Rowman and Littlefield, 2017) and *Europe Beyond Universalism and Particularism* (with Sergei Prozorov and Mika Ojakangas, Palgrave Macmillan, 2014). In addition to this, she has published many academic articles in the leading journals.

Artemy Magun is Professor and Director at the Center for Practical Philosophy at the European University at Saint-Petersburg. He has a PhD degree in Political Science from the University of Michigan (2003) and a doctorate in philosophy from the University of Strasbourg (2004). Magun is author of many books and articles in Russian, English, and French. He is the editor of *Stasis*, a peer-reviewed journal in social and political thought. Among his English-language works are books: *Negative Revolution* (2013), *Politics of the One* (2013, ed.) *The Future of the State* (2020, ed.); articles such as "Illuminated by Darkness. Two Symbolist Masterpieces," "Hysterical Machiavellianism. Russian Foreign Policy and the International Non-relations"; "Marx's Theory of Time," "De Negatione," and many others.

Boyan Manchev is a philosopher, Professor at the New Bulgarian University (Sofia), former Director of Program and Vice-President of the International College of Philosophy in Paris and Professor at the Berlin University of the Arts. He is the author of fifteen books, among which are *Freedom in Spite of Everything. Surcritique and Modal Ontology* (2020), *The New Athanor. Prolegomena to Philosophical Fantastic* (vol. 1, 2020), *Clouds. Philosophy of the Free Body* (2019), *Logic of the Political* (2012), *Miracolo* (Lanfranchi, 2011), *L'altération du monde: Pour une esthétique radicale* (Lignes, 2009), *La Métamorphose et l'instant – Désorganisation de la vi*e (La Phocide, 2009), *The Body-Metamorphosis* (2007), *The Unimaginable* (2003). *https://boyanmanchev.net/*

Michael Marder is IKERBASQUE Research Professor in the Department of Philosophy at the University of the Basque Country (UPV-EHU), Vitoria-Gasteiz, Spain. His writings span the fields of ecological theory, phenomenology, and political thought. He is the author of numerous scientific articles and monographs, including *Plant-Thinking* (2013); *Phenomena—Critique*—Logos (2014); *The Philosopher's Plant* (2014); *Dust* (2016), *Energy Dreams* (2017), *Heidegger* (2018), *Political Categories* (2019), *Pyropolitics* (2015, 2020); *Dump Philosophy* (2020); *Hegel's Energy* (2021); *Green Mass* (2021) and *Philosophy for Passengers* (2022), among others. For more information, consult his website michaelmarder.org.

Dieter Mersch, Emeritus Professor at the Zurich University of the Arts, studied mathematics and philosophy in Cologne, Bochum and Darmstadt. Between 2004–2013 he was Full Professor of Media Theory at the University of Potsdam; 2013–2021 director of the Institute for Critical Theory at Zurich University of the Arts, Switzerland and Professor for Aesthetic Theory, also between 2018–2021 president of the German Society for Aesthetics. Recent publications: *Epistemologies of Aesthetics*, Zurich / Berlin 2015, *Manifesto of Artistic Research. A Defense against its Advocates*, Zurich / Berlin 2020. Several essays on media philosophy, art theory, image theory, and Digital Criticism.

Aïcha Liviana Messina is Professor at the University Diego Portales. Her work focuses mainly on the topics of law, criticism, and on the relation between violence and language. She is the author of an essay on Marx, *Amour/Argent. Le livre blanc des manuscrits de 1844* (Le portique/La Phocide, 2011), of a book on Levinas, *L'anarchie de la paix. Levinas et la philosophie politique* (CNRS, 2018), of a book on Blanchot, *The Writing of Innocence. Blanchot and the Deconstruction of Christianity* (SUNY, 2022). She has also written books related to contemporary political issues and to artistic experiences such as *Poser me va si bien* (POL, 2005), *Feminismo y revolución* followed by de *Santiago 2019* (Metales Pesados 2020). With Constanza Michelson, she has co-written *Una falla en la lógica del universo* (Metales Pesados 2020).

Ginette Michaud is Professor Emerita at the University of Montréal. As a member of the international committee responsible for the edition of Jacques Derrida's seminars, she has co-edited *The Beast and the Sovereign* (University of Chicago Press, 2009 and 2011), *Le parjure et le pardon* (Seuil, 2019 and 2020), and Derrida's writings on the arts, *Thinking Out of Sight* (University of Chicago Press, 2021), and architecture, *Les arts de l'espace* (La Différence, 2015). She has dedicated several essays and collections to Derrida, Nancy, Cixous and Kofman. Her latest publications include: *La vérité à l'épreuve du pardon* (PUM, 2018), *Sarah Kofman et Jacques Derrida. Croisements, écarts, différences* (with I. Ullern, Hermann, 2018), *Lire dans la nuit et autres essais – Pour Jacques Derrida* (PUM, 2020), and *Ekphraser. Nouvelles poétiques de l'*ekphrasis *en déconstruction* (PUM, 2022).

Helen Petrovsky is head of the Department of Aesthetics at the Institute of Philosophy of the Russian Academy of Sciences. Her major fields of interest are contemporary philosophy, visual studies, North American literature and culture. She is the author of a number of books devoted, among other things, to a theoretical exploration of the image. Her most recent book is *Disturbance of the Sign: Culture against Transcendence* (*Vozmushchenie znaka: Kul'tura protiv transtsendentsii*, 2019), for which she was awarded the Alexander Piatigorsky Literary Prize (2020–2021). She is also editor-in-chief of the theoretical and philosophical journal *Sinii divan*.

Jacob Rogozinski is Professor Emeritus of Philosophy at Strasbourg University, where he succeeded Jean-Luc Nancy in 2002. His research focuses on contemporary French philosophy, political philosophy and the phenomenology of the self or "ego-analysis." He recently published: *Le moi et la chair – introduction à l'ego-analyse* (Cerf, 2006, English translation: Stanford University Press, 2010), *Guérir la vie – la Passion d'Antonin Artaud* (Cerf, 2011, German translation: Verlag Turia + Kant, 2019), *Cryptes de Derrida* (Lignes, 2014), *Ils m'ont haï sans raison – de la chasse aux sorcières à la Terreur* (Cerf, 2015, English translation forthcoming: Fordham University Press), *Djihadisme – le retour du sacrifice* (Desclée de Brouwer, 2017), *Moïse l'insurgé* (Cerf, 2022).

Philipp Stoellger studied Protestant Theology and Philosophy and received his doctorate with the thesis "Metapher und Lebenswelt. Hans Blumenbergs Metaphorologie als Lebensweltthermeneutik und ihr religionsphänomenologischer Horizont," Tübingen 2000, and his *habilitation* with the thesis *Passivität aus Passion. Zur Problemgeschichte einer categoria non grata, Tübingen 2010*. Since 2015, he is the Chair of Systematic Theology: Dogmatics and Philosophy of Religion at the Faculty of Theology, University of Heidelberg; in 2007–2015, Chair of Systematic Theology and Philosophy of Religion at the Faculty of Theology, University of Rostock, founder of the Institute for Image Theory (IFI) at the University of Rostock, the founding spokesperson of the DFG Research Training Group 1887: Interpretive Power: Religion and belief systems in interpretive power conflicts; Fellow of the Marsilius-Kolleg, Heidelberg; Advisory Board of the International College for Cultural Technology Research and Media Philosophy (IKKM), Weimar; Director of the Forschungsstätte der Evangelischen Studiengemeinschaft (FEST), Heidelberg.

Peter Szendy is Professor of Humanities and Comparative Literature at Brown University and musicological advisor to the Philharmonie de Paris. His recent publications include *Pouvoirs de la lecture: De Platon au livre électronique* (La Découverte, 2022); *Pour une écologie des images* (Minuit, 2021); *Bendings: Four Variations on Anri Sala* (Mousse, 2019); *The Supermarket of the Visible: Toward a General Economy of Images* (Fordham University Press, 2019); *Of Stigmatology: Punctuation as Experience* (Fordham University Press, 2018). He curated the exhibition *Le Supermarché des images* at the Jeu de Paume (February–June 2020).

Marita Tatari is Associate Professor of Philosophy at the University of Patras, Greece (impending appointment). She specializes in continental aesthetics. She earned her PhD at the University of Marc Bloch in Strasbourg with Jean-Luc Nancy and her *habilitation* at the Ruhr University Bochum. She was a Feodor-Lynen Fellow of the Humboldt Foundation at UC Berkeley and at the ZfL Berlin. She has taught at the Humboldt University Berlin, the University of the Arts in Berlin, and at the Universities of Basel, Bochum, Dresden, Leipzig, and Crete. She was visitng Professor of Contemporary Aesthetics at the University of Music and Performing Arts in Stuttgart. Among her publications are the books: *Kunstwerk als Handlung–Transformationen von Ausstellung und Teilnahme*, Fink 2017; *Orte des Unermesslichen–Theater nach der Geschichtsteleologie* (ed.), diaphanes 2014; *Heidegger et Rilke – Interprétation et partage de la poésie*, L'Harmattan 2013; *Ästhetische Universalität – Vom fortbestehenden Wir*, Metzler (forthcoming).

Georgios Tsagdis teaches at Leiden University, Erasmus University Rotterdam, the University of Groningen and is founder of the theory network *Minor Torus*. His philosophical work is transdisciplinary, ranging from technology and ecology, to aesthetics and ethics, while remaining attuned to foundational theoretical questions. His essays have appeared in numerous international journals, including *Parallax*, *Philosophy Today* and *Studia Phaenomenologica*. His recent editorials include: 'Of Times: Arrested, Resigned, Imagined' (*International Journal of Philosophical Studies*, 2020), and *Derrida's Politics of Friendship: Amity and Enmity* (Edinburgh University Press, 2022).

Gert-Jan van der Heiden is Professor of Metaphysics at Radboud University, Nijmegen, The Netherlands. He is the author of *The Truth (and Untruth) of Language: Heidegger, Ricoeur, and Derrida on Disclosure and Displacement* (2010), *Ontology after Ontotheology: Plurality, Event, and Contingency in Contemporary Philosophy* (2014), and *The Voice of Misery: A Continental Philosophy of Testimony* (2020) and he co-edited *Saint Paul and Philosophy: The Consonance of Ancient and Modern Thought* (2017), *Continental Perspectives on Community: Human Coexistence from Unity to Plurality* (2020), and *The Gadamerian Mind (2022)*.

Aukje van Rooden is Assistant Professor in Philosophy at the University of Amsterdam. She is the author of numerous works on the role of literature in contemporary French philosophy in general and the work of Jean-Luc Nancy in particular. Van Rooden has published the following books: *L'Intrigue dénouée. Mythe, littérature et communauté dans la pensée de Jean-Luc Nancy* (2022), *Literature, Autonomy and Commitment* (2019), *Literatuur, autonomie en engagement: Pleidooi voor een nieuw paradigma* (2015), *Re-treating Religion: Deconstructing Christianity with Jean-Luc Nancy* (2012, co-edited), *De nieuwe Franse Filosofie: Denkers en thema's voor de 21e eeuw* (2011, co-edited), *Maurice Blanchot: De stem en het schrift* (2011, co-authored).